This Book is forever

"The School for Gods"

All rights reserved
Copyright © by ESE Ltd London

visibilia ex invisibilibus
European School of Economics

ISBN13: 978 0 9560716 2 0

The School for Gods

Recounted by Stefano E. D'Anna

To the Dreamer in me
Who urges my dream
to heights beyond reason
and deeps beyond emotion
who rules me
and compels me
to be free

TABLE OF CONTENTS

This Book

This book is a map and an escape plan.

Its aim is to show you the path followed by an ordinary man away from a hypnotic view of the world, and an accusing and plaintive interpretation of existence, to escape the rut of a programmed destiny.

This book would never have come to be, nor could I have written a single line, had I not encountered the Dreamer and His teachings.

I owe my infinite gratitude to the Dreamer for having taken me by the hand into the world of the 'dream', into the world of courage and flawlessness, where time and death do not exist and where wealth knows neither "thieves nor decay".

On this journey back to the Essence, I have had to abandon so much ballast: destructive thoughts, negative emotions, second hand beliefs and ideas. I have had to 'conquer myself', acknowledge and challenge the darkest parts of my Being.

All that we see, touch and feel, reality in all its variety, is nothing more than the projection of an invisible universe which exists vertical to our world and which is the true origin of it.

With great difficulty, we can be aware of being surrounded by invisibility, of living in a world which has its source in dreams, where all that counts and is real in a man is invisible.

All our thoughts, feelings and fantasies are invisible. Our hopes, ambitions, secrets, memories and imaginations, fears and uncertainties and all our sensations, attractions, desires, aversions, loves and hates belong to the impalpable but very real world of Being.

The invisible is not something metaphysical, poetic or mythical, nor is it mysterious, secret or supernatural; it is not a steady part of the world of phenomena and events, of categories of elements of reality. In every epoch, the change from one period to another in the intellectual climate and the discovery and implementation of new, more advanced technologies, constantly alter its boundaries making even larger parts of what was invisible in the past, the subject of legitimate scientific research today.

This book is the story of the 'rebirth' of a common man who is the epitome of a fallen, defeated Humanity. His journey back to the essence is a new exodus in search of lost integrity.

The first thing one needs to be aware of to make this journey is one's own condition of enslavement.

The root, the primary cause of all the world's problems, from the endemic poverty of vast regions of the planet to criminality and war, is that Humanity thinks and feels negatively.

Negative emotions rule the world we know. They are unreal and yet they occupy every corner of our life. In order to change man's destiny, he needs to change his psychology, his system of convictions and beliefs. He needs to eradicate from deep within himself, the tyranny of his fragile, mortal, fragmented mentality. The planet's most terrible illness is not cancer or Aids, but man's conflictual thinking. This is the foundation upon which the ordinary vision of the world is built: the real planetary killer.

The direction indicated to us by the Dreamer is both terrible and wonderful, difficult and joyful, but as necessary as the journey made by the salmon, returning upstream against the current.

At first, His philosophy appeared to me to be a transgression of the natural laws that govern all of Humanity; yet it showed itself to be envisaged and desired by the universal order of things and representing the peak of man's possible evolution.

The book is the story of years of study and preparation spent alongside an 'extraordinary Being'. From Him, I received as a gift the most unbelievable task: the creation of a planetary 'School' a University without boundaries.

I've dreamed of an Individual Revolution
Capable of overturning the mental paradigms
of the old Humanity
And freeing it for ever from all conflicts,
From doubt, fear, pain.

I've dreamed of a School that teaches
A new generation of leaders
To harmonize the old apparent antagonisms:
Economy and ethics, action and contemplation,
Financial power and love.

Growing and changing before my eyes, like a being in gestation, day after day, 'The School for Gods' was being built, as I was building myself. To all appearances, I was writing this book, but in fact it had always existed.

The Dreamer's laws, and ideas, keep digging into me, and for the most part, still remain misunderstood.

Like Prometheus, I have seized a fragment of the Dreamer's world and hold it tightly so as to give it one day to men and women who, like me, want to abandon the hellish circles of ordinariness.

Once I believed that writing, and above all teaching, were the truest form of giving. I know now that teaching is only a stratagem to know oneself, to discover one's own incompleteness and heal it.

One can only teach if one doesn't know – says the Dreamer – *Those who truly know don't teach!*

What we have 'learned' what we truly 'possess', cannot be transferred. Happiness, wealth, knowledge, will and love, cannot be acquired from the outside, cannot be 'given' but only... 'remembered' They are the inalienable gifts of Being, and therefore, the natural inheritance of every man.

No political, religious or philosophical system can change society from the outside. Only an individual revolution, psychological rebirth or internal healing, man by man, cell by cell, will lead us towards planetary well-being, towards a more intelligent civilization, truer, richer, happier.

In recounting the lessons I learned from the Dreamer, I have deliberately avoided including episodes, events and revelations which might go beyond the reader's acceptance, referring only to those that, though still 'revolutionary' seem to me to be within the grasp of humanity in its present state.

CHAPTER I

The encounter with the Dreamer

1 The encounter with the Dreamer

At that time I was living in New York. My apartment was on little Roosevelt Island, in the middle of the East River, between Manhattan and Queens. The islet seemed like a ship about to slip its moorings and drift out on the current towards the freedom of the ocean, yet day after day it stayed where it was in the wavy darkness of the river. I came into the bedroom to say goodnight to the children, but they were already asleep. I tiptoed back into the living room. The silence of the night cloaked me and I had a sudden sense of revulsion, of not belonging to that place and felt like a thief stealing into the life of a stranger. I stopped and looked out at the jagged profile of lights along the Queensborough Bridge. It was cold and impending, like a threat.

Jennifer had just retired to her room, ending our marital argument in the typical American style. I had come home late that evening.

I'd been to the J. F. K. airport to pick up a friend I hadn't seen for some time. As soon as we greeted each other, I immediately sensed that his life was somehow more fulfilling and joyful than mine. Instantly, feelings of jealousy, envy, and a blind rivalry, which I would never have admitted, not even to myself, burst forth in a mechanical torrent of words, a compulsive need to talk incessantly. In the car, I spun one lie after another, creating a fictitious version of my years in New York. I told him how impossible it was to attend all the parties I had been invited to, the art gallery openings, the first night performances. I spoke of my own professional triumphs, my hobbies and, above all, my great relationship with Jennifer. However, the words were already dead when they reached my throat. A cry was building up inside me. The nausea I felt at that river of insincerity kept on flowing, dense and unstoppable, and my sense of helplessness at being unable to control the string of falsehoods, became unbearable. I wanted to cease my absurd display, but the more I tried, the more I felt the impossibility of separating myself from that automaton, the man that I was. The more disgust I felt at my words, the more I realized it was impossible to recover the situation.

There were two of us in one body. I was petrified at the thought of being trapped inside a split creature: Siamese twin, centaur, androgyne; forever imprisoned in a fierce and grotesque symbiosis.

Darkness fell. I realized I had made a wrong turn. We were penetrating more and more deeply into a labyrinth of dimly lit streets that were growing increasingly desolate and filthy. My words died away, and a cold silence took over, filling the car. We had slowed to walking pace, in heavy torrential rain. I noticed the headlights of a car tailing us, then caught a glimpse of shadows moving under the pillars of an overpass, and turned to look at my friend and froze. He was shaking. His face was full of fear. I accelerated. My heart was beating rapidly as I instinctively swung into the first street I found. With a sharp swerve, I managed to avoid a group of tramps huddled around a burning oil drum. The shadows of the buildings gaped like monstrous jaws, ready to swallow us up.

The shriek of a siren split the air. I cast nervous glances into the rear-view mirror to check on the car following us until I saw its lights fade away and disappear into the darkness. Once reached a safer part of the city, I recognized some street signs that finally led us home.

I never saw that friend again.

I took the elevator up to the sixteenth floor in the company of a huge black man whose mumblings stayed with me all the way to my apartment. At that time, Roosevelt Island was an experiment in social integration so it wasn't unusual to meet disabled people who lived there with their caregivers.

The sight of Jennifer welcomed me, her hair just unwound from big curlers was slithering like Medusa's snakes. She was brandishing a cigarette between her fingers as she ranted and nervously paced the living room. This was my final indelible impression of her in the mirror of my life. I felt the great void between us and the gnawing ache of my existence, as if the anaesthetic that had numbed me for years was finally wearing off. That apartment, my relationship with that woman, and anything my gaze fell upon spoke of an unredeemable mediocrity. Those choices that I'd believed to be my own, and taken as expressions of my own personality, were revealing themselves as traps from which I could see no hope of escape.

This wasn't the life I'd dreamed of! I was disgusted by my impotence. A numb feeling of despair gushed over me drowning my lies and compromises and washing me up onto desolate shores. I rested my forehead on my arms and sadness gave way to sleep.

The interior of the villa was plunged in darkness and just beginning to be tempered by a hint of dawn. An antique painting occupied the wall at one end of the big hall. In the dim light I could just make out a woodland scene with a dreaming figure at its centre. Like the painting itself, every other aspect of that room, from its furnishings to the architecture, conveyed an intense message of beauty. Finding myself in that villa, at that uncertain time between night and dawn, was very strange, and yet I was not surprised. Everything seemed familiar to me, although I was quite certain I had never been there before.

The villa was silent, as if deep in thought. I climbed the ancient stone stairs and came to a solid wooden chamber door. I noticed that I had dressed elegantly, as though prepared to meet some unknown figure of authority. I don't remember what was distressing me, but I was anxious and grumpy. A swirl of emotions was feeding my internal monologue like dry twigs in a fire. I took off my shoes and left them at the entrance. This action too, seemed perfectly natural to me. These necessary and familiar movements were clearly part of a ritual I had performed on many other occasions. I felt as though I already knew what was waiting for me beyond that door, though I didn't have the faintest idea what. But when I knocked I felt a kind of apprehension and awe as if something inside of me knew. Without waiting for an answer, I pressed down the wrought iron handle and pushed open the door.

I glanced at the fireplace. The dazzling brightness of the flames hurt my eyes so much that I had to look away and blink hard to stop myself from crying. *He* stood next to it with his back to me and I saw the shadow of His profile projected onto the wall. The room, which the firelight had left mostly in shadow, had imposing arches on two sides framing ancient windows, like stone eye-sockets with wide-open eyes into the night. Through those facing East, I could see a section of the sky becoming tinged with the gentle colours of dawn.

I had only taken a few cautious steps across the wide expanse of the white tailed floor when His voice rang out, forceful and terrifying, freezing my every movement and paralysing my thoughts.

«Your life is a disaster! – He said, without turning to face me *– I can sense it by the way you came in, by your footsteps, and above all, by the stench of your emotions. You are a multitude, a mob of thoughts. Where do you think you are going in this state? Shattered into a thousand pieces as you are, you can barely manage to live the existence of a clerk.»*

«I'm not a clerk» I retorted, raising my voice as if to defend myself from a sudden physical attack. Whoever this person was, it seemed appropriate to draw certain lines between us. But the impact of my words was lost, as if muffled by padded walls. Seized by an unreasonable fear, I barely summoned up enough voice to retort weakly:

«I'm a manager!»

The spreading silence that followed grew enormous and penetrated to my very core. A derisive laugh echoed somewhere inside me for an infinitely long time and I remained painfully suspended, uncertain which part of me was being mocked and which was doing the mocking. After what seemed like an eternity, I heard the voice again.

«How dare you say 'I'? – He said with such contempt that it hit me like a slap in the face – *In my world saying 'I' is blasphemous. 'I' is the conflict you bear inside... 'I' is your host of lies... Every time you utter one of your little 'I's you are lying. Only he who knows himself, who is master of his own life... only he who possesses a real will, can say 'I'.»*

There was a pause. When He continued, His words were even more menacing.

«If I ever hear you say 'I' again, you will never be allowed to come back here!

Observe yourself ... Discover who you are!

To be a multitude means being trapped in an unreal, inescapable system of false beliefs and lies that you yourself created. Lack of unity leaves man imprisoned in ignorance, fear, and self-destructiveness. It causes illness, degradation, violence, cruelty and war in the outer world.

The world is as you dream it... a mirror. Out there you find your reflection, the world that you have made, that you have dreamed. Out there you can find yourself! Go, go out into the world and see what you are. You will discover that others are the reflected image of the lie that is living inside you, of your compromises, your ignorance.

Change!... and the world will change.

You create a sick world, and then you fear your own creation, the thing you yourself gave birth to. You think the world is an objective fact... but the world is as you dream it. Go into the world and accept yourself. Meet the poor, the violent, the lepers that dwell inside you. Accept them... Do not avoid them, do not blame them... Surrender to your world. Go and consciously accept what you have created: a world that is rigid, ignorant... lifeless.

Man's power lies in his capacity to master himself while at the same time surrendering to himself.»

Abruptly, His voice took on the sharp tone of an order:

«In My presence... pen and paper! – He commanded – *Don't ever forget them!»*

His peremptory tone and the sudden change of subject disconcerted me. But my confusion quickly turned into fear and then into panic.

I felt as if a mortal threat were hanging over me. Every fibre of my Being was on edge when I heard His voice transformed into a powerful hiss:

«This time you must write. Pen and paper will be your salvation – He said – *Writing down My words is the only way for you not to forget... Write! This is the only way you can scrape together the scattered shreds of your existence.»*

Then as if He had never strayed from the subject, He took up my last assertion and said:

«*A manager is an employee who struggles to believe in what he does; forcing a faith upon himself... he is the high priest of a cult that, however mediocre, nevertheless gives him a feeling of belonging, the illusion of having a direction. But you don't even have this! Thoughts, sensations and desires, in the absence of will, are crazed splinters of Being and 'you', a meaningless fragment at the mercy of the universe.*»

Those words poured over me like a bucket of cold water leaving me gasping. The temperature seemed to plummet and I was suddenly freezing. A profound embarrassment, such as I had never experienced in my entire life, pervaded me slowly and cruelly. I started at the sound of His voice in my ear, so incredibly close I could feel His breath. His tone was a hoarse, dry murmur.

«*Among American Indian tribes, there was a caste of men at the very bottom of the scale: men who were neither witch-doctors nor warriors; they neither hunted nor competed for rank or for women. They were assigned the hardest and most humiliating tasks. They were the ones who would back away from trials of courage and incorruptibility.*»

Here He stopped, then lunged. Paralysed, I could do nothing to deflect or cushion that blow.

«*In any tribe, primitive or modern* – He whispered fiercely – *that is where you would be: on the lowest rung of the ladder.*»

It struck me full in the chest and I was full of shame. Now I didn't even want him to stop. I just wanted to escape; to find enough strength to simply turn my back on Him and go. If only a telephone or an alarm clock would ring and save me from all this... But I could not move a muscle, nor muster a single twitching motion. An inviolate law, there in the Dreamer's world, prevented me from making a single gesture or even taking a breath that was without dignity.

«*I know you would like to escape from this 'dream'* – He continued relentlessly – *But I am Reality. Your life, which you believe to be real, and your world in which you think you are making choices and decisions, are unreal... they are a terrible nightmare. Marrying, having children, a career and a house, making money... everything you believed in... all this is a meaningless fetish which you idolize and place above everything else.*»

«*Only the 'dream' is real* – He affirmed forcefully – *The 'dream' is the most real thing there is. Learn to live within the world of the real. Here your habits and convictions, your old codes, no longer apply... What you call reality is only an image that must be completely overturned. Nothing of the old world can be brought with you. You will have to learn a new way of thinking, breathing, acting and loving...*»

«*You have led a purposeless existence... a painful life. Hidden behind a job and the protective illusion of a paycheck, you are perpetuating the poverty and suffering of the world* – He diagnosed with a sweet yet grave voice, as if He were assessing some serious damage – *Life is too precious to waste in dependence and too rich to lose! It's time to change!*»

A pause amplified the force of the words that followed.

«*It's time to abandon your conflictual vision of the world. It's time for you to die to all which is lifeless. It's time to be reborn. It's time for a new exodus and a new freedom. It is the greatest adventure a man can possibly imagine: the regaining of his own lost integrity.*»

My eyes had almost become accustomed to the half-light. Outside, the dawn began to dissipate the night. Before the cold, pale earth re-emerged from the shadows, a shaft of sunlight struck the great mahogany mantel supporting the stone hood over the fireplace. Carved in great gilded gothic letters, the words: *Visibilia ex Invisibilibus* appeared.

2 Work is slavery

«Who are you?» I barely found the strength to enquire.

«*I am the Dreamer* – said He – *I am the Dreamer and you are the dreamed. An instant of sincerity, a crack in the wall of your lies, like a flash of lightning, allowed you to see Me.*»

The silence which followed spread like ripples in infinite circles. His voice became a rustle.

«*I am freedom*! – He announced – *Now that you have met Me, you will no longer be able to live such an insignificant existence.*»

The following words would remain forever engraved in my memory.

«To be dependent, even if involuntarily, is always a personal choice. Nothing and no one can force you into dependency, only you can do that to yourself.»

Staring at me steadily, He stated that the propensity to lay the blame on the world and to complain about one's lot were the most irrefutable evidence of the fact that these principles had not been understood. A man does not depend on a company; he is not limited by a corporate pecking order or by a boss, but by his own fear. Dependence is fear.

«Being dependent is not the effect of a contract, it is not related to any role nor is it the result of one's social class... Dependency is the consequence of lowering your self-esteem, abdicating your dignity. It is what happens when you allow yourself to be crushed.

In the external world, this internal condition, this degradation, takes the form of a job, and assumes all the aspects of a subordinate position. Dependency is the effect of an unsound mind, enslaved by imaginary fears, by its own apprehensions... Dependency is the visible sign of having surrendered one's 'dream'.»

This conclusion, the way He pronounced the word 'dependency' each time and the slow enunciation of each syllable, unveiled the real meaning of the word and all the pain, the lack of self-love, masked by the banality of its common usage.

«Dependency is a disease of Being!... It is the result of one's incompleteness – the Dreamer revealed – *To be dependent means ceasing to believe in oneself. To depend means to stop dreaming.* »

The more I pondered His words, the more I felt them eating into me like acid. My resentment sharpened into a rage. The way His words cut a swath through the human condition was intolerable. What could a man's life or his work have to do with his feelings and fears? For me these two worlds, the inner and the outer had always been separated, and so should have remained. I firmly believed that it was possible to be dependent in the outside world and yet remain free on the inside and this certainty fueled my indignation.

«Like millions of other men you, have lived your life hidden in the folds of lifeless organizations – He said to me accusingly – *You have bartered your freedom for an illusory assurance. It's time to wake from your hypnotic sleep... from your hellish vision of existence!»*

No one had ever treated me like that before.

«Who gives you the right to speak to me in this way?» I burst out defiantly.

«*You*»

That simple, unexpected response left me frozen in a state of utter impotence. I felt crushed by an overwhelming sense of guilt and I wanted to hide. An inexplicable feeling of shame made me feel naked in front of that as yet faceless being. I had a sudden desire to flee. With my last remaining strength I tried to recover a situation that seemed to be catapulting me beyond the boundaries of my world.

«But how can organizations possibly work without employees?» I asked, feebly trying to redirect the conversation back to what I considered coherent and reasonable.

The Dreamer did not respond. Encouraged by His silence that I took for perplexity or an inability to answer me, I continued:

«If they did not exist… the world would come to a halt!»

«*No, just the opposite*! – He replied sharply – *The world comes to a halt because there are men who are dependent, men who are frightened to death. Humanity, in its present state, cannot conceive of a society free from dependency.*»

Recognising that I'd reached, indeed gone beyond, the limits of my comprehension, He softened His tone and became almost encouraging.

«*Don't be afraid*! – He said with sarcastic concern, flashes of irony crossed His severe gaze – *As long as there are men like you, the world of dependency will continue to exist, and be densely populated.*»

The pause that followed chilled the air between us. His light amused tone suddenly turned steely.

«*You!… You will no longer be able to be part of that world… because you have met Me!*»

I felt a burst of light piercing painfully through my gloomy thoughts and emotional mist.

«*Dependency is the negation of the dream* – He continued – *Dependency is the mask men adopt to conceal their lack of freedom, their denial of life.*»

I had used and heard that word 'dependency' many times, but it was only after that first meeting with the Dreamer that I realized all its painful significance. The condition of being an employee, dependent on a company, revealed itself to be a modern transposition of ancient slavery: a state of inner immaturity and subjugation. I suddenly imagined crowds of human beings condemned to the destiny of Sisyphus, chained to endless drudgery, tasks they'd never chosen; labouring without creativity.

In a flashback I once again envisioned the facade of the Rusconi building in Milan, on Viale Sarca, with its sign, 'Ingresso Dipendenti', towering over the long line of entrance slots reserved for employees. I imagined a host of stooped individuals filing through those narrow portals as the defeated Romans were once obliged to do in the Sannio when forced to pass in humiliation under the Caudine Forks. A planetary procession of men and women who had abandoned belief in their own uniqueness. A premonition of the death of the individual darkened the air, and all the sorrow that accompanied that fate clenched my heart.

The Dreamer cut through this vision with the delicacy of someone drawing together the edges of a gaping wound. His words had a solemn intonation when He announced:

«One day there will be a society that merely dreams and will no longer have to work. A humanity rich enough to dream, and infinitely rich because it dreams.

The universe is bountiful in the extreme, a cornucopia overflowing with all a man's heart desires... In such a universe it is impossible to fear scarcity. Only men like you, racked with fear and doubt, can be poor and perpetuate dependency and poverty in the world.»

«But I'm not poor!» I shouted indignantly.

«Why would you say that?»

Inside I defended myself with all the reasons I could muster to demonstrate the absurdity of His accusation. The Dreamer was silent.

«I'm not poor! – I shouted again – I have a beautiful home, a manager's position, friends who respect me... I have two children to whom I am both father and mother...»

Here I stopped, overwhelmed by the intolerable injustice of His groundless attack.

«*Poverty means being unable to see one's own limits* – the Dreamer explained – *Being poor means you have bartered your right to be the creator of your own destiny for a job you do not like and did not choose.*»

«*You*! – He added, just when I was hoping he had finished – *you are the poorest of the poor, because you still do not know who you are... You 'forgot'. To no one else have I given so many opportunities as I have given to you. This is your last chance.*»

All at once, that feeling of having been offended and unfairly treated, disappeared and all my defences gave way in the face of that battering ram. I felt the hinges holding together my very existence beginning to creak and my most deep-rooted convictions began to crumble like ancient temples shaken to their foundations.

«*Open your eyes, contemplate your condition. See how far a man can stray from magnificence. We appear to be here in the same room, and yet we are separated by infinite eons of time.*»

With those words, as though illuminated by a flash of lightning slashing across the darkness of the night, I understood the distance that existed between Him and I. I appreciated the falseness of my offended dignity and the insignificance of the 'I' I pronounced in the presence of the Dreamer like a tiny squeak in the universe. My illusions of belonging to a decision-making class, an elite of responsible men, possessing free will and independence and in control of their own lives fell like a curtain after the first act of a comic opera. My eyes were open now. Without realizing it, I had been sinking into a mire of self-pity.

Providentially, the Dreamer intervened, launching a harsh command which seemed to be directed at the very depths of my Being.

«*Wake up! Start your own revolution... Rise up against yourself!*» he ordered sharply, offering me a way out of the tight corner of contrition into which I had retreated.

«*Dream of freedom... freedom from all constraints... You are the only obstacle to everything you desire! Dream, dream... Dream without end! The 'dream' is the most real thing there is.*»

3 "I am a woman..."

His voice, so deep and forceful only a moment ago, was now as soft as a woman's. This transformation made my blood run cold. It could not be! That voice was... it was... the thought fell into a vortex, and although the words uttered were no longer violent they nevertheless remained unbearable.

«I'm a dying woman» murmured the voice.

The pause that followed gave me enough time to suffer the nausea of an unknown terror. I was paralysed, incapable of even looking up. A pitiless eye, as huge as the horizon, was opening upon my past.

«I'm a woman suffering from cancer who curses you for deserting me and being unable to face her impending death.»

I listened intently, my body quaking and shivering, and I felt that every word was pushing me closer to the edge of an abyss. Luisella was speaking to me, with her disarming sweetness, reaching to me across time, from beyond the boundaries of life and death. The terrible circumstances of her death, at the age of 27, were now once again confronting my guilty conscience. The sordidness of so many episodes of our life together, the selfishness that drove me to trade everything and everyone for some crumbs of security, my fixation with money, my career and my inability to love her, flashed and exploded painfully within me, and my soul was flooded with an overwhelming disgust as I tried to break away from the man I had been.

«This is 'your' death – He told me – *It is the death of all that you have been and the death of the old debris you carry within you... Don't run away from it... confront it once and for all! To be 'reborn,' a man must first 'die'.»*

«What does 'to die' mean?» I asked submissively, making me realize how much my attitude had changed.

«'To die' means to overturn your own way of looking at things. 'To die' means to disappear from a coarse world, ruled by suffering, to reappear at a higher level.» He spoke enigmatically.

I still did not understand. A part of me somehow wanted to resist. These ideas expressed in words never heard until now, were tearing me to pieces, shattering my memories, friendships, and most deeply rooted convictions. For years I had studied, desperately trying to be top of my class, working tirelessly to make a name for myself, driven by the ambition to be someone who counted. To fight and win, to struggle and win... to overcome any obstacle that got in my way. The guiding principle of my life and the only one I had ever believed in, had been to work hard to 'make it'... my greatest satisfaction... was to win in this world, to get ahead of the competition... And now, did I have to reject all this? It seemed unfair that the Dreamer should condemn my efforts. Dashed by the new powerful current, I still clung to the desire to rise above the rest and hang onto the detritus of my will which I believed to be the healthiest, most vital part of me.

«*Whatever happens outside yourself has to have your inner approval to manifest. This means that anything happening in your own life is the faithful reflection of your will*» He said, and I swallowed these words like gulps of oxygen after a long dive. The effort to understand rationally the implications of what I had just heard from Him made me lose concentration for a moment and a mortal anguish followed.

«Was I then responsible for Luisella's death, had I asked for it?»

«*The world around you dies because you die inside... A very dear person dies to make you realize your mortal vision of existence as the very cause of all your troubles. Do not let her sacrifice be wasted through your incomprehension and self-pity ! Anything that allows you to understand and know the truth about yourself, even if unbearable, is always good.*»

«How could I remedy this? – I asked – I would give my life, now, to change this tragedy.»

«*You are a liar and your past is the reflection of your hypocrisy and your sick imagination. The slightest change in your Being would project an entirely different past. This moment is the only point of physical experience where you can change your past history and with each change in your Being, you become a different person living in a different world. With the slightest change of your inner states, the memory of your past, your future and the entire universe will simultaneously change. Your past history, which you believe to have really lived, and feel to be so familiar, is just an imaginary experience that you produce in this precise instant.*

Remember! All possibilities lie in Now!»

4 A dying species

«*No one can prevail over the others around him* – said the Dreamer, insinuating himself into my thoughts, which were scattered like flotsam from a shipwreck – *The idea of dominating others is an illusion... a prejudice of the old conflictual, predatory, and failing humanity...*»

The pause that followed gave me the illusion of respite but the hammer had rested in the air only to strike a harder blow.

«You are the emblem of this dying species – He pronounced *– a species that is making way for a more evolved one.»*

His words were tunnelling through many layers of old ideas and values. I felt the spasms of a creature making a supreme effort to be born, despaired of ever succeeding. My universe had first become malleable and then liquified. I was swimming in deep water.

«What you perceive as a sensation of death, is the suffocation of a humanity that is shedding its skin, a species on the edge of an abyss, forced to abandon its superstitions and old tricks which no longer work.»

Those words were carved into the air like the universal epigraph of the human condition. I saw myself floundering in an immense ocean of bobbing heads, shipwrecked souls resigned to their watery fate.

«From their earliest years, men are taught to live in the most desolate parts of their imaginations... Confronted with too large ideas or anything which surpasses the limits of their imagination, they will resist it and try to reduce it to a size small enough to fit into the tiny container of their consciousness.» These words brought to mind images of the primitive tribes of Borneo who shrank the scalps of their enemies in order to exorcize their power. His voice tore me sharply away from such thoughts.

«It's time you prepare for your 'journey'» He announced with paternal solemnity.

There was, in His words, the tenderness, sorrow and authority of those who 'know'. I noticed that His tone reflected exactly the way I was listening to him, as though each moment my attitude were being reflected in a sonic mirror. When I resisted, His voice became as hard and violent as my stubborness, and when I 'surrendered' as sweet and gentle as my attitude. With a theatrical gesture, He put His hand on the corner of his mouth, as if to share some secret with me, and whispered:

«Until now, when faced with life's challenges, you have found nothing better to do than numb yourself with work, or take refuge in sex, sleep, or some hospital bed.»

Then with intentional harshness, to shake me from the self-pity into which I was sliding, He said:

«To bend under the weight of unpleasant situations and misfortunes, to take these things terribly seriously, is to reinforce a miserable 'description' of the world, and perpetuate its events.»

«Then what should I have done?» I asked, my voice breaking with desperation.

«If a man changes his attitude towards the things that happen to him, over the course of time, this will change the very nature of the things happening to him.»

«Our Being creates our Life» He concluded while taking a step towards me. His advance, of only a few centimeters, was nevertheless unsettling and put me on my guard, in a state of anxious vigilance. I didn't know what to expect, as I had never been so alert. It felt as if all the cells of my Being, suddenly awakened, were eyes and ears, intent on listening. The Dreamer waited until my attention peaked, and then spoke the most devastating words of all.

«The death of your wife was the materialization, the dramatic representation of the scream of pain that permanently echoes within you. States of Being and events are the two faces of a single reality.»

An unbearable sense of guilt was making me feel faint. A chasm opened up ready to engulf me. With all my remaining strength I was resisting this most simple and unbearable of truths: that I alone was responsible for every event in my life, I was the sole cause of every suffering and misfortune.

It was as if the lights of the world grew dim to the point of being extinguished. I was on the edge of limbo. Slowly, I slipped towards it…

5 The awakening

As soon as I awoke, I could think of nothing else. Outside it was still night. The Manhattan traffic streaked past like bright lava flowing from the mouth of an unseen volcano. I remained still for some time, watching the 'world' below floating in my conscience. It seemed pale and insignificant. A new and pitiless clarity of thought was sifting through me, scouring every corner of that apartment making every piece of furniture, every book, every decoration, reflect the ache of an insignificant life lived without joy. All my possessions suddenly seemed to be orphaned and soulless. That distinctive melancholy emanating from ownerless objects clenched my heart. I felt the enormous weight of existing and the daunting impossibility of change. I feared meeting my children and seeing in their eyes the same death that permeated everything that surrounded me and feared they might fade and disappear along with everything else.

I spent many hours writing down everything that had happened during my encounter with the Dreamer, and all He had told me in that mysterious villa, in the chamber with the white tiled floor. I only had to half close my eyes to see every detail emerge from my memory in perfect clarity. Never had I been as lucid as in that timeless time spent with Him. Now I knew I belonged to a dark welter of divided and unconscious humanity. I was part of a planetary mob of sleepwalkers who were unable to love. I could no longer ignore it.

In the weeks that followed I diligently read and reread my notes, searching for some clue that might lead me back to Him and His world.

From the terrace of the *Café de la France*, I watched Western tourists going into the Souk, wandering in the maze of streets like white corpuscles in the veins of El Fna. They made slow progress, assailed from all sides by noisy merchants, by begging hands browned by the sun and water sellers, heavily laden with fleecy goatskin bags. Young girls selling ornate jewellery besieged foreigners as they passed by, stroking them as if they were talismans from whom they could magically extract a few dirhams. I was familiar with their watchful eyes – blades of black fire – and their imploring smiles, like players in the game of love.

For three days I went back to that café, surrounded by the pulsating life of Marrakech. I waited, reading and drinking tea while a pair of chameleons I had bought when I arrived kept me company. Every so often, I would stop reading, and get up to observe the kaleidoscopic spectacle of the street life, the brouhaha of commerce, the intense activity of the locals plying their trades. Then I would go back to my table. I began to lose heart. The thought of returning to New York, of taking the first plane out, without looking back often came to me as the hours and then the days passed. I was still trying to figure things out, trying to find a gauge with which to measure what was happening to me. I had left to look for Him without any indication but the name of this city – a scattering of palms and houses clustered between the blazing lips of the Sahara.

After receiving His message, I had hesitated a long time before leaving. It seemed utterly insane to cross the ocean to go and meet a fantastic character whose name I didn't even know. So many difficulties had arisen and conspired against me taking that journey. Above all, I couldn't think of a way of justifying it to Jennifer. Day after day I had put off making any decision. But the need to feel that sense of healing that I uniquely felt near Him, and my fear of missing the only opportunity of seeing Him again had got the better of me and I had decided to go. I was helped in reaching this decision by my closest confidante, Giuseppona, the only person to whom I had ever spoken about the Dreamer, and my encounter with Him.

«Go, my son» she urged in her direct way of speaking, with her strong Neapolitan accent, when I went to talk to her about it in her little room.

«Find him! This Dreamer sounds like a good person.»

Giuseppona had always been part of the family. She had been there when I had taken my first steps, and it was with her by my side that I had faced my first days at school. Every morning when she took me there I would listen to the stories of the streets and the people of Naples, ancient tales which were forever new. It was through her that I soaked up the spirit, legends and exploits of the heroes of that city. A city with an ancient heart, pulsating through timeless layers of many civilizations, wearing one on top of the other in shabby splendor, like Pulcinella's tiered costume. With the passage of time, these had become the strata of the city's living skin. In Giuseppona's company, I could still feel their vitality; beneath the patches and tatters I could see the gleam of gold and precious silks. I still remember my embarrassment when, on rainy days, she would burst into my classroom halfway through the morning, having rushed past caretakers and janitors, to change my wet socks and shoes. As I grew older, I didn't want her to hold my hand anymore, so for some time she continued to accompany me but following at a distance. From my teenage years on, she became my advisor in matters of the heart. I remember her terse judgment, "She wasn't right for you anyway!", that comforted me in my romantic misfortunes. She had adored my wife Luisella from the very first, and when we married and had our first child Giuseppona came to stay with us. She was the best nanny we could ever have had for Giorgia and Luca for whom she still had a boundless devotion.

Giuseppona was short and stocky, self-taught, resolute and pugnacious, with a rough, despotic manner. Her robust physique and strong features gave her the look of an American Indian, something between an old squaw and a tribal chief, and she had all the dignity and bravery of a chieftain. She was slow and heavy but wherever she went she put things in order. With her, one never felt the lack of anything. Her judgment, which I had asked for on so many occasions in my life, was an inimitable blend of good sense and popular wisdom. Her presence had brought joy and good humour wherever she had followed me, and she had been a solid rock throughout my life. When Luisa fell ill and died, Giuseppona became a second mother to my children, never missing a day. I will never be able to repay that debt of gratitude nor express what she has represented to four generations of my family. Dear Giuseppona, I will hold you in my heart, forever.

Having reached Marrakech, all my efforts to find the Dreamer had come to nothing, and by the third day, I wasn't even sure whether the enigmatic note which brought me there had really been written by Him.

While waiting, I had spent many long hours roaming the city, looking for some clue. For two nights, on my way back to the hotel after a full day of fruitless searching, I had mentally gone over every detail of our remarkable encounter, trying to find the slightest trace that would lead me to Him.

That morning I was once again wandering through the heart of the Souk. In the shadowy labyrinth of its spice-perfumed alleyways, the Levantine smiles of a hundred merchants invited me into their emporia –small shops piled high with the most improbable of merchandise – mostly of trinkets arranged haphazardly like debris cast up from a shipwreck. The endless succession of these commercial, often inhospitable caverns as lightless as the cells of a beehive, formed what looked like the banks of a river of people which dragged along with it men and women of different nationalities and backgrounds.

A picturesquely dressed, corpulent Mustapha who could have been created by Walt Disney, succeeded in enticing me into his shop, to the envy and disappointment of his competitors. He had the clever, shifty eyes of a rogue, set in a good-natured and intelligent face. The shop turned out to be surprisingly large. With the help of two assistants he literally turned everything in the shop upside down to find something that might interest me, something I might buy. He unrolled a hundred carpets, and offered me a veritable bazaar of silver and brass objects, first polishing them on his arm before offering them to me for examination. Following lengthy discourses on the merits of all these items and innumerable glasses of mint tea, which local custom does not permit one to decline, I was about to leave.

It was at this point that he extracted from the top shelf, out of a bundle of knick-nacks, a jewel box made of wood and ivory. It was so finely inlaid, so perfectly formed that I could not take my eyes off it, and the merchant, noting my interest, increased the praise he heaped upon, as well as the price. On the lid of the box, engraved in Gothic characters, I read the inscription: *Visibilia ex Invisibilibus.* All that we see and touch, all that is visible is born from the invisible.

6 Changing the past

I had left the Souk and returned to the Cafe de la France to pick up my scaly, green chameleon friends and as I leaned on the terrace railing, I reflected on what had just happened.

«The first rule of the desert is to travel light» I heard someone say behind me. I startled at the sound of that voice. However much I had longed for that moment and however much I had wished to see Him again, I could not help but feel frightened. I felt the terror of the unknown and his miraculous breath on my neck. Only with great effort, turning very slowly, did I find the courage to face Him.

The Dreamer was smiling at me. His look was that of a rich, aristocratic traveller from another time. He had the bored attitude and the languorous movements of a snob, but his voice betrayed a boundless energy. When He began to speak, I once again recognized His decisive tone, with its apparent roughness.

«It takes a huge amount of work to lighten your Being – He announced, launching in without any preamble – *You have to leave everything behind: all that your parents and your teachers, your*

masters of misadventure and prophets of doom have imposed on you. From them we have learned how to get into victim consciousness; how to get into misery, poverty and sickness…»

Then, slowly moving His face towards mine, He added:

«From them, we have learned a thousand ways to die. From the dawn of civilization, by means of a 'generational contamination,' millions of men, sealed into a hypnotic sleep, have learned to believe blindly in scarcity and limits.»

«Why – I asked – why… shouldn't we choose vastness without limits… why shouldn't we choose life?»

«Because man is irretrievably hypnotized. Behind his every misfortune, there is the most evil of evils: his unshakable faith in the inevitability of death…

The first and most difficult step towards freedom is realizing that this fear tyrannically governs his entire life.»

These words, together with the solemnity of his tone and his moving closer to me, thrust me into a state of agitation. As in the cults and sacred rites of ancient civilizations, His theatricality transformed the simplest act into a magical gesture, into a unique cosmic event of creative power.

As I felt my heart sink, I could tell that He was about to make a decisive judgment.

«Your past is a calamity!» He declared, in a hoarse voice. Then He stopped. This pause was particularly long, as if, before proceeding, He had to wait for a signal that was slow in coming. Then He said:

«You need to redeem it… to reclaim it… you need to change it!»

«Change… the past?» I asked.

«In your past, there are still too many holes… unsettled accounts, inner debts that have not been paid off, feelings of guilt and self-pity, and above all, dark corners where dirt and rust reign.» He listed these things as if rummaging through me like a drawer full of superfluous, old possessions.

«Your Being is like a badly managed shop, with articles priced at random – He observed – *those things which are of great value you sell cheaply, but the junk has ridiculously high price tags. To keep on like this means certain failure…»*

I would have liked to raise a shield to block those words streaming mercilessly towards me.

«But how is it possible to change the past? How can one change situations and events that have already taken place?» I asked, trying to defend myself, and divert what was becoming an unbearable sense of responsibility.

«There is a place in your Being, where thoughts, sensations, emotions, actions and events are archived forever, and even after many years have passed we can still find them, like things which are apparently inert and harmless that we have put away in an attic. In reality, these things continue to live and condition the whole of our existence. That is where you have to go» adding that all this would have taken a long period of preparation.

«How long?» I asked, with all the excitement and apprehension of someone about to embark upon a great adventure.

«You will need at least as many years as have already been spent mismanaging your life» was His stony reply, simultaneously reprimanding me for my past conduct and my present question. A stinging feeling of offence, like a conditioned psychological reflex, overcame me mechanically. Then, just as quickly as it had appeared, it shrank to a mild complaint before vanishing altogether.

The Dreamer had taken a seat at one of the tables and I sat down next to Him. The silence that followed lasted a long time and became even deeper as the approaching darkness muffled the clamour of El Fna.

7 Inner forgiveness

The setting sun was offering its last rays and Orion was already visible in the fading blue cobalt of the night sky. The temperature was dropping but the Dreamer gave no sign of noticing, nor of wanting to go inside. All indications were that a new, important chapter of my apprenticeship was about to start. Although the terrace was growing dark I took out my pen and notebook, determined to take down every word He said. I understood the importance of always having pen and paper at hand. They were all I needed to re-member and recover the wholeness that I had lost in an outside world far away from Him. Writing with Him in front of me, taking down his every word, was like tiptoeing into a higher level of Being. His voice caught me in the act.

«It takes years of working on yourself – He said – *to achieve this special condition of freedom, of knowledge, of power, called 'inner forgiveness'.»* He emphasized this term with a particular inflection in His voice, which instantly struck me as quite different to the warrior-like character and the uncompromising language of the Dreamer.

With a glance He verified that I was faithfully writing down His words. He waited for me to finish, and then continued:

«Inner forgiveness means delving into the folds of your own existence where it is still torn...it means washing and healing those wounds that are still open and...paying off all unsettled debts...»

Then, assuming a theatrically conspiratorial pose and lowering His voice as if about to share a valuable secret, He confided:

«Inner forgiveness has the power to transform your past and all its dead weight.»

Time after time, I turned over in my mind those incomprehensible words.

«Everything is here, now! In this very instant, in the life of every man, the past and the future are interacting simultaneously.»

These words filled me with an inexplicable, irrational joy. I found myself facing a limitless vision. The past and the future were not separate worlds, but connected and indivisible, a single reality. 'Inner forgiveness' was a time machine… which gave you the ability to access events of your life that in your ordinary way of thinking were forever gone, and future ones that were yet to come…

«I understand how the past might affect our lives, but the future?…» I asked.

«The future, like the past, lies right before your eyes, but you cannot see it yet.»

He spoke of 'vertical time' and of a 'time-body' where the past and the future were compressed in this very moment. He told me that the portal to gain access to this 'timeless' time, was this instant. The secret is never to be distracted, never to venture far from it. Accessing the 'time-body' meant being able to change the past and create a brand new destiny.

I was thrilled. I wanted this adventure to start immediately… I wanted it desperately…but my enthusiasm didn't have time to bud before I felt it put out by the Dreamer's harsh words.

«For people like you it is impossible to achieve inner forgiveness!» He announced. His tone was that of a judge passing a sentence for which there was no appeal.

«To enter into your past and heal it, you need a long preparation.»

«Without the ideas and the principles of a School, this achievement is impossible; you wouldn't even know where to begin.»

In a tone of finality, He said:

«Inner forgiveness is a return journey to oneself, the real reason why we were born. Men should never interrupt this healing process.»

The Dreamer warned me that this would require an extensive effort on my part and, first and foremost, a lengthy process of self-observation.

8 "Self-observation is self-correction"

«Self-observation is self-correction... A man can heal anything from his past if he has the ability to 'observe himself'» said the Dreamer. Then He went on to remark that man's condition was nothing more than the result of his inability to observe himself, and consequently, know himself.

«Self-observation is akin to taking a bird's eye view of oneself and one's life! – said the Dreamer, defining this concept, and sharpening his observation He went on – *It is like putting events, circumstances and relationships from the past, under a bright ray of sunlight.»*

As far as I could understand, the crucial prerequisite for self-observation was the ability to conduct it impartially, without passing moral judgment. Self-observation for the Dreamer meant letting one's life flow, not before a panel of courthouse judges, but under the x-rays of one's own objective intelligence, becoming a neutral witness to one's own self; a witness whose duty was limited to observing without ever passing judgment or formulating criticism. This vaguely reminded me of some of the experiments in organizational psychology I had studied at the London Business School. Some large firms had dramatically improved productivity by means of 'wandering management' (as the researchers had called it). This approach was based on attention and advocated the adoption of a system which kept the management constantly on the move within the organization. The duty of a *wandering manager* consisted precisely of 'roaming around' and making his presence felt in every corner of the company, no matter how remote.

His voice abruptly broke into my thoughts and memories, tearing me away from the London's LBS classrooms.

«*Self-observation is self-correction* – repeated the Dreamer – *If you are able to observe yourself, you will automatically self-correct... Self-observation is healing... a natural consequence of the detachment that is created between the observer and the observed.*

Self-observation allows a man to see everything that keeps him glued to the conveyor belt of the world: obsolete ideas, guilt, prejudices, negative emotions, prophecies of doom... It is a matter of detachment, de-hypnotism, awakening...

The most minimal suspension of the hypnotic effect the world has on you would shatter everything you ever believed in and would unravel the apparent equilibrium and illusory certainties of a lifetime.»

«*This is why most men will never be able to observe themselves* – He pronounced – *To distance oneself from the description of the world, if only for a moment... is an effort too great for most men.*»

He fixed me with a long intense stare. He was redirecting the focus of the conversation towards me. A knot in my stomach anticipated the pain of what was about to follow.

«*Put the observer within you to work! Self-observation is the death of that multitude of negative thoughts and emotions that have always ruled your life. If you observe inside yourself, the right things will start to happen and those that are not right will gradually melt away.*»

With a glance He noticed my look of dismay and added:

«*No one can do this alone. To meet with yourself, with your lie, to venture into the labyrinths of your Being without impeccable preparation, would kill you in an instant.*»

His words sounded like an irrevocable judgement and I was afraid He would abandon me. I feared He would consider mine to be a lost cause and conclude that any further effort to help me would be in vain. A desperate and heroic determination rose inside me. My readiness made Him reflect. Slowly He extended the forefinger and middle finger of his right hand and holding them together, pressed them against His cheek. Then He laid his chin down on the hollow of His thumb and bent His head slightly forward. He remained like this, deep in thought, for what seemed an eternity. He didn't seem to be looking at me, but I was certain that not one of my thoughts escaped Him. I was playing the final game of a decisive set, quite possibly the last. Everything depended on me, and me alone. I waited.

Finally, the Dreamer emerged from His stillness.

«Look... it's a full moon – He said, pointing to the heavens with a slight movement of His chin – *A man might see at most a thousand full moons in his lifetime, but it is very likely that, by the end of his life he will never have found the time to observe even one of them...*

And yet the moon is external. Imagine how much more difficult it is for a man to see himself, to focus inwards the direction of his attention. Self-observation is only the beginning of the Art of Dreaming.»

We remained silent for a long time. The terrace of *Café de la France*, stretched out into the darkness like the prow of a spaceship about to cross the star-filled heavens. We were the only ones on board... solitary Argonauts of the invisible.

«Get ready – He said, with the resolute tone of one used to getting things done – *It won't be an easy ride.»*

I listened carefully to His last words of advice. The Dreamer would stay at my side, but everything would depend entirely on me. He coldly explained that I risked finding myself trapped in a sort of mental limbo, a place where the past is abandoned but not yet understood, where the new world has yet to take shape. I would have no way of returning to the Dreamer's world from that band of space-time. He made it plain that this might therefore be our last encounter.

«The past of an ordinary man... a man who hasn't yet taken even the first steps towards the unity of Being, is strewn with barbs – He said – *These will snag him at the slightest attempt to enter and make changes...»*

These were the last words I was able to listen to. I had the sensation that the terrace was drifting like a boat away from the shore and the objects around it were beginning to fade into the distance.

"This is it" I thought, gathering my courage.

It was hard for me to hear what the Dreamer was saying. It was as though for long periods His voice was drowned out by the noise of invisible engines. The terrace turned into a time machine in which He and I were the only crew members. The universe was suspended, the time-tape rewound itself, and nothing else in the world seemed more important than our voyage back into my consciousness and past. I had the impression of slipping into the impenetrable darkness of a tunnel, as if our 'machine' was passing through an inner geology, and layer upon calcified layer of the strata of existence.

The first fragment of my life came into view, like an island, out of the darkness. As I watched it coming closer and looming larger I had the feeling that I was entering a world that was at the same time both familiar, yet arcane and mysterious, at the edge of the unknown. In linear time, only a few years had passed since the events I was revisiting with the Dreamer had taken place, and yet, that part of my past seemed incredibly remote.

9 "Death is no solution"

Luisella had died at the age of twenty-seven. Like a child at the beach digging a hole in the sand, a melanoma had slowly carved a hole in her leg. The edges of my world became ever more blurred, as if I were seeing them through the battered eyes of a boxer. For months I'd felt only rancor: a numb resentment somewhere between anger and fear.

Stupor,
pain…
darkness!...
A criminal complicity of thoughts and emotions…
Crazed splinters of Being…
A blade of light pierces
the darkness of my existence.
Pain,
stupor…
darkness!...
Torn apart
Behind: darkness…and pain…still!...

I fly towards it, closer, larger,
the opaque planet of my past years…
Landing…but where?
There is no space, no opening,
Not a square millimeter of sincerity
In the stony desert of my thoughts.
A gut swallows me….
Darkness…
Pain…
Stupor!...
The room of a provincial hospital…
the smell of disinfectant…
the stench of disease and helplessness.
A grief-stricken figure is kneeling by someone
lying down, still…
I move closer …
that frightened man…
is me!

This is the scene I was observing with the Dreamer. The austerity of that already distant, marmoreal presence, cast a pitiless light upon that small, dejected man, revealing his anachronism. I listened to the confused multitude that assailed his Being: the seething mass of thoughts, insignificant desires and emotions jostling within him, all offering an illusory semblance of a soul. Through the eyes of the Dreamer, as if under the influence of a hallucinogenic, I could 'see,' beyond appearances, the lump of selfishness and fear to which this man had been reduced.

«He is a ghost weeping over his own death» commented the Dreamer pitilessly, raising His chin in the direction He was indicating.

«Fear, suffering and anxiety are not the effect but the true cause of all his troubles.»

The Dreamer was revealing to me the most evil of all evils, the source of every misfortune - individual or collective, provincial or planetary.

«The chaos that every man carries within himself, his hell, is projected onto the world and takes the form of strife, discrimination and wars between races, ideologies, religions, and beliefs.»

The excitement of this discovery mingled with my horror, pity and shame when I saw the distinctive signs of premature ageing in this man.

«This man suffers, not because he is facing an event which brings him pain and grief, rather he is facing this event because he has chosen suffering as his natural state» announced the Dreamer conclusively.

I realized that everything that my life had been and everything it would become was already there, in that instant, just as the life cycle of an oak tree is contained in its acorn. Every detail proclaimed the negligence, carelessness and staleness of this life. I would have liked to have done something, to warn the man I once was, of our presence. I would have liked to have gone inside him to put things right, to give him a little dignity, to make him straighten his hunched back and wipe that pained expression off his face…

«It is impossible to intervene! You cannot do anything to help» said the Dreamer, holding me back. The tone of His voice had become imperceptibly sweeter.

«That man loves to suffer... he might swear to the contrary, but in reality he would not leave his hell for anything in the world.»

I was astonished, unable to believe such a monstrous claim. The Dreamer caught the expression of incredulity on my face, and added,

«Indulging in that state allows him to cling to the world. It makes him feel secure. Even with the pain of his condition, he is comforted by the illusion that some help might come to him from the outside…

If only he could observe himself... make even the most microscopic adjustment to his attitude and reactions… if only he had the capacity to raise the level of one single thought or emotion by one single millimetre, then his entire life would be transformed…»

Then, theatrically, He turned his voice into a powerful whisper. That sudden change of tone sharpened my attention.

«A man cannot change the events in his life, but only his attitude towards them.»

«But you said it was possible to change the past…» I protested. A searing disappointment, a wave of desperation, was welling up behind my eyes like tears.

«What you see here, this fragment of your existence which you would like to step into and change, is not your past – countered the Dreamer sharply – *It is your future!»*

«Everything repeats itself in your life... Events repeat themselves, remaining the same, because you don't want to change... Yet you complain, you accuse the world, convinced that someone from the outside can harm you or be the cause of your misfortunes...

The ordinary man imprisoned by the circularity of time doesn't have a future, only a past that repeats itself over and over again...

Now you are 'seeing' through My eyes! One day, when you are able to bear the responsibility, you will understand that pitying yourself is not the consequence but the origin of your misfortunes... and that you, and you alone, are the cause of all this... only then will you be able to bring light into your past and heal it.»

We were in the morgue. There were other bodies lined up next to that of my wife. None were as young as Luisa. Then, in that silence echoed the words that I would never forget.

«The death of this woman is the mirror image of all your states of Being, of your own inner deaths.»

The Dreamer had warned me about the difficulties I would encounter in revisiting the furrows of my past, and experiencing them again with Him by my side, I felt crushed by the weight of His vision. The resulting sense of responsibility germinating within me was unbearable. How could I accept that I was the creator and director of this horror film that I called my life?

«Death is immoral – He announced, in a firm voice – *and unnatural... Physical death is only the materialization of millions of deaths which take place inside us every day; it is the crystallization of a faith borrowed from a humanity which indulges in pain and loves suffering.»*

«Men have made death into their escape route – He continued relentlessly, taking no notice of my discomfiture – *They know exactly what they have to do to kill themselves... they know all the tricks... The body is indestructible!... And yet, they have managed to turn the impossible into the inevitable. A man cannot die, he can only kill himself! To succeed in this a man has to give it his all and make full time occupation of self-pity and self-destruction...»*

At this point He stopped, searching for the right words to overcome my resistance, the rudimentary level of my perception and the psychic wall I had raised up against the mysterious power of these revolutionary ideas.

«Death is always a suicide – He declared, roaring the phrase with the force of a battle cry – *Once this way of thinking has become your own flesh, it will overturn your vision of the world, and with it, your reality.»*

The Dreamer was attacking age-old beliefs, the unshakable faith shared by all mankind, held together in brotherhood by the shared condition of mortality, by the universal belief that death is inevitable. These words made me violent, absolutely vicious, as if someone was suddenly robbing me of everything that was most precious to me, as if something was tearing into my very flesh. An uncontrollable, silent scream arose within and echoed from the depths of my Being.

«In this very moment, billions of human beings are thinking and feeling negatively, trapped as you are, in their own resentment» He said. I felt Him seeping into the most secret and inaccessible recesses of my Being and I was deeply ashamed, as if I had been caught in the act of stealing.

«It is this state of Being that denies humanity any hope of escape from the most painful circles of existence» He declared with a trace of bitterness.

Then, in a tone of finality; gathering the threads of that most memorable lesson, He said:

«Men worship death and would never give it up, even if they could, because they consider it to be the answer to all their problems, the end of their suffering and of the thousand psychological deaths they inflict upon themselves... but death is no solution!»

The mesmerizing fog lifted, and my vision became clear. And, while the words of the Dreamer became real, the death of Luisella, in that room draped in black, with the other bodies lined up in those little beds surrounded by candles, seemed unreal to me, like a macabre scene from a play.

10 Healing comes from within

We continued on that trip into my past until we docked at the period of Luisa's last months of life. I saw myself once again unconsciously playing the obtuse role of the grieving husband, the head of a household not yet at thirty, already bent under the weight of such terrible misfortune. I watched that little man full of self-pity, blame, regret and recrimination. I saw his rancour and how he was caught in the grip of hatred and resentment; how he was throbbing with anxiety, lost in a sick imagination, his heart held in the ruthless clutches of guilt. I listened to his song of pain, that unremitting accusation against everyone and everything until I could stand it no more.

«Why all this? What am I doing here?» I cried to the Dreamer, crushed by the shame of this vision. I would have liked to turn on my heels and run away, but I couldn't move a muscle.

With unexpected gentleness the Dreamer brought me back to the purpose of this journey: to shed some light on my past, to revisit it with a new understanding. It was an unrepeatable opportunity.

«As with every true healing, the process has to start from within» He said sweetly, happily removing me from that state of self pity that was threatening to overcome me at any moment.

«It is our Being that creates the world, and not vice versa!»

«Like all men, you have always believed that events create your state, that external circumstances are responsible for your condition. Now you know this is a distorted view of reality.»

I was recovering. I waited a few seconds and then indicated to the Dreamer that I was ready to continue.

The next stage of our journey took us to Via Bolognese in Florence where, at that time, I had been involved in management training. During those months a sort of emotional symbiosis had been established between my colleagues and me, which had combined my natural tendency towards self-pity with the support they provided for me at little cost. Without being aware of it, my misfortune had made them feel better and faced with the precariousness of life, they were, for a while really able to appreciate their mediocre ration of existence. They treated me with the kindness and solicitude usually reserved for the seriously ill, the injured, or the beaten. I 'saw' the full horror of this exchange and felt a deep discomfort. Whichever way I looked at it, my past was full of shadows and I could not find a scrap worth saving.

I wandered about like a desperate man arriving at a disaster scene, looking for something to save: a loved one, a relationship, anything that might have some use or value but, to no avail. I was breathless with horror. Without the Dreamer next to me I would not have found the strength to carry on.

«Don't blame events – He said, seeing me tottering under the weight of these emotions – *To be a widower at twenty-nine with two children is not a curse. An event is neither good nor bad. It is just an opportunity. If you had had the discipline you could have transformed that event into something luminous. You could have moved it to a higher level... If you had had the courage to know yourself, it would not have been necessary for Luisa to die... it would not have been necessary to have experienced so many misfortunes.*

Our level of Being creates our life... everything that you see and touch is the reflected image of your Being and comes from your incompleteness, from that gap you bear inside. In existence, there are no empty spaces. If you do not fill them intentionally, by forcing yourself to think and act in a different way, then the world will do it for you mercilessly.

If you do not see, or do not want to see, then the disease becomes acute, and the travesty of your life will become ever more painful. Everything happens to reveal to you the cause of that tragedy, to take you back to the source of all this... and allow you someday to intervene and change this mortal vision of existence.»

11 The Landlords

Other fragments of my life, images from the past, streamed before my eyes like a film on fast forward. The streets and faces of people made me recognize the hundred cities in which I had lived, the hundred houses in which I had slept. And finally I caught a glimpse of…the shadow!... The dark presence that had always followed me, whenever I had chosen a new house, every time I had moved. I felt the vice-like grip of apprehension.

In every one of these houses I had found ogres: unreasonable landlords, argumentative characters. An ironic fate, a recurring destiny of admirable pedagogy, required me to have these neighbours.

«Look carefully... observe them closely! – ordered the Dreamer, firmly but kindly, anticipating the painfulness of what he was about to show me – *Those landlords were all the same person. There was no change... You didn't want to 'see' that the person behind the mask, disguised as a landlord, was you. You, meeting yourself!»*

Something broke inside me. A heavy door slammed shut and I heard the metallic click of the lock. I had the terrifying certainty that once I had heard these words I would never be able to turn back and nothing would ever be the same again. I fell apart inside, weeping without tears: my life had been that of a ghost, a reflection that I could see fading in the mirror of the world and disappearing without trace.

On the edge of that abyss, the words of the Dreamer came to my rescue.

«These are the guards, the jailers that you yourself have paid to perpetuate your state of dependence. Until you banish forever that song of pain which has always directed your life, those ghosts will keep coming back.»

The silence that followed lasted so long that I began to fear that the golden thread which joined us would break and I felt a pang of anxiety at the thought that He might have cut me out of His 'dream.'

It was a terrible feeling. For what seemed like an eternity I experienced that emptiness, that absence, and I ceased to exist. I understood then how much the Dreamer had become an integral part of my existence. I was connected to Him by a precious cord as if it were a vital organ from which I drew life, a third lung from which I breathed 'pure air'.

Then, new images from my past began to pass before my eyes, as though I were watching my life in an editing room. Somehow, I began to learn to control them. Now I could stop them, enlarge them, zoom in or out to gain a perspective. I could include or exclude myself from the scene. I saw the villa at via Fortini again, too large and silent now that Luisa was in the hospital at Via Venezian in Milan and Luca and Georgia were with their grandparents in Piedmont. I watched those days quickly rushing by, dawning and waning. At sunset, the shadows of the pine trees took possession of the old house, insinuating themselves like thin fingers into the innermost part of my Being.

I did not know the reason why the Dreamer had taken me to this exact spot. I did not know which part of my life I was to live through again. But I began to shake uncontrollably.

«We are about to go into the cellar of your life, the dark corners of your existence – He said, encouraging me – *It's time to do some tidying up... to clear things out.»*

«Get rid of that man! – He ordered, hardening His tone into a scornful sneer – *Get him out of your life once and for all!»*

I grasped what courage I had with both hands and once again climbed the steep road leading to the large gates of the entrance. I recognized the wind that blew down this hill and reached its fullest force in that precise spot. Like a gale, it rushed down the gully of that twisting alley, brushing its rough dry-walls, speckled here and there with the green and white of wild capers. I went in by the little metal door and saw the Citroën I had had at that time parked at the far end.

The villa appeared before me unexpectedly, the inner driveway being very short. Just as unexpectedly I came upon the stairway of terracotta tiles and stone. As I began to make my way up I turned my gaze towards the bottom of the garden beyond the house. I stopped to look at the illuminated windows of the guest cottage. Our only neighbor lived there.

Memories rushed into my mind, bumping into each other and I felt my breathing quicken as the frames of my affair with Judith began to flicker into view.

12 Judith, 'la signorina'

Giorgia and Luca called her 'la signorina.' Judith was tall, attractive, quite reserved and just a few years older than me. She lived by herself in the little house at the end of our garden. An intense batting of her eyelashes animated her expression as if in a constant state of astonishment. In reality she lived in a state of unperturbed detachment. Nothing truly surprised her, and nothing seemed to interest her beside her books and her music.

I checked to make sure that the Dreamer was still by my side and went up to one of the windows in the small living room. My heart was in turmoil, as it had been when at night I would go to her, seeking comfort in her body through fear and my inability to bear what was happening to me.

Once again I saw that small room, its walls covered with books, the sofa in the middle upholstered in a flowery fabric, and Judith, whose long fingers would dance across the keyboards while I told her about Luisa's illness and the deterioration of her condition. Her music was filling the room, making every atom of it vibrate. A crescendo drowned out those words full of egoism and false concern for my wife.

Now I could feel the full horror of that man's intentions and even smell the nauseating odour of his thoughts. For the first time I clearly saw the kind of struggle that was churning in my guts, torn as I was between the pain of Luisa's impending death and the wild and secret joy I felt at the prospect of freeing myself from my wife and the weight of that unbalanced and immature marriage.

At some obscure level, I had been blaming her for my unhappiness and frustrations, for the restrictions and obstacles I had encountered in my professional life.

«Death is never an accident – interrupted the voice of the Dreamer – *like sickness, unhappiness, and poverty. For years you prayed this would happen... without even admitting it to yourself, you intensely desired and even invoked it. Dreams always come true, even the darkest ones.»*

The curtain of pretence was lifted. I could no longer hide, it would no longer be possible. Behind the tears and desperation of that small man, between his skin and the mask he wore, I saw the smirking face of my own criminality. The horror took my breath away and an unassailable force held me there unable to move, in front of Judith's window.

Once again I saw the scene of our first meeting. Luisa was dying and I was clinging to this woman, in search of a little company, compassion and her body. When Judith understood my intentions, her attitude didn't change; she was not upset. She took my hand and led me into her bedroom to give me what I had come begging for: sex... to forget, escape and find relief from the fear which tortured my soul. From then on, we met frequently. We did not talk a great deal and there was no need for ceremony. At night I would go to her in order to soothe my anguish but our embraces would end in orgasms as insignificant as sneezes.

The Dreamer did not spare me even a single one of those scenes and I stayed there, watching that spectacle, tasting the full bitterness of its squalor.

Luisa was in the house, a few yards away from us, at the other end of the garden. This man could not be me…My disgust became unbearable and I felt faint at the recognition of the fact that I would stoop to any level to save myself. And so, cruelly, the wounds left open from my past were healing themselves.

Judith saw our sexual relationship as a task to be scrupulously fulfilled, with dedication and seriousness, but she never allowed not even one atom of my Being to attach itself to her life. Our affair flowed over her without her life being influenced by mine at all. It was frustrating not to be able to truly possess her, her independence made me feel insecure. I persuaded myself that Judith lived for no one but herself, that her love for books and music was only a cloak for her egoism. And so, sealed under glass and labelled by my judgment, I relegated her to the closet of past memories. Only now, through the eyes of the Dreamer, was I able to see exactly what Judith had represented for me. Only now was I able to see from her reserved nature, so devoid of any hypocrisy, the detached attitude of an impeccable being and the pure love of a sincere woman.

Judith was better than me. She had rescued me like a desperate soul from the wreckage of my life. I cannot imagine what I would have done without her. She had clearly seen who I was! She had seen my senseless life turn horribly upon itself. She had recognized me as a bearer of death! Keeping me out of her life had been her salvation. How could I have judged her so harshly?

No longer occupying such a dark corner of my life, Judith shone!

Her music was life…

And yet something did not make sense. How had I come to meet her? How had a creature like Judith entered my hell just when I so desperately needed her?

I turned towards the Dreamer. My legs were giving out from under me. An absurd notion, a glint of total insanity, was planting itself in a small crack in my rationality. From there I felt it pushing inwards, penetrating, slowly, inexorably. I had to stop it before it destroyed every one of my faculties. It wasn't possible! Judith was… a gift from the Dreamer!... Judith was the Dreamer!… How many times had He already come into my life to save me? How could I have been so blind? How could I not have noticed such perfection?

The thought whirled at the edge of this precipice and then dropped over.

«Each one of us is given an immense margin of salvation» were the words the Dreamer used to bring me back. His tone was surprisingly sweet.

«But we use it up, we waste it quickly, through our constant negligence, our irresponsible way of ignoring the signs, the warnings, the 'traffic-lights' of existence... and we believe ourselves to be fragile, exposed to every peril, at the mercy of chance...»

The voice of the Dreamer became severe and resolute once more and His intensity made me shudder.

«Life is very powerful, and the body is indestructible. In order to die, you must make the impossible possible.»

Referring to the man I had been as if talking about someone else, He said:

«Forgive him! Forgiving him will heal your past and replace it with the light of today.»

Something inside me began to melt and then give way. I cried like a baby. A magma of pain, of unpleasant thoughts and emotions flowed freely while regrets, accusations, resentments and feelings of guilt came to the surface.

«Men and women are all like you, ruled by negative emotion, they are like fragments floating in the universe... Accusations, complaints and dependency are all part of the story of their lives... and the only way they can make sense of things!... Suffocated by anxiety, they try to forget about death through death.»

13 Thank you, Luisa!

The journey into the past started once again. The scene slowly changed and the Dreamer took me back to the period when I was making constant trips between Florence and Milan to visit Luisa who was hospitalized at the Institute on Via Venezian. I was immediately trapped in the same mental cage and I found myself in the same state I had been in at that time. I experienced the same pain

I had felt then, becoming more acute as the moment of each of those departures drew closer.

I was torn between a moral obligation to be near her and a repugnance I felt whenever I entered that place crowded with suffering people. Crossing the wards, meeting them in the corridors, I could flick through their faces as if I were turning the pale pages of a book. I painfully entered into their storylines, into the words of their expressions and the ink of their suffering, fearing that one day I might be condemned to the same fate.

And then I would feel an irresistible urge to flee, to leave them behind and forget them forever. Outside there was what I called life: people lost in the triviality of every day, the hubbub of the traffic, the sound and reassuring flare of futile laughter. Having hurriedly performed the ritual of the grieving husband, as soon as I had absolved my guilt by conferring with one of the medical staff, asking for updates and displaying my concern, I would find some pretext and run away. I would wander around the streets of the city centre seeking refuge in the crowds; losing myself in the confusion of the traffic, wrapping myself in the colours and lights of the city. I was numbed by the smiles of the well-dressed women and the shop window displays, nursing the illusion of a world without problems, populated by people who were miraculously invulnerable and happy. In that psychological bubble I could breathe. Thoughts of Luisa would break in without warning from time to time and disturb my drunken state. Apprehension, fear and a sense of guilt came to roust me out, like the Furies and the vengeful gods, from whatever momentary distraction I had chosen, whether it be theater, café or vernissage.

Only then the thought of the fragility of life, the impotence and distress I felt at its precariousness terrified me.

Accompanied by the Dreamer, I arrived at Luisa's bedside. Her eyes were closed. She was alone. The Dreamer had chosen a day when I was at work or walking around the city trying to escape from myself. Luisa's laboured breathing lifted the edge of the blanket at an inhumanly fast rate. I recognized that symptom with an aching heart. Her days were coming to an end.

A nod from the Dreamer encouraged me to move closer.

I carefully moved a chair from next to the metal bedside cabinet and remained watching her for a long time. Locks of hair soaked in sweat covered her brow and the part of her face that was not covered by the sheet. The months and days of our brief marriage spooled quickly before my eyes, vividly, loaded with events and memories. Our first apartment. The stories I brought home from work and the pride I could read in her eyes on hearing of my first successes. The birth of Georgia. Her endless crying at night, which seemed hopeless. The birth of Luca. And then, her illness.

Our immaturity had soon turned into incomprehension, jealousy, arguments, regrets and recriminations. We were two weak people, clinging to one another; two incomplete human beings who had deceived themselves into thinking that together they could complete each other and form a whole. But the result of the union of two incomplete people is incompleteness squared. These thoughts, and others, came to my lips forming words which I whispered in her ear. I spoke to her of life, beauty and happiness. It didn't matter whether she heard me or not.

A bitter pain was lodged in my chest. An urge to weep tightened in my throat. Yet I was joyful. I felt in love, a passionately as never before. Up until that day, hypnotically caught up in my activities and by a thousand illusory tasks, I had experienced the time spent with Luisa as pure suffering. The waiting without either past or future, the hours ticking away while nothing happened, the stillness, the silence and calm which reigned supreme in that world, overwhelmed me. The vision was intolerable. I felt only one, overwhelming desire: to flee and protect myself from the creeping intrusiveness of a reality which froze the very blood in my veins.

«This woman is your past which is dying» said the Dreamer from behind me. The force of these words, and the delicacy with which He pronounced them, caused a tension within my Being which moved me and set me free.

The feeling of death I had experienced for months next to her, was not something outside myself. It was my death, the death which I had always carried within me. Luisa had enabled me to see it, feel it, and touch it, and at that supreme moment, she had given me the opportunity to defeat it. In return, I had sullied her with every bad thought, every accusation.

«Ask her forgiveness! – ordered the Dreamer in a fatherly tone – *Her life was special, it has made you recognize the death that is inside you – your sense of victimhood, your feelings of guilt and the destructiveness which have guided your existence.»*

«Thank you, Luisa – I murmured, smoothing the wet hair away from her face, and wiping her brow – What senseless ignorance. I didn't know. This is our resurrection…I will change, forever, and our children will change with me!»

The hours went by but I was not in the least a bit tired. I wouldn't have wanted to be anywhere else in the world but there, by her side. I reflected that I had been coming to see her and the others in this hospital for so long, and I had felt detached, convinced that I was the only healthy one among the sick. Week after week I had lived alongside those people who, like her, were clinging to a scrap of life, without understanding what they had to give.

Then, it would have been impossible for me to see that all these men and women were not outside of me, but were merely the projection of an unhealthy vision of existence…reflected images of my own sickness, of my own separation, of my irresponsibility. This world was revealing to me the death, which I carried within myself. Accepting this and taking responsibility for it, was part of a process which had not even started yet, and which the Dreamer called 'inner forgiveness'.

Self-observation is self-healing.

Observing all this, and feeling thankful for the realization of how much even the smallest detail of this world belonged to me, alerted me to the first signs of my healing process.

It was night. The corridors of the hospital were silent. I no longer knew for how long I had been by her bedside. I had used up everything there was to use up: words, memories, tears. There was one thing left to do! I folded back the sheet and uncovered her. Under her nightshirt, she had enormous swellings. Her stomach in particular was swollen and hard, as if she was ready to give birth. I bathed her chest and her legs with a damp, lightly perfumed cloth. I examined her wound, dark and deep as a nest. Lucidity, judgment, and a cool professionalism I would never have imagined possible, guided my hands as I applied her medication. Years of incomprehension, the incrustations of so many unkind actions and betrayals, were scraped away along with the cells and dead tissue. I disinfected the area, applied a new gauze bandage and taped it with plasters. I drew the covers over her once again and kissed her.

«The past needs to be blessed and healed... Go into every fold! Bring light into every corner! Transform the past with a new understanding… Your past will be healed when you cease to indulge

in anxieties, doubts and fears. This is the real meaning of 'inner forgiveness'.»

The air was still echoing with the Dreamer's words when I felt the pavement suddenly give way under my feet as though a trap-door had opened beneath me. I fell on my back and began to slide down an invisible chute at great speed, until a whirlpool of colors swallowed me up.

When I opened my eyes I was in my hotel room in Marrakech. That same day I made arrangements for my return to New York. An extraordinary feeling still coloured the recollection of every moment spent with Him, from our encounter at the Café de la France to the journey into my tormented past and the night spent with Luisa.

They had already taken my luggage down to the car that was waiting to drive me to the airport, yet I lingered. I couldn't tear myself away from the place where I could still breathe His presence. I sent a grateful thought towards the Dreamer for having escorted me into my past, helping me to get rid of so much useless ballast.

Only a few shreds of my former self were still attached to my Being. I had kept one particular fragment, just one, which I still gripped in my fist. However painful, I held it tight, reluctant to let it go: my last look at Luisa, that kiss of love exchanged between the past and the future, at the edges of existence.

CHAPTER II

Lupelius

1 Encounter with the School

It was late morning and I was going down an elegant street full of antique shops. The hot sun on my back seemed to be pushing me towards an open space that I could just catch a glimpse of at the end. I noticed that I was walking at a brisk pace, as though hurrying to an appointment without knowing where it was, nor whom I was going to meet. The pavement I was walking along led to an Italian café and the open space revealed itself to be a large piazza, one of the most beautiful I had ever seen.

The Dreamer was seated at one of the little tables, from which to best admire both the square and the spectacle of the passers-by. He was surrounded by a small cluster of obsequious waiters who were intent on serving Him and listening to his suggestions. As I arrived they were drawing up a second table and making space to set down the contents of two large trays. A constant aura of wealth surrounded Him and every aspect of His presence emanated refinement. He delighted in abundance, yet His every expression was marked by the sobriety of a Macedonian warrior, and his diet with extreme frugality.

He seemed pleased to see me again. With a slight nod of His head He both greeted and invited me to join Him. From that moment on the Dreamer's attention seemed entirely focused on the tiny pastries and delicacies neatly arranged before Him.

I had not seen Him since our last encounter in Marrakech but I had been waiting impatiently for this moment. Now, in His presence, a thousand questions crowded my mind. Some had echoed down the centuries - raised throughout the history of the world and remaining still unanswered. Religions, schools of thought and prophetic traditions, generations of scientists, researchers, philosophers and ascetics had all tried in vain to find responses. I reflected on the fact that modern man, the most recent link in this chain of research tracing back thousands of years, remained as naked as ever in the face of the enigma of his own existence, like Oedipus before the Sphinx.

Tea was served and the Dreamer followed the execution of this operation with scrupulous care, directing the waiters according to a ritual known only to Himself. He hardly touched the food. The Dreamer seemed to derive nourishment from His own attentiveness, His impressions, and the harmony and rhythms of each tiny movement. After the tea there was a long pause. I waited eagerly for Him to begin speaking and in the meantime opened my notebook. My pen was at hand. When He spoke, His tone was solemn.

«With Me at your side you can leave the tracks of your inflexible destiny – He said – *At My side you can break the mechanical cycle of your routines, your feelings of guilt... beside Me you must give up your doubts, your fear, and your destructive thoughts... you must abandon the lie that binds you to a mortal description of existence.»*

«In order to change, you must fight a lifetime of indoctrination!– He continued – *You must overturn your way of seeing things. Only in this way, and through hard work, can you change your destiny... But a man can never achieve this alone.. He needs a School.»*

The emphasis He placed on the word 'School,' and the context in which He used it, made me realize, intuitively, that it held a meaning which went beyond the conventional. I felt I was hearing it for the first time. I discovered a power in it that I had never felt before and the sweetness of a long forgotten promise. A thought passed through my Being like a shiver, and reached my lips in the form of a question.

«What is the 'School'?» I asked. My voice was trembling and I found myself surprised by my emotion.

«The School is your voyage of return» said the Dreamer. His dark eyes glowing with a secret joy.

The School is the quantum leap from Multitude to Integrity.
from Conflict to Harmony, from Slavery to Freedom.

«Finding the School means binding yourself to the 'Dream' with a steel cable...it means being able to access the highest levels of responsibility. Only few can endure such an encounter» He concluded.

Those words and His gaze triggered something hidden inside of me into action, like the click of a changing gear. I was filled with regret as I realized the immorality of having lived for years 'away from home'. How miraculous it was to find myself with something, someone that I had been so desperately seeking.

«How does one go about finding the School?» I asked, with a whisper of a voice, full of reverence, feeling the exceptional nature of that event.

«Don't worry... the School will find you» replied the Dreamer. Then, seeing my bewilderment, He softened His blunt response adding:

«When a man is hopelessly disappointed by his life... when he realizes its incompleteness, and his impotence; when existence grips him in a vice so he cannot breathe, only then will the School appear.»

2 "The world is a legend"

Sitting in the café in that unknown city, I listened to Him, while accumulating pages of notes. I sensed that my apprenticeship, which had started in that unknown villa, and continued in Marrakech, was following a secret path of learning, the outline of an uninterrupted design.

«Discovering the 'School' is the most extraordinary event in a man's life; his only opportunity to escape collective hypnosis – explained the Dreamer – *to understand that everything that you see, everything that surrounds you is not the world... but only a description.»*

«But I am listening to You, I can touch this table. I can see people passing by… and know that every one of these men has a life, a job, a family… how can all this be just a vision of mine?»

«The images that fall upon your retina are not the world, but its narrative: a story repeated to you many times; a legend... – responded the Dreamer laconically – *The world has been described to you.»*

I marvelled at what I was hearing, but was even more astonished when He added in a whisper:

«The true creator of the reality that surrounds you, is you!... But you have forgotten...»

«What have I forgotten?» I asked. I could hear a trace of hostility in my voice, emblematic of the distance growing between us.

«The world requires you so that it can exist. You have forgotten that you are the creator, you have become the shadow of your own creation.»

His tone of voice bridged the distance and brought me back into line, like a schoolboy.

«The world is subjective, personal!... It is the mirror image of our Being...Vision and reality are one and the same thing, the only thing dividing them is 'time'.»

I would have liked to have said 'yes,' to have accepted His vision. But something inside me objected. The rational part of me faltered, but did not give way. How was it possible to confront the same object, landscape, event or person, and yet have differing perceptions?

«But surely there is such a thing as objective reality! – I declared, to shore up my long-held convictions – After all, a thing cannot be anything other than what it is...»

I was still trying to defend 'my' beliefs, but I knew that, no matter how deeply rooted they were, they would not hold. They were bound to be overturned by contact with the Dreamer's vision. This time too, as on every other occasion, the unforeseeable miracle would occur and everything would suddenly click into place; in His company I would inevitably understand things without ever being able to know when or how. I wanted, and expected, this change and when it finally came, I felt the walls of my Being expanding vastly to make room for a clearer, freer, and more intelligent vision of the world.

Seeing me still perplexed, He unleashed another decisive blow against my vision of the world, and added:

«We can only see what we are.»

Then, with His inimitable and subtle, sarcastic humour, He said:

«If a thief would encounter a saint, he wouldn't see past his pockets.»

This witticism enlightened me and I lingered for a moment over that comic and instructive image. But the Dreamer had already resumed His lecture with a scowl, as if this digression, minimal as it was, had distracted Him or caused Him to deviate too much from the purpose of our meeting.

«Only contact with the School will allow you to escape the rigidity of the vision held by common minds.

Only 'School work' will one day enable us to 'see' the world behind its false description.

Only a man who 'works on himself' will one day be able to access a harmonious vision, a state of wholeness. And only a harmonious and complete vision can heal the world.»

3 A School for overturning

The Dreamer revealed to me that Schools that prepared exceptional men had always existed, in every age and society. Apart from the philosophical and cultural differences that seem to have distinguished them from one another, these 'schools' were, in actual fact, only one single School. Its voice remained as it had always been, and its thought had crossed every age and civilization. He called this school the 'School of Being', a forge, a universal hotbed where Dreamers are formed, and where visionaries and luminous utopians had always refined their intent.

«A School of Transformation» the Dreamer elaborated, and then paused.

He breathed in deeply the aromas spiralling up from His tea, and then, in a hushed voice added:

«The School for Gods... where one learns to govern oneself before governing others.»

His voice made my spine tingle. It had become the martial cry of a warrior in action.

«A School for overturning – He said – *where ideas and beliefs are overthrown... first and foremost, the idea that death is inevitable. Death is the ultimate resistance to truth, harmony and beauty. Death destroys whatever is incapable of becoming truth. If we are true in every cell of our body we will never die.»*

I thought back to the classical tradition, before the age of Homer, which divided humanity into two species vastly removed from each other: the heroes, who were the champions of a dreaming humanity, individuals capable of making the impossible happen, and an indistinct and faceless multitude without will and without dreams. The former, guided by Fate, were destined for a great individual adventure and the latter, ruled by the laws of Accident and Chance, were doomed to a life of insignificance.

I was enlightened by the thought that in reality the great myths, from the most ancient times, narrated the actions of men who had encountered the 'School.' Their adventures, their battles against monsters and giants, sung by the aoidoi, the wandering bards, were the stages along the way - part of an 'inner journey' back into the depths, into the most obscure and secret recesses of their beings. The Dreamer explained that it was there, in the most hidden corners of existence, where the river of destructive thoughts and guilt coursed, and negative emotions festered. There one could find the origin of all those monsters, the source of vulgarity, every failure and all our deaths.

«You need, above all, to cast out the enemy within your own flesh. And no sooner will you finish rousting him out than you will find him confronting you again in an even more ruthless, cruel and powerful way.... The Antagonist grows as you grow! There are not thousands of enemies, there is only one, and victory is only one... that over yourself.»

«The 'journey of return' is the great opportunity for a man to heal his past» He said, as His gaze slowly surveyed the piazza, the twin churches, the patrician palaces and the statues around the ancient obelisk. He looked at the people crowding it.

«The world is the past –He pronounced, coining one of His most admirable maxims – *Whoever you meet, whatever you encounter, is always the past. Even if it appears to be before you at this moment, what you see and touch is only the materialization of your inner states... Past is dust. The world you see and feel, in this precise moment, is the materialization of all that you have been... There is nothing that can happen in your life that has not already been accepted in your thoughts. The world is dust. With a puff you blow it away.»*

The Dreamer moved His chair slightly back to suggest that we should rise. His movement distracted me abruptly from the effort I was making to keep up with Him and these new ideas. I had a knot in my stomach. I would have liked to pour this exuberant and irrepressible new wine into the old skin of my convictions but it was like trying to contain an ocean in a chalice. I felt my rationality crumbling and yielding under His assault. I wandered into empty, intellectual posturing to hide from myself the evidence that His teaching was penetrating ever more deeply, becoming more dangerous, perhaps even fatal for my old equilibrium.

In the meantime the Dreamer had stood up. With a nod, He invited me to follow Him. I was reluctant to leave that quiet corner where His words still resounded in the air. It felt as if I were leaving an ancient temple, a venerable ark of knowledge. Every detail of that meeting would be forever fixed within my cellular memory, including the carefully laid tables, the movements of the waiters, and even the freshly baked *sfogliatine*.

I walked across the piazza with Him and followed Him into a church. Passing between the transept and the altar, beyond the central nave, we came to a little chapel. I could make out two giant canvasses in the semi-darkness, one facing the other. I glanced around. From our position, the church seemed completely deserted. The Dreamer asked me to put a coin in the meter. A strong light was cast onto the two works of art. He suggested I look at them from the centre of the chapel, from a point equidistant from both. I did as He suggested, then carefully examined the two masterpieces. The painting on the left showed Peter being crucified upside down; the other was of Paul's fall on the road to Damascus.

«*It is no coincidence that these two paintings are facing each other* – He said – *They are indissolubly linked in a single message.*»

The Dreamer stopped talking and we remained there in silence. I took this pause as an invitation to reflect and try to discover the secret of the symbolism. I could feel time passing, scanning my futile efforts, until the Dreamer liberated me from my bewilderment by pointing out that these two works were the most powerful iconographic representations of the idea of 'overturning'.

«*These works exude the breadth of thought that comes out of a great School of responsibility* – He said – *Only a School like that can fight prejudice and age-old beliefs in order to overthrow old humanity's mental paradigms. It can heal it forever from its conflictual thinking and free it from pain... Vision and reality are one and the same thing. The world is your reflection. Turn your beliefs upside down and the world will follow like a shadow. Reality will take the shape of a new vision.*»

The timer on the lights ran out, and the paintings sank back into darkness like steel blades returning to their sheaths. In that semi-darkness scented with beeswax candles, I listened as the Dreamer told me of a School that had remained silent for more than ten centuries. He paused for a long time; and then He told me enigmatically that it was time for its voice to be heard once again. I was astonished. The idea of a thousand-year-old School reappearing after centuries of silence to carry on its mission dazzled me. It was then that the Dreamer told me about a legendary warrior-monk and a precious manuscript that had been lost.

«For you, and for those like you who believe they can find the truth in books... it would be useful to seek out the traces of this ancient School» He said.

Suddenly His voice became imperious.

«Find that manuscript!» He commanded.

Beyond the roughness of His voice and His peremptory attitude, I knew that He was assigning me an important task and I was grateful to Him. A decisive 'Yes', solemn as an oath, echoed in my chest. I would dedicate all my efforts to this task. The more I thought about it, the more my enthusiasm grew for this enterprise, which promised to project me into a familiar and congenial world.

The Dreamer noticed I was reverting to my old habits, falling back into the melancholy *cliché* of the scholar, and said:

«One day you will realise that there is nothing you can bring in from the outside, there is nothing you can add to what you already know... and there is nothing that teaching and experience can add to your understanding... True knowledge can only be 'remembered'... Man's knowledge cannot be greater or smaller than he is. A man 'knows' what he 'is' and never the other way around. To know means, above all else, to be... The more you are, the more you know.»

Years later, the Dreamer would talk to me about a memory beyond time, a 'vertical memory', made up of states and levels, the container of infinite knowledge. This is the inheritance of every man; we all have it, but we have lost the key...

Re-member.

The ancient mosaics on the floor began to expand, and the distance between us began to increase, imperceptibly at first and then visibly. I felt an aching sense of loss as I listened to His final words.

«Knowledge is the inalienable property of every man... it is as ancient as humanity...

One day, you will realize that there is nothing to add... but a great deal to eliminate... if you wish to know.»

I drank in those words. I had been waiting to hear them all my life. I recognised them. A slight tremor under my skin heightened the sensation that I felt of containing all things. I was a perfect, universal measuring system. I experienced a feeling of wholeness, of understanding, of connectedness, with all and with everything. The Dreamer's invulnerability and faultlessness was palpable. Nothing could erode or corrupt that integrity.

«Find that manuscript!» He said again austerely. The outline of His face had already begun to fade away.

«When you have found it, we will meet again.»

4 Lupelius

That same day I began my research on the ancient school and my quest for the manuscript of which we had spoken. The work He had asked me to find, 'The School for Gods', had been written in the ninth century by the philosopher-monk Lupelius, a free spirit of the Dark Ages, and a native of Ireland, in those years a refuge for learned men, a land at the crossroads of cultures and traditions, tormented by every war and conflict imaginable.

Little was known about the life of Lupelius and the information that did exist was uncertain. The documents I was able to find were few and contradictory in facts. Since his youth Lupelius had been trained in the art of war by his father who hired the greatest masters available and brought him up under the strictest discipline. While still very young, he embraced the monastic life and sought solitude in the mountains of Bet Huzaye, today called Kazakhstan, which was at that time a favourite destination for Anchorites from all parts of the Christian world. Of his religious and spiritual training, it is known that he entered the nearby monastery of Shaban Rabbur, where, cloistered for years in its formidable library, he fervently studied the sacred Scriptures, the Greek Fathers and the great mystics of every time and place, from Origen to Giovanni of Apamea, down to the Desert Fathers. In the weeks that followed I was able to speak with a few scholars of medieval philosophy who confirmed that all traces of Lupelius' only work, and of the original manuscript, had been lost for centuries.

I researched the libraries of the great universities, contacted various institutes of philosophy and met with scholars and researchers after which I extended my search to the rest of Europe, without success. Finally, in Ireland, at Dublin's Wrighter Museum, following yet another trail, I ascertained that they had kept a copy, the only known one in existence. However, it turned out that this one too had been swallowed by the quicksand of time.

The obstacles and difficulties I met increased my commitment and determination while every clue and new encounter along the trail of that lost teaching, spoke to me, shaping my very existence into a new order. As if following the outlines of a precise design, the fragments of my life, once scattered pieces of an unknown mosaic, were now coming together, each one finding its rightful place.

Finding that manuscript and going back to see the Dreamer, became for me one single task. There was no other way of seeing Him again. This thought constantly rekindled my desire to continue with the research He had entrusted to me.

From the information I was slowly gathering and the elements of Lupelius' philosophy that I was able to laboriously piece together, the thought and character of a great School began to emerge, its principles as powerful as the walls of an immortal city. After more than a thousand years, the fragments of that lost teaching still shone forth a light at odds with the social and moral dissolution of that era.

The figure of Lupelius, servant to the world, immediately made a great impression on me. From the beginning of my research I had felt a growing admiration for this unknown philosopher. The more I learned about him and his mission, the more I saw this thinker towering alone above people and events. His School stood out like a rock in a sea of ignorance and superstition. His thought was woven like a golden thread through the fabric of a history filled with crime and misadventure.

I was unable to learn much about his life apart from the period of time he spent at the court of Charles the Bald in France. Certainly Lupelius was an unusual character, a philosopher and man of action unlike any other. He had no habits or routines. It was said that he could stay awake for inordinate amounts of time and no one had ever seen him sleep.

"Sleeping makes you weak, in your mind, and in your body – he said to his followers, and with his typical Irish humor, added – *Sleeping is nothing but a bad habit."*

One of his particular practices was to wander around the markets in the most dangerous and disreputable parts of the cities of Europe. There, in the most apparently unfavourable conditions, he initiated his followers into new ways of thinking and feeling, overthrowing conventional and narrow-minded views of the world. There, his shining madness transformed that world of cheats and criminals, of snares and ambushes, into a school of integrity. He used the cleverest tricks to eradicate their ingrained beliefs and erase the emotional slime from their minds.

His school forged remarkable men and invincible warriors. Lupelius made use of creative methods he invented for teaching and purification. He would disguise himself as a slave, a vagabond, a politician, a banker or a wealthy merchant and he would use these roles strategically. Whether it was the king's crown or the robe of a monk, Lupelius assumed them and had his disciples wear them too, teaching them how to 'become' the characters they were inhabiting, to explore and understand their every detail and secret, but without ever forgetting that they were playing a game and becoming trapped by it. He led them into the Souk where he involved them in wild intrigues with bandits and criminals. He encouraged them to enter into the most deprived and needy sectors of society and pushed them to undertake the most foolhardy excursions, almost beyond the point of no return. The Lupelians enlisted as mercenaries in pointless wars, revolutions and feuds in distant countries without even knowing the reasons for these conflicts. They went into battle, not to defend the weak or the oppressed, not to support abstract principles or ideologies, nor to defeat external enemies or seek revenge but to become masters of themselves, authors of their destiny.

Real warriors do not fight for supremacy or control over others.
They do not fight for glory, nor for any possession or reward,
but to gain the only thing which truly matters:
their own inner freedom.

For the Lupelians, the fields of battle offered the most practical way to apply the principles and ideas of the School – the real proof of their conscious transformation and understanding. Only he who had conquered an inner integrity could remain unharmed by any attack. The Lupelians' invulnerability sprang therefore from this flawless integrity – death might be near, but it could neither take hold nor enter.

Lupelius' teaching was a discipline of invulnerability founded upon the development of the will. His aim was to achieve freedom without limits.

Free forever from all human conditions and natural limitations

The Lupelians practiced the art of 'self-mastery'. The supreme victory is to 'conquer oneself'; never permitting any external event or condition to produce internal wounds, to tarnish one's Being. Lupelius trained his disciples to maintain their serenity and calm under the most extreme conditions. He urged them to seek offence and encourage hostility in order to test their integrity. Even when crossing cities or regions afflicted by epidemics and contagious diseases, they would always emerge unscathed.

Incorruptibility and purity make a warrior invulnerable,
impervious to attack from even the most dreaded of evils.

I tried to confront the question of the difference between impassivity (*apatheia*) advocated by the stoics, and the indifference of the soul towards passions and external thoughts championed by the mystic Lupelians. For Lupelius, impassivity was characterized by the recovery of integrity, by that unity of Being which is a natural condition forgotten by man. From the vacuum that the soul creates in freeing itself from the ballast of external and carnal objects, without any illusion that there is anything outside ourselves, is born a state of Being that is a continuous, natural motion towards eternity, immortality, and infinity.

All that we synthetically call 'the world',
the events and circumstances of our life,
are but our own projections.

If we are aware, we can project only life,
prosperity, victory and beauty.
If we are alert and attentive we can project freedom,
a world without limits,
without constraints, without old age, sickness or death.

The School of Lupelius fascinated me. I studied it and loved it passionately. I felt as though I was breathing its air. It was in my daydreams. I recognized those visionary men and women, student warriors, lonely heroes of an ineffable spiritual battle, as extraordinary Beings, incomparable models of courage and determination. I secretly observed the glimmer of madness, the feverish quest that marked their steadfast pursuit of the conquest of the self. I kept on searching incessantly, and found persuasive evidence that many of the mercenary heroes of that time, in the turbulent years after Charlemagne that saw the slow dissolution of the Holy Roman Empire, were Lupelius' disciples in disguise. Without ever revealing their true identities, those warrior monks were the legendary protagonists of unparalleled epic deeds often capable of turning defeats into glorious victories.

Then, abruptly my research came to a standstill and for weeks I was unable to add anything more to the small amount that I had already painstakingly gathered. I gave up hope of ever finding that legendary manuscript and, with it, the way back to the Dreamer.

However, one day, during one of my many sorties on the trail of this lost teaching, I came to hear of a Dominican father of boundless culture who might be able to help me with my research. He was, moreover, the author of an encyclopedic work on the medieval history of the Church.

5 The Meeting with Father S.

I arrived a few minutes early for my appointment with the person who, after so much searching, had been recommended to me as one of the living fathers of the Christian doctrine.

Father S. lived in an ancient Carmelite convent. A tribe of tiny nuns, strict and protective, watched over his scholarly meditations and his contemplative old age. Two of these nuns ushered me into a small ante-chamber where I stood and waited.

From the half-open window I could see a corner of the delightful cloister. The thick expanse of greenery enclosed by the geometry of the arcades and the quality of the silence intensified the sensation I had experienced as I passed through the ancient gates. Rather than just crossing the threshold of a convent, I felt I had somehow passed into another time. In an instant my mind flew back to the courtyard of the Collegio Bianchi, the Barnabites' parochial School in the heart of Naples. The air rang with the sound of swift footsteps, of children shouting and chasing each other under the arches; I could smell the food from the refectory and thousands of memories came flooding back to me from my childhood.

At the appointed time, I was granted permission to enter. Regretfully, I turned away from that lost kingdom of my childhood and the little crowd of my schoolmates that had run to greet me. Their smiling faces faded and disappeared into the shadows of my memories.

«Father S. is completing a new volume of his immense work on medieval Christianity» said one of the miniature sister-guardians who was escorting me. I guessed from the austerity of her tone that she was issuing a veiled warning for me to make sparing use of my host's time and patience.

I went up a spiral staircase made even more constricted by the walls of books surrounding it. More than going up a ladder, I felt instead that I was somehow ascending a steep metaphor. Every detail of the setting struck me as vaguely threatening, charged with symbolic warning. I was about to meet one of the great thinkers of Christianity and the very concept filled me with a sense of reverential awe. I also felt the slight pain of regret, a passing melancholy. I had at one time wanted my own life to be like this, dedicated to research and study and I felt a sudden resurgence of my old, blind faith in teachers and books.

The harsh and providential words of the Dreamer interrupted these thoughts:

"There is nothing you can add to that which you already know... True knowledge cannot be acquired, it can only be 're-membered'."

I recognized my sickness: the propensity for depending on the world, and in particular, for idolizing knowledge gained from books. Once again, I was making the external world my god.

Coming face to face with some fetish was enough for me to elect that man to be my leader, even though I had never met him.

I imagined Father S. to be the epitome of a mankind trapped by intellectualism, a humanity that had stopped dreaming. The champion of a Christianity that had forgotten and had placed bookish men and intellectual pride at its summit.

"All the world's books are contained in a single atom of one's Being – the Dreamer had said to me – *They cannot add anything to your knowledge... books cannot lead you to life. Knowledge depends upon Being... the more you are, the more you know!"*

A powerful, psalm-like voice reached me from above, as though it had broken through a breach in the rows of books.

«Come in» it said. The intonation resembled a passage in the liturgy. The invitation echoed very close to me giving me advance warning of the modest dimensions of the place I was about to enter.

As I climbed up the last steps, I felt my Being tense, gathering itself like a warrior approaching a known danger. Again I heard the words of the Dreamer: "*Every man occupies a rung on the ladder of human intelligence and is an ineluctable guardian of the higher levels... If you remain intact, every encounter will be an opportunity, a rung for you to step on and go beyond. If you forget, you will find yourself trapped in an external, virtual game which will throw you back into the infernal disorder of your life."*

Father S. was a portal of existence. This was who I was really about to meet: a guardian-examiner, a Minos, the strictest of judges, whose infallibility would assign me the post I deserved on the ladder of Being.

The large head of an old man, bald and clean-shaven, emerged from behind the waves of books that covered the table.

He scrutinized me for a long time.

His dark eyes appeared so extraordinarily young to me that I had the impression they were not his own; that they had surely been borrowed and placed in the face of an old man. By what extraordinary circumstance had those eyes found a way to avoid the ageing process, leaving the rest of the face to its biological destiny? He must have realised that I had noticed this. Slowly, he looked downwards, shielding his eyes like a tortoise. When he looked at me again, his gaze was that of an old man.

This impression was reinforced by another contrast: the ceremonial expression of someone welcoming a guest with the stern frown of a master. This ambivalence was the constant background of our encounter, as if to remind me of the distance that separated us. His tone of voice, his clothes, and his gestures were setting the rules for our meeting. Father S. apparently wanted to establish the purpose of our encounter as soon as possible and the limits within which it would take place.

I shook hands with him and I felt the same energy I had seen in his gaze. Father S. was studying me. His smile barely concealed the fact that he was gathering and evaluating information in order to classify me. His visitor was not an academic animal but someone who looked more like a young businessman, the type of man that Father S. probably did not encounter frequently.

«The only thing I know about you is that you are interested in moral philosophy and that you come from an American university… from New York… if I'm not mistaken» he said, pronouncing the word 'only' with an almost reproachful tone, revealing his nature and professorial attitude.

«I specialized in Business Ethics» I corrected him courteously, as I handed him a copy of the letter Fordham University had sent a few days earlier. The document confirmed that I was a researcher, a scholar of business ethics. It was the letter of introduction that I had used to set up this meeting. I felt perfectly at ease in this role. I remained silent. I preferred not to give him any more information about me for the moment, and instead leave him feeling slightly unease, caught between curiosity and unfamiliarity. I didn't want to make his task too easy.

As he read, I noticed an expression of growing interest on his face. He gave a visible start as he read about the studies I was pursuing on Lupelius and my hope that our encounter would help to further my research. With great self-control he contained his emotions at this discovery only allowing himself to express mild surprise at my choice of topic – such an extraordinary school of thought, so far from the familiar scientific themes.

I did not tell him anything about the Dreamer but justified my interest in Lupelius by talking about the importance his ideas might have on modern business theory and for the training of a new generation of leaders. I told him about the high expectations I had for that branch of studies, which would advocate the application of the educational methods, value systems, and philosophical principles that belonged to the ancient Schools of Being to the world of business. What I had found of particular interest were the teachings of Lupelius, and his research into invulnerability and invincibility, because of their relevance to the challenges of the modern economies, no less difficult or fatal than those of the military. The research and experiments on immortality conducted in Lupelius' School could be extended to modern enterprises.

For a long time, scholars and economic thinkers had been helpless in the face of an alarming phenomenon of planetary dimensions.

«Companies die young. Companies all over the world have too short a life cycle, only a handful of years – I told him – Even the giants of finance and the economy, the largest multinationals on the planet, struggle to survive for more than forty years.»

Drawing on the Dreamer's teachings, I passed off as my own the idea that a durable company is born from a durable founder, and that an immortal company can only be born from the dream of an immortal Being. Once, while talking to me about the polarity of love/fear, the Dreamer had revealed that the true meaning of love *amore* could be found in the etymology of the Latin word, 'a-mors', which means the absence of death. Not by chance, 'Roma', the name of the eternal city, is the anagram of a-mor. Its destiny to be immortal was codified in its roots, and sealed into the name given to it by its founder. I cited Rome, which had recently celebrated 2,800 years of uninterrupted life, as an example of a long-established enterprise that could not be explained without reference to its founder and his qualities as an immortal Being (Romulus was deified and worshipped by the Romans as the god Quirino).

I gave Father S. other examples of extreme longevity in business, from the thousand year old House of Windsor to the largest multinational on the planet, the Catholic Church itself. Again drawing on the teachings of the Dreamer, I maintained that a rich economy was always the expression of immortal thinking.

Vision and reality are one

The merest fragment of eternity is enough to broaden a country's vision, to expand the horizons of its economy. The concept of immortality is sufficient to raise the financial destiny of individuals, organizations and entire nations.

This was the direction my research was taking. I claimed that these discoveries would soon change the way business was done and would revolutionize teaching and scientific research in all universities of economics.

I could see Father S.'s interest visibly growing as I spoke of economic theory related to immortality and of the little I knew of Lupelius' philosophy. The global economy stood out against the backdrop of an immense battlefield where every day entire nations, companies as large as huge regiments, confronted each other in order to establish new economic frontiers while modifying existing ones to their advantage. Only one victor emerges from these conflicts. The others, all the defeated, are chained to his war chariot and condemned to slavery. To survive, they have to adopt the habits of their new owner and learn his language. They have to serve him.

Encouraged by a gesture from my host, I continued, telling him everything I had discovered about the mysterious monk-philosopher. Without trying to conceal my fascination with Lupelius and his extraordinary teachings. I quickly reached the point where my research had come to a standstill. I also told him about my efforts, thus far entirely fruitless, to find the manuscript entitled the 'School for Gods' and the mysterious disappearance of every single copy. I didn't hide my astonishment at what seemed to be a deliberate attempt to sweep away all trace of Lupelius' work and his School for immortal Beings.

6 The doctrine of Lupelius

Father S. listened to me intently, his head bowed on his chest.

When he raised it again, he was glowing and once more I saw those extraordinarily young eyes which had so impressed me when I first came face to face with him but this time he made no attempt to hide them. His face took on the expression of someone expecting to be recognized.

I did not retreat from the game and concentrated on his gesture. The solution to the riddle came suddenly and was dazzling. That man disguised himself as an old man… but yes… he was using his apparent age as a mask… a strategic mask… Father S. was a man who was feigning old age. My heart leapt in my chest. Father S. was… a Lupelian. I was sure of it.

I could hardly contain my emotion at this discovery… I felt subtle pleasure at the complicity that was being established between us… A ten century-long cord linked us to that race of warriors who had known how to live strategically, who had understood the art of disguise. His chameleon-like talent had allowed him to live tucked into the folds of his order, hidden in the bosom of Christianity. A tunnel had opened in time and more than a thousand years had been compressed into an instant in order to lead me to the doors of the School. Before me was perhaps the last of its immortal custodians. A question pounded at my temples, pulsating with my arteries. Did Father S. know the Dreamer?… I was tempted to tell him about my encounter with the 'Dream' and the extraordinary adventure that I was experiencing at that time.

«Lupelius is the prophet of physical immortality, the birthright of every man – Father S. imparted, interrupting my feverish thoughts and shedding his initial reserve – A right that we have relinquished and which we must reclaim.»

Then, as if he were taking his cue from an invisible book, rather than quoting, with his eyes closed he read the following words:

«*The body is the spirit made flesh. If the spirit is immortal, so then is the body.*»

The joy he felt as he remembered the School and listened once again to the words which he seemed not to have heard for years, was evident. He told me that Lupelius had been banished from Christianity for his ideas and that it was a miracle that he had avoided being burned at the stake. The worst threat Lupelius posed was his faith in the immense power of the individual and the final victory of life over death. For the Catholic Church, and all religious institutions aimed at the masses, there could be no more dangerous philosophy: the 'revolution of Being', the rebellion to which every man is called to overturn his fragility, his mortal destiny. A struggle against inner demons, dragons and chimeras, against psychological monsters and giants which men have called 'doubt', 'fear' and 'pain'. For Lupelius, these were the true cause of every evil and every misfortune.

It was not surprising that such subversive ideas should have resulted in persecution and attempts against his life. In effect, every trace of Lupelius and his work had disappeared. This now seemed to me to be the effect of a deliberate strategy on the part of Lupelius himself rather than the result of implacable hostility towards him.

To be accepted by his School meant being put to the severest test and living with him required being able to withstand great effort for long periods of time. Lupelius wanted his followers to have direct awareness of physical immortality and invulnerability, by experiencing how it might be possible to survive the gravest of dangers unharmed. In effect, having left with his blessing, not one of his men ever returned even slightly grazed.

I asked him to what he attributed such an extraordinary thing.

«A man's shield is his purity and his love for life and his Master» said Father S., his eyes half closed. Rather than reflecting on how to respond, it seemed to me that he was remembering.

«For Lupelius, purity is the fundamental quality of a man, and the way to achieve physical immortality: the supreme asymptote of the human parabola.» He paused for what seemed to me an extremely long time. I had noticed that whenever he referred to Lupelius, Father S. always used the present tense, as though he were speaking about a contemporary… or about someone who had never died. In the conversation that followed he led me by the hand into the extraordinary world of those few men and women who were ready to do anything to push themselves beyond the inviolate boundaries, the Pillars of Hercules of the common description of the world.

«In the school of Lupelius every effort is made to free the mind from the belief that death is inevitable and invincible – said Father S. – Everything forms part of a strategy of purification intended to conquer within oneself that mysterious desire to die which in the common man takes so many forms: it imbues his psychology until it becomes second nature and an inevitable part of his life.»

The belief that death is invincible is unhealthy for humans.
Your longevity is determined by your mental state, by your life urge.

«Your longevity is determined by your mind – asserted Father S., summarizing Lupelius' thinking for my benefit – This means that if you die, you are the only one responsible!»

A tiny nun quietly came in, carrying all that was necessary to serve us tea. From the looks of astonishment she furtively cast in my direction while transferring the cups and teapot onto the table and pouring the steaming tea, I realized how rare it must be for Father S. to spend this much time with a visitor. My host remained silent and only when the nun had left did he resume his point, explaining to me how the Lupelians knew that by questioning the inevitability of death, even only ironically, its power would be weakened.

«For his assertion that immortality is the right of every man, for his struggle to denounce death as the most horrible and unjust of all human prejudices – announced Father S. with an epigraphic tone – Lupelius will be remembered as the most important mystic of physical immortality.»

He continued, claiming that the Lupelians' thinking was connected to that which emerged from the physical, corporeal religion which Christianity had been in the beginning and had become its epigone, at the same time a herald of spiritual materialism and of its message of the body's indestructibility.

«Lying, hiding, complaining, and evading responsibilities are the psychological stigmata, the indelible marks of a man who has fallen into immorality and fragmentation; of a man who has forgotten the reason for his existence – said Father S. in a conclusive tone – Once man has abdicated his birthright of immortality and forgotten his integrity, he 'invents' death to put an end to his misery. Man prefers to die rather than take on the immense task of conquering himself and his incompleteness… In any case, death is no solution. A man always starts again from wherever he has left off.»

Lupelius created the School for Gods, a school of responsibility, a means of showing fragmented humanity, the way back towards simplicity, integrity, and his buried will.

7 Offer a rooster to Asclepius

Through the fragments I had been able to glean of the lost works of Lupelius, and backed up by the words of Father S., I recognized the Dreamer's inspiration ever more clearly. I could hear His voice. It was louder and more ancient than that of Lupelius. I thought of Him with gratitude.

Father S. was now reading some phrases to me from a little book which he was holding with reverence and which he evidently always carried with him. His voice trembled with emotion. His impassioned tone gradually became more intense as some of the more scandalous of Lupelius' beliefs came to light from this treatise, truths which were unacceptable to any rational mind or canon law. As I listened and wrote them down in my notebook, I felt the impact of their unsustainable difference and their striking contrast with the most deeply-rooted, universally accepted beliefs.

«Old age, sickness and death are insults to human dignity, the pillars, which for thousands of years have supported an illusory description of the world.

Evil is at the service of good. Always!... Everything comes to heal us... even physical death is actually healing. The final chance!»

This statement, Lupelius' unbearable paradox, released a secret mechanism. My mind returned to the words pronounced by Socrates as the hemlock was about to reach his heart and stop it from beating forever. Their meaning burst within me with an intolerable brilliance. It lasted only the blink of an eye and then disappeared but it was enough for me to grasp. For over two-and-a-half thousand years the meaning of Socrates' last wish had been an unfathomable mystery. Surrounded by his closest acolytes, Socrates swallowed the hemlock and the paralyzing effect of the poison spread rapidly from his legs towards his heart. He had only a few seconds left to live but in that supreme moment he uttered the following words: "We are debtors owing a rooster to Asclepius: give one to him, and don't forget."

How could Socrates ask his friend Criton to offer a rooster to the god of healing when his life was slipping through his fingers and death was by then inevitable? For twenty-five centuries these words have represented a riddle for generations of sages, learned men and exegetes.

Lupelius' philosophical statements had ripped open an impenetrable curtain and now, from the depths of time, the meaning of that message and its enormity was finally emerging. Like a castaway putting his message in a bottle to save it and pass it on, Socrates had entrusted his understanding to the oceans of time so that it would eventually reach us. Sealed in his last words is the fruit of his tireless search: even death is a healing… it is the ultimate medicine! It comes when all else fails.

As a consequence of the extraordinary circumstances of his death, Socrates reached a state of inner unity never previously achieved, a height of integrity that allowed him access to the greatest of all misteries: why mankind still had to die and how one day this would no longer be necessary. Behind Socrates' last words towered the dream of a future mankind which would be healed and made whole and would never again need that extreme act of purification.

"*Death is the last resort to which existence turns when every other attempt to heal and to become whole has failed* – the Dreamer would one day tell me – *Socrates used death to understand! In the supreme moment he discovered that it was just one step on the road to healing, another step on the ladder of wholeness. And this was the last, and greatest, of Socrates' teachings.*"

Socrates was the epitome of a humanity in unstable balance between two visions. He was a seeker, an explorer and although unable to overcome death he could at least use it to understand. He showed the way.

8 Forbidden to kill yourself inside

«Unity of Being is only the beginning for a mankind that has chosen to live forever – summed up Father S. – Like attracts like. Death attracts death and cannot affect anyone who is connected to Life.»

Armed with their wholeness, the Lupelians would return unharmed from their most audacious exploits. No instrument of war seemed able to touch them, as if connection with death had been eradicated forever. Without proselytizing, and without advocating any philosophy, Lupelius' warrior-monks knew how to rise up, and knew how to make men and events rise up around them, to a higher level of Being. They had won before they had even begun to fight. Winning meant conquering themselves, overcoming their doubts, fears and ignorance. External victory was only a sign of their internal victory. Thus, by taking care of their own Being, by ensuring their own flawlessness and making themselves impervious to evil, they would meet impossible challenges and carry out astonishing feats.

«The first cause of death is precisely our separation from God, the fact that we have expelled the divine and transferred it outside of ourselves» said Father S., taking a piece of paper out of a drawer and making a note on it. Then he went on:

«Lupelius says: You can hate God because you are sick, because you are suffering or because you are poor, but I can assure you, the reason for your illness, suffering or poverty is your separation from God. Men have forgotten this and they have transformed the planet into a world of death. They have made death into their reason for living. Every thought they have and every action they take is dedicated to it.»

«*Love and serve* is the motto… To serve mankind one must love… and before anything else, one must love one's self and one's own life…»

At this point Father S. lowered his voice… I guessed he was about to confide in me the most secret and unacceptable teachings of the School.

«Lupelius would remind his followers…» he said, pausing for a few interminable moments. His lips were trembling as he prepared to quote his master's words.

«You are gods who have forgotten… you are gods in a state of amnesia.»

«Even orders centuries old can forget» said the old man, his eyes becoming moist at the thought of the warrior spirit which had inspired him to become a monk.

«Forgetfulness weakens the warrior in every man. Once, we Dominicans were vegetarians, we ate only once a day; we cultivated the body and the spirit as one entity…The message of Christ and our Mission was very clear to us: the victory of life over physical death.»

Only unceasing work on oneself
can allow a man to overcome death.

I detected in his voice a nostalgia for the discipline of times past, for the memory of the buried brilliance of the School. I admired him and I was happy. I did not think that men like Father S. could still be found in the bosom of the Christian faith, crusaders dedicated to the holiest of wars: the war of putting death to death.

«Schools and churches, religious orders and government institutions stopped training responsible individuals years ago. Today they only produce polluted minds and bodies» said Father S.

He finished covering the page before him with crabbed handwriting. Then he folded it several times and handed it to me without saying a word. Symbolically this gesture seemed to me like the passing of the baton in a never-ending relay across the time. He was entrusting me with a portion of the race that humanity had been running for centuries, in search of an escape route from its prisons.

When we parted at the door of his tiny study he gave me a smile and winked, infecting me with that joyful and inviolate complicity that I'd only found amongst the little warriors, the bright Neapolitan street kids of my neighborhood. I asked him to tell me which of Lupelius' commandments best represented the sum of his research, the secret formula for defeating physical death.

«*It is forbidden to kill yourself inside!* – said Father S. without hesitation – It is the thousand psychological deaths that undermine us every day that lead to physical death…Believing death to be invincible is what kills us. The belief in its inevitability is the true killer.»

9 The School for Gods

I had climbed up the steep slopes of the plateau as far as the peak of its imposing volcanoes. Through the clear, dry air, across the vast expanse, my eyes swept over the vegetation of the steppes, a landscape without trees. Once I reached Everan, I left the statue of Mashtots behind me and crossed the square towards a bunker-like structure of grey basalt at the top of a bare hill. I was in the heart of Armenia. I had faithfully followed Father S.'s instructions on how to reach this place, and now I was climbing towards a severe looking building which housed the ancient library. Here, stored in thousands of books, were the memories of a people who had lived for centuries on the verge of extinction. Here, where copyists and translators were venerated like saints, from the second half of the fifth century until the present day, thousands of classical, Christian but also pagan works had been conserved or copied. Seminal texts and masterpieces, which had been considered lost forever had been saved by being faithfully translated into classical Armenian and I knew that Everan was my last hope of finding Lupelius' manuscript, or at least a copy of it.

I spent many days questioning the archivists and exploring entire sections of the library in depth. Like an archaeologist in a buried city, I walked down endless corridors with walls lined with books and dusty folders. The curator had assigned me two young librarians who were assisting me in my search. I am still not sure whether they were there to help me or to keep an eye on me. With them I went into labyrinths of papers, I examined parchments and yellowed rolls of sheepskin, bringing them out into the light for the first time in centuries.

Whenever I thought I had identified something promising I would select the volumes or rolls and the two young scholars would take them off the shelves and open them for me. They never touched these precious relics with their bare hands but only with a preciously embroidered cloth, following an almost sacred ritual.

One day, in the catalogue of the Institute of Ancient Manuscripts, I discovered that the original copy of an untitled volume was conserved under register number 7722. Having been ransomed for its weight in gold from the hands of the Seljukians in 1204, it had been kept and protected in a monastery perched in the craggy, snowy peaks overlooking the Black Sea. By the end of the eighteenth century it was part of the collection of spiritual and ascetic-mystic texts belonging to Paisij Velichovskij who had a Slavonic version printed in Moscow. After many vicissitudes it was again miraculously saved from destruction at the hands of the Turks and brought to Everan in 1915. My heart beat became as strong as a hammer when rolls of parchment covered in the author's handwriting emerged from the safe.

I only needed to read a few lines to be sure that it was Lupelius' work. I could hardly contain my joy as I avidly explored its content.

The language of Lupelius revealed itself to be a mixture of vernacular English and Latin, a kind of European Esperanto of striking inventiveness. These words had the power to cancel out time and transmit intact, after more than a thousand years, the precious energy that had inspired generations of warrior-monks.

During my stay in Everan, I became friendly with a couple of Welsh scholars. The man was a historian and his wife a Latinist. It was to them, in the small lounge of the inn where we were staying, that I revealed my discovery one evening. We talked about it excitedly for most of the night. Their help later turned out to be providential. Only the Dreamer could have arranged such an extraordinary 'coincidence'.

The one thing that seemed most surprising to these researchers was not the way in which I had tracked down the book so much as the fact that I knew its original title. A title which had been lost for centuries and that no one knew. With their help I immediately started to transcribe some passages and begin work on the translation. We studied the manuscript together for weeks and the more I read, the closer I felt to Lupelius' philosophy and the more I felt my passion grow for that forgotten teaching. The interpretation of one of the passages, the exegesis of a symbol, made me cross the sacred threshold of that school of men and women, inexhaustible seekers in the quest for immortality.

I commissioned expert copyists to produce a faithful reproduction of 'The School for Gods'. The result was a genuine masterpiece: a fine leather bound edition with pages of vegetable parchment identical in every detail to Lupelius' original work. I kept that copy with me at all times and at night I kept the book under my pillow as Alexander used to do with the Iliad. It was a present for the Dreamer and I could not wait for the time when I would be able to give it to him. I knew that day by day, every small advance I made in my understanding of His principles brought me closer to Him.

I was often overcome by uncontrollable enthusiasm culminating in moments of ecstasy at the thought of the wonderful outcome of my enterprise, at the limits of the impossible. I had 'miraculously' found Father S., I had found the original manuscript of 'The School for Gods' and I had met two scholars who, with boundless devotion, were working on the translation. I had no doubt that I would soon find the Dreamer again. For the moment, nothing mattered other than immersing myself in the manuscript, delving into King Solomon's mines, venturing down those venerable tunnels and ceaselessly searching for 'precious material'.

In order to choose life, we must choose the thought that
death is not invincible.
And so, we must find the principles of
aliveness, longevity, and eternity in our Being.

This and other rules, which I learned from Lupelius' manuscript, would one day become the cornerstones of all my future activities and the fundamental principles of many enterprises in the world of international business.

An enterprise is only as vital, rich and enduring,
as the ideas and principles of its founder.

For Lupelius the real inequality between men, the root from which every other visible difference arises, is that they belong to different levels of inner responsibility. Differences in the quality of thought place men vertically on different levels of the ladder of Being. There exists an inner hierarchy that no war or revolution can ever erase because the true difference between men does not depend on wealth, creed or race. It is a difference in states of Being. It is a psychological, vertical, evolutionary difference of rank. For this reason, it can only be overcome by a radical change in the way a man thinks and feels.

A real improvement implies change of Being.
A real improvement means evolution or growth towards
unity of Being
which is the result of a new way of thinking
and the abandonment of the old, mortal mentality...
Only a change of being can raise a man to a higher level of
freedom, understanding and happiness.

10 Mea Culpa

For Lupelius the Earth was a cosmic penitentiary, a prison as vast as the planet itself, where men lived like convicts on death row. Instead of drawing from this vision the conclusion that defeat was final and irremediable, his brilliant madness devised the most audacious plan. Lupelius dreamt up an adventure for man that took him beyond the boundaries of the possible: an escape from the laws that govern the planet, a flight from his apparently inexorable mortal destiny. Man could break through the confines he himself had established, defying nature and crossing over those limits which, like the Pillars of Hercules, he dared not go beyond even in his imagination. Lupelius gathered around himself a few brave men and prepared a detailed plan of escape.

You always encounter the same events
because nothing changes in you!
Like attracts like.
A particle of paradise moves towards paradise,
a particle of hell towards hell.

According to Lupelius' philosophy our states of Being attract the events that correspond to them, and events cause us to return to those same states. Only the will can stop this endless circle, this never-ending mechanical game and break the hypnotic cycle in which man's existence is circumscribed. *Thought is creative. Thought creates.* Events are the materialization of our thoughts, of our states of Being. Therefore, states and events are the same thing. States are produced in the Being of every man and events manifest themselves in his life, over time, and seem to originate independently of his will. In reality we are the ones who have intensely invoked them and unconsciously created them.

Whether positive or negative, a man's thoughts are always creative and they will unfailingly find a way to materialize. Our thoughts, like hand-written invitations, sent and then forgotten, attract events that correspond to them. In due course, when we are no longer even thinking about them, circumstances, meetings, events, problems and accidents, downfalls and failures, knock at our door like unwelcome guests with a secret and longstanding invitation nevertheless. Only neglect of our states of Being, which are the true cause of such events, makes them appear to be sudden and unexpected.

The unexpected always requires a lengthy preparation.

No external event can happen to a man without his consent, albeit unconscious. Nothing can happen to him without it first passing through the filter of his psychology.

Therefore, thinking is a very powerful process.

What we then call facts, events, experiences and all manner of occurrences in one's life are states of Being which are already marching towards those who are in tune with them. Inner states are external events just waiting for the right occasion to manifest.

The quality of our emotions, the breadth of our thoughts and the states of mind that we experience this very instant will decide what will then become visibly manifest and the nature of the events that will materialize in our lives.

Thinking is Destiny.
The higher our Thoughts the greater our Life.

The fundamental tenet of Lupelius' philosophy is that inner states and events are two aspects of a single reality. This does away with any distinction between an external and an internal world, thereby making it possible for every man to guide his own destiny, through knowledge of his own inner states and self-mastery.

Existence is our own invention
and as such depends on us alone.

Guided by Lupelius, I was discovering for the first time the vertiginous power, the 'concreteness of doing' which lay hidden in the Christian phrase *mea culpa.* For thousands of years, as though locked in a treasure chest, the very epitome of human intelligence had been conserved in these two Latin words. *Mea culpa, mea culpa, mea maxima culpa.* Only now did I recognise this as the most concise and potent expression of the idea of responsibility: m*ea culpa*. This formula, capable of harnessing the universe, from the hierarchy of the planets to the movement of the atoms, holds the secret of boundless energy. Modifying your states of Being can transform the events that happen to you. This is how a man, by studying himself and changing his way of thinking and feeling, can transform his horizontal, temporal existence.

Existence on Earth is our great School... A School of life which in the eyes of ordinary men appears to be a prison.

We need to learn how to turn our vision upside down.
Whatever men normally perceive as difficulty and misfortune,
whatever they curse and try to avoid at all costs,
is actually the most precious material
for transforming their psychology of death into a psychology of life.

Life through this world is a School for Gods.
Confusion, doubt, chaos, crisis, anger, despair and pain
are all propitious conditions for growth.

11 States and events I

A man's Being is made up of states and his life of events. Our existence therefore runs along two parallel tracks: 'events' which are the sequence of circumstances that come towards us during our lives on the conveyor belt of time and space, and 'states' which are the impulses of our spirits, moods and emotions which arise within us in a mostly unconscious way.

A man's personal history is therefore composed horizontally of events and vertically of states of Being. However, people usually think about their life and talk about it as if it were only made up of external events. In reality, the type of events that occur, and consequently the quality of a person's external life, depends upon the quality of their thoughts and states of Being.

Life is therefore made up of events but more so, of states.

We all believe, for example, when we go to a conference or the theatre, that we are the ones who choose our seats; we are all sure that this morning we chose what we were going to wear. However, in reality, the choice of seat and clothing was not made by 'us' but by our states of Being. Everyone has a suit, a shirt, or some other item of clothing in their wardrobe which for some reason they never feel like wearing. However they do not throw that garment away because they know that, sooner or later, they will find themselves in a state of mind, a mood, a level of Being, which will be in tune with it. When we 'feel' that way, we 'choose' that garment.

The relationship between states and events, inner circumstances and outer events, the mysterious relationship between a man's psychology and the things that happen to him, are at the core of the question of free will and the age-old enigma of whether destiny is determined by chance or necessity. Around this enigma, through the ages, men have accumulated the knowledge of a great science that is today unknown.

The ancient Greeks maintained that there was a causal relationship between inner states and external events. This archaic civilization firmly believed that a man's destiny was the projection of his inner world or Being. They founded a science and an art on this conviction that for them had the highest value. In the pre-Homeric age, a wise man was not someone rich in experience or in possession of great knowledge but someone who could predict the future and reveal what was unknown. For the Greeks, shedding light on darkness, defining the uncertain, was true knowledge and also an art.

Other civilizations also exalted divination and prophecy but no other people elevated it to the extent where it became the central tenet of their lives. All over the Hellenic world sanctuaries sprang up dedicated to the cult of Apollo to whom, more than to Dionysus, was attributed the dominion of knowledge, understood as manifestation and communication of human destiny.

This Greek vocation and the art of predicting the future found its greatest expression in Delphi, which was why the god of Delphi was a unifying image for that civilization and a symbol of Greece itself. The pilgrim who often travelled great distances and faced grave dangers to ask the god about his future would find the Delphic inscription 'Know Thyself' engraved on the tympanum of the temple, as if to say 'Do you want to know your future? Then know yourself!'

In this apparently mocking paradox the Greeks set out the solution to the oldest riddle of humanity, the answer to the age-old question concerning the existence of free will. A question that led all the philosophers in the world to ponder feverishly whether to follow a fatalistic view of a predetermined and inevitable future or the belief in the *homo faber*, man as maker of his own destiny. Sculpting this Delphic motto onto the very temple dedicated to the most sacred art and the greatest of sciences, divination, the Greeks revealed the secret relationship between the inner and the outer world, between states and events. They entrusted this discovery to the oceans of time, like a message in a bottle, so that it would reach us. The man who knows himself, his own Being, the container of his thoughts, ideas, and attitudes, also knows his own future; for our psychology is our destiny.

Thinking is Destiny

Apollo is the symbol of the world as a mirror of man's inner self. The world is our reflection.

Classical tradition tells us that Homer was a blind prophet and this is yet another message that has come down to us from that age of wise men which ended with the death of Socrates, the last of the sages. The blindness attributed to the author of the Iliad and the Odyssey, the two great bibles of the ancient world, is emblematic of the attention paid by the Greeks to psychology, self knowledge and states of Being. Looking inside oneself is the key to knowing the world, the road to understanding it and foreseeing its events.

Noticing how some men were capable of exceptional deeds and of undertaking enterprises well beyond ordinary capacity, and observing how they seemed to enjoy some special protection, even in the most dangerous circumstances, and how their lives seemed to be at the centre of extraordinary events, the ancient Greeks recognized that these men had a special nature, a luminosity of Being and inner qualities that were almost divine. They therefore concluded that there existed two species of man: heroes and demigods, on the one hand, common men on the other.

In the age of Homer only demigods and heroes, thanks to their extraordinary deeds, could gain the right to an individual destiny. Their unique and original lives were not ruled by any divinity and were free from chance and the randomness of events. All other men were condemned to a repetitive existence. They were ruled by the laws of Accident and Chance and their lives, whether short or long, were like their actions: aimless and doomed to end without leaving any trace.

For Lupelius the difference between these two kinds of human being, and between men in general, was that they belonged to different levels on the ladder of Being.

Wherever they meet, for a few moments or years,
men inevitably form a pyramid,
arranging themselves on different levels of an invisible ladder,
according to an inner, mathematical order,
like planetary hierarchies organized according to their brightness,
mass, orbit and distance from their sun.

We may not be aware of it, but our destiny, the quality of our lives and the events which affect us, respect this hierarchy.

Being aware that everything emanates from the Being and that the individual destiny of man, like that of an entire society, is nothing but a projection of the Being, the classical Greeks used every possible means, from religion to politics, from science to philosophy, art and even war, to raise the spirit. The wonderful architecture of cities like Athens and works of art like the masterpieces of Phidias, displayed in public squares, were machines that transmitted messages of beauty, pride and harmony to the Being in order to elevate it. Only the Ancient Greeks had a word for poetry (*poiesis*) through which we can unearth the secret, sealed within its etymology, of doing through Being. All Greek theatre had a therapeutic, cathartic function for society to purify audiences and free their souls from burden. For the Greeks the ultimate purpose of the tragedy was the purification of the passions in order to achieve, through this, the elevation of Being.

12 States and events II

Many times, as I reflected on the significance of this information and on everything I was learning about states and events, I considered how absurd it was that we should spend a quarter of our lives at school and university and let our entire life slip away without knowing anything about the 'Being' and the power our states of mind have in determining the events and circumstances of our lives.

The first education we receive does not provide us with any sense of the distinction between what is external and what is internal, nor does it prepare us to manage our thoughts or be aware of our emotions. Without any deliberate intent, ordinary culture has relegated emotions, feelings and thoughts to the ephemeral and intangible sphere of myths, fables and dreams, considering them to be separate phenomena and extremely far from what is commonly called 'reality'.

Following the path of classical civilization, discovering its mythology – more useful and reliable than history in every respect – and studying Lupelius' manuscript, I made the thrilling discovery that in reality, between states and events there is no relationship of former and latter or cause and effect, but only of total identification. States and events are two sides of the same reality placed on different levels of existence. They are the two ends of the same stick positioned vertically.

What prevents us from seeing that states and events are one and the same thing is that they are separated by the factor of time, which acts as a sort of shock absorber. Between our inner states and the occurrence of corresponding external events, is a lapse of time and, like a smoke screen, it prevents us from recognizing that events are nothing but the materialization of our inner states in time-space.

Thoughts, emotions, feelings and all our states are like invitations for the corresponding events. To be more precise, they are already events. It is only a question of time before they happen. It may take more or less time before they occur, in one place or another, but they invariably reach us.

A man's emotional states are in reality events
seeking an opportunity to happen
and become visible.

Time distances states from events and masks their biuniqueness. Time squirts a sepia wash over events, which hide and lurk behind the screen, taking us by surprise when we have forgotten, or never even realized, that our emotional states alone were responsible for them.

Nothing happens suddenly.
The unexpected always requires a lengthy preparation.

There is nothing that a man could possibly encounter, no event that could present itself to him without first having, knowingly or unknowingly, journeyed through his Being or psychology. The world is connected to our emotions, passions and thoughts which are the drive belt between the inner and outer world. By managing our emotions and thoughts, along with everything that we feel and experience in a specific moment, by mastering our states, we can take control of our existence and set the direction of our destiny. This is where the Roman concept of fortune and of *homo faber* had its roots, in contrast to the Greek and Middle Eastern vision which represented Fortune as a blindfolded goddess distributing events at random and directing them by whim.

It is commonly believed that external events condition our attitudes and determine our moods. Something happens, we meet someone or receive some news, and we believe that the psychological state we experience, irritation, anxiety or surprise, is a result or a consequence of that event, meeting or news. In the same way as, until the invention of photography, it was impossible to determine, for example, the exact sequence of the hooves on a galloping horse because the movements were faster than the eye could see. So it is that thoughts, emotions, perceptions and feelings travel like electronic flashes through the mysterious forest of our neurons at the speed of light, making it seem impossible to establish the exact temporal sequence in relation to external event. Something happens and we believe the psychological state we feel to be the result of that event. So we justify our state of Being by reference to that external event while in fact exactly the opposite has taken place. In reality, it is our states of Being which announce and determine the external events of our lives. Our negative emotions in time turn into the adversity of which we then complain. To encounter a certain kind of event, be it good or bad, we first have to create the conditions within ourselves that allow it to happen.

Man's biggest illusion is to believe he can change external conditions and change the world. We can only change ourselves, work on our own attitudes, modify our reactions and not express the negative emotions we feel.

The universe is perfect the way it is.
The only one who must change is you!

We are convinced that a man's energy and good will count for very little compared to the events that happen to him in life, which appear to be largely fortuitous and inevitable. The rush of events that continuously overtake us is too varied and confused to be foreseeable and much too powerful for us to imagine that we might be able to direct it.

According to Lupelius we need to 'see' that our own self always lurks behind events and states of Being. No solution is possible unless we first change ourselves.

Who knows how to produce the slightest change in his level of Being
can move mountains
and project himself as a giant in the external world.

By acting on our inner states and on the quality of our thoughts and feelings, starving some and nourishing others, we will not only change our attitudes and the way we react to the events which confront us in the external world, but we will also change the very nature of the events that we encounter day after day.

Our first task must be one of *self-observation.* The scrutiny of our thoughts and the way in which we 'take' events, will allow us to discover that humanity thinks and feels negatively.

It is only apparent that man wishes himself wealth,
health and good fortune.
If he could observe and know his inner self,
he would hear within an almost constant chant of negativity,
like a prayer of misfortune composed of worries,
sick images and the expectation of terrible events,
both probable and improbable.

But how can we act upon inner states of Being, on our own moods, emotions and ways of thinking?

The energy that could move a mountain is not enough to modify a thought, let alone lift oneself out of a bad mood or negative emotion. The force needed to redirect one's thinking or gain control over an emotion is produced at a higher level. In order to accumulate this special energy, it is necessary to eliminate all possible flaws in the system – the thousand tiny fissures consisting mostly of the expression of negative emotions and wrong interior attitudes through which, like a colander, we lose energy. If an event happens in the external world and we do not connect it to the states of our Being that created it, we will have missed a valuable opportunity.

If one observes carefully, many of the events in our lives repeat themselves and it is possible to try to gain a better understanding of their nature by looking at the way they correspond to particular states of Being. For instance, take the cluster of emotions that are generated by 'being late' for a meeting. 'Being late' triggers a feeling of anxiety. We have to be aware that these external conditions correspond to inner states that have not yet arisen. There is a part of my Being which connects me to those events. There is no other way to eliminate them from my life other than by modifying this inner condition that I call anxiety, fear or worry, but which in reality is nothing more than a sickness of Being, an inner fault.

In one way or another, that kind of worrying event will repeat itself in my life for as long as I harbour within me the psychological states which produce it. Those events are actually the signs which indicate that a recovery may take place, if we have the intelligence to connect them to the emotional states that gave rise to them. Paying attention to our own psychological states, means reversing the process and going back from the event to the state which produced it. This is where we can access understanding and the concrete possibility of transforming our own lives.

Making excuses, justifying oneself, blaming an external event and not recognizing that the cause lies in the shortcomings of our own Being, of our inner states and ways of thinking, feeling and reacting, means that we have not understood. Not understanding means that in some way the event will have to repeat itself over and over again. The circumstances may change with the events presenting themselves in different guises, but we will continue to blame external circumstances and in doing so miss the opportunity to free ourselves from them forever.

Take the blame for everything,
accept responsibility for everything that happens to you.
The power of this attitude is compressed in two eternal words:
Mea Culpa.

I reflected upon the fact that entire nations live in states of Being which attract corresponding events. For example, in the United States, it has taken tens, even hundreds of years for racial prejudice or the dislike of people who are different for reasons of creed or culture, to be recognized and to create the conditions for these prejudices to be overcome.

The premature deaths of martyrs, and leaders such as Malcolm X, Martin Luther King, and John F. Kennedy, have shortened the time and hastened the conditions needed to change the psychological states and ways of thinking and feeling of nations and entire civilisations, so that they become capable of attracting new events and new opportunities.

Our states can make us win or lose in life. They can make us rich or poor. They can make us ill or heal us. Self-observation, the study of the self, is the means by which we can know them. The mere act of observing ourselves makes us more aware and more intelligent.

Self-observation is self-correction

13 "Put God to work!"

Reading Lupelius' manuscript put me in a state of feverish excitement. Leafing through those pages which had been passed down through the centuries made me feel I was wandering among the desks of a classroom in the School for Gods. I listened in rapture to the School's timeless voice. Every day was an intellectual adventure and my research was rewarded with the treasure of immortal thought.

There is nothing that man needs to introduce from the outside...
neither food, nor knowledge, nor happiness...
it is his birthright not to depend on anything outside of himself...
Man can feed himself from the inside,
nourish himself from his own intelligence,
his own will and his own light.

For Lupelius this idea was the central element of physical immortality and the cornerstone of every philosophy and religion. From a recess in the memory came the most ancient words in the world; the words that man's lips had pronounced, like those of a child, four thousand years ago, even before he knew how to write them. *Thou shalt have no other God before Me!...*

An understanding grew and spread inside me, initially with trepidation, like a lamp dispersing the darkness of ages. Then it flared up as powerful as a roaring fire. *Thou shalt have no other God...* meant that man, unaware of being the creator, makes the external world his God and elects it as lord of his Being and master of his destiny... That centuries-old warning handed down the first and greatest of all the commandments: do not depend on anything!… Remember that you are the one who created all of this!... Believing in a world outside ourselves means depending on it and being trapped by the laws of one's own projection. At this point my thoughts overlapped and became confused like the voices of small children excited by a joyous discovery… '*Love your Lord God. Thou shalt have no other Gods outside yourself*'. You are the lord and master, the maker and creator of all and everything. You project all this… You 'are' all this… Never again will you be this close to the breath of a more real and concrete God… Here my thoughts stopped and remained suspended…

From the translations I received every day from the team of scholars and researchers I had assembled in Everan, emerged a dialogue between Lupelius and Amanzio, one of his warrior monks. Their message darted out from between the lines, still alive and fresh, as if the disciple had asked his questions at the very moment I was reading them. Time became compressed and I found myself within the venerable walls of that School.

Lupelius: *"If you believe in the external world*
as something real, then you are lost
and destined to fail in whatever you do.
Anything coming from 'out there'
can only help you to recognise in yourself
the true source of all your troubles,
limitations and misery.
Therefore, let all outer incidents,
circumstances, events and relations with others
fall in a place within yourself,
where such trash can be transformed into
a new substance,
new energy, new life…
You have made existence
and the external world your god…
But existence is not real…
it is a device that serves the 'dream'
so as to help you return to the source
to find out what is really real…
There is nothing outside ourselves
which is not ruled by the 'dream'."

Amanzio: "Then what about this castle we are in
and these rooms which are more than three hundred years old?"

Lupelius: *"They are a creation of yours...*
now, in this moment!"

Amanzio: "And what about my mother and father?"

Lupelius: *"They are also your creations...*
there is nothing outside of you that is before you!
Life doesn't come from our parents,
but stands Real, Eternal, Magnificent,
with neither beginning nor end,
neither birth nor death."

Amanzio: "So... then... is man... God?"

Lupelius: *"No!... He is much more!...*
He has God at his service..."

Amanzio: "What does that mean?"

Lupelius: *"That you could ask him for everything you desire...*
and God will satisfy all your requests...
without constraint...
God is a good servant but not a good master...
God loves to serve... he loves to love...
God is total surrender at your service...
God exists... because 'you' exist...
If you are not there then
He has no reason to exist...
God is your will in action."

Amanzio: "I don't understand"

Lupelius: *"The mind cannot understand... it can only lie...*
The mind... is mendacious...
The mind that is not mendacious annuls itself

and makes way for the totality of the Being.
You cannot change the past
if you don't understand that
it is this present which gives form to the past.
Whatever you attain in this istant
is simultaneously transferred in all directions.
If the present is made perfect,
everything in your past will be aligned
with this perfection.
Each event of the past
is just a resonance of vibrations
that your body is sending right Now.
It's Here that everything happens...
It's Here that everything is touched...
It's Here that everything is moved...
Here where Truth,
Innocence, Beauty and Power dwell.
Here... in this infinite, everlasting,
indestructible Body."

14 The art of vigilance

The battlefield is the Body I read in the manuscript.

This authoritative statement by Lupelius echoed inside me like the war cry of a great crusade. The battlefield is our body. The name of victory is integrity. The goal of a man's life, his aim, is wholeness, the unity of Being. In this way Lupelius summarized the sense of mankind's millennial quest and explained the very reason for his existence, the meaning of his entire history. According to Lupelius, this achievement is physical. The body is the most visible part of the Being and integrity of Being is a victory that takes place in our very cells.

Expand your vision until your whole body,
every organ, muscle, fiber and cell down to the very last atom
is overwhelmed by the light of your dream.
Once dreaming is set in motion all things are possible.
Your dreaming contains all the principles and power
needed for the establishment of a kingdom of heaven on earth.

There is no war so holy as that in which one 'conquers oneself',
no greater victory than exceeding one's own limits.
Integrity is the healing of Being.
It requires the overthrowing of age-old beliefs,
transforming negative emotions and destructive thoughts,
achieving self-mastery and control
of one's eating, sleeping and breathing...

Studying this and other passages of 'The School for Gods', I perceived the nature of the experiments that Lupelius and those around him were conducting, in that glowing laboratory that was his School in Ireland one thousand years ago. There his warrior-acolytes trained themselves to master dependence on sleep and food, reducing their reliance on them day by day, as a fundamental part of their training to become invulnerable and immortal.

According to Lupelius, sleep was a poor surrogate for breathing, it was a contrivance that the body had devised to free itself, if only for a few hours, from insufficient and inefficient breathing. As I delved even further into Lupelius' thinking I realized that nothing is as close to us, and at the same time as mysterious and unknown, as our breathing. We are creatures living at the bottom of an ocean of air. And although we are submerged in this element and every square centimeter of our body is under pressure from this ethereal ocean, we still absorb an insufficient quantity of oxygen into our lungs... Lupelius made the astonishing discovery that the amount of air we all breathe in is hundreds of times less than we actually need.

In his manuscript he examined and accurately described this condition of near suffocation to which man has been reduced, referring to it as 'underbreathing'.

According to Lupelius, the consequence of this strange phenomenon is that there are vital parts of our organism that do not receive an adequate supply of oxygen and are undernourished. Anticipating by many hundreds of years the discovery of the importance of respiration in catabolism and organ regeneration, Lupelius concluded that mankind was seriously polluted. He considered that it was necessary for a man to dedicate several hours a day to breathing fully, deeply and completely, and he predicted that one day every school, organization and community would teach breathing techniques as a way of training people to take in much greater quantities of oxygen, thus fulfilling our body's real needs.

I noted with regret that, ten centuries later, that prophecy was still far from being realised and that men continued to 'underbreathe' unperturbed, behaving as if oxygen were subject to heavy taxes or counted amongst the rarest and most costly commodities in the universe.

According to Lupelius, deep breathing cannot be done mechanically but only through an effort of will. From him I learned that the destiny of a man is linked to his breathing by a double thread.

The deeper a man's breathing, the richer his reality...
If you want to change your destiny, work on your breathing....
dedicate time to intentional breathing.

One of the cornerstones of Lupelius' doctrine was that in order to deserve an individual destiny, to be the hero of a great personal adventure, a man needs to breathe consciously and deeply, to be frugal with food and sex, to steal time from sleep. All necessary efforts should be directed towards this goal. On this subject, I found a letter in the manuscript written by Lupelius to one of his students providing advice in a familiar and informal tone.

People fall asleep in the same way as they hope to die...suddenly...
But, whatever time it is, however long your day has been
and however hard your battle,
make sure you 'fall asleep awake'...
Those who do not know how to manage their energy,
fall into bed exhausted at the end of the day, more dead than alive...
If you really have to sleep for a few minutes,
then you must approach sleep from a state of wakefulness.
This will prevent you from falling into the infernal depths.

It seemed as if these words from Lupelius were directed at me, indirectly reprimanding me for my then quite frequent habit of falling asleep suddenly in front of the television or while reading a book. Their force and suggestive power was such that upon reading those words I immediately decided to redeem myself and from that day on I adopted 'falling asleep awake' as a password and a rule for life. According to Lupelius the way in which a man goes to sleep is like a litmus test, a way of revealing the quality of his life. The moment we feel we are succumbing, when our eyes are closing and falling asleep seems inevitable, for Lupelius is the time when we must exercise our will, rising up and using every possible means to conquer sleep… Lupelius suggested swordplay, bathing or dancing and devised all sorts of tricks and stratagems that could serve this purpose.

According to Lupelius "*To sleep is to die!*"

With his inimitable black humor, universal jester and master of disguises that he was, he claimed that every night men play out the dress rehearsal for their own final exit from the scene. Persevering in their 'bad habit' of sleeping, half the planet goes to bed, its inhabitants bidding each other good night without even realizing what a macabre ritual they are performing. The philosopher-monk who dared to dream the impossible, the head of the School of invincible warriors, concluded the following letter to his disciple with some extraordinary advice on the art of staying awake.

When you know that sleep is the representation of death,
you can no longer approach it as you did before…
In any case, whatever precautions or methods you adopt,
you must never let anyone, not even your woman, see you sleeping…
Exercise the art of staying awake!...
A warrior knows that to be caught napping
is to expose his vulnerability…
It is like inviting the world to attack
and mortally wound you.

15 Bad habits

Lupelius had discovered a mystery in man that the mind cannot even begin to conceive: the existence of a black hole that collects a 'psychological scum' that pollutes his cells.

By using the techniques of fasting and breathing, by adopting a new vision and new ideas and by making special efforts, a man can change himself and the situations he finds himself in. He can make the transition from an incomplete Being, mortal and ridden with conflict, to one who is whole, harmonious and immortal.

Every deprivation, every effort made towards frugality, is part of the preparation for our escape from the hell of ordinariness, freeing us from the pileup of emotional debris built up over the years. According to Lupelius, only a man from the School, guided by a flawless teacher, can confront such a healing process and overcome the hurdles and obstacles of such an undertaking.

Man is generally incapable of understanding the signs that announce and accompany an act of purification. Ordinary men read these in reverse and see them as signs of sickness rather than healing. The pain involved in the effort required is something no one wants to face which is why, according to Lupelius, we abandon every act of abstinence just when it is starting to have a positive effect.

Through his long voyages, intense study and tireless research, Lupelius had come to know the ancient schools of initiation and had met extraordinary men who belonged to the great ascetic and mystic traditions. In every age and in all civilizations, *otium,* the art of not doing, had been the mainstay of every discipline and inner search; the golden thread that tied every man who desired to conquer the highest levels of responsibility to the great adventure.

Following the ideal map indicated by the manuscript, the abstinence of the ascetic, the solitude of the hermit and the frugality of the monk, revealed themselves to be expressions of a single School, different aspects of one, timeless quest that was connected to the martial disciplines and wakefulness of the warrior.

Upon further investigation, I discovered that Arrian, one of the two historians who wrote of the exploits of Alexander the Great, had, in the 'Anabasis Alexandrou', summed up the dietary rules and the secret of his boundless energy in a single sentence:

"…he had been trained to be frugal: for breakfast, a march before dawn; for dinner, a light meal."

The Macedonian warriors themselves, considered throughout all antiquity to be the unmatched models of bravery and strength, were of legendary frugality. They slept on the naked earth and, even at times of extreme endurance and while undertaking the most daunting endeavors, would eat only a handful of olives. And yet, they were tireless, the most fearsome of warriors, a true nightmare for their enemies.

The deliberate elimination of just one gram of food and abstinence from just one minute of sleep were, in Lupelius' opinion, so powerful as to cast serious doubt on man's entire system of beliefs and upset his artificial equilibrium. His School advocated the absence of sickness, old age and death as an inalienable birthright and natural condition of man.

A diseaseless, ageless, deathless man.

Since the beginning of time, throughout the centuries and in all traditions, the quest for self-mastery had required practice and discipline, and was intended as a means by which to bring to the surface what Lupelius called 'emotional slime'. It was an essential procedure in order to discover inner wounds and drive out all the shadows lurking in the folds of the Being.

One day, while working on the manuscript, I discovered the incredible secret which Lupelius had exposed. His announcement was the manifesto for a revolution in thought that did not appear to be directed at his contemporaries but at a scientific assembly of the future:

"...It is time for mankind to wake up from an ancestral, metaphysical sleep... It is time to shake off the dust of ages from its belief system ..."

And the document ended with these forbidding words:

"Food, sleep, sex, disease, old age and death are 'bad mental habits'. We must rid ourselves of them."

In several places in his manuscript these words were also referred to as 'superstitions' or 'illusions.'

"The battlefield is the body – said Lupelius – Every refusal of food and every minute rescued from sleep, is a victory in the battle against death... Physical death is immoral... unnatural... unnecessary."

Lupelius believed that lack of frugality in food, sleep, sex or work, was the primary cause of any loss of energy and vitality, leading man to annihilate himself, thereby achieving the impossible of abdicating his birthright to immortality and making physical death first, possible and secondly unavoidable. Throughout the ages, in every civilization and religious tradition, an elite few have awakened from the hypnotic sleep vilified by Lupelius and tried to follow a discipline which placed the idea of physical immortality at the centre of their system of thought, claiming it as the origin of all prosperity and longevity.

The Dreamer would one day say to me that the idea of physical immortality was a fundamental element in the psychology of a new humanity, and of leaders in particular. Unless he passed through these Pillars of Hercules, a man would sooner or later be put under severe pressure by his limitations and succumb to his own demise. And if that man was in charge of an organization then the whole enterprise would fall with him. The idea that death can be defeated uproots every constraint from our psychology, increases our responsibility and is an essential requirement for the establishment of a vital, prosperous and durable enterprise. According to the Dreamer, the philosophy of physical immortality should be taught in all schools, universities and institutions. The idea of a life without end is the strongest antidote to poverty, crime and death.

Leaving Everan and the Institute for Ancient Manuscripts, I returned to New York bringing with me, as my most prized possession, the copy of 'The School for Gods' which I had made for the Dreamer. From the mountain of notes I had compiled, two words in particular gave me pause for thought for the duration of my journey: *Die less,* a recurrent aphorism and perhaps the motto of the Lupelians. These words seemed to me to be the ultimate synthesis of the School's philosophy.

Die less and Live forever.

I thought of the devastating discovery hidden behind the apparent simplicity of this formula. Man dies inside thousands of times a day. Destructive states and thoughts and negative emotions burgeon and reproduce ceaselessly within our Being while distilling the slow poison that kills us. We may not know where to start in order to live forever, but following Lupelius' age-old aphorism we can certainly resolve to '*die less*'. Many times I chanted the Lupelian song of immortality:

Eat less and Dream more.
Sleep less and Breathe more.
Die less and Live forever.

16 "You won't make it!"

I emerged as if from a journey underground. I recognized the room and the great painting on the far wall. This time, it was an hour later in the morning in the Dreamer's world, and the light was such that I could easily observe the architecture of that part of the house. I looked up towards the high ceiling and followed its line to the point where it dropped sharply forming an imposing archway of bare bricks.

It was in that moment that I sensed a presence. I gave a start. On each side of the arch, two naked people, a man and a woman, were observing me like motionless guardians. A shiver flew down my spine before I understood what was before me. They were life size statues placed opposite each other and were so perfectly made that I thought they were copies of Hellenic originals. The chest of the warrior, so high and smooth and strong as armour, conveyed to me a message of irresistible pride. I stood up and straightened my back as if responding to a military order.

I instinctively ignored the steep stone stairway that led to the Dreamer's rooms and, went unhesitatingly in the opposite direction, towards a large, unusually shaped door made of glass and wrought iron. Beside it, a large painting covered the entire wall. I stopped to look and recognised an opulent representation of the myth of Narcissus, depicting him as he admired his reflection in a pond, shortly before being swallowed into it. I kept admiring this work which would not have looked out of place among the seventeenth century masterpieces of an important museum collection. Then I carefully pushed open the glass door and stopped spellbound on the threshold of a fairytale setting.

Without taking my eyes off this scene, I bent down to untie my shoelaces and left my shoes there, where I stood, as I had done on my first visit. I proceeded cautiously in bare feet across the large terracotta tile floor and went into what seemed to be a large greenhouse. There was a rich variety of plants, for the most part tropical, and the walls consisting of long rows of glass arches, reinforced this impression. Outside, the deep green of the garden pressed against the chestnut window frames like a sea of plants against the sides of an ark. But the elegance of every detail, the works of art, the valuable paintings and the modern sculptures in white marble, left me pleasantly perplexed as to the true nature of this extraordinary place. The first light of morning flooded in from two large skylights. I looked at the huge beams that supported the roof and I tried to imagine what titan had been able to carry and place them there. I scored the room several times but could find no trace of the Dreamer. I had not seen Him for over a year. Just the thought of meeting Him made my heart race and my breath quicken. As I carried on I saw an expanse of water in the middle of the hall floor. Rather than a pool it appeared to be a small light blue pond dug into the terracotta tiles, a constant movement shivering across the surface of the water. I gazed along the edge until I saw His reflection rippling in the waves.

I looked up slowly. The Dreamer was putting a silver flute to his lips. He bent forward elegantly and lifted his face, and the shining instrument, towards the light. The air was filled with a string of notes, threaded one after another, like pearls on a necklace all of varying sizes and value. It was ageless, timeless music, ageless and timeless like the villa, like that room, like that moment. I remained motionless as I listened.

I felt the joyful thrill of my childhood, permeated with the salty fragrance of the sea, and its forgotten happiness; the foolish races along the rocks, the taste of freshly caught crabs and shellfish, the way my heart pounded before diving off the big rock, the cool shade of our summer house in Ischia, Carmela's sweaty kisses when she returned hot from the market, heavy bags in both hands…

Finally one note remained suspended in the air longer than the others, fluttering on the breath which had created it, clinging a little longer to the molecules of air, before freeing itself from the music and becoming a single, quivering, sonorous sound. Suddenly it stopped. For an endless moment the flute was held crosswise, attached to the Dreamer's lower lip, and then it softly followed the hand that laid it down on a cushion nearby.

He was younger than I remembered Him, and seemed even thinner. He looked up and examined me at length. He certainly knew how much effort I had made to return to Him… He knew about my extensive search for the manuscript and the success of my mission, the passion with which I had studied which had brought me closer to the thought of the School. Following the stormy meeting that marked the† beginning of my apprenticeship and the journey into my past, this time I was expecting words of encouragement, if not of praise. I took a few steps towards him.

The Dreamer continued to stare at me without saying a word.

Initially I felt a vague sense of unease that quickly turned into pain. Under His gaze, my attention reversed its direction. I was looking inside myself for the first time. The spectacle was far from agreeable: a mass of dark thoughts was forming within my consciousness, along with a sense of guilt and other feelings twisted into an emotional jumble which was never disentangled. His eyes bore into me, churning up a psychological sludge that I never wanted to see or confront. He stopped just as the pain was exceeding the limits of my endurance. But He didn't relax His grip. What was to follow would be much more painful.

At the end of His examination, as if He had reached a final, definitive judgment, He passed sentence:

«You won't make it!»

The silence which followed that verdict flooded into the greenhouse, filling every corner. Disappointment, dejection and anger closed in on me merging into a single, quiet agony. I felt myself spent of all energy. I wanted only to collapse and be left in peace. But I did not dare do that, nor did I request it. Holding my breath, like an accused man, I awaited the final sentence of this judgement. The pause was cruelly long.

Finally, like a researcher observing the results of yet another failed experiment, an expected but no less disappointing outcome, He announced:

«No one can make it... It is humanity that cannot make it!...»

He was addressing me as if I were a representative of a defeated race, a species on the brink of extinction.

«There are too many laws which compel you to remain as you are. You have even turned the quest I entrusted to you into something which feeds your vanity, your egocentricity.»

I experienced a powerful feeling of resentment, that mixture of loathing and self pity that results from perceived injustice. After months of travelling and research in the United States and Europe, after having found Lupelius' manuscript, that scholars, researchers and archaeologists had deemed lost forever, and after having courageously confronted my tormented past, I did not deserve to be treated in this way. I would have liked to rebut the Dreamer's words in some way, but the muscles of my dignity were still too weak. Besides, deep in my heart I knew that He was right. I tried to conceal my mood behind a false appeasement.

«I can't change» was all I allowed myself to say. However, my voice betrayed the rancour of my impotence and my tendency to cling and be dependent.

«STOOOOP IT!» shouted the Dreamer, drawing out the 'o' in a hideous tone of voice.

The passing seconds were filled with terror like the countdown to a harrowing event. I felt an empty silence form inside me, carved out by that inhuman wail, terrible as a battle cry heard among the clashing components of war in the middle of lethal combat. Something in my Being was triggered which sharpened my ability to listen.

«Do you remember when you used to cry for hours until you were hoarse?» asked the Dreamer suddenly in a low voice yet somehow distilling ferocity in His tone. Image after image rushed through my mind, points of access to a distant past that overlapped and mixed together like shuffled playing cards. The images all shared the same characteristics. They all possessed the same light and magical atmosphere of my Neapolitan childhood, where Lares and Penates had even more ancient names, given to them by age-old superstitions. I recognized the old house, Carmela's room and the wardrobe with the mirrors on its doors. A boy of may be six was sitting on the floor, crying desperately, endlessly… It was me.

«You are still there, nothing has changed, except that your childish tantrums have become a lasting tendency to complain and indulge in self-pity».

He fell silent for what seemed an interminable length of time…

«No one changes... it is impossible to change – commented the Dreamer at last – *At the age of seven, a child is already recruited into that sad army of adults and, like a little Spartan... he has already received an inverted vision of the world along with a complete set of all the beliefs, prejudices, superstitions and ideas that give him a lifetime membership in that planetary club of miserable souls.*

A man's thoughts, emotions and body are concentric universes... everything is connected. Deliberately changing the tone or inflection of one's voice, straightening one's back by even one millimeter or modifying one's most insignificant habit, means changing one's entire life. It is almost impossible.»

He scrutinized me intensely, severely, and I endured His examination. I knew that not even the slightest impulse in my soul would escape His notice and that there was no possible way of cheating in this game. I was betting on all or nothing... The possibility that, one day, I might conquer myself, be touched by the 'dream' and transform my life into a great personal adventure, or else fall and lose myself forever, with no hope of recovery, was there...the alternatives co-existed. My life was hanging by a thin thread suspended over the mouth of an abyss. One word, a change in inflection, the length of a pause, could make it fall into the swarming mass of a collective destiny.

With a quick movement and the agility of someone who keeps his body in shape, He rose from His reclining position. The light blue of the pool caught His movement like the reflection of something in flight and rocked it on its trembling surface. Slowly, He took a few steps in my direction. I held my breath and waited for what seemed an eternity. Then, with a firm tone, but this time devoid of harshness, He announced:

«You can make it only if you remember Me!»

17 "Turn your convictions upside down!"

In the meantime, He had settled Himself comfortably, carefully arranging a few cushions around Him. He looked as though He were bracing Himself to resume a lengthy task that He thought already completed and left at His side.

«Overthrow your beliefs!» He exhorted, emphatically.

The idea of inviting me to take a seat must never even have crossed His mind, and He left me standing on the same spot where I had been from the beginning of our encounter. I thought this was lacking in consideration and felt resentful and offended. At the time, it was inconceivable to me that one could live every moment as purposefully as the Dreamer. He did not so much as bat an eyelid without it consciously serving His purpose. Brooding over my resentment, I carried on listening to Him, not moving from the terracotta tile on which I was standing, next to the trembling waters of His pool.

«A man's present, past and future... the events, the circumstances and the experiences he encounters on his way, are

shadows projected by his beliefs – continued the Dreamer – *His existence and destiny are the materialization of his convictions and, above all, of his indulgences...*

'Visibilia ex invisibilibus'. Everything you perceive, see and touch comes from the invisible. The life of a man is the shadow of his 'dream', it is the visual manifestation of his principles and all he believes...

Everyone invariably sees what he has firmly believed in come to pass... A man always creates. The obstacles he encounters are the materialization of his own limitations, his fragmented thinking and his impotence...

There are those who have faith in poverty and those who only know how to believe in sickness... There are those who have an unshakable belief in misery and scarcity... and there are those who have staked everything on crime... Man is always creative, even when he is imprisoned in the dungeons of his Being.»

According to the Dreamer, no man has any more faith than the other. Every man has his own allocation of faith to manage, to invest... everyone has been apportioned exactly the same amount.

«What differentiates men... what really gives them a different destiny, is the direction of their beliefs, the different quality of their goals, be they conscious or not... »

I was more than a little disconcerted by the Dreamer's claims as I had always believed that faith was a rare commodity, and, what was more, that it was precisely their varying capacity for believing that differentiated men. One of the ideological constraints on my vision of the world certainly included the belief that Mohammed, Alexander, Socrates, Lao Tzu, Churchill or Napoleon could be set apart from other men by the strength of their convictions.

«But if everyone has faith... and furthermore, the same quantity of faith – I asked, using the Holy Scriptures to support my case and drawing strength from their authority – what then is the meaning of the words 'if you have faith like a mustard seed...'?»

The discussion which followed imprinted itself forever in my consciousness. Not so much for His memorable words but for the authority with which He delivered them. The Dreamer was not giving me an interpretation of that passage from the Gospel, He was creating it. The dreaming essence of that age-old message and the intelligence compressed in its atoms, was being released there and then, in that moment. The words I was listening to were new and alive, and had never been uttered before in the entire history of the world.

«If a man were able to shift the direction of his faith by even one millimeter, if he could only redirect the strength of his convictions towards life rather than death... he could move mountains in the world of events.»

Like a flash of lightning that tears through the darkness and illuminates what a few moments earlier had been steeped in shadows, did this evidence leap across my mind. Now I understood vividly just how much energy was contained in a single atom of faith. I understood that the elimination of the smallest particle of hell would destroy that total faith in death - the most deeply rooted of all men's beliefs. I also realized the enormity of such an undertaking. Grasping this idea alone required an effort equivalent to a Titan carrying the weight of heaven and earth on his shoulders.

For the first time I asked myself what I had believed in, to what had I attributed value until my meeting with the Dreamer... His voice reached me while I was immersed in these thoughts and helped me as they turned irreparably towards the dark morass of my past. Although I already knew, it was embarrassing for me to have renewed confirmation of the fact that I was an open book to Him.

«Until today your reason for living, the goal of your existence, as for all men, has been to kill yourself inside. Sickness, Old age and Death are the gods that mankind has worshipped for thousands of years... Thus has man painfully renounced life... and his infinite dream.»

'If you had faith like a mustard seed...' meant that the slightest raising of our vision, the most minimal change, could divert us from our mortal destiny.

The dream is the most real thing there is.

To 'see' one's own limitations and circumscribe them, means to free oneself from them! For how long will you be able to remove these constraints and escape this condition of impotence? Man's life is ruled by negative emotions. The anguish he carries inside is the real cause of all his troubles and unhappiness. The Dreamer rose and, turning His back to me, took a few careful steps past the large pool towards the opposite corner of that extraordinary greenhouse.

From there He spoke, still with His back to me, and I heard His voice as strong and clear as if He had been right next to my ear.

«It is only a question of time – I scrupulously wrote down in my notebook – *before every one of us will reach the goals we have set for ourselves... In the end we will all win... we will all become what we have believed in... and each of us will achieve everything we have clung to most faithfully... you, your misery, your immorality, your death... and I flawlessness, infinity and immortality.»*

18 The Narcissus Syndrome

«Your most unshakeable faith... your most harmful belief, is that a world exists outside of yourself, that there is someone or something on which to depend, someone or something that can give or take from you, elect or condemn you» said the Dreamer.

«If a warrior believed, even for a moment, in outside help, he would immediately lose his invulnerability» He said. Then He fell silent and shut His eyes.

I tried to fill that moment by writing down His words in my notebook. But the sense of a void expanded. I struggled to overcome my discomfort at suddenly feeling irrelevant and superfluous by mentally rereading parts of my notes. Finally, the Dreamer broke His silence and with His eyes still closed, recited:

There is nothing out there...
There is no help coming from anywhere at all...

«Man's most serious disease is dependence» He announced in a severe tone. I immediately became very wary. I unerringly felt in my bones the importance of this statement and the central role that I should give it in my new system of beliefs.

«There is nothing worse than dependence on others, on their presence or their judgment... and to free oneself from this requires extensive preparation... One must train for it...»

Later, when I recalled my attitude on that occasion and similar ones, I realized that when the Dreamer referred to mankind in general, what I accepted immediately and unquestioningly, provoked in me a response of unassailable resistance when His criticism was aimed directly at me.

«People like you... only feel alive when they are among others... they prefer crowded places... they find work in government offices or large companies... wherever they feel the reassuring presence of the crowd... They celebrate all the rituals of dependence and gather in its temples: cinemas, theatres, hospitals, stadiums, courthouses or churches, just to huddle in a group with others, to escape from themselves and the unbearable burden of their solitude» continued the Dreamer.

An irrepressible hostility darkened my Being, almost as if those words had threatened something vital or upset a plan which had been made a long time before. Mentally I lined up all the harsh words, like a row of mortar shells I would have liked to lob at Him. I tried desperately to clear away the negativity, but could only manage a pained grimace. The Dreamer was testing the walls of my resistance and He knew how to breach them. He gave me a ferocious smile, as if He were about to strike me, and whispered:

«A man like you falls ill and is willing to be cut to pieces by surgeons... by the shamans of a still primitive science just to draw attention to himself...» I gasped, as if I had been punched in the stomach. The Dreamer let a few seconds pass as if he were counting me out, as if he were referee and adversary at the same time.

«Do you remember the painting?» He asked suddenly, completely changing His tone and demeanor. He knocked me off balance every time. I would never get used to these abrupt changes, performed with a suddenness and mastery I had never seen in anyone before. I was amazed by His ability to transform Himself entering into a totally new state of Being without transferring even one atom from the previous one. I immediately understood that His question referred to the painting I had admired before coming into the greenhouse where we were now. I recalled the picture of Narcissus admiring his image in the pool moments before being swallowed up by it.

«It is the symbolic story of a man trapped in his own reflection» explained the Dreamer, barely concealing His mirth at my vain attempts to change my facial expressions in response to His sudden change of topic and mood.

«The fable of Narcissus is the metaphor of a man who becomes a victim of his own creation»

He continued, explaining to me that, contrary to what is commonly believed, Narcissus was not in love with himself but with the image reflected in the water, while unaware that it was his own. In fact, believing he was looking at somebody else, he became infatuated, fell into the water and tragically drowned.

«Once you realize that the world you see is the projection of yourself, you are free of it» concluded the Dreamer.

I was in a state of shock… How had it been possible for one of the most crucial myths of our civilization to be misunderstood for thousands of years? How on earth had it been possible to miss an explanation that was so simple?

Alongside the Dreamer, I distinctly heard the voice of ancient times, of the classic age when most audacious ideas were forged, conceived by that race of gigantic thinkers, lofty philosophers who died out with Socrates. The resonance of their knowledge, which was eventually replaced by the consolatory invention of philosophy, still crosses the ages to reach us but we continue to neglect or misunderstand its warning myths. We do not want to know of their merciless message about the true condition of man and we still present Narcissus as the archetype of vanity, whereas instead his myth is a warning signal alerting us to the stupidity and danger of the conventional vision of the world. What the Dreamer had repeatedly tried to make me understand was finally penetrating a little deeper. The story of Narcissus was a message from a School of Overturning which had existed thousands of years before Caravaggio and which had inspired him to paint those pictures of the crucifixion of Peter and the conversion of Paul stricken on the road to Damascus.

«To fall in love with something outside of ourselves, forgetting ourselves, means becoming lost in the wanderings of a world of dependence… it means forgetting that one is the sole creator of his own personal reality…»

«A world outside of ourselves does not exist – He stated again – *All that we meet, see and touch is a reflection of ourselves. Other people, the events and circumstances in a man's life reveal his condition.»* Blaming the world, complaining, justifying and hiding, are therefore the surest signs of dependency and the absence of a 'true' will.

«This is not the only message which has come down to us across the ages which man has consistently misunderstood in order to escape its unbearable proposition» said the Dreamer.

«Like Adam, Narcissus also bit into the apple!» He said, catching me by surprise. It was difficult for me to keep pace with Him, when with a single step, He crossed the abyss of time and space between distant worlds, placing the four thousand year old story of Genesis alongside one of most ancient Greek myths.

«He too, like Adam, believed in otherness, in the existence of a world outside himself.»

Narcissus wasted away, victim of his illusion that there was someone outside himself and Adam was cast out of Eden and condemned to death for having bitten into the apple and for believing in the existence of an external world.

However culturally distant they may have been, in both traditions the message was the same: to believe that the world is outside us means to become its victim, to be swallowed up by it.

«The world is created by you, every second! – said the Dreamer – *The pool in which Narcissus saw his reflection is the external world. Believing it to be real and relying on it means depending on one's own shadow... it means becoming smaller than the world we project. From creator, you become a creation, from dreamer you become dreamed, from master you become slave, until you are suffocated by your own creation.»*

It occurred to me that the message conveyed by these myths, as the Dreamer was helping me discover, could also be found intact in modern as well as ancient fables, from Frankenstein to Blade Runner, from the Gospels to Alice in Wonderland.

«The fall of Adam and Eve from paradise happens every moment» concluded the Dreamer.

«We are thrown out of Eden each time the description of the world takes hold of us... the moment we forget we are the creators. Then the creation rebels and rises up against us... This is the original sin, the unforgivable, mortal sin: mistaking the cause for the effect. A man that is whole and true... is such because he governs himself... And in spite of the apparent dynamism of events and the variety of situations he finds himself in, he knows that the world is his mirror.»

«Whether good or bad, ugly or beautiful, right or wrong, everything a man encounters is just his reflection and not reality»

said the Dreamer, and from His tone I understood our meeting was approaching its end. He was about to leave me.

«Everyone always and only reaps what he is... You are both the seed, and the harvest.

This is why all the revolutions in history have failed... they tried to change the world from the outside... they believed the image in the pool to be real.

Do not rely any more on the world for help. Go beyond it! Only those who have gone beyond the world can improve it.»

Here He stopped for a few moments.

«Go beyond it!» He ordered and then fell silent once more.

Transcend the world, go beyond it! What could this mean?

«For centuries man has scratched at the screen of the world, believing he could change the images of the film he himself had projected onto it.»

The explanation for the failure of so many generations of men who had attempted to change the course of history was being handed to me on a silver tray.. That bitterly comic vision summed up the infinite succession of atrocities, defeats and heroics, passing upon it just one judgment: that it had been a colossal useless folly.

«You... get out of this madness! – He ordered with unexpected kindness – *Forget about wars, revolutions and economic, social, or political reform... concern yourself with the one who is truly responsible for everything that happens... Stop thinking about the dream and take care of the dreamer in you. The greatest revolution, the most difficult of all undertakings, yet the only one that has any sense, is changing one's self.»*

19 A man cannot hide

«Those who depend on the world remain mired in the lowest levels of existence – the Dreamer warned – *For your whole life, you have looked for ephemeral certainties, satisfactions and security outside of yourself... constantly suspended between fear and hope which are the roots of dependence... »*

As He spoke the Dreamer fixed His gaze on me with a severity that did not permit me to blink or draw breath, as He would do when He had to overcome my barriers and reach me at a deeper level.

«Your life, like that of all those who are dependent, is horrible. It is the life of a slave... Years and years in an office, perpetuating mediocrity and scarcity, without even having the slightest desire to escape from that prison.»

Like a war reporter, I took note of what He was saying, writing amidst a hail of gunfire.

«There is nothing out there... there is no help coming from anywhere at all – repeated the Dreamer to impress this statement on the core of my most deeply rooted beliefs – *I will never stop repeating this; nothing is outside of you... What you call the 'world' is only an effect... what you call reality is the materialisation, the mirror image of your dreams or your nightmares... »*

This vision would reveal itself to be the backdrop to all His teachings and, on several occasions in the future, the Dreamer would elaborate and expand on it, as my ability to understand and support its subversive force developed. I remember how that first time had been a shock for me, a reversal of everything I had believed in up until that moment.

«Realize that the world is in you, and not vice versa! What is in the world, or belongs to it, can neither help nor save you!»

Then His words became an exhortation, an appeal that I felt was directed not only to me but to every man. His words were laced with the disappointment of one who knows he is offering something of great value to someone who can neither appreciate nor use it.

«Aspire to freedom, leave this desperate multitude behind... Impose a new way of feeling upon yourself. Conquer the immensity within you and the galaxies will become grains of sand...

Broaden your vision and you will see the world become small... Vision and reality are one and the same thing... Look for integrity and what are insurmountable mountains for others will become tiny bumps for you.»

I interpreted the pause that followed as an invitation to make a comment and, carelessly, I ventured a few observations. I said something about the difficulty of accepting the idea that we are the cause of every event or circumstance in our lives. I took care to avoid anything contentious and adopted the impartial tone of one who tries to introduce a wise neutrality into a casual conversation with a stranger. Like a blind man, I could not perceive the unfathomable distance which separated the Dreamer's words from mine on the ladder of responsibility.

«It seems impossible to believe that everything that can happen to a man, from a cold to a plane crash, is the materialization of his psychology» I concluded. I felt simultaneously fascinated and threatened by the Dreamer's vision. Following the trail of my reflections, I was digging down to the roots of our civilization, as far as those two contrasting positions which have divided our world to this day. Classical Greece believed in a goddess of Fortune who blindly bestowed favours. They represented her wearing a blindfold. The ancient Romans, on the other hand, believed in *homo faber.* Fortune to the Romans was a goddess who had the most perfect sight and respected the virtue of the individual. In my mind I classified the Dreamer among those who supported the Roman conception of the world.

However, I hardly had time to formulate this idea, when I heard His voice transform itself into a roar which froze my blood, as in the most terrible moments I had previously experienced with Him.

« ...Do you think you are here to make small talk with some poor slob like yourself?... Hear me well – He said, and reinforced this order by tapping His right ear with His first two fingers several times, in a slow and deliberate way – *The world is a reflection of your states of Being' means this: Luisa did not die of cancer. Her death is the theatrical representation of your interior drama, your mortal anguish... That event, like all events, is only a manifestation of your states of Being... Even though you try to conceal it through endless blame and complaint, in reality your song of sorrow is a fertility rite in reverse. It has invited all the troubles and difficulties of your entire existence.»*

Suddenly everything fell silent.

An inexplicable anxiety was welling up inside me. A part of me gave way and a cavern opened wider and wider until it engulfed me. My heart was throwing itself against the walls of my chest and my breathing was blocked by an everlasting exhalation. I felt sickened and dizzy, trapped in an endless fall, while a mute cry of terror, desperation, shame echoed throughout the fibres of my Being, as if all the pain of my existence were compressed into a single point.

Only when He began to speak once more was I finally able to breathe again. Greedily I gulped in all the air I could.

«A man cannot hide» whispered the Dreamer, as if imparting a secret teaching. I listened like a child, without disagreement or opposition.

«Our most insignificant action, perception, thought, gesture and facial expression is recorded in eternity.» He told me that the way we live every moment, like a frame in the film of our lives, signals a heightening or lowering of Being and attunes us to everything that will happen to us.

«A man cannot hide!... Here with me you stand alone facing existence... Here there are no political affiliations or trade unions. When you enter this room you cannot bring anything with you from your past, not even the lie of your name or your role in life. Here there is no guard rail for you to hold onto... Here you are alone facing yourself...»

He noticed that I was trembling visibly; my teeth began to chatter as if I was coming down with a fever, and He said:

«Stop being afraid and stop hiding! There is a part of you that has to die because it is absurd. This death is your great opportunity. Only you can do it...»

Physically, painfully I felt that the Dreamer was penetrating layer upon layer into my ignorance, through the psychological detritus which had accumulated over time and hardened.

«If you work tirelessly and for as many years as you have spent damaging yourself – He said in a whisper as sweet as a promise – *one day time will split open. A tunnel will open up and guide you to the part of yourself that is the most real and true... a part with which sooner or later every man must reconnect: his dream.»*

Only at this point did the Dreamer take His eyes off me, allowing me to catch my breath. His figure rippled like a watery reflection. He was about to leave me. All at once I felt impossibly tired, as if I had run for miles and miles on a single breath of air. My legs refused to support me so I knelt down on the carpet, which had just become visible by the light of the new day, and fell to the ground like a dead man.

CHAPTER III

The Body

1 "You are the world"

A few months had passed since my last meeting with the Dreamer and the words I had heard in the shimmering atmosphere of the greenhouse by the pool still troubled me. More than anything else, His unforgettable and inhuman cry '*Stoooop it!*'... kept resonating inside me; along with the feeling that it had emptied me completely. For quite some time I found it hard to think of anything else. I repeatedly looked over the notes I had taken, and each time the powerful chemistry of His words permeated me.

Then gradually, increasingly, New York took hold and my life started to flow again along the usual lines, its rhythm marked by my business commitments at the ACO and the daily routine of looking after the children and tending to domestic affairs with Jennifer. The precious substance I had gathered grain by grain during my meetings with the Dreamer evaporated; and my states of Being, my thoughts, my attitudes, and my language reverted to what they had been before I met Him.

One evening, I was having a drink with a few people from my work team, in the semi-darkness of a bar on Madison Avenue – the usual New York after-work ritual. We were celebrating someone's birthday. Suddenly, the bar and its customers sank into complete silence, as if the world's audio system had somehow broken down. Time slowed. I observed my companions' faces swollen with alcohol, and I 'saw' expressions of pain concealed behind their silent laughter. I reflected with a mildly ironic lucidity on what an evolved sense of the grotesque it took to call that joyless ritual 'happy hour'. Suddenly I felt a sharp sense of having missed something; a sudden feeling of having neglected something essential and irreplaceable. The yearning desire to see Him alternated with the nausea caused by that emptiness until it invaded every recess of my Being. I desperately and silently appealed to Him. Never before had such an SOS been sent out to literally save a soul.

A few days later, Valerie, my assistant, came in with the ritual 'white coffee' to start off the day in one hand and a mysterious envelope in the other. Wordlessly she removed a plane ticket from it and, ostentatiously, slapped it down in front of me, as if she were a wife confronted with the evidence of an undeniable infidelity.

«So – she said resentfully – you're going to Barcelona, are you, and you didn't even tell me! Thanks a lot.»

And in that woman's words, tone and attitude, I heard the distillation of thousands of compromises that had spoiled my life.

I passed through many rooms before finding Him. He had his back to me, and seemed to be busy stoking the flames in the stone fireplace. A preciously carved coat of arms dominated the mantelpiece and in a large grisaille toned painting which depicted some peons walking lazily, I thought I recognized the hand of Ortega.

I could see the Dreamer's profile in the firelight and I had the impression that its brightness and luminosity did not come from the flames, but His own tawny skin. He was wearing a light silk dressing gown and His demeanor was that of an aristocratic gentleman whose privileges and high birth permitted Him to lead a life of leisure.

The secret thread of my mood took me back to our first meeting. On that occasion too he had His back to me and I registered this similarity with apprehension. I could still feel the sting of the words he had used towards me then, and I did not relish the idea of undergoing a similar experience.

The silence continued with the Dreamer giving no sign of having noticed my presence. I tried to stifle my growing anxiety by looking at the surroundings, the extensive suite of rooms and halls which housed *Mas Anglada*'s imposing library. A vast collection of books densely covered the walls from floor to ceiling. The floor was entirely made up of little diamond-shaped glazed terracotta tiles that composed a colourful painting by Chagall. I was trying to catch a glimpse of the titles of some of the books closest to me when His voice broke the silence.

«*When you are far away from Me you degenerate, you revert to your plan of death*» and as He turned to face me, I felt His steely gaze pass over me like a sword.

«*When you forget Me you fall back into the rut of repetition. And every time you go through your life again, you become troubled by it without realizing that you have already lived it.*»

In those words there was a flavour of eternity, the forgotten reminder of a boundless freedom behind the threatening tone and unbearable pain. Almost as if life had been suspended, the Dreamer was resuming His speech from where He had left off months before, and it seemed only now that it was able to flow again. I drew out my notebook and took down every word.

«*Nothing is external!... Yet you still seek reassurance in the eyes of others... you are still seeking happiness and solutions in a world that suffers from the same disease as you do... The world is your skin... the world is you!... You meet always and only yourself.*»

«And what about the others?» I asked.

«*The others? They are you 'outside yourself'! They are fragments of you distributed in time; reflections of a disintegrated psychology...* »

I took pages and pages of notes during that meeting, especially about the fatal illusion which makes us believe in otherness and the existence of a world outside of ourselves that is independent of our will and on which our destiny depends.

«*This is the sin of all sins*» concluded the Dreamer. The original sin. When you wish for something and stretch out your hand, even to reach for an apple, wholeness is gone, paradise lost.

2 Psychological dwarves

According to the Dreamer, our 'first education' teaches us to perceive the world as an external entity capable of deciding and acting, and able to impose its own will upon us. This is why man confronts a world that constantly threatens and irremediably victimizes him...

«This is how men become psychological dwarves... smaller than insects. Wandering through the world with their tail between their legs... nourishing a sense of guilt... they're afraid...

Once a man reaches this level of degradation, all he can do is betray, blame, complain, feel sorry for himself... and lie... lie to himself, believing that the problem is limited... that his life is perfect apart from a few insignificant details, an occasional problem or a passing moment of adversity.

He is so blind that he cannot see that behind an unpleasant aspect of his life, behind some seemingly insignificant detail, lies a disease of the whole Being. In order to change a single atom of his existence he needs to change everything... he has to overthrow his way of thinking, his ideas... his ordinary vision of the world!»

At the end of His speech, the Dreamer revealed to me that the five wounds of Jesus symbolized the five senses of the horizontal man which nail him to the lowest part of existence.

«When you realize that you are the creator of the external world, that you contain the world and not vice versa... when you remember that whatever you see, hear and touch are the fruits of your own creation, you can no longer be afraid of them...»

«The world is a chewing gum; it takes on the shape of your teeth» He said. I immediately loved that expression. It was so unusual and impudently expressive that I wrote it down among His most memorable maxims.

«Do not forget that the world and the others are the most honest and sincere expression of what you really are... The world is such because you are such.»

He pulled back the heavy curtain to reveal a long glass wall and I gazed out across distant hills, dense green vineyards, and the dark lines of the freshly ploughed furrows. The property of *Mas Anglada* seemed to go on forever. The Dreamer's voice had the sweet ring of a promise.

« ...Remember Me! Remember the 'dream'! This is how you will find a perfect world, a healed world. Earthly Paradise is the projection of a state of Being, a 'portable paradise'... In order to keep it intact, to hold its atoms together, one must be constantly on the alert, one must constantly 'intervene'... »

I was filling the pages of my notebook so fast, and yet I could hardly keep up with Him. I had circled one particular verb many times to highlight it, and as soon as I had the chance, I asked Him what He meant by 'intervene'.

«It means knowing how to access the darkest parts of one's Being and bring light there» replied the Dreamer, giving these words a special intensity, as if He were revealing a vital secret.

He paused for a long time and seemed to be hesitating before telling me something that might exceed my powers of understanding. I held my breath and hoped that He would be able to trust me.

«If I were to allow one single grain of hell to enter my paradise... all this would disappear» He said, accompanying His words with a wide gesture that encompassed first the ancient fireplace, the lake sized of pool surrounded by the vibrant green of the park, the huge estate and the books and the works of art that were all around us.

«Some day, to deserve paradise and be able to sustain it, you will have to learn how to shield yourself from mediocrity, from neglect... from your inner deaths... A solar man can project his light, a world that is joyous and complete and he lets nothing cloud it...»

It was then that I started to fully comprehend what the Dreamer meant by 'being alert'.

" ...If I were to allow one single grain of hell..." Those words dug deeply into me and as they reached my bones, something clicked. In a flash, I understood what incorruptibility was; what it meant to be an honest and faultless leader, and how immense was the task of watching for the slightest shadow in one's Being. I understood His severity and why even a grimace, attitude or the slightest sign of negativity would trigger the harshest of reprimands from Him.

The Dreamer explained that human thoughts and emotions have a physical nature made up of colors and smells, which reveal one's states of Being and level of responsibility, even at a distance. I turned bright red as I thought of all the times I had brought my miasma of doubts and the acrid smell of fear into the Dreamer's world.

I recognized we were incomplete Beings who conduct our lives without even imagining that anyone might be able to detect the reek of our psychological rubbish, our thoughts and negative emotions which, like the smell of gas signaling a leak, have the function of exposing our states as warnings of imminent disaster.

«The world is the perfect representation of your states of Being. The world is such because you are such, and not vice versa.»

3 A song of sorrow

We had left *Mas Anglada*. The pool, the park, and the rural beauty of the landscape no longer surrounded us. Now I was walking with the Dreamer through the narrow streets of an unknown town while the pungent humid smell of a port drifted along them as though channelled down invisible rivers. We proceeded on foot into that watery world which the Dreamer seemed to know so well and as we went further into its liquid body, I felt, amid the reflections and echoes, a sensation of lightness growing inside me. A little rack-rail train was laboring up the hill and we came out on a terrace suspended between the rocks and the sea; an ancient corner of the world cradled in the amniotic fluid which spawned those myths and fables so dear to the infancy of humanity.

«A man only apparently aspires to good health, prosperity and well-being» said the Dreamer gravely, and in His voice was the solemnity of a speech addressed to the most authentic part of every man.

«If he could observe and know his inner self, he would hear a song of sorrow, the constant recital of a prayer of misfortune, in the expectation of some terrible disaster, however probable or improbable...»

There was a man some distance away, who seemed to be absorbed by the all-embracing panorama of sea and sky. He was wearing a black T-shirt and dark sunglasses and had an excessively large belly, while his arms were turned inwards as a result of his bulging underarms. He was constantly plunging his hand into a huge bag of crisps and taking out generous handfuls while continuing to stare.

«You see? – He said gesturing with a slight movement of the chin – *that man is killing himself. A gentleman from another age, or of a different temperament, might have chosen a pistol. We would have seen him aim it at his temple with dignity and bid farewell to the world, while taking a last look at this extraordinary landscape.»*

I was troubled by this comment about the stranger. I was still trying to understand what it was that had so upset me about His words, when I heard Him add:

«The only difference between the gun and that food is the speed of the method chosen to end one's own life!»

Had those words been uttered by anyone else I would have considered them to be a cruel joke; an overstatement made in dubious taste. But the Dreamer was not one to joke. Why did His words upset and annoy me so much? At the time I thought that my state of mind, poised halfway between amazement and indignation, and my ongoing pain, had been provoked by the Dreamer's cynicism but I was a long way from guessing the real cause of my uneasiness.

The only way I found to escape that malaise and stop, or at least hide, the inexplicable hostility growing uncontrollably inside me, was by resorting to a quip.

«Then in both cases we should call the police, have them disarm him before it's too late» I said with a smile that was already dead when it reached my lips. I should have stopped, but I couldn't resist saying ironically.

«In this instance we would warn the police that a man is trying to commit suicide with a bag of potato chips.»

His face, which was already severe, turned to steel and froze the blood in my veins.

«You too are suicidal» He announced coldly. Then He whispered:

«That man is you!»

He waited a few seconds for me to recover from the blow, like a boxer who had been knocked out. Then He must have decided that I was TKO, so He stopped and said:

«The life of an ordinary man is a one-way street. He only knows the way towards limitations. His only faith, his only absolute loyalty is to death. The choice of how he kills himself is his only true freedom. This body is indestructible. We ourselves allow it to be destroyed. The very thoughts and feelings we impose upon it are the causes of ageing, disease, failure and death. Whatever happens in your body happens to the world. The world is what you are; and you are this birthless, deathless body.

You, like millions of men, have chosen to use your fears and destructive thoughts to kill yourself.»

«But what can one do?» was all I could stammer. I wanted to ask this question in the name of all suicidal humanity. I wanted to say "What can I do?"... but this would have required energy, and all of mine had drained out through some unknown crack in my Being leaving me with barely enough strength to stand up.

«Were we to try and stop them and thwart their project of death, they would not see us as rescuers or benefactors – said the Dreamer – *On the contrary, such an attempt would turn them into mortal enemies, and in the end would only postpone their self-sabotage.»*

He examined me carefully as if trying to discover how ready I was to shoulder the responsibility of what He was about to tell me. Then He whispered:

«Man inherited a dark side of his Being from the 'first education', an embrace of destruction, an impulse to harm first himself and then others.»

He told me that self-sabotage and loyalty to death were the dominant features of the old humanity's psychology, a shadowy second nature which manifests itself in the ordinary man as an irresistible urge to kill oneself. Once he forgets that he is the maker, creator and absolute master of anything and everything, man becomes prey to an insidious notion of the world as miserable, wretched, futile. He lives like a beggar, afflicted by a sense of guilt and a constant feeling of failure; a victim of the song of sorrow he sings inside, the negative imagination and destructive thoughts ceaselessly echoing inside him.

«Observe yourselves! Self-observation opens up the darkest corners of your Being. Circumscribe every kind of doubt and fear inside yourself as soon it arises. Be brutal with yourselves. Impose happiness, well-being and certainty upon yourselves. It is not the circumstances and events of the world that make you unhappy; it is your unhappiness that creates all the miseries in the world. Poverty is a mental illness.»

4 The body cannot lie

«Look at yourself – the Dreamer went on brusquely – *you've just turned thirty and you already have an old man's body.»* The blood rushed to my face and I felt I would die with embarrassment,

as if He had put me on display naked, right there, in front of all the people who were crowded together on the belvedere.

He continued mercilessly.

«The body reveals the Being. It should always resonate with pleasure, joy, like that of a child... but you have forgotten... The body cannot lie!»

There was no hint of accusation in His voice, only the cold assessment of a disaster. I felt the stinging blow; a pain that was true and clear, without resentment or accusation. I composed myself. I tried to straighten up but it was only at that moment that I realized how accustomed I had become to live hunched over, and how guilty I was of not having loved and looked after my body. At that point my natural disposition would have inclined me towards my old habit of self-pity. But the Dreamer did not allow it. The opportunity He was offering me was too great. I should have grasped it but I was not ready so I adopted a defensive attitude; a reflection of an unconscious refusal to change. I quickly mustered all the good reasons which had prevented me from taking care of my body: my job, the endless trips, city life, family needs, Luisa's illness and, last but not least, the kidney stones that had plagued me since I was very young.

His voice blocked my planned apology and confused my arguments. Suddenly I felt myself catapulted out of my condition and I saw myself through the Dreamer's eyes. It was the humiliating vision of a small man concerned only with saving himself by seeking good reasons to acquit himself and wriggle out of any responsibility in order to stay as he was. I would have liked to hold on to that vision which, however painful, had the purity of detachment, the healing clarity of integrity. But this freedom lasted only a few moments.

«Your body, your pale face, your swollen eyes and your flabbiness are evidence of the fact that you have given up living; that you have already dropped out. Everyone knows about your unconscious plan to hasten your physical death, everyone that is, except you!

In order to reduce his body to such a state, a man must first profane himself... He is like a wounded animal leaving a trail of blood so as to be caught and killed by his predator.

The laws of existence outside the jungle are no different.

The Being, the body and the world are one and the same thing!»

This last statement astounded me. While I was just nearly able to rationally grasp the possibility that the Being and the body were a single entity, the idea that there existed a causal relationship between the body and the world went far beyond my limits of acceptance.

«*Everything that you see and touch is solidified light, whatever you perceive is nothing but a projection of your organs* – the Dreamer confirmed – *They are not only the part of you which is closest to the world... they are the real builders, makers and creators of your universe.*»

Then, He closed His eyes, as he often did, and recited some lines which I faithfully transcribed:

The Body is the true Dreamer...
The Body dreams, and its cells and its organs dream.
The Body is the real maker of your personal world.

The Dreamer explained to me that what a man sees of himself through his physical eyes is what he calls a body, whereas what he cannot see, since it vibrates at a higher frequency, is what he calls his Being.

«*Actually the body is the Being... it is the Being made visible.*» He said, and started to scrutinize me again, as if evaluating my condition. Then His tone became harsh.

«*Faith in a divinity outside ourselves... the idea that there exists an entity beyond our body, is the most widely accepted superstition in the world and one of the biggest killers of humanity.*» In many religious traditions this external god has been replaced by belief in a spirit-guide, a soul, an invisible entity within man. According to the Dreamer this belief was also fatal. One way or another we have been led to disown our body and reduce our life to an endless series of attempts to suppress it.

«*This is how man has fallen into iniquity, into the immorality of death.*»

My thoughts whirled around the revolutionary concepts I was learning from Him.

«*The body cannot lie* – He repeated, raising His voice with a harsh tone that immediately drew my attention – *The body is the most honest and sincere part of our Being. The body reveals what we are... In our present state, it reveals our incompleteness and conflictual nature.»*

I cleared my throat and coughed slightly. The Dreamer slowly came a few millimeters closer to me and in His eyes I could see the innocent ferocity, the mercilessness of a wild creature. The air grew dark and it was as if I had come face to face with a mortal enemy… I fell into an uncontrollable anguish.

«Coughing is your way of saying no... of digging in your heels and resisting Me – He said in a terrible voice – *I am what stops you from growing old; what protects you from your plan of falling ill and dying. I am what stops you from returning to the vulgarity of your past... to repetitiveness... and chance... With Me you cannot degrade yourself. This is why you see Me as your worst enemy... It is easier to follow hypnotically the old path towards degradation and suffering than to climb upwards and go against the tide, rebelling against poverty, the tyranny of old age and sickness, and the immorality of death.»*

He gave me a short break and I grasped it eagerly like a shipwreck victim taking his first gulp of air above water. These words threw me into despair and drained my body of all its vitality. Nobody had ever spoken to me in such a way or made me feel so wretched. Who was that Being? What was that love of His, so merciless and sharp?

«Here with Me you can never grow old… you cannot get sick or die» He said, as I listened in amazement to those timeless words.

«Learn how to raise the vibrations of your body to a higher level, and you will disappear from the sight of a harmful, threatening, mortal world. The battlefield is the body.

However, to those of you who have chosen death as your guide, light and life appear to be gruesome things, this is why there is an open struggle between you and Me…»

By saying 'those of you', He broadened that extraordinary message and extended it in a masterly fashion to encompass all the human Beings in the world. Standing on the belvedere of that unknown city surrounded by a breathtaking panorama, I was no longer alone in front of the Dreamer. The rest of humanity was there with me, listening to Him too.

5 Be frugal!

«This struggle between us will end only when you will change forever – threatened the Dreamer with a cold calmness – *If I appear hard... merciless... if you feel pain... if you see me as a monster with bloodshot eyes, this will only be a reflection of your incomprehension and resistance to change. With me, if you want to, you can change your unavoidable destiny and that of thousands of men and women...»*

A new determination, a certainty, was making its way into my Being, like a hand slowly forming a fist: I no longer wanted to depend on the world and others as I had done so desperately up until that moment. I did not want to be a shadow anymore, a bio-chemical puppet jerked by the horrible strings of circumstance and chance. I swore to myself that I would do anything to faithfully apply the principles that the Dreamer was arduously trying to impress upon me.

«Use all your strength to fight your self-fulfilling prophecy of doom while you still have time. You have been programmed for defeat and dependency all your life. Overthrow that vision and free yourself from the description of the world you were given by adulterated adults and all the masters of misfortune you met in your life. Renounce your faith in sickness and old-age. Stop lying!... Rebel against all this and get rid of the dead weight... Straighten up, lift your neck and hold your head up high... Shed the superfluous weight, the fat and the lies.»

Why was He talking to me as if I were obese? The insult stung me, and I felt a mute resentment as if I had been dealt an unbearable injustice. In actual fact I weighed just over eighty-five kilos, not an excessive weight for a man of my height. This apparently small disparity between the Dreamer and myself was distilled into an inexpressible physical pain. Differences of opinion that are normal and accepted among friends, and even considered as signs of intellectual independence and strength of character, were inadmissible and outlawed in the Dreamer's presence.

I realized now that invisible threads connected me to Him. In a flash I saw our Beings crossing cosmic distances and slowly being woven together. A mythical being, brought forth by the invisible, appeared and took the shape of a centaur galloping across my imagination. For a moment, the creature stood out against an ancestral horizon as a vivid memory of the future and I recognized it to be the new Being, the archetype of a new species: half man-half dream. I do not know why, but suddenly I felt that I had to shake that image out of my mind. A kind of modesty, an inexplicable sense of guilt, made me feel as if I had stolen it or inadvertently spied on it, like Actaeon who once saw what a human should never have seen. I was afraid of being caught red-handed. However, the Dreamer seemed to leave my imagination free to roam. During the pause that followed I gathered my thoughts and tried to recover at least some fragments of my old certainties.

He assured Himself with a long glance, that I was accurately noting His every word, then He uttered a phrase that cut me to the quick.

«*Food is death*» He announced peremptorily.

And, before I had time to recover from my surprise, He added:

«*Your body is the evidence that you are being blackmailed by food. Ageing reveals your lack of frugality, intelligence and love.*» And while He spoke, His eyes were examining every part of me. Suddenly, I saw Him laughing at my comically pathetic expression of dismay.

«*Man's attachment to food is only matched by his loyalty to death*» He remarked sarcastically. Then He urged me:

«*Abandon these superstitions!*»

Until that moment I had never heard food, much less death, referred to as a superstition. In Lupelius' manuscript, ignorance of one's Being, negative emotions and food had been indicated as among the principal causes of death; but to hear this from the Dreamer was a challenge to my beliefs and an attack on man's most unwavering convictions. I was overcome by dizziness, as if tottering at the edge of a chasm. If I'd ever had the conviction of being part of a particular group or of belonging to the mainstream of human society, I was now losing my membership. I felt the inconsolable desperation of a creature driven out of his herd, cast out of his nature.

The Dreamer seemed extremely amused by my confusion, obviously considering it to be a good sign and, in any case, a more advanced and productive state than my fruitless 'normality'. Then the expression on His face became more intense.

«*Eat just once a day* – He repeated *–and be frugal.*»

His request sounded so absurd, even subversive to the natural order that I started to wonder whether I was facing a diabolical figure or even the Devil himself. My father, Giuseppe, had told me many times that, during war years he had endured long periods in which he ate just once a day; however, he had always referred to that experience as a time of hardship. I knew of practices and periods of ritual, asceticism and religious fasting, mostly connected to cultures and traditions of the past, but I had never thought, or even imagined that such discipline could be applied by an active man, with the commitments and pressures of modern business. And to what end? Even Ramadan, in the Islamic faith, when observed in its strictest form, only lasts for a month, the ninth in their calendar. The Dreamer's demand seemed unjust, cruel, and even dangerous for my health. I reacted with an immediate and radical sense of revulsion.

«Eventually, when you are more advanced, you will realize that even one meal a day is excessive. A man's organs were not created for processing and disposing of food.»

«So what are they for?» I asked, barely managing to stop my voice from breaking with emotion.

«A man's organs... all his organs... are made to dream! This is their natural function – He said with sweet assertiveness – *When the body is free of food, our features become more refined... the mind is clear, ready... quick... the cells are grateful and they regenerate. The healing process is underway, a rebirth of the Being starts and manifests itself first in the body and then in the world of events»* added the Dreamer.

I listened, amazed, as He told me about the ancient schools of invulnerability which knew the secret of a sustenance more subtle than food. Even centuries before Alexander's conquests, the Macedonian warriors' habits were considered to be among the most frugal. At the same time, they were renowned for their courage and unequalled valor. Alexander himself, who endured the same trials as his men, even the most arduous, ate hardly anything and only once a day. His invulnerability was legendary; he could emerge from hailing arrows unharmed, whereas his companions would be decimated around him.

«The secret is that when organs have no food, they start to perform their real and natural function again: they dream!... and through the power of dreaming, every day they produce whatever a man can desire.

So long as you see any part of your body as worthy of anything less than eternity then you are casting a death sentence on your entire organism.»

The menacing shadow which had darkened every fiber of my Being at the beginning of His discourse on food, began to dissipate.

«Beware! – He said, realizing that a chink had finally appeared in my comprehension – *abstaining from food does not mean fasting. What I'm talking about is a substitution...»*

6 A world without hunger

«Once you have stopped believing that the external world is the source of your sustenance, you can no longer draw nourishment from the lower levels of life and you will no longer be able to feed yourself on coarse substances... When humanity raises the quality of its Being through new ways of thinking, feeling, breathing and acting, this more responsible humanity will discover an alternative source of subsistence. This food, our true nourishment, originates from ourselves and will only become accessible again when it is our will that governs our lives and not the description of the world.»

Suddenly, even before His explanation had become clear, my internal dialogue subsided. Only something like a sob remained, like the tail end of a childish tantrum; then even that ceased.

I thought back to the myths of classical antiquity and the ancient Greeks' belief that the Gods' table was abundantly laden, not with the food of mortals, but with nectar and ambrosia. I remembered that making their bid for freedom during the Exodus, the Hebrews had been fed with 'manna from heaven'.

I conceived the inconceivable: a civilization without food; a world without hunger. I realized how much space and time food takes up in our lives and the absurdity of the resources consumed in this way. We live in the conviction that unless we are nourished from outside we cannot survive. Haunted by the specter of hunger, without realizing it, we have based our lives on food and turned it into an obsession, a relentless activity of planetary dimensions. I felt overwhelmed by the thought of billions of people stubbornly working to cultivate, produce, raise, buy, cook, distribute, consume... and digest.

I wondered what cities would look like without grocers, restaurants and supermarkets. I had an apocalyptic vision of life with desolate larders, empty refrigerators, bare tables… a life without business lunches, candlelit dinners or the rhythm of mealtimes ruling the family's day. What in the world could ever fill the abyss of time and space opened up by this absence?

«Turn your vision upside down – suggested the Dreamer – *Think how many resources could be devoted to beauty, art, music, entertainment, the search for truth and self-knowledge… A society free of food would be a society free of sickness, old age and death… In a world without slaughter-houses and farms, without the need to produce food or cultivate fields, there would be no crime or poverty, no ghettos, wars or conflicts… nor social workers. A world without food would be a world without ideological divisions, superstitions or religions. There would be no starving children or hospices. There would be no tribunals, hospitals or graveyards. It would be a world where resources could be directed towards realizing humanity's greatest dream… Once man succeeds in defeating the industry of death and the economics of disaster, which are materializations of his fears, he will be able to regain his birthright and achieve the supreme aim of his existence: physical immortality.»*

Now I could raise my eyes. I looked at the Dreamer. I realized that, for the whole time that I had been internally resisting His vision, my body had been tense and I had kept my head bowed, as if I had been using all my strength to physically fend something off.

«A society, which had given up believing in food and was free of the need to eat, would leave behind the ancestral obsession with hunger and all its terrifying consequences and would face an even more implacable enemy – said the Dreamer – *the boredom of not eating.»*

Even if human Beings were persuaded to give up eating as an extremely harmful habit; they would still have to face the abyss of time carved into their lives by its elimination.

I thought that this was the key to understanding why, regarding all the disciplines and austerities, the one concerning food had always been the most unbearable and assiduously avoided. So much so that, throughout history, only saints and ascetics had succeeded in conquering the need for food and, very often, this had proved to be only a partial and temporary victory. I remarked on this to the Dreamer.

«*It will require long preparation and a new education* – He said – *A coarse zoological mankind, still frightened by the specter of time, still convinced of the inevitability of death, can only be nourished by a coarse, external and mortal kind of food. Nourishing oneself internally will be the natural outcome of a different way of thinking and breathing, an evolution from the conflictual man ruled by his negative emotions, to the vertical man.*»

«So what happens to the economy? – I asked – How can we compensate for the loss of such a large part of our business activity?»

«*What you call the economy is actually nothing more than a system of survival, even in the richest countries. And yet the cost of such a system has become unsustainable... A society that recognizes the creative power of thought and its capacity to nourish, will produce better goods and services for both the individual and all of mankind* – He announced prophetically – *A society that dreams, one that is light and flexible, will devote itself to the education of every individual and the improvement of its every cell.*»

I imagined an army of men and women dedicated to the re-education of a humanity that had long since forgotten its origin and its purpose.

«*A revolution like this cannot be performed by the masses* – the Dreamer asserted – *Humanity must be educated on an individual basis, man by man, cell by cell, to open up to a new vision... to rebel against its destiny and fight against the real root of all evil: the beliefs that the outside world can sustain it and that something external can heal it.*»

These superstitions find their most conspicuous expression in the pharmaceutical and food industries. Having forgotten the primordial game, man becomes the last link in an infernal production cycle. Under a spell yet to be exorcised, as if trapped in some gruesome tale or horror movie, men are condemned to spend half of their lives eating and the other half undergoing therapy and taking drugs. Man's supreme task is to transcend himself through the art of dreaming. For this he has to reduce the need for nourishment to an absolute minimum.

«*It is an inside-out process. Only a new education can remedy a misunderstanding of such vast dimensions...*»

According to the Dreamer's vision, with the gradual disappearance of food, sickness, old age and death would also disappear.

«Don't be afraid to announce it! – He encouraged me, noticing my hesitation at even writing His formidable revelations in my notebook – *The change will be gradual, but it has already begun in the richer countries. People will eat less and less, until they discover they are actually swimming in an infinite plankton, surrounded by an inexhaustible amount of food which is theirs alone, and for which they need neither to toil nor to fight.»*

«Is it possible for man to live without food?»

«I'm not talking about living without food, but about replacing it. When man succeeds in turning over a new leaf by changing his vision and everything he has believed in up until now, then a more evolved humanity will substitute a more intelligent sustenance for food. Once free of this need, this dependence on food, man will be able to choose whether to eat or not, treating it entirely as an option.»

The Dreamer's words made me think of the Homeric gods, who, wishing to experience man's joys and sorrows, occasionally chose to debase themselves, coming down from Olympus and transforming themselves into mortals or animals…

I remembered that when I fell in love with Luisella, and the scent of her youth saturated every molecule of my life, I would go for days without feeling any need to eat. I told the Dreamer about Carmela's comic distress at seeing me refuse my favourite dishes, even her most irresistible desserts: *struffoli* and *pastiera*.

«You were substituting a more subtle and internal nourishment for mortal food – He said – *And this will be possible for all men when they are no longer ruled by the description of the world but by themselves, by their own will… by the 'dream'.»*

«But what about anorexics?»

«Anorexics are not sick people but the forerunners of a more advanced and longer-living mankind. They are the real rebels against the industry of death.»

«And those who die from anorexia?»

«People do not die of anorexia. They are only victims of primitive medical practices, and families who are not equipped to recognize that they are precursors of the new humanity.»

On this occasion, as He had already done before, the Dreamer spoke to me about young people: their calls for help, their desperate and vain attempts to announce the new direction, the exodus to the obsolete and adult, adult-erated, humanity.

«You, give up 'bad habits' – He said – *Be frugal!»*

«But remember – He warned – *Until you are truly ready for such an undertaking, never dare to fast or stay awake all night. I will tell you when you can eat one mouthful less or stay awake for an additional minute... It takes years and years of work...»*

In fact, in all the time I had spent with the Dreamer, I had never undertaken a fast or any kind of abstinence, nor had He ever said anything about privations. On the contrary, I always saw Him surrounded by prosperity and abundance. Frugality, for me, was a slow process and a natural consequence of His presence. Despite being so close to His philosophy, it took me years and a great effort to understand that in the Dreamer's vision, food was only the sign, the most visible expression of man's dependence on the external world.

«It is not food that poisons man, but his belief that he cannot do without it. Saints and ascetics have also missed the real aim of the discipline of frugality, which is not about eliminating food but about an emancipation from the need for food, an escape from addiction.»

I pointed out that, in the end, nourishing oneself from the inside also constituted a form of dependence.

«To depend on what is within, to depend on oneself is not dependence – He said – *but self-government».*

According to the Dreamer, those who have not questioned the idea of the inevitability of death hide their self-sabotage behind self-improvement regimes, diets, fasts and extreme exercises of all sorts. Man often hides his self-destructiveness, his desire for annihilation, behind the smokescreen of religious and spiritual disciplines relating to food and sleep.

«You will discover that scientific temples, humanitarian organizations, pharmaceutical laboratories, food industries, ascetic sects, beauty farms, schools proposing exotic and austere regimes are all unconsciously at the service of death; they too nourish, and are nourished by the economics of disaster. Behind their messages of well-being, happiness and longevity, health and wealth, there lies

an unwitting, undaunted loyalty to death and the most intense and devoted activity in its service.»

«But isn't it possible that there are institutions sincerely devoted to mankind...people who are capable of leading a revolt against every form of dependence?» I asked worriedly. I felt suddenly exposed to the coldness of a strange and inhospitable world.

«What about all of the saviours, heroes and saints from long ago?»

«Heroes, saints and benefactors and the institutions founded or inspired by them are at the service of mankind, but it is a self-destructive mankind – answered the Dreamer – *They are themselves the victims of their own lack of understanding. They do not know that no help or healing can come from outside and that only the individual can provide his own solution by healing his own vision and recognizing that the true cause of every calamity is within himself.*

In a more advanced society philanthropists and benefactors will disappear or their deeds be considered illegal because their distorted altruism and corrupt philanthropy can only perpetuate poverty and sickness.

Healing the world means healing yourself... Your vision of the world creates the world...

It may sound absurd and completely illogical to you, but the world is actually just as you dream it. It is you who makes it sick. You are the only one responsible for the conflicts, disasters, hunger and crime which ravaging it.

Regain your integrity and the world will be healed forever!»

7 The world is as you dream it

From this point on, the Dreamer made me carefully note principles and practices, as well as activities and techniques, which might appear many and diverse, but in reality formed a complete discipline, a system. A unique and fascinating cosmogony was taking shape before my eyes like the outline of an unknown continent. I spent days diligently studying in the impressive library of *Mas Anglada*, where I found and consulted rare books that held the key to understanding 'The School for Gods'. In particular, I asked Him the meaning of drawings and formulae I had found in the manuscript.

Lupelius considered the body and spirit to be a single, indivisible reality. He recognized the 'body' as the creator of the phenomenal world which included everything from microbes to God. I have to make it clear that, as I write, the use of terms such as 'spirit', or occasionally 'soul', are my own; it is done as a means to assist the reader's understanding. The Dreamer never made use of them. The more I learned about Lupelius' theories regarding food and the body, the more shocked I became and the more I drew back from the extreme implications of what he was postulating. Some of the warrior-monk's most unsustainable propositions stuck in my mind, like splinters of irrationality and caused me disquiet. I really wanted to speak to the Dreamer about this and had the opportunity to do so on the third night, when He invited me to visit the wine cellars of His astonishing residence.

The way in which He had arranged His wine by country, quality and vintage was quite amazing. I had never imagined the existence of such a vast and complete collection. As we savored one of His most precious wines by the fireplace, the Dreamer asked me how my studies were going and whether I had discovered anything important. I told Him about the most difficult and unsustainable points of Lupelius' theories on the body. More particularly, I drew His attention to a dialogue which had particularly disturbed me, between Lupelius and one of his disciples, the central argument of which concerned the way the body and its organs could create the world.

As soon as I mentioned this topic, I realized that I was not ready to hear what He was about to say. I wanted to flee, but when I recognized that it was too late, my heart started to beat rapidly, in anticipation of some serious danger. An iron vice closed round my temples and started to squeeze. I could neither accept such a bizarre vision nor refuse it, and I tried to avoid what the Dreamer was telling me with such authority. Once more I felt my thoughts perched on a precipice.

«Between dream and reality there is neither distance nor division, just as there is no distance between being and having, or believing and seeing – said the Dreamer – *Whatever a man dreams is already true. It only takes a little time for it to become visible…»*

Dream + Time = Reality

«The dream manifests itself through time. It is only because of our limited perception that we need time in order to see it.

Time, for man, is like a magic paint that reveals what otherwise would remain invisible to human eyes.

Behind everything you see and touch there must be a dream in order to exist... A world of wonder or a world of pain must be dreamed in order to become real. The dream is the most real thing there is; and behind the dream is our body....

Our cells, our organs... dream!» concluded the Dreamer.

«But if the body can dream and create the world, why can't I change a single atom in the way I'd like to?» I asked, venting my frustration.

His look travelled far beyond the little flames from the large silver candelabra, through and beyond the centuries-old walls of *Mas Anglada*. For a long time He remained absorbed, His chin resting on the palm of His left hand, then He said:

«There is no fixed, objective world that is the same for all. The world is as you dream it. And even what may appear negative and destructive to you, is only the reflection of a conflict-ridden dream.»

«And to change things that don't work?»

«If you don't like your life, change your dream!It is impossible to climb out of the ruts of repetitiveness and recurrence, unless you change your dream.

You have to abandon your destructive way of dreaming.

You have to dream a new dream, you have to learn a new way of dreaming where the power of will commands, where the power of love creates, where the power of certainty wins.

Be more sincere and honest with yourself and you will realise that behind your false belief of wanting to change your life there is the secret plan to keep perpetuating it just as it is.

The world is such because you are such.»

8 No war within, no war without

«The world is the materialization of the 'dream.' Your thoughts create your personal reality.»

The Dreamer was talking to me whilst doing a series of physical exercises, alternating between the sophisticated machines in His gymnasium. This room occupied the top of an ancient tower which overlooked the immense expanse of *Mas Anglada*. Through the panoramic windows, the centuries-old stillness of the hillsides and vineyards contrasted with the strong and silent equipment and the glinting reflection of steel. The broad skylight framed the heavens, which were crossed by light cirrus clouds.

«So… everyone dreams and everyone creates the world.»

«Exactly! Their own world.»

«What about pollution of the planet?… Wars and crime?»

«These are part of your personal reality too... The world is as healthy or as sick as you are! Only you can pollute it... by obstructing and dulling your organs!Even those who pollute their bodies, create!... They invent a degenerate world, the events and circumstances of which are the mirror image of their diseased bodies, but first and foremost, a reflection of their states of Being and thoughts.

Thoughts are always creative at any level.

Thinking belongs to your way of dreaming and is the basic factor in shaping your destiny.»

«What about wars and poverty?» I asked, distressed by such an enormous responsibility.

«Suffering, poverty and all the conflicts, persecutions and carnage in the world, have all been dreamed. They have been secretly desired by a humanity that has seriously polluted its Being and has no idea of the power of thought.»

«While we are talking, hundreds of factories throughout the world are producing and storing armaments to feed conflicts and even destroy humanity. How can we protect ourselves from such a destructive power?»

«Remove yourself from any form of hypnotism, dependency, superstition. Do not lean on anybody's knowledge, fantasy or prophecy. Know that there is no power out there that can destroy you. Out there nothing can happen without your consent.

The world of events and circumstances is totally depending upon you. If you integrate yourself, if you become a unity, than the world will be safe.

So don't worry about the world, worry only about yourself. This is the only way you can help. No war within, no war without. This is the law.»

The Dreamer picked up a towel from the neatly folded pile and dried His face, then draped it around His neck like a treasured scarf, crossing the ends over His chest with an elegant gesture.

«By learning to master his own body, a man can master the universe» He said.

At this point He raised His eyes and stared at me intently for a long time without blinking. My thoughts faded away, one by one, with increasing speed until my mind was completely clear.

«Do you remember your time in California... that friend of yours in San Francisco?» He asked, continuing to hold me in his stare.

That was all I needed to hear. I knew perfectly well to whom He was referring. It was surprising how quickly that name, Corrado, came to me so easily.

We had been great friends when I lived in San Francisco. He was a fine musician and when still very young had fallen desperately in love with a belly dancer and married her. Apart from this, however much I wracked my memory, there was nothing else I could recall about him that could possibly justify such a close connection to the Dreamer's idea that every man was the inventor of his own world, the absolute creator of every event taking place in his life.

At that point, the particulars of a distant memory became increasingly clear, and a curious story began to take shape. Corrado had always felt a natural affinity for blacks. He used to imitate the way they spoke and behaved, their laid-back style and movements. He worshipped their music, which he considered superior to all others, and loved their culture. He hung out in the same places they did and even attended their churches and whenever he passed a black person in the street, he never missed an opportunity to show how close he felt to their race by way of a wink, a greeting or some witty remark. He dragged his wife into this particular obsession; and they had black friends, couples with whom they socialized in the restaurants and clubs favoured by the black community in San Francisco.

One night he and his wife were on their way home when they were mugged and viciously beaten up by a black gang who seemed to have no motive, not even robbery. However, they were so severely beaten that they had to spend several days in hospital. I remember Corrado weeping with rage while he told me about this misadventure.

The Dreamer was watching me, obviously looking for some signs of comprehension on my part, but the seconds elapsed and not even a hint of a clue occurred to me. I knew that He considered musicians and artists in general to possess a low level of responsibility and personal weakness. For the Dreamer, the bohemian world, even those whom history has consecrated as geniuses, were actually dependent on their own art. They were puny men frightened by the unbearable discovery that the individual is the creator of his own personal reality, the supreme Artist, the origin of everything that we see and touch. Aesthetes and artists have not recognized the reason for their existence; indulging in something that is only a distant gleam of the 'dream' from which it originates. Instead of using art as a bridge between man and the dream, a way to touch the innermost part of the self, they clung to their own creations, as if they were gods, aggravating that state of dependence on the world which rules their whole life. A man who has reached a degree of higher freedom and is on his way towards unity of Being, can no longer be an artist. When you realise you are the artificer and creator of an entirely separate world, you can no longer paint or compose music. You abandon that intermediary known as art, just as a lame man who is healed throws away his crutch. According to the Dreamer, freedom from any dependency and slavery was the very meaning of life itself. Roles were prisons to be transcended and left behind.

However, none of these considerations was leading me anywhere either. Corrado was a professional musician. He certainly earned his living from music but I still could not see the connection that led the Dreamer to recall such a memory.

«That episode is life which comes, with both violence and compassion, to show you what you do not want to see, to make you touch what you do not want to touch within yourself. There is no crime outside of us, other than the one we project – said the Dreamer, interrupting my thoughts at that point, considering it a waste of time to wait for the improbable outcome of my pondering – *That incident allowed your friend to see his lie, his latent racism...*

to overcome his conflictual self, the violence that he had always carried inside him... and finally set him free.»

The Dreamer mentioned a few other important aspects of Corrado's life, presenting them as different facets of the same disease: hypocrisy and lying to oneself. Even his rushed marriage had been determined, not by any real feeling for that woman, but by his desire to remain in the United States and become an American citizen.

He stopped. Then, He changed the weights on one of his machines and adjusted the programme on the computerized system to do some more exercises. I was amazed. I was sure that I had never told Him anything about Corrado. I wondered how He could know such things about the life of a friend I had not seen or heard from for years. Meanwhile the Dreamer stopped doing His exercises.

«There! – He said, tying the sash of His kimono with the pride and grace of a martial ritual – *This 'thing' which is hidden in the folds of one's Being, this lie that covers and conceals egoism, prejudice, vanity and racial hatred, constructs that event, and is the real cause of all the atrocities in the world.»* His tone was like that of a scientist announcing the discovery of a virus that he had pursued to the farthest perimeters of life.

«Suffering, poverty and all calamities... have been dreamed. They have been obscurely desired and unconsciously projected... They are the materialization, enlarged on a pantograph, of the shadows and monsters that are harboured in the darkness of the Self.»

«Today, if your friend has understood the lesson, he is now surely a man more honest and free than before – concluded the Dreamer – *In time he will recognize his lie... and one day he will also be able to heal it.»*

I recalled mankind's constant song of sorrow; the ode to misfortune that the Dreamer had made me listen to and recognize in myself. At last I understood the vital importance He gave to self-study, to being watchful and ruthlessly attentive to one's own states; particularly to self-observation which, like a ray of light, prevents any monstrosity from hiding in one's Being.

Self-observation is self-correction.

I remembered His aphorisms: '*States and events are one and the same thing...Vision and reality are one... Thinking is Destiny... The world is such because you are such...*' and among the most surprising: '*life is a stick of chewing-gum, it takes the shape of your teeth'*. I noticed the golden thread connecting them as different expressions of the same message... A message that summed up all His teachings and at the same time was at the last frontier that human intelligence had dared to approach.

In a moment of lucidity, a bright truth came to me like the announcement by an almighty god: *the world is the mirror of the Being!* A laser beam penetrated the sedimentary layers of my description of the world... I 'saw' that each molecule was wonderfully connected to everything. And that 'everything' was a personal and subjective entity.

«You are the only obstacle preventing the world from changing. Change yourself and you will see the world change before your eyes! Each atom of clarity, freedom, and absence of death will take shape in the world and free it from all evil.»

I understood scientifically, without moral or metaphysical frills, the importance of self-knowledge and of working tirelessly to elevate one's own Being.

«Whatever journey a man takes, whether historical or mythical; whatever exodus he undertakes, whether real or imaginary, leads towards one single goal: self-knowledge! Self-knowledge makes you the master of yourself and the world.»

9 Thinking is Destiny

«If man would recognize the creative power of his own thought, and pursue beauty and harmony with the same determination for as many years as he has dedicated to poverty and suffering, he could transform the past and his own destiny. The world would be Heaven on Earth.»

I could feel eternity pulsing in those words. Once time was removed from the equation of vision and reality, of states and events, of having and being, then the indivisible nature of opposites, the hidden unity behind every apparent conflict was revealed.

«If a man's thoughts create his universe, his personal reality, how can he change them?»

«You can only improve or control the quality of your thoughts if you know how to raise the quality of your Being. In order to do this you will have to work and study in a special School and apply its teachings and ideas to yourself.

Man, as he is, cannot 'do' unless he overcomes his own inner violence through enormous efforts. Man cannot 'do' unless he understands that all planetary evils and individual miseries are none other than the dramatic result of his own destructive inner states and negative attitudes.

So long as man is ruled by external circumstances he will never be able to see where all the violence of the world is coming from.

The world is your mirror. Anything coming from the outer world breathes with your breath, everything is as alive as you are.

There is nothing in the universe that is not you.

Thinking is Destiny.»

The sound of these words echoed inside me, as sudden and savage as a primal scream and louder than the anthem of a hundred revolutions. No event would ever appear so devastating to me or seem such a transgression as the crossing of that fine line… of the new threshold to humanization. I was witnessing, with my own eyes, the exodus of a species still at the primitive stage of consciousness, on its evolutionary passage from a hominid race to a humanity endowed with a real psychology, free of conflict, doubt or fear.

«There is a fable that everyone knows as 'The Sleeping Beauty'» He announced abruptly.

That sudden change of topic took me by surprise. My attention was sharpened and rapt. Then He whispered:

« …but its real title is 'La belle au bois dormant'. The Beauty in the Sleeping Wood.»

The essence of the mission that He would one day assign to me was to be found in that apparently trivial detail. The sleeping wood is the world as it has been described to us, plagued by poverty and conflict, sealed into a hypnotic sleep. The beauty is the reawakening of the will, the reawakening of the Self, the 'dream'.

The School that I was soon to establish would allow a new generation of young people to overthrow the old paradigms and enter into a new vision of reality.

«The only way to help others is to awaken yourself from that sleep» said the Dreamer that evening. His tone was unusually calm and His words were mellow, like dates ripened in the sun. I tasted their woody sweetness with all my Being.

That time spent with Him, which had been unexpectedly long, was coming to an end. The last candelabras flickered out and the splendid hall of *Mas Anglada*, with its elegant furnishings, works of art and glimmering silver, retreated into darkness. Along the days I spent near the Dreamer I felt that I was the only fragile link between His impeccable world and the tainted world of ordinary men. Now, in the silence, I was watching Him. He remained still for a long time. His eyes were half closed and he held His body very straight.

When He began to speak again, His words struck me with the power of a premonition.

« ...Slowly, mankind is shedding its skin... One day, it will stop rummaging through the shadows of the world and will give up worshipping food, medicine, sex, sleep, work... The value of frugality will grow in its consciousness, until it achieves a wholeness of Being which will signal the end of poverty, calamities and conflicts. It will take time... because humanity is time. For now, study, observe yourself and know yourself! And one day you will take part in the most magnificent spectacle on earth: your own integrity!»

Once I had left the Dreamer there was nothing to keep me in Barcelona and that night I took the first flight back to New York. Throughout my journey I went over everything I had heard in those extraordinary days spent with Him. My body was still vibrating with a sensation I had never felt before: a state of wholeness, order and celebration.

The whole universe was breathing with my breath.

Everything was connected to the whole and nothing remained separate.

CHAPTER IV

The Law of the Antagonist

1 Running

"The body cannot lie. Yours already looks like an old man's body..."

The Dreamer's words were still echoing in my mind, renewing the pain of their first impact.

"I don't need geriatrics at my side..."

Those cruel words had split the thick crust of my defenses and were now invading my living tissue. I felt their explosive power sweeping away my attitudes and beliefs. In particular, the things He had revealed to me at the end of our meeting stung me like spurs:

"Organs are made for dreaming. The body creates the world. Even those who pollute their body create; but their creation is a polluted world... The world is your reflection: it is as sick as you are. Everything is connected, nothing stands alone."

The Dreamer taught me that the destiny of a human Being and all that he possesses is closely linked to the health of his body. In the future, following these revelations, I would do research into the fields of economics and business to find that even the financial destiny of a man depends on his physical integrity and the impeccability of his body. The financial fortunes of great enterprises and industrial empires, just as that of nations and entire civilizations develop and prosper, or fall ill and die, along with their leader and founder-creator.

"An organizational pyramid is inextricably bound to its leader's breath. A golden thread binds his image and personal destiny to that of his organization and his people. His corporeal

identity coincides with his economic identity, just as it did for the rulers of antiquity. The King is the land and the land is the King."

I could no longer elude such a direct, poignant message and decided to take the first steps in the direction indicated by the Dreamer to combat my physical decline. I resolved to commit to a thorough physical training regime, following the guidelines I had received at our meeting in *Mas Anglada*, encompassing everything, from diet and breathing to sex and sleep. I examined all the options available to me and prepared a plan of action, a plan for striking a decisive blow to my existence. The difficulties seemed insurmountable. The very idea of changing my habits, of making physical efforts or any sacrifice at all, was enough to arouse inner resistances of varying degrees and nature within me, to the point of repugnance. The thought of the austerity that would be required made my moods quarrel and chase one another like swallows.

The attention I gave to my reactions caused my inner map of difficulties to surface as though they'd been plotted out on a radar screen: the mountains of rigidity, the steep slopes of doubt, the bottomless pits of fear, and the deserts of incomprehension and loneliness. Only by studying and observing myself in this way was I able to locate the part within me which felt most conflicted and pained at the idea of changing. And precisely there, where I felt that knot, is where I plunged the sword of my will. From that day on began the struggle… a mortal challenge, a holy war between me and myself that was to last for years.

That winter was one of the harshest in the meteorological history of New York. The city was covered with a thick blanket of snow, and swept by polar winds that seemed to have magically transformed the metropolis into an arctic country where the skyscrapers had been changed into icy slides for the children of a race of Titans. In the early morning, before mustering the courage to go out for my run, I would peep through the Venetian blinds to check the weather. I was one of the lucky ones as living on the 16th floor with a view over the East River and the city gave me immediate access to information on weather conditions. Most New Yorkers had to switch on the television if they wanted to peer out and decide what to wear.

For weeks, the Manhattan skyline, with its snowy spires and pinnacles was a white gothic universe sealed in a crystal bubble. At that sight one's determination would falter. Every morning I had to face a hard battle. At the sound of the alarm, the idea of making a journey out into those polar conditions would trigger an epic struggle between my resolve and my lazy, degraded body which did not want to hear about change. Disheartened by years of abuse and neglect, my body said 'no' to every attempt to halt its atrophy. Threatened by the run, my body exposed its true condition. Only today, looking back, can I see the impossibility of my endeavour, as impossible as Baron Munchausen's attempt to escape from a quagmire by pulling himself up by his wig. Only the sound of the Dreamer's voice and the memory of His words, sustained my ambition and gave me courage.

If we want to advance even one millimeter towards integrity,
we must turn our vision of the world upside down.
It requires an inhuman effort.
Yet there is no greater blessing.
The conquest of that millimeter of Eternity
can swallow oceans in the world of events.

The program I had set for myself involved running once around the island and getting back in time to dress for work and exchange a few words with Giorgia and Luca over breakfast before they set off for school. I was always tempted to stay in bed and let Giuseppona take care of them.

Many times I tried to identify that voice attempting to dissuade me from taking a run every morning. "After all – it said – in weather like this, who could blame you for going back to bed? Haven't you already done enough? It's not the end of the world if you miss your run just this once…" And so on. On other occasions, going to bed too late or needing to make an early flight would become the day's pretext for trying to avoid the effort. So every circumstance sought to widen the rifts in my determination, and become a good excuse for abandoning the discipline I had set myself. Whatever its origin, that exasperating inner voice was always ready to sabotage my plans, and I fought to suppress it. And this was just the tip of the iceberg. By maintaining the discipline of running, by fighting my resistance and defying my habits, the most unknown and obscure part of my Being was emerging.

"Remember... Nothing is external... You are the only obstacle to your evolution! – the Dreamer had told me many times – *There is no difficulty or limit that does not originate in yourself"*. But it would take me years to 'understand' these words and transform them into my body's vital lymph. I had to decay, fall, and rise up again a thousand times… to die and be reborn, before I learned to bless every difficulty that I met on my way and recognize that my only antagonist lied within.

In order to justify his mortal destiny and his life infested with disastrous events, man persuades himself that there are external forces that thwart him, and that these are responsible for his every ill. He complains, makes excuses; and blames events, external circumstances, without ever suspecting that the world is a reflection of himself, or realizing that to change one's mirror image is impossible without first changing oneself.

There is no help coming from anywhere at all.
You have to make your own individual revolution
which is based purely upon you.

If some day it were possible to encapsulate the Dreamer's teachings in a method, to configure a doctrine or a new philosophical system, what He describes as the intentional tripping up of mechanical behavior would deserve an entire chapter to itself. According to the Dreamer, this kind of displacement is an ambush of self-repetition or self-deception, a trick we play on our *routines* and habits to get around the iron defences behind which we protect our calcified mentality.

Only with time, as my apprenticeship progressed, would I realize that the benefit of running was not so much to be found in the physical exercise itself, or in learning to endure the effort required, but in its nature as a 'tripwire' or stratagem for breaking a mechanical pattern composed of apathy and repetition. Running helped me to block, albeit for just a few seconds, the dark stream of my thoughts; it collided with and interrupted that pathetic, mournful description of the world that men call reality. Running opened a chink in that prison-like order and through that physical effort a breath of freedom loosened the shackles of my slavery. Like an ocean gathering to drown every hollow, determined not to leave a single void, the world rebelled and marshalled a tide of events to flood that one small space that was its mortal enemy: a kind of intolerable transgression of thc planet's natural law. Only the memory of the Dreamer and my awareness of His presence, supported me by providing a prodigious energy.

At the time, my own obstinacy, rather than any strength of will, helped me persevere. I made myself believe in the absolute necessity of that effort, and without any other rational explanation, I gave my morning run top priority, as if my life depended on it. The Dreamer used the phrase 'first things first', to remind me of the importance of giving oneself priorities and maintaining goals. Now I know that the early morning hour, deliberately stolen from my daily routine, was a space of power, a leverage point from which to change the world.

A man who aims high,
impeccably committed to his improvement,
can move mountains,
find solutions to apparently impossible situations,
and transform adversity into events of a higher order.

2 The keepers of Main Street

When I think back to that time, I see myself again, hooded and padded out like Bibendum the Michelin Man, walking past the doorman's niche in my apartment block on Roosevelt Island. The head shaking and bemused smiles of the security guards lit up by the livid lights of the monitors, were the first signs of ironic disagreement to my daring morning enterprise. Only now am I able to see that their attitude was nothing but the world's reaction, the mirror image of my resistance and the half-hearted commitment I had at the time. Among the Dreamer's teachings, one in particular had laid siege to my beliefs and crushed the bastions of my certainties as if under the blows of a battering ram.

The world is such because you are such.

The world is a faithful image of our states and those doormen were my reflection! Behind their sarcastic smiles, Jennifer's skepticism, my colleagues' comments, and the reactions of all those who knew about my morning exercise regime, there was my own frailty. Behind all these attitudes, my lack of determination showed through, along with the doubts and lies that 'the others' promptly sent back to me in the form of grimaces as if I were making faces at myself in the mirror of the world.

Always remember this! Nothing is outside you...
The world you see and touch is only an effect.
It shares your breath...
it lives if you're alive and dies when you die.

Without the Dreamer's teachings, I would have kept on believing that those men were security guards; poor devils who were just earning a living. Going out of the building, coming in every day, I would have exchanged greetings with them, I would have mirrored in their irony and skepticism without never imagining that they were not guards; they were not even men. They were nerve endings: highly perceptive instruments, sensory organs of the world.

A man cannot hide... The world knows! It reveals you!

Ideas like these gradually began to penetrate deeply inside me, and over the years transformed me.

You can evolve or degrade at any moment. It's up to you.
Each of your thoughts, attitudes, words and glances,
even the slightest wince,
announces to the whole world your degree of
responsibility and level of freedom.
This is what unmistakably places you where you are
and determines your destiny,
financial status and role in the theatre of existence...

I imagined a universe that knew everything about me, an apparatus made up of countless sensors, updated in real time by the slightest movement of my Being and the quality of my thoughts and my states. If we paid attention to these clues, as if interpreting the prophecy of some ancient oracle, we would know who we are, what we could know, what we could and couldn't do, what we could keep and what we should lose.

Never missing my daily appointment with my run and myself, I remembered and fortified my intent, unburdening myself of a lifetime's accumulation of waste. The drumbeat of my existence was sending out new messages to the universe. Its rhythm was spreading the news that another man was making a break for freedom. His bold attempt to escape the horror of ordinary life was underway.

3 The walls

My first attempts at running around the whole island required a heroic effort. Even later, when I was fitter, overcoming fatigue was a constant battle, especially at certain critical moments of the run. I noticed that the difficulty and exertion required did not increase in a linear progression, as I had expected; instead, it swung like a pendulum, back and forth in waves. Over the course of each run, I felt moments of calm, where almost no effort was required, alternating with periods of unbearable pain. In these crucial phases it seemed as though real 'walls' were being raised, barriers which required a superhuman effort.

A key part of my apprenticeship with the Dreamer had trained me for the painstaking task of self-observation: a constant attention to my states, thoughts, feelings, emotions, and to everything that seemed to attract or repel me. Observing myself in precisely those moments when I lacked energy, I had noticed that the critical moments were always preceded by the construction of a psychological wall, by a shadow that darkened my Being. Pessimism and mistrust would then seize control, and the inner antagonist's voice would make itself heard more forcefully, always finding new reasons to abandon my resolution.

Running taught me to grit my teeth, to realize that in those difficult moments all I had to do was hold out just a second longer to get back to a state of ease and as soon as I overcame the temptation to let myself go and give up, new reserves of energy would open up to me. It would have been impossible to approach them, or even know about them, without having conquered the battle with myself and demolished those walls which just a few moments earlier had seemed insurmountable.

The more I studied the mechanism that generated those moments, the more running appeared to be a precious instrument, a conceptual model, for an explanation of the world. In that alternate motion I recognized the essential element, the dynamic principle of every physical reality. From the atom's nucleus to the edges of the universe, everything moves and expands with the undulating movement that I had discovered in my body. Life itself is a wave-like motion with neither beginning nor end.

The 'walls' that running made me face at certain times, and the extraordinary effort required to overcome them, were making me aware of a universal paradigm recurring in life. On so many occasions it would have been enough to hold out just a little bit longer to climb them, to conquer them for good and go beyond. But something had always urged me to give up, to surrender. Defeat, which I always blamed on external events, was instead revealing itself to be an inside-out process, a mechanism that unmistakably obeyed an inner command, an act of self-sabotage. The shadow is born and spreads within the Being; then it finds the right moment to manifest in the form of unfavourable circumstances, events and encounters. Awareness of this mechanism and the sensitivity to detect this obscurity in my Self, the prelude to every defeat, gave me the golden opportunity to circumscribe and eliminate it, not only from my run, but from my existence.

I generally ran alone. The gulls that flew overhead and the occasional barges going up the East River that flanked me for a time until leaving me in their wake with a whistle, were my only companions. While I was running, I often dreamed. I liked to believe that sooner or later I would meet other escapees, other rash people who, like me, had decided to flee from a mediocre existence.

On one occasion I joined a group of five men and two women. We started our run with enthusiasm. The morning was bright and the Manhattan skyline stood out on the horizon and we ran side by side all the way around the island. I had never seen any of them before, but I felt an immediate understanding and got the impression that they were already a bonded group. For a short time, a man wearing black and grey jogging shoes and a track suit that glistened like silk, set the pace. Suddenly, he increased his speed. Unable to keep up, we dropped out one by one. Our overburdened and discouraged bodies revealed their shortcomings, and we lost sight of him. This made it painfully clear how much work we all still had to do. We carried on, running in a group until we reached the playground where we sat down to catch our breath. A glorious fire engine parked nearby, was now reduced to a mere attraction for the few children living on the island. The fate of that vehicle, an emblem of past heroic deeds, seemed to act as a reminder of the flabbiness and physical decline of man in our civilization. Tacitly I promised myself that I would increase my efforts and rise above my present condition. Nobody spoke; there was no need. Cleansed by our exertion, we shared the pale sunlight, as if it were unleavened bread; enjoying the special complicity of our improvised sodality. Then each of us took our leave with a nod, jogging off for a hot shower before beginning a typical New York business day.

It was still early and I played with a ray of sunlight between my half-closed eyelids, catching a glimpse of the red cable cars as they shuttled tirelessly between Manhattan and Queens.

4 The law of the Antagonist

«Fear not the Antagonist! Behind his fierce mask lies our greatest ally, our most faithful servant.»

On hearing these words I gave a start. With my eyes still closed, I remained suspended between hope and disbelief.

"It's impossible!" I thought. I couldn't believe it. Yet that voice was unmistakable… those were His words.

Slowly I turned around and opened my eyes. The Dreamer was sitting next to me. An unearthly shiver ran down my spine and spread under my skin to the roots of my hair where it nestled like a light but insistent vibration. He was wearing the silken tracksuit and those futuristic jogging shoes. I had run almost all the way around the island with Him, without ever suspecting that He was the Dreamer! I guessed that the men and women in the group were His students. Once I had recovered from my astonishment, I confided in Him what I proposed to do. I told Him how attentive I had been to my body recently, about the results I was achieving in my experiments with food, sleep and breathing… I told Him about my running, the discovery of the 'walls' and the mystery of this inner voice that constantly urged me to give up, to yield, to fail and relinquish my goal.

«The voice you hear is the antagonist that you have inside» stated the Dreamer, starting a discussion that would reveal itself to be one of the most demanding issues tackled in my entire apprenticeship. He accompanied these words with a hint of a smile that made Him appear even younger. This benevolent expression was so rare in Him that instead of giving me courage it had the opposite effect. I became apprehensive. I knew I was nearing a crucial passage so I straightened up and took a deep breath: whatever I had to overcome, I would have dedicated every drop of my strength.

The Dreamer reviewed all the most emblematic events of our history, the disasters that have troubled man and societies over the centuries. Analyzing the reasons and penetrating into their roots, He told me in detail about a planetary force that was the psychological equivalent of friction. As if subject to the same laws that govern a body in motion, man's impulses inevitably meet the contrast of an equal and opposite force. It was on this occasion that the Dreamer introduced a system of propositions, a set of principles He called 'the Law of the Antagonist'.

«Everything, from the simplest to the most complex, from one man to an entire civilization, every organism on its evolutionary path meets an 'apparently' opposing force, an Antagonist of strength and ability equal to the breadth and scope of its own project.»

In time, upon further investigation, all those ideas would reveal the outline of a veritable 'general theory of friction', capable of disentangling centuries of history and making sense of the endless series of difficulties and disasters that have vexed humanity ever since its birth. I gazed down on a 360 degrees view of the human condition, and saw how painful man's life had always been. It made me gasp as if on the brink of a bottomless pit.

My notebook came miraculously to hand. I clutched it, it was my lifeline, my last hope and there, in the open air, I carefully annotated every fragment of that unique lesson. The park bench where we were sitting was sealed in a timeless bubble and it seemed as though the whole of Roosevelt Island had turned into a spaceship ready for liftoff at the speed of thought. Manhattan and its swarming life could not have been farther away.

The Dreamer explained that every man is a 'Dreamer'. And as a Dreamer, he becomes the crucible of good and evil, the creator of his own personal reality and destiny. In time man will see the materialization of every dream and thought that springs from the depths of his Being.

«The world is an effect... a projection, not only of your 'dreams' but also your nightmares. It can be a heaven or a hell. You alone decide.»

5 Love thy enemy

«In reality, behind the mask of the Antagonist, beyond appearances, lies the face of our greatest ally» He explained. Then He added:

«Contrary to what everyone believes, it is not possible to be opposed by anything whose forces are greater than our own... the antagonist is never stronger than we are!»

«What about David and Goliath?» I asked, citing the most famous story and one of the most symbolic examples of a mismatched fight. My mind flipped through dozens of icons that, over the millennia, have reiterated the challenge of the heavily armed Philistine giant against the young shepherd with only a slingshot in his pocket...

«A slingshot... and also the 'dream' of becoming king! – corrected the Dreamer, breaking into that throng of images – *Beyond appearances, the fight is always fair!... »*

«No one can meet an Antagonist greater than himself, or superior to his own intelligence and ability... Beyond the apparent disparity in strength, the contest between David and Goliath respects the universal laws of the duel – said the Dreamer as if he were conducting a mathematical demonstration – *The one and only aim of the Antagonist, concealed by his mercilessness, is your victory. The Antagonist has all the instruments and methods at his disposal to allow you to achieve your 'dream' and it is he who can show you the quickest way to success.»*

No matter how paradoxical these statements seemed, I reflected that, in actual fact, no strategies or allies could have led David realize his dream more quickly. The Dreamer assented in silence, encouraging these first signs of comprehension by nodding His head. Then He concluded:

«No one on earth can love you more than the Antagonist.»

I couldn't speak.

My temples were throbbing with fever. The height of human intelligence, expressed in Christian thought by "love thy enemy," was now surpassed, two thousand years later, by the Dreamer's simpler and more revolutionary announcement: it is the enemy who loves you!

Man should no longer force himself to love his enemy (something which by now was demonstrably unworkable, if not impossible, even after two thousand more years of revenge and reprisals). For a new humanity it would be enough to recognise that it is the enemy, the antagonist, who loves you.

The more I thought about it, the sharper became my perception of the great spiral ascent of human thinking that was born out of the Dreamer's message. The millenary announcement *"Love thy enemy"*, that cornerstone of Christian teaching, had been left behind in a flash, demonstrating all its rigidity. Like all the religions of the world, the Christian faith, worn down by the centuries and divisions amongst its churches, had forgotten that truth is not static and cannot remain still. Yesterday's truth not transcended degrades and becomes today's lie.

In the meantime, we had left the playground bench and the old fire engine behind us, and were heading north along the riverbank. I walked with the Dreamer and listened to Him while He put in place the last pieces of His astonishing theory.

«Forgiving the enemy outside is a demonstration of man's infinite vanity and inability to understand. The only enemy is within you. Outside there is no enemy to forgive, nor any evil that can harm you. The Antagonist is your most precious ally; an instrument to improve and perfect you and make you whole; the unique key that grants access to higher zones of Being.»

We passed by the Chapel of the Good Shepherd, the old gothic church which lay in ruins. The stone bust of a suffering Christ still stood in the silence of those remains.

«That ancient 'school' also failed» said the Dreamer, and I perceived a faint hint of sorrow for the umpteenth epilogue to this timeless drama.

«Even Christianity missed the target… »

The Antagonist

The Antagonist, the enemy, is a special propellant.
The greater our degree of responsibility,
the more ruthless the Antagonist's attack.

The Antagonist measures us, reveals us, completes us...
The higher our degree of freedom, the more subtle his action.

Fear not the Antagonist!
Behind his apparent ruthlessness hides
your greatest ally, your most faithful servant.

The Antagonist's sole and unique aim
is your victory...

The Antagonist employs every artifice, every strategy,
to achieve his final goal: your integrity.

No one in the world can love you more than the Antagonist.
You are the sole reason for his existence.

Fear not the Antagonist!
Your perfection will grow with his mercilessness.
Your immortality with his apparent immorality.

Your intelligence will grow with his power.
Your power with his intelligence.

Because the Antagonist is you!

6 Learn to smile inside

I thought about the greatness of this revelation: if such a truth had been recognized by humanity it would have revolutionized and transformed our way of thinking and feeling forever. One day I would transfer the force of this vision to my students: the fiercer the Antagonist's attack and the graver the insult, the greater the opportunity to go beyond.

Learn to smile inside while the attack reigns down
and the offence manifests itself without mercy.
The Antagonist should be fought outside,
and simultaneously forgiven inside!
Forgiveness can only happen inside you.
Impeccably 'perform' the fiercest combat ...
but without believing in it!

Finally, a tiny chink was opening up to throw light on that thousand-year-old, impenetrable paradox: if you love him he is no longer your enemy, and if he is your enemy how can you love him?

'Love thy enemy' is an idea that comes from
a higher level of intelligence.
Only a man who is whole can understand and apply it.
Only he who has extirpated all interior conflict and division
can do without the Antagonist.
For those who have a dual logic,
still seeing and thinking through a system of opposites,
healing can only present itself wearing the ferocious mask of the Antagonist.

«*The attitude of a leader in the face of difficulties should be this*» said the Dreamer representing the concept in mime by rubbing his hands together, like someone who finally has in front of him the very thing he has been waiting for.

«*A leader knows that, however terrible the Antagonist may seem, the fight is always equal and the difficulties only apparent. The Antagonist's mask, his apparent brutality, conceals access to the highest levels of responsibility.*»

«No one has ever explained the game to you more clearly than this!» announced the Dreamer, addressing His words to an invisible audience as vast as the planet.

He added that without this understanding, without a School, most men would stop on the threshold of this passage, refusing to pay the price. We constantly come up against obstacles and internal voices that dissuade us from continuing, physical and psychological antagonists that test the strength of our aspiration, the clarity of our intent, our readiness and our determination.

The impossible always opens the door to the next possibility.

The more I immersed myself in the Dreamer's vision, the more I felt the power of a special training. From Him I was receiving the teaching of a martial art capable of transforming every attack and apparent adversity we encounter in life into a propulsive force. Enemies and obstacles now appeared in a new light.

The Antagonist, whether man or event,
has the thankless task of revealing every emptiness,
every shortcoming, every weakness or fear that you carry inside;
uncompromisingly denouncing your lack of preparation,
your faults and the limits that you yourself have imposed.
Once you recognize the Antagonist inside yourself
it will disappear from outside.

The Dreamer ironically emphasized that in exchange for his precious services the Antagonist receives from us only spite and rancour.

The figure of Father Nuzzo filtered into my memory and dominated the tiny crowd of Antagonists encountered during my childhood years at the Barnabites' 'Collegio Bianchi'. I felt a stinging melancholy and slight remorse at the memory of all the ill will we had felt for him. Only now, beside the Dreamer, could I 'see', beyond the mercilessness and severity of that teacher, the smile and love of someone who understood the 'game.'

«The teachers we most hated are the ones who gave us most» pronounced the Dreamer, sweeping away my thoughts and clearing away all the ghosts and shadows generated by those useless feelings.

From the Dreamer's exposition I could see a system emerging, a recurring cosmic model that could be applied to all human actions, both individual and collective – a kind of universal law that could be observed on any scale. I was particularly struck by his mention of the possibility of escaping the laws of the Antagonist. On this point I expressed my difficulty in imagining a world without friction, where it would be possible to reach out towards any goal without resorting to the precious and ruthless help of the Antagonist.

«How can we?» I asked, fascinated by the prospect of transforming life into an earthly paradise into which the antagonist would finally have no access.

«It's like expecting to live on this planet without having to submit to the law of gravity» answered the Dreamer in the brusque tone of someone who dismisses a question out of hand. Then, softly, as if he had been trying to keep the information secret, he added:

«Man could choose the influences on his life and entrust himself to the power of something higher, but he lives in pain and as a result knows nothing of the Art of Dreaming! He suffers because he does not dream.»

«Through the Art of Dreaming, a man stops suffering… stops dying – He said enigmatically – *only one who has stopped killing himself inside has a 'right' to the ineffable revelations of the Antagonist.»*

He paused at length, during which time He seemed to be focused on that part of Roosevelt Island and the seagulls that wheeled across its sky. Then He said:

«For the moment, learn to consider the Antagonist as your closest ally… and hope that he is increasingly fierce and strong. The higher our responsibility, the more ferocious the Antagonist's attack. In time this vision will overturn your life and create the world you have always wanted.»

The Dreamer noticed that I was still waiting for an answer for to how to make every threat and attack disappear from our existence.

«What is apparently opposing you is only a sign, a luminous arrow pointed towards the real cause of all your troubles and difficulties. The Antagonist is you! If you could just draw near to this understanding, the 'game' would be revealed and disappear, and the Antagonist would lose his form, his apparent cruelty and power. In reality, the Antagonist appears in your life to point out

everything that you should change inside, everything that you do not want to see, touch or feel in yourself...»

In view of the obvious difficulty I had in following Him, He decided I was not yet ready to tackle that question. He said that, for now, I would have to consider the law of the Antagonist as a universal and inescapable principle:

«Man as he is, cannot escape the law governing the world of duality, where everything happens and is created through conflict: the game of opposites» the Dreamer affirmed with an air of finality. I found myself reflecting on the unrelenting nature of our destiny and how the salvation of only one man could extend itself to all humanity.

«What business of yours is the salvation of the world? – said the Dreamer, interrupting my thoughts with a terrible voice – *when all the world needs... is to save itself from you»*

«For now, mind your pain and suffering – He ordered – *Stay there. Don't turn away. Observe them and lay bare their roots. Only when you become free of the world's description will you be able to set it free. The whole world, its way of thinking and doing, its conditions, precariousness and danger, exactly mirrors your interior fragmentation.»*

«Only you, living permanently Here and Now can liberate the world from all opposites. Only you, abandoning your inner conflictuality, can free it from all contradictions, violence and wars» He said, definitely concluding that part of our meeting.

I had to wait several months before He resumed the discussion; it was one evening in London when, at a dinner with some unforgettable people, He introduced me to the secret of *'pro-activity'*.

At the end of that peripatetic lesson, walking and listening to Him, I found myself in the park, near the bench we had started from. The Dreamer sat down and I took my place next to Him at a respectful distance. The sun appeared from behind a cloud, and the sudden glare made me close my eyes. It was pleasant and I stayed like that for a while, savouring the moment. The Dreamer's words, attenuate, seemed to arrive from a distant world.

«Man has forgotten he is the dreamer, the creator of his own reality and this is what makes the action of the Antagonists in his life essential *and symbiotic...»*

«Turn your vision upside down! Force yourself to be free!» He said. The tone was paternal but had the harsh, strict forcefulness of an order. Initially it shocked me, then the drowsiness I was feeling took over once more, weakening all my faculties. I just managed to hear Him say:

«Turn yourself into a man who dreams, who creates, who loves! Only he who has decided to conquer himself meets the Antagonist. A falling man has no Antagonists. His descent is free and painless.»

7 The suite at the St. James'

I set my bag down on the thick carpet and looked around. The luxury of that suite, the austere opulence of the brocades and the furniture made me uneasy. I wondered what the Dreamer had in mind in requesting that I transfer to that exclusive hotel. With him, nothing happened by chance; yet at the same time nothing could ever be planned ahead. For the Dreamer even the smallest movement was part of a strategy. Over the course of my apprenticeship I had met him in the most remote countries as well as the world's main capitals. Each time without advance notice and without any need for appointments or scheduling. Every meeting had been an irreplaceable experience, a luminous step on the ladder that was transforming my life into an extraordinary adventure.

This time I had received His message at the small hotel where I usually stayed when in London. We were to meet at Veronica's. In making the appointment for that evening, the Dreamer had asked me to leave Eaton Place and move to a suite at the St. James in Mayfair. It was there that I found myself now, trying to pass the endless minutes that separated me from our meeting. Flowers, a triumph of fruit, champagne, two bathrooms… a study with an antique desk, a luxurious sofa… the thought of how much all this cost actually made me feel ill.

I knew that anything the Dreamer had in mind, anything he asked me to do, including transferring to one of the most expensive hotels in London, was undoubtedly part of a strategic plan; yet I couldn't rid myself of that discomfort. I imagined the face Mr. Lyford of the administration department would have made at the appearance of the bill for a luxury suite on my expenses account…

I would surely have to pay for it out of my own pocket. It was in fact, quite out of the question for me to get the ACO to reimburse me as just a few nights at the St. James' would have devoured my entire New York salary. That thought transformed itself quickly from a psychological pain to a physical one as at that time, the conviction that circumstances and events controlled every aspect of my life was too deeply rooted in me. I blamed the others, the external world, for my unhappiness and malaise.

«You would have felt the same resentment and bitterness if instead of a royal suite I had asked you to transfer to some squalid hovel in the poorest neighborhood of London – the Dreamer said to me later – *What you were facing has nothing to do with the external world, nor with events or circumstances. It is something that you have always brought with you, that you carry inside, and this is the real cause of all your difficulties and infernal existence.»*

I look back with shame on the thoughts I'd had that day which had dangled in my mind like hang men. An unsupressable nausea flooded my Being and pervaded every cell. I had to sit down to recover a breath of life. I looked everywhere for the hotel rates but couldn't find them. I picked up the phone to ask the price of the suite. Perhaps it wasn't too late for me to cancel. I would have given anything to be able to get out of that situation, that desperation. Snapshots of a fragile, powerless and senseless life flashed through my mind. I remained motionless for a few seconds, as if paralyzed, then slowly put the phone down. A new lucidity had taken over, lifting me out of the quicksand of my dread.

I remembered an extraordinary phrase that He had once whispered to me, and which, fortunately, I had been able to catch and write down:

"*Style is conscience… Invest everything you have… and even what you don't have… on yourself… always! You will see your life become richer and broader in every sense. If you bet on yourself, life will bet on you.*

Don't worry about money. Worry about yourself, about your integrity. When money is needed, it will be right there. Trust yourself. Trust your dream and you will have all the money necessary to match a beautiful life. The masterpiece of your very dreaming is… you.

The outer world is only a pale shadow of your inner creativity, a very faded manifestation of your uniqueness."

8 Before the cock crows

I felt a sudden change in my body chemistry and I became as euphoric as a convict whose prison gates had just been flung open. I reflected on how little it took to scare me, to cast a shadow over me and dishearten me. This was the exact measure of my Being and the real reason for every difficulty in my life. Yet I only needed to connect with Him, to look at Him, just to cast a thought in His direction, to feel myself transformed and see the solution emerge. That suite at the St. James', as on other occasions created by His inexhaustible teachings, was revealing itself to be a classroom of the School in which I studied and assimilated the foundations of the Art of Dreaming that the Dreamer very often called the '*Science of Doing*'.

The Dreamer was preparing me for an extraordinary undertaking, even if I still had no idea what it was. I was sure that the mission He would one day entrust to me, required a total 'revolution', a burden of responsibility that, in my current condition, I could never have borne.

I felt a mounting sense of gratitude flooding my Being. I half closed my eyes and drank deeply of that luxury, absorbing every detail of the setting with its richness and beauty.

Nothing is external

The presence of the Dreamer was revealing completely unknown parts of me. Something extraordinary happened in that suite in the St. James'. Eons of time compressed and atoms of prosperity enriched my Being. I sensed infinity. Even if for only a few seconds, I stopped being a victim, a frightened, doubtful and defeated man, and became an architect, the artist who had conceived that hotel. I realized the eternal distance between the dreamer and the dreamed, between a free man and one who depends.

The world is a projection of Being. That is the source!

I looked for the Bible and I found it in one of the bedside drawers. I opened it 'at random' and read the passage in which three times Jesus asks Peter "Do you love me?" And three times, initially embarrassed but in the end slightly annoyed, Peter answers, "Yes, I love you!"

He should have answered "No! Not yet".

Had he known himself just a little better and been just a little more sincere and honest, he would have said "I'm trying to love you!"

With that thrice-repeated question, Jesus was actually asking:

"Do you know yourself, do you know who you are?... Do you love yourself more than anything else? Have you stopped killing yourself inside?"

He was asking him to transfer his teaching to the innermost parts of his Being, to overthrow his vision, transform his way of thinking and soften his rigidity. Perhaps it is for this rock-hard attitude that Jesus named him 'Peter' (from the Greek *petros,* meaning rock). This new name prefigured his later transformation from a fearful man into the founder and cornerstone of the Church. Yet Peter was the man who believed he could lie and hide. I too was that man.

I read this, and wept. Three times Peter had been given the chance to avoid his betrayal. If only he could have observed himself, he would have discovered that his betrayal was already there, in his Being, just waiting for the favorable occasion to reveal itself. Poor Peter! If only he could have observed himself he would have understood that those questions, repeated three times, were not external but came from within his own Being: You, Peter, do you love yourself? Have you eliminated any division, any inner deaths? He would have discovered the lies, fears and doubts in himself and could have put them to flight like a thief.

Loving oneself inside is an act of will, it means knowing oneself.
Loving oneself inside means celebrating life unceasingly,
in its totality.

I remembered these words of the Dreamer and realized that if Peter had heeded the request to look inside himself so that he might know and love himself, it would have changed his mortal destiny. If he had been able to upend his convictions, he would not have been crucified upside down... as he himself requested of his executioners, offering a symbol of his late but genuine understanding of Christ's subversive teachings.

From that step, from the message transmitted by that great School of early Christianity, I was retracing the steps to the greatness of the Dreamer's teachings. Being is the origin of all that we then encounter in the world of events.

Look at yourself inside and you will know your destiny!

The three 'yes' are the lies that Peter did not want to see, that became manifest in the event of his martyrdom.

If we want to change something,
we can only do so by elevating our Being.
The destiny of a man, as well as of an organization,
nation or entire civilization and its economy,
is the projection of his Being and vision.
The broader a man's vision, the richer his reality.

No school of economics could ever have taught me such an all encompassing law.

These were for me the great lessons in true economics, management and high finance. In these teachings, I recognized the milestones of a new education founded on Being, the manifesto of a psychological revolution capable of overthrowing the mental paradigms and vision of the old humanity, capable of turning its vision upside down and of freeing it forever from its conflictuality doubt, fear and pain, the real causes of all the crime and poverty in the world.

9 Dinner with the Dreamer

I had to control my impatience so that I wouldn't arrive at Veronica's too early. The dining room was packed. Sitting at a richly arrayed table, the Dreamer was surrounded by an excited swarm of diligent waiters and a careful, attentive hostess. From time to time they would crowd around to listen religiously to His orders and detailed recommendations; then, in unison, would resume their working dance. The Dreamer was wearing a black suit of timeless style and His long hair was gathered at the nape of his neck. Under the satin lapels was a resplendent shirt set off with a black velvet ribbon.

I was surprised to see that he wasn't alone. There were four men and three women with him: Bruno and Rebecca W., owners of an important advertising agency in Zurich; Klaus E., from Frankfurt, founder of Robotronic and president of an international foundation operating in the field of biological research; Ben F., Dean of a British university, the oddest looking member of the group. The oriental cut of his suit accentuated his imposing athletic physique, surprisingly unlike the build we commonly expect of an intellectual. Next to him was Linda, an attractive and determined-looking human resources specialist, founder and owner of two head-hunting agencies with offices in London and New York. Finally there was a young Irish couple, Peter C. and his wife Susan, timid and reserved. I took to them instinctively. He, a Catholic, and she, the daughter of a Protestant minister, were working together on a European project based at a historic college in Regent's Park.

The group's attitude towards the Dreamer suggested both simultaneous deference and familiarity. In the unexpected presence of those people I was overcome with emotions that I hadn't felt for a long time and which I thought I had eradicated forever: resentment at the intrusion, but also jealousy and envy of their opulence and the aura of success that surrounded them. That splendor overshadowed me. Of course, I had always thought that the Dreamer had other 'students', and many times I had imagined meeting them, but actually doing so like this, without advance warning, had caught me off guard. I was ashamed of my reaction and the emotions I was feeling, and this added to my pain. In covering the infinite distance separating me from the Dreamer, which was in reality no more than a few steps, I felt compelled to change. I reversed the focus of my attention, turning it from outside to inside. The instant I observed those negative emotions, they faded and vanished like the illusions they were. In the end, it was the fascination of the discovery that remained. I recognized the value of the opportunity of finally meeting men and women who, like me, had encountered the School for Gods.

I felt to be in a virtual theatre, where the line separating the actors and the audience was constantly infringed upon, remaining intriguingly uncertain during the whole performance. The curtain was going up on a Theatre of the Absurd revealing the contours of a separate reality. We were the living pages of an unknown script, the fresh brush strokes on a painting none of us could see in its entirety… And now, gathered before the Artist-Author-Creator, we were waiting to learn our destiny.

I concentrated my attention on the dinner. Every one of those men and women was a recognized authority in their own field. Bruno W. was a middle-aged, big fellow, blunt in his words and actions, but at the same time decisive and constructive. His stylishly unkempt, salt and pepper beard gave him a relaxed air of a rather simple and childlike character. His wife, Rebecca seemed delicate and almost frail, but with the concentrated energy of an international businesswoman. She spent part of her time in Tuscany where she managed a vast family estate and winery. Klaus E. was cosmopolitan and luminous, looking like a gentleman-adventurer of elegant demeanor, and, like a blade in its sheath, beneath his frivolous appearance and witty conversation was a sharp intelligence at the service of a fierce ambition. Peter C. turned out to be a vibrant André Chenier, refined in his expression and visionary in his ideas. His young wife, Susan, watched him ecstatically and hung on his every word.

Before the Dreamer, we were naked. He knew all our qualities and limits and the place each of us occupied in the overall economy of a perfect masterpiece. Together we formed a kind of keyboard on which he was creating and composing the opus conceived by His genius. Only He knew the complete score by heart, the precise notes, the unique and irreplaceable part that each of us had to contribute to His great composition.

No one seemed to notice my arrival. There was neither ceremony nor introductions. I joined them in silence taking the place that had been left free, and concentrated on what the Dreamer was saying. As I sat down at the table, I heard this fragment of His remarks.

«A real man doesn't belong to any philosophy, ideology or religion. A real Dreamer has no labels. He cannot belong. He cannot be confined... He knows that the Antagonist comes only to allow us to overcome our limits… For this he blesses every apparent obstacle... every apparent adversity... If, one day, walking in a garden, you happen to step on a thorn – He concluded – *never forget to give thanks.»*

10 The dishonest administrator

The Dreamer's reference to the Antagonist and His concluding epigram, served as an introduction to an ancient story of obscure meaning: the parable of the dishonest administrator. The Dreamer presented it still wrapped in the enigmatic mystery that had enveloped it for two thousand years.

A rich man discovered that his farm bailiff was squandering his assets. He summoned him, and, having established the facts, dismissed him from his administrative responsibilities. "What will I do? – cried the desperate bailiff – I'm no good at tilling soil, and I'm too embarrassed to beg." So he called his master's debtors one by one and falsified the documents thereby reducing the debt. One hundred barrels of oil became fifty, one hundred sheaves of grain became eighty, and so forth. In this way he counted on earning their good favor and finding a job once relieved of his office. His master also found out about this dishonest practice and in response… 'praised' him.

«Throughout the centuries, the behavior of this master has puzzled the most learned Bible scholars and challenged generations of theologians and sages» concluded the Dreamer pausing.

Some of us took up the challenge and tried to offer explanations but all of them seemed improbable and were thrown out by the others. It was an enigma wrapped in a riddle. In the end we turned towards the Dreamer in defeat. We knew that even the Gordian knot would loosen easily in his fingers. His gloss of that biblical conundrum was a model of simplicity and cast light on the millennial darkness.

He explained us that the master's apparently convoluted reaction was as solemn and important as a cosmic event for the human race: the crossing of an evolutionary threshold for humankind. For man's psychology this was a quantum leap of importance comparable only to the ability to stand erect or the loss of his ancestral tail. The master's reaction in the parable signals the birth of the '*sapiens sapiens*' species, the birth of man after man. It represents the beginning of an exodus that will lead the species out of a psychology which is still wedded to its primal animal condition.

«Man discovers pro-activity, the management of the moment and the transformation of every offence to his advantage, of every

insult into fuel for his journey... And he buries this treasure map in a small story of unimaginable profundity.»

«Feel the offence in your guts!» This sudden order from the Dreamer, pronounced in a loud voice, in fact almost shouted, jolted me and sharpened my attention.

«That is the battlefield... and it is there that the victory will be decided... The secret lies in winning before fighting.»

I reached for my notebook to record every word:

«The praising of the dishonest administrator is the cry of a humanity healed of every internal wound, of humanity that has forgiven itself inside, that wins without having to fight... because it no longer needs the beneficial but terrible intervention of the Antagonist.»

He told us that, when a mature man reaches the end of his great performance in the spotlight on the stage of life, rather than thanking those who showed him friendship and affection, he should solemnly thank all those who impeded him; those who were despotic and offensive towards him.

At this point, the Dreamer suspended His discourse and, with a nod, signaled that the first course be served. With simplicity and the same authority, He passed from the analysis of that obscure parable to a commentary on the various dishes as they were uncovered in turn. Following a digression into the realms of history and gastronomy, a succession of delicacies of regional English cuisine, previously unknown to me, was laid before us: from dishes based on sixteenth-century mustards to the more modern recipes, but all from before the Second World War.

The Dreamer, as usual, didn't touch the food, and His plate went back to the kitchen practically intact. Even though He was a refined guest and an extremely attentive and generous host with a great connoisseur's knowledge of food and wine, the Dreamer was the personification of frugality. He observed the most refined food related etiquette and rituals, serving himself and offering the dishes, which He'd comment on, to the others. Yet He consumed virtually nothing, every once in a while chewing a mouthful, but without swallowing it. The Dreamer seemed to feed on ceaseless attention to every detail. A waiter's gesture, the presentation of a dish and its decoration, the color and aroma of the food, the design of the restaurant and every aspect of the room seemed for Him like a flow of plankton, a subtle nourishment made up of feelings, perceptions, and sensations that were His alone, and which our organs no longer knew how to recognize or assimilate.

11 The victim is always guilty

«Apparently, everything on this planet is kept in balance by the 'law of opposites': to everything there is an opposite through which it exists and by which it is counterbalanced – recited the Dreamer – *An individual's life, like that of a nation or an entire civilization 'seems' to be rigidly governed by the law of opposites.»*

That topic lit up the conversation as if by magic. At the Dreamer's direct invitation, everyone indicated who or what at that moment he felt to be his own antagonist. The Dreamer listened to each one attentively. I couldn't help but ask myself what he had meant by starting with the adverb, 'apparently', and by using the expression 'seems to be'.

In the meantime He had begun to speak again so I set aside my reflections to listen to him. The secret of proactivity, barely touched on in New York, was finally about to be addressed.

«Everyone senses a force that places itself between one's wishes and the fulfillment of those wishes... the presence of a kind of universal friction» said the Dreamer, adding that, at least judging from history and from the infinite adversities that man has had to overcome, the antagonist could be recognized as the very driver of his evolution.

«If you want to do something in life, you have to meet the opposing force known as 'the Antagonist'.»

He paused, as if to summon the right words from the air around Him, and said:

«However, there are some secrets concerning the Antagonist that are only known to a few.» Following His mysterious preamble we all prepared ourselves to listen with heightened attention.

«The Antagonist measures us. It measures our AIM, our goal, the scope of our 'dream'. AIM is the anagram of I AM.»

AIM = I AM

«No one can have a goal that is greater than himself – He revealed, and added – *an ordinary man can dream of a small*

apartment; another of a house on the beach, but only a king can dream Versailles.»

I was completely bewitched by the magic of the equation the Dreamer had just outlined, between what a man asks for and what he is. I considered how this contrasted with the common belief that man's desire knows no limits, and that everyone could set themselves any goal if it were not for limits self-imposed by their own good sense and awareness of their lack of resources. Without these restrictions anyone could nurture the grandest dreams or harbour the highest aspirations.

The Dreamer moved on to demonstrate the groundlessness of this general belief.

«The amplitude of one's own Being sets the limit of what he can ask from life and the culmination of his every desire. At the same time it is also the limit of all that a man can receive and possess.»

This struck me as a fantastic discovery. Fragments of His teachings which until then had been scattered, began to connect. In a flash I perceived the magnitude of the revelations I had received. When I emerged from my thoughts, I realized that I had lingered there too long and without realizing, had fallen behind in the conversation. I hurried to catch up with the others, as I used to do as a child at the Collegio Bianchi, when, having been distracted by some stuffed wild animal or the depiction of ancient myths enclosed within austere frames, I would have to race after my classmates who were marching on in orderly file along the corridors.

« ...The Antagonist is the most precise measure of our thinking and feeling» affirmed the Dreamer, leaving us a few seconds to draw our own conclusions. Then He added:

« And this is why the antagonist is never stronger than we are. However horrible, menacing or unbeatable it may appear, the confrontation with the Antagonist is always a fair fight and the forces in play are always equal.»

At this point he lowered his voice transforming it into a threatening hiss that made us tremble and gather around Him as if we were one single Being.

«It is only 'apparently' that a man confronts external obstacles, or meets enemies and adversaries outside himself. In reality, the antagonist is always the materialization of a shadow, a dark part of ourselves that we neither know nor want to know –

continued the Dreamer – *When it manifests itself in the form of an attack, adversity, or a problem we are taken by surprise. In reality we have unconsciously cultivated it within ourselves. Because of our inattentiveness, a tiny symptom has had time to become acute, and due to our inability to identify it and intervene, it has materialized into a real threat. For this reason, a more attentive humanity, one which has eliminated self-pity and victim consciousness from its Being, will have the slogan 'The Victim is Always Guilty!' inscribed in block capitals on the walls of its courtrooms.»*

«But how should we consider a persecution that resulted in millions of deaths as in the case of the Jews? – interjected Bruno W. in a heated tone – I really don't see how, in the case of the Holocaust, the victim could have been the creator of his own executioner. What responsibility can millions of innocent people have for the extremism of a group like the Nazis, and their aberrant theories such as the idea of racial purity?»

At this point, the *sommelier* approached us discreetly and went around the table, pouring the precious content of a bottle of vintage wine into our glasses. The Dreamer stopped and waited for him to complete his task before resuming. It was then that Klaus E. burst out, as though he were reflecting out loud, saying:

«Of course, over the centuries, it has always been hard to be a Jew… In 600 BC Nebuchadnezzar had already razed the temple of Jerusalem to the ground and deported all the Israelites to Babylon… Then there were the Egyptians… the Romans… Whether they were called *Führer*, Caesar, Pharaohs or Satraps, the Jews have never lacked antagonists...»

The Dreamer rotated his glass with a movement of the wrist and watched the wine as it slowly swirled around the sides, 'breathing.' Then He inhaled the bouquet and, dismissing the *sommelier* with a look of approval, said:

«The opposite is a fragment, a part which has separated itself and moved away from the whole... The apparent antagonist is the silver talent lost by the woman... it is the lamb lost by the shepherd... Whoever fails to recover his integrity, whoever fails to reintegrate that atom of his Being, must encounter it outside himself, monstrously enlarged, in the form of a limitation, obstacle or adversity.»

At these words Linda lit up and interjected animatedly:

«But of course! – she exclaimed – Separate nurseries, schools and hospitals… separate butchers, grocers and restaurants… separate holidays, traditions and rituals… You could say that the Jewish religion, the philosophy, work and life-style of this race are effectively founded on a discriminatory vision of the world: there are the Jews and then there are the others…»

«In the temple of Jerusalem, there was a wall separating the Jewish courtyard from that of the Gentiles – mused Peter – and the penalty for any pagan who crossed that line was immediate execution.»

«The ghetto was born and the barbed wire was already twisted into the Jewish psychology – he said, before adding in a quiet voice, as speaking to himself – only waiting for the right circumstances to be transformed into a terrible reality…»

Bruno latched onto Linda and Peter's reflections and as though making an unexpected discovery, exclaimed:

«I had never thought of it before but in its Hebrew roots, the etymology of the word, 'sacred' means 'separate'… In their sacred vision, the Jews divided the world into what was sacred, that is to say whatever respected their own beliefs, and everything else, which was profane... impure.»

He slumped back in his chair as though he had taken a blow which was hard to bear...

«But then?…» he gasped, unable to carry on.

«Then... – resumed the Dreamer, recovering that fragment of understanding and proceeding to give voice to the thought that Bruno had not dared express – *our incompleteness produces monsters in the external world. Our division creates the violence that then we meet outside. The Antagonist is us... Feeling oneself separate from the others is the effect of a disintegrated psychology, which feeds an internal criminality. One day this will manifest itself in the world of events in the form of violence, crime, conflicts and persecution.»*

We were stunned. We were crossing a divide before which our thoughts had come to a breathless halt.

«The Shoah was not an accident of history nor the result of the mercilessness of a regime, nation or, even worse, a man or tyrant – He said – *It was the materialization of the vision of people who still had not forgiven themselves inside; the mirror image of a divided and conflictual way of thinking which was the true cause of*

the concentration camps, deportations, extermination and every other atrocity. The only enemy lies within ourselves!... Outside there is no enemy to hate or to forgive, and no ill that can harm us.»

«Now I come to think of it – said Rebecca – the lamentations of Jeremiah, the tragic chant of the Israelites who were enslaved in Babylon, begin with an expression of painful surprise. The first word is 'eckah' which means, 'why'?»

«The unexpected always requires a long preparation... a long incubation period that occurs in our Being, in our states – announced the Dreamer – *Therefore, recognize the Antagonist within you... become attuned to him... recover your integrity. Becoming whole means 'forgiving oneself inside'... it is the part that joins the whole... it is the return of the prodigal son. Love your neighbour... Then life will always say 'yes' to you... It will display a constant generosity towards you which others will put down to good luck.»*

That evening the Dreamer told us that at a certain stage in its evolution the human species found itself at a crossroads, a fork which generated two distinct races, two psychological species, each profoundly different from the other.

There are men who depend, who blame external conditions, they complain and they commiserate. The Dreamer called these people 'reactive'. They see things by contraposition and have a bipolar consciousness.

If you see the external world as something real,
then you are lost and destined to fail no matter what you do.

Then there is another type of man who is aware that there is no adverse world outside of ourselves, no external antagonist ready to block our path. The Dreamer called such men 'proactive.' They see the unity behind the extremes, the harmony behind the apparent antagonisms.

«Proactive men enter into the darkest parts of their own Being and fight their shadows, ghosts and most deeply hidden fears before they can materialize and one day present themselves as adversaries. Whatever comes from outside must be transformed. Let events, incidents, circumstances and relationships fall into a place

inside you where junk and rubbish can be transformed into a new substance, new energy and new life.»

These personal victories were defined by the Dreamer as 'creative victories':

«These represent the way to make one's dream materialize. Iphigenia's sacrifice, Ulysses' journey, the offering of Isaac, the battle of Arjuna, the temptations of Christ, all still hand down the secret of creative victories achieved by men who were able to overcome their internal antagonist, the only true obstacle to the fulfilment of all our aspirations.»

Then with the bitter tone of one who announces a situation to be without solution, He added:

«The real malady of the reactive man is that he is perennially 'away from home'... 'outside of himself'. For him the inner world does not exist and he has made the external world into an idol to be worshipped, a fetish to adore and upon which he must depend. Do not ever expect anything from anybody.»

At the end of that dinner, the Dreamer highlighted certain signs of ageing and degradation which were unacceptable in anyone who was part of a School of Being and He pointed out the lack of progress and slow pace of each individual's 'work'. He expressed His displeasure through harsh and unforgettable words. The Dreamer's strength and energy, which, in the space of just a few years, had enabled those people to achieve extraordinary things and reach the top positions in each of their worlds, were now only feeding their arrogance and vanity. Having forgotten the real reason for being with the Dreamer, their promise to be the precursors and forerunners of a new humanity, they had reduced themselves to being clones of the old leadership, lifeless matrices of a species on the verge of extinction.

As we were leaving Veronica's, we stood around Him listening to the end of that unforgettable lesson. His words were biting and His conclusion unbearable.

«I have given you fame, wealth and power. You have achieved everything you dreamed of. Now there is a new adventure, a new expedition... It is time to dream a new dream, to dream a new world... Abandon everything you believe you have and put someone else in your place... Dedicate yourselves entirely to the Project.»

I will not recount His speech, which today only a few people would be able to understand or accept, but I registered everything that He said to us and carefully treasured it.

«Your lie is lurking behind the mask of age – He thundered – *Delegate to your subordinates! Give up your roles! Do it intentionally before life does it for you.»*

In the eyes of those men and women I could see consternation and dismay and I remembered the parable of the rich, young man.

One day I will write about those who heard the Dreamer's words, the ones He abandoned that night and what became of those individuals I had been able to get to know so well personally. The Dreamer's conclusion struck them like a mallet and their worried faces distorted in pain.

«I will not intervene again – He said – *'Real' freedom cannot be given. A man must conquer it for himself and want it absolutely and at any price. Only then will he achieve it!*

In my world there is no room for even a single atom of your horror and indolence. Everything one is, everything one has, must be left behind and transcended... in order to be and to have more.»

A stony, solemn warning sounded and sealed the end of that speech:

«Whatever you do not understand through my words, life will explain to you with its own laws and instruments of healing. I therefore give you back 'your' freedom, the freedom to surrender to pain, degradation, disease, ageing and death...»

I took this as a premonition that darkened my soul. I was listening, years ahead of time, to the words that one day would be branded on me in some of the most difficult moments of my life.

I waited for all the others to leave and lingered in order to be alone with Him. I'd have liked to have asked Him the meaning of those harsh words and above all else understand why they had struck me with such force. Obscurely I sensed that I was witnessing something that had a lot to do with me and that one day it would be my turn to choose between the 'dream', and the 'dreamed', between true life and the attachment to the shadows projected by the dream. I wondered what I would have done had I been in their place.

That evening I only wanted a little of His attention so I limited myself to requesting to see Him once more before going back to New York. He fixed an appointment with me for the following afternoon. We were to meet at the Savoy. Then, as if to make the most of that impromptu opportunity, He asked me to get two tickets for the hit musical of the moment, *Les Misérables*. I was surprised at His request but didn't say anything, and I promised that I would deal with it that very morning.

12 The tickets

I arrived punctually for what would prove to be one of our most extraordinary meetings. The Thames foyer at the Savoy was crowded at that hour. Sitting with a steaming cup of tea before Him, which He was on the point of bringing to His lips, was the Dreamer. The little table was heaped with pastries of every kind, and both the table setting and silver service were immaculate. As usual, He had hardly touched a thing. I greeted Him with the customary deference and quietly took the seat next to Him, trying to stay 'up' and keep a smile on my face, despite my burning sense of defeat.

I struggled to let myself be taken in by the Deco atmosphere and the discreet piano, but a recurring thought, more troublesome than the rest, continued to vex me. The hundred justifications which had crowded my mind along the way had now turned into a maelstrom. I was desperate. I knew the Dreamer was not a man to take 'no' for an answer and my indecision over how I would tell Him had become an unbearable anxiety. His cool, calm voice intruded into my thoughts and made me start.

«You couldn't find those tickets!» He said flatly.

His serious tone confirmed my worst fears: the Dreamer considered of vital importance the task He'd assigned me, and in an instant my fear, humiliation and impotence turned into rage and an uncontrollable smirk of arrogance. If He had known I would not have been able to procure them then why had He asked me? I had spent the whole day searching in vain for those two tickets. But *Les Misérables* was the most successful West End musical in years so it was an impossible quest. I told the Dreamer how my search had begun early that morning with the St James' Hotel concierge laughing derisively in response to my innocent request that he reserve two seats for that evening's performance.

"Why, sir, don't you know? – he chortled – For tickets to a hit show like that, I'm not even sure that booking three months in advance is enough!"

From that moment on, as the hours passed, my search became increasingly feverish. As I confessed to the Dreamer, I suspected at various moments that He had deliberately set me an impossible task.

He remained silent, His chin lightly resting on His chest. He seemed to be absorbed, listening to the tale of my fruitless mission, and I interpreted this as soliciting a full account of my failed endeavours. I had vainly scoured every box office kiosk and ticket office but, confirming the concierge's information, from even the most restricted view side seats to the stage boxes, the theatre had been entirely sold out for months. Finding those seats seemed to be the most difficult thing to do in the whole of London. In a confused way, something inside me had known that the challenge went way beyond the apparent futility of the task and this had urged me to redouble my efforts in order not to leave any option untried. As tea time approached, and with it the feared moment of truth with the Dreamer, I had even contacted some influential friends in show business. I told Him about how I had paid a visit to Lady Ellis during an interval between parliamentary votes at Westminster, and how even that had proved unsuccessful. To fill every space, I was dragging out more episodes from my odyssey, expecting an unleashing of His wrath, or worse, His derision, upon me at any moment, when suddenly the Dreamer interrupted me repeating His initial words.

«'You'couldn't find those tickets!» He said in the same tone, this time laying the emphasis on the 'you', with the irritation one feels for those who are being stupid. He brought His face imperceptibly closer and added:

«To find them you would have had to derail your own destiny... finding them would have changed you forever!»

He revealed to me that, contrary to my belief, at the very moment when He had asked me to find those tickets, the job was already done. This statement astonished me. Could I possibly have been persuaded that the difficulties I had encountered were not objective?... Who better than myself could know that I had stopped at nothing to try and get those tickets. It was all very well to talk about it there, sitting at a table at the Savoy, but who else could have done better?...

«You are still a man hypnotized by the description of the world... For you the world is the truth! – He hissed while the irritation in His voice emerged with greater force – *When that man told you that it would have taken three months, you were already defeated. From that moment on you no longer looked for the tickets.»*

I tried to break in to protest that... But a severe gesture from the Dreamer froze me in my tracks before I could even open my mouth.

«From that moment you did not look for the tickets... but for every way possible to confirm the world's description... to reinforce your conviction that that was really how things were, that it was impossible to succeed... Every attempt you made was preceded by your resignation... each time, the 'no' you were convinced you would hear, was already there waiting for you, even before you knocked at the door... to reinforce your prophecy of doom and allow you to honor the promise you had made to yourself.»

«What promise?» I stammered. A little light was making its way through my horrible certainties. A glimmer of humility, and therefore of understanding, made me feel the wretchedness of my long line of excuses.

«The promise of coming before me defeated but with a claim of having done everything possible to succeed» replied the Dreamer. He allowed a small pause before pronouncing the words I would never forget.

«Believing what that man said is part of your blind obedience to the voice of the world. From the moment you accepted his description, you no longer worked to win but rather to justify your failure. It's the story of your life... a prophecy of defeat.»

The whole day flashed before my eyes like the final images of a dying man. Not the temporal sequence of events, however, but the states of mind, the thoughts and everything I had gone through while trying to find those tickets... Once again I saw my lack of faith in my own abilities, that sensation of inadequacy, the fear of being beaten, the determination to blame the world which was so inexplicably hostile, and the 'others' who seemed to be deliberately withholding those tickets from me, and finally the sense of guilt. I became aware of this mass of unpleasant emotions which had pervaded my Being throughout that day. The Dreamer's words were making me confront my habitual attitude. That apparently banal undertaking had exposed my innermost wounds and revealed limits which I felt more painfully as I realized their meanness. The Dreamer's skill had altered the world and put the universe to work so that I would be able to recognize and overcome them. As I realized the enormous and unique value of that opportunity, my sadness at not having succeeded in my task increased. In the tug of war between reality and its illusory projection, between the Dreamer's vision and the world as it had always been described to me, illusion and non-existence had won out again. The world was still reality, its hypnotic power was too strong and the Dreamer's presence still too faint.

«Yours was not a failure but the result of a failure, the reflex of an internal fault, a condition of your Being. There are no failures in life but only effects.»

«To find those tickets you would have had to change your past!» the Dreamer continued, with a tone reflecting my new attitude. What had seemed to me to be an over-statement now appeared as the clearest of all truths.

«Had you been able to remain faithful to the 'dream' you would have changed your destiny» He said with pitiless sweetness as addressing the representative of a permanently defeated humanity.

Then, in a whisper, He added:

«The sleeping beauty is the dreamer inside you who knows.»

Whoever He was, I felt that I loved Him more than anything else in the world… I loved the lucidity that I was now experiencing with Him… and I would have held onto it tooth and nail for fear of losing it… The world of integrity and solutions had said to me: 'go… it is already done!' The world of division, of conflict and complexity, had told me: 'it's impossible!' And I had obeyed the superficial description of the world, believing and identifying with its lowest and most miserable part.

The Dream is the most real thing there is. But I constantly forgot.

«In order to avoid corruption, you would have had to defeat your scarcity, your victim consciousness and the hypnotic sleep that makes you into a dependent, fearful, doubting and unhappy Being…

The unshakable faith men have in the description of the world is the source of their fragility, the ultimate explanation for the events in their lives and the role that each one is assigned in the theatre of existence...»

«Disease is another one of the world's lies! We fall ill because the disease has been described to us, and so we get old and die, through imitation, without ever questioning the reality of it all» raged the Dreamer. His raised tone and the usual delivery made His words resonate, indicating that they were no longer only directed at me but at an immense and invisible audience.

«The ordinary man does not dream, he blindly obeys a hypnotic tale of existence. He has forgotten his uniqueness, his nature as creator because he does not have access to himself. He does not know himself!... Whatever you dream, happens and if you begin to know yourself, you will understand why the world is as it is. Now you know why the world is as it is!... Because you dream it so!»

Not having enough pages left in my notebook, I recorded these words on the Savoy menu and, for a few minutes, covered it in dense notes using all the available space. I was still writing when I saw Him motion to attract the head waiter's attention.

«Let's go» He instructed bluntly, as He rose.

13 At the theatre with the Dreamer

As soon as we were outside, we set off on foot. I imagined that we might have caught a taxi in the street, but the Dreamer continued accelerating His pace and I followed. It was the first time I had seen the Dreamer in a hurry. I considered myself fit, and yet several times I had to speed up to keep pace with Him, nevertheless each time the Dreamer pulled away, forging ahead. How, when I ran every day around my island on the East River, when I had taken part in the most testing of marathons – the Oakland marathon, and extreme competitions like the Pepsi Trophy in Central Park – when I had biked for 24 hours non-stop, how did I have such trouble keeping up with the Dreamer who seemed to be making no effort at all?

Where were we going? Who was expecting us, so important to make the Dreamer hurry? I wanted to ask, but never dared, nor would I have found the breath to do so. Suddenly, with the agility of a boy, the Dreamer raced and caught up with a bus, an old double-decker which was leaving just in front of us. I accelerated my pace but I would not have made it had the Dreamer not stretched out a hand to drag me aboard. I was still clutching His hand when I looked into His eyes.

Suddenly I was thrust back into my Neapolitan childhood. I saw my band of urchins again, our desperate tests of bravery in Mergellina, the races on the tracks and how we leapt onto the bumper of the tram. At the age of 10 one had to be an expert at this in order to be admitted into that gang of warriors and share in their exciting and risky life. One time something went terribly wrong. Running at breakneck speed I had grabbed the bumper, that sort of metal buffer at the back, and I was ready to jump on but the tram accelerated unexpectedly. I didn't dare let go nor could I quite jump on. I felt my desperation grow as my legs began to give way… But then a thin but strong arm reached out from the back window and grabbed me by the wrist. At last I jumped and was saved. The eyes of that young boy, laughing calmly… were the same ones… they were His eyes. How many times, in how many different circumstances had I already encountered the Dreamer? How many times had He already intervened in my life?

This time my surprise exceeded my ability to disguise it and, while I recovered my breath, my expression must have seemed so funny to Him that He felt compelled to reveal at least part of the mysterious journey.

«*We're going to the theatre* – He said in a cheerful manner that I had never seen before – *and I wouldn't want to miss the start of the show tonight.*»

I imagined we were going to see a play by Samuel Beckett, Brecht or Chekhov. The only ones for which two tickets might be available at that time. Unless… The explanation dawned on me like a flash of light. Yes, it could only be this… I was suddenly quite certain of it. And, when I recognized the theatre in the distance, I had no doubt. What a coup! The Dreamer had made me turn London inside out and He'd had the tickets in His pocket all the time. When I told Him of my discovery He couldn't stop himself from laughing quite openly.

«I don't have any tickets!» He said, approaching the door of the bus and preparing to get off. I was crestfallen. Could it be that He had not believed me? Might I have failed to convey to Him how completely impossible it had been to find any sort of seat for that performance?

«It's impossible – I said, supporting myself by clinging to a handle and preparing to get off the bus with Him – We have no chance of finding a ticket, especially at this time.»

The Dreamer silenced me with a gesture of irritation.

«Worrying, doubting and suffering are for those who do not dream, who do not love. These are the daily pursuits of those who are hypnotized by the world of rationality, the world of superstition – He said, resuming His severe tone – *They are the symptoms of a fragmented psychology, evidence of a fault in the Being which pre-announces disasters, failures and defeats which are already underway in the world of events.»*

Those words gave me a sense of burning shame. In the theatre of existence I was doomed to the role of the killjoy, typecast as the 'rational', consistent man, for whom I had already begun to feel a certain revulsion, but whom I was unable to abandon.

He got off the bus and I followed. After a few steps I saw the lights of the foyer sparkle before me and felt the magic atmosphere of a great theatrical event. There was still a crowd of people in front of the posters which, against a background depicting a heroic image of the Parisian insurrection of 1832, showed the revolutionary flag and, in the forefront, the ragged but undaunted figure of the young heroine, the urchin Gavroche.

The show was about to begin. As I watched the ticket-seeking crowd finally disperse and noted how many people moved away disappointed, I suddenly felt that mean sense of satisfaction, that ephemeral triumph enjoyed by easy prophets of doom when they see their predictions confirmed. Along with this, I also experienced that collective mood of wretchedness that the rabble, the mob, feel when they see heroes executed. Suddenly I realized that, over the centuries, one dark angle of my Being had been the true culprit of horrible crimes; that from this shadow lurking in a fold of my soul, wars and atrocities, destruction and immense suffering had sprung forth. For a few moments, overcome by my own sense of revulsion, and horror at myself, I held my breath observing the true fabric of my Being through this tear in my consciousness.

In the meantime I had lost sight of the Dreamer. I found Him again and stayed beside Him observing the crowd thinning out until only one couple remained in front of the entrance to the theatre: a short and stocky middle-aged woman accompanied by a tall, strapping young lad, who we were later to discover were an American mother and son who were there waiting for friends. They were elegant and of noble aspect, with the authoritative and confident air of those who are in control of their own lives. The young man, clearly more accustomed to country than city life, was putting up with the uncomfortable elegance of his bow tie and tuxedo with stoic dignity but evident affliction.

In his hands he held some tickets.

14 Le Misérables

Once the crowd had dispersed, only we and this couple remained in the foyer. Our eyes met and I spotted their fleeting look of reverence towards the Dreamer, an almost inward bow, as occurs between men and women who recognize that they belong to different rungs in an invisible hierarchy.

I thought back to all the times when I had seen the world 'recognize' the Dreamer and, on each occasion, show signs of respect towards Him, like a plant that senses the presence of and offers gratitude to whom tends and feeds its roots. These reflections reminded me of an episode which had occurred in New York. I had been with the Dreamer in an elevator which was stopping at the various floors and filling up with people. As we got out, the Dreamer made me note that the real difference between those men and women, their belonging to different levels of being, could be visible in their attitude, measured by the greater or lesser degree of embarrassment they had experienced during that fragment of eternity elapsing between floors. He explained that in that elevator a hierarchy had formed amongst the individuals, if only for a few seconds, without their being aware of it; an invisible pyramid on the steps of which they had taken up positions corresponding to their level of inner responsibility.

Wherever they meet, for a few seconds or years,
men will arrange themselves
on the different levels of an invisible pyramid
respecting an inner, mathematical order,
like planetary hierarchies made of light,
orbits, mass and distance from their sun.
There are degrees and levels of Being.
It is a universal law.

We struck up a conversation with the American couple and they told us that, curiously, their friends had not yet arrived. As we chatted I noticed that the woman's expression was changing and I watched her become increasingly relaxed, serene and almost euphoric. The show was about to start and there was no longer any point in waiting. Turning to the Dreamer with a broad smile which revealed how she was not at all unhappy with the change of plan, the woman invited us to go into the theatre with them. They had the best seats in the house, which they had reserved even before leaving the US. All my attempts to offer them the price of the tickets were met with a polite but firm refusal. We were their guests.

I would never get used to that indefinable sense of the miraculous that constantly hovered around the Dreamer. I would have liked to have said something to Him, to apologize for my skepticism, but the Dreamer did not even glance at me, so apparently deep in conversation was He with the woman who was now going into the auditorium with Him, resting her hand lightly upon His arm.

How had it been possible for the tickets to have been there waiting for us? I felt I was losing my mind: had the American couple, their friends' delay, even their entire trip to Europe, all been created by the Dreamer, materialized by Him at that moment, there, before my very eyes? His mastery was permanently overturning my vision of the world.

When we were comfortably ensconced in our front row seats and as the lights went down, I heard Him whisper in my ear:

«Seeing and believing are one and the same thing. In time you will see everything you believe in and you will realize everything that you dream.»

In the half-light of the theatre, those barely whispered words evoked the magic of an ancient chorus and I felt my soul rise. I sensed the purity and freedom that herald the advent of the healing solution; the alchemy of catharsis which the antique tragedies elicited in their audiences; the denouement unfolding according to the principles of justice.

«To believe you must be impeccable and whole. The smallest flaw in your Being, the merest shadow of a doubt, will cause you to be cast back among the ranks of the defeated and the mortal, with those billions of Beings who have given up their rights as authors of their own destinies, trapped in the hell of those who need to see in order to believe...»

The Dreamer had been preparing me for a long time and yet, a direct experience of the fact that the world is created by us, was making me falter on the edge of a crevasse.

Every man is a creator...
The world is a chewing gum...
Whatever you dream happens...

I understood that humanity suffers because it sees the world upside down. Believing and seeing are one and the same thing; but men perceive them as separate, divided by time, and they wait to see in order to believe. Pain and suffering exist because they are the only ways in which humanity knows how to bridge this illusory gap. When believing and seeing merge in a man, he is then also able to eliminate pain and suffering from his life, banishing them forever from his personal universe.

«Believing in order to see: this is the law of the creator» continued the Dreamer.

«It is the principle of those who rule; it is the ineluctable law of kings – He said as the curtain began to rise – *Believing belongs to the art of dreaming and is the intimate quality of the Dreamer... In the roots of 'cre-do', 'cre-ed', there is 'cre-ation'... The dream is the most real thing there is...»*

His voice became even softer until it was hardly more than a mutter. I had trouble making out His words but I could distinctly pick up the severity of His intimation. Referring to the story of *Les Misérables* He said:

«Pay attention. Beyond its eighteenth century pathos, this story contains an important lesson about the antagonist... It is a universal parable applicable to all humanity. It is the story of a man who doesn't know how to 'forgive himself inside'... just like you!»

Les Misérables was the musical version of the story of an implacable antagonism: the search carried out over many years by a policeman with an uncompromising sense of duty, the fanatical Javert, to enforce an unjust sentence on the escaped convict Jean Valjean who had been condemned to 20 years in prison, and subsequently to life, for having stolen a piece of bread. In the story, the wanted man, Jean Valjean, comes to symbolize generosity, the goodness of the humiliated individual, brutalized by society's injustice and the mercilessness of its laws. In the background, we see the glorious and desperate epic of an entire nation, the life of the Paris slums, the insurrection of 1832 and the battle of Waterloo.

I knew that story. My father Giuseppe used to tell it to me when I was a child and I still had a vivid recollection of how moved he became every time he reached the part where Jean Valjean finally releases himself from the pursuit of the fanatic Javert, but instead of leaving his tormentor to die, against all reason, he saves his life. The generosity of this act so disrupts the policeman's rigid vision of the world that, once his most deep-rooted beliefs about good and evil have been overthrown, unable to live with his old values, he kills himself.

«Javert/Valjean, even the names sound similar... They are the same person – the Dreamer then affirmed to me – *When he finally forgives himself inside... when he saves Javert's life... and thus brings the opposites within himself into harmony,only then is he ready for a more intelligent and powerful Antagonist. Once understood and overcome, the old Antagonist no longer has any reason to exist, so he disappears... he commits suicide. In reality he had never existed except as the materialization of a shadow, an incompleteness of his Being...»*

These words of the Dreamer's timeless teaching reverberated powerfully and found resonance in every atom of my Being.

«The only enemy is within you! Outside there is no enemy to blame or forgive and no ill that can harm you... Do not fear the antagonist. He is your greatest ally. He is the one who will show you the shortest path to success. His one and only purpose is your victory.»

When the lights came up again, the Dreamer had gone and I spent the rest of the evening with our new American friends... but my thoughts turned to the Dreamer and His extraordinary lesson. From the darkest ages, since the time when the first spark of thought crossed the mind of man, there have been seekers of truth and schools of Being, schools for inner preparation. The school of Pythagoras, Plutarch, Plato's Academy, Aristotle's Lyceum, early Christianity and all the greatest schools of classical antiquity, were forges of the spirit and found their highest expression in the Dreamer, the very reason for their existence and the continuation of their mission.

CHAPTER V

Goodbye to New York

1 On the streets of Manhattan

The headquarters of ACO occupied an elegant nine-storey building, a jewel of marble and stainless steel among the skyscrapers of Park Avenue. From Roosevelt Island I could reach 60th St by aerial tramway in four minutes and would then walk the last few blocks through the pulsing heart of Manhattan. Along the way, an immense crowd of people swept me along the streets and sidewalks like a river whose banks were buildings with thousands of glass eyes.

A few weeks had passed since our last encounter, but His words, like a precious living substance, were still working their mysterious power over me. I felt them turning into glands, tissue and organs. Everything was beginning to get clearer. Humanity which until then I had perceived as an indiscriminate mass, now appeared to be composed of different colours, energies and frequencies. Observing the people around me through the eyes of the Dreamer, I realized that every minute detail revealed the position that each one of us occupied on the ladder of Being, and the roles we were to play in the world.

Everything is connected to everything else.
Nothing is separate.

As I walked, I sensed that multitude breathing along with me, as if we were one single immense Being. I could sense their fear. I could feel their moods and hear their thoughts, and I observed how faithfully they revealed themselves through their clothes, their attitudes, their gait and the work that awaited them and towards which they hurried. Their vision and aspirations were as limited as the roles into which existence had meticulously confined them.

Our level of Being creates our life and not vice versa.

I held these words of His close to my chest like a talisman as I made my way through that well of humanity to which I had never previously realized that I belonged. I heard the chant of sorrow coming from each one of these people. For the first time I was listening to the ceaseless inner monologue of a humanity who doesn't know and I felt its painful solitude as I passed by. I heard the buzzing of that swarm, like the sound of millions of insect wings. Before having met the Dreamer, I used to like the feeling of belonging, and I loved this city. I'd adopted all its rituals. I would dive into the most crowded street fairs and wait in line for tickets to the most popular shows. Working in a big corporation, living with millions of other people in a metropolis and rubbing shoulders with thousands of strangers had always given me a sense of security.

Now a new lucidity was eliminating every trace of compromise. I 'saw' them, and through them, as if in a distorting mirror, I saw myself. I recognized the common condition of Beings imprisoned in a role: tragicomic masks marked by a perpetual grimace of pain that remained the same, even when they laughed; machines activated in sleep by pitiable fantasies and futile desires.

From the Dreamer I had learned that others are nothing but our own inventions. All these men and women were myself. I was lost in a hall of mirrors! Reflected to infinity, fragmented into thousands of images that were all, painfully, still myself. And as I walked, I observed the dribble of emotions, the trail of thoughts that every human leaves behind him like the luminous slime of a giant snail.

I too was one of these distracted Beings passing by, wrapped in a cloud of worry and self-interest. I was a droplet in that Stygian river of oblivion, flowing past the skyscrapers, invading the streets and wending its way towards its fatal destiny. Only one thing set me apart. I had met the Dreamer. Now I knew that there was a revolution to be made, and with His help, I was taking my first steps in that direction.

Not one in a thousand faces was looking up at the sky. In vain I searched for signs of life, for a single face with an expression of gratitude for being a human Being here in this world, for being a part of this marvellous universe. In vain I hoped for the mirror of my attention to be blurred by the breath of another being gasping for life.

The enchanted vision came back in flashes; a child, clinging tightly to Giuseppona's side, captivated by the kaleidoscopic circus of the world. Then, as now, I would look around me to see if I could find some playmates in that game. But Manhattan had as many children as Herod's kingdom.

One snowy morning, I noticed a young, black man who was slim and well dressed with a European look about him. A special light made him stand out in the crowd. Snowflakes had settled on the halo of curls framing his face, as on the surrounding hedges in Central Park. We only had time to exchange a smile as we passed each other but I had the impression that he too 'knew' and that he 'recognized' me. It was a fleeting sensation, but for that moment I entertained the hope that I was not alone in that huge city, that amongst all those sleepwalkers, within the torpor of that inert humanity, there might be some pulsating corpuscles, some living cells.

Since the Dreamer had opened my eyes to the fact that employment was, in effect, a modern form of slavery, that army of men and women going to work appeared to me like a horde of insects, driven by blind instinct. Every morning, I saw them crowd into entire floors of skyscrapers, occupying millions of cells, cramped as honeycombs, and fill them with the sound of their buzzing. Within their glands, they carried a sort of life in the form of a thick sludge: a heavy burden of dark thoughts and a dense syrup of emotions. And while I too made my way towards my little cell, I thought of the infinite number of people on this planet, destined to spend the better part of their life working for organizations, just as I was; selling themselves out for a pay cheque.

I asked myself what might be the evolutionary purpose of the travail of so many people locked into the cages of their hypnotic roles, and where all their efforts were leading them. Whether within organizations or out, wherever I looked I saw men in the grip of fear. In them I recognized my own anxieties and unhappiness, and under the thin film of apparent rationality, I saw the conflictual logic, the destructive thinking and that death urge relentlessly driving us to hurt ourselves first and then those around us. Under layers of centuries old emotional sediment, I recognized an inner pollution produced by anxiety, doubt and insecurity, as well as by an unlimited fear of both living and dying. I was sliding into a feeling of absolute terror at the thought that without the Dreamer, I would have come back to join this multitude of the living dead.

Once I asked Him what He meant by 'ordinary' or 'horizontal' men, as He often called them.

"They are the men and women who study, teach, and work... who have children and raise them... who plan and build roads and skyscrapers, write books, found churches, have jobs in private and public life, even at the highest level – was His unforgettable response – *and all in a state of hypnosis."* And after a studied pause for suspense, He added:

"They grope in their sleep, permanently sealed in a bubble of oblivion and unhappiness."

When I remembered these words, and felt this overshadowing destiny, always ready to suck me back in, my Being clenched into a fist, in one single immense desire to avoid this fate, to cut through the bars of this prison and escape.

"Once you have 'seen through' the game you can no longer take part in it" the Dreamer revealed, and I felt that, no matter how painful it might be to overturn the ordinary vision of the world, my life was changing and it would be impossible for me to go back. Now I knew that it was indeed possible to take possession of one's destiny and at last I felt that I could contain and control my existence. That corporate business world that had always fascinated me with its merciless practicality, and everything I had been working at for years: career, success, family and money, were now all taking on a new meaning. Even New York, which I had so loved and desired, now often appeared to be like a *papier-maché* world, as noisy and pointless as a circus, with the same intense smell of dusty poverty and vagabondage.

For the Dreamer, the physical universe, meaning everything outside ourselves, from insects to galaxies, a visible world – which also includes things we cannot see or touch – was the microcosm, and the world of Being was the macrocosm.

In the microcosm, everything is slow.
There are obstacles, limits and priorities which must be respected...
It is the domain of Time... where men proceed in single file
and where it is impossible to break free and pass beyond....
Dedicate yourself to your Being...
Only within yourself, with your eyes shut,
will you be able to fly and dream...
lift yourself above the plain of ordinariness and go beyond.
Real action comes about through 'not doing'...
If you lose one millimetre of ignorance,
you will feel a quaking of the foundations of business and finance,
with their pyramids and temples,
and armies of slaves and high priests.

Poised as I was on the edge of this world, I stared with eyes wide open at what was to come and my position within it. I would have liked having held onto that vision, to sustain this marvellous and terrible state of detachment, which was making it possible for me to 'see'. I feared I could lose it at any moment and be swallowed up once more by the machine of the world and sucked into its vortex.

I was sure that if I had been able to maintain that state of detachment for even just a short time, I would have finally become a stranger to that world, like a termite removed for two days from the hypnotic influence of its mound.

To change the nature of events we have to change our vision.
One day the material universe will become our masterpiece,
the mirror image of our rediscovered will,
the perfect materialisation of the Art of Dreaming.

The constant memory of the Dreamer's teachings, my own work of self-observation and study, my experiments with diet, breathing and sleep, my regular morning runs and the other physical exercises and silence, were cracking to open the cocoon which had confined me, and the light of a new existence was already filtering through that crack.

2 The Tools of Dreaming

For days Jennifer acted as though she hadn't noticed anything happening. On hearing the sound of the alarm calling me for my morning run, at first she did no more than roll over and continue sleeping. In her view it was simply a case of waiting for laziness and old habits to take hold of me once more, like a game bird in the jaws of a retriever, so I tried to explain. Without mentioning the Dreamer, I tried to make her understand something of the revolution that had exploded within me and the invisible world into which I was taking my first difficult steps. It was all in vain.

I speeded up and the faster I went, the more time became compressed. It was incredible how much I was able to accomplish in that hour and how much more I could fit into it. The faster I went, the more energy I had and the more I was able to do in furthering the research which had become the main focus of my life. As I got faster at running and even ordinary tasks, I began to steal time from time itself. Miraculously, that hour in the morning expanded and, with it, so did the work I was doing on myself. In the end, a moment of reflection on some thought of His which I had recorded in my ever-present notebook, occupied the last minutes of my morning and connected me with the Dreamer, providing me with guidance, a *viaticum* for the day ahead.

For the Dreamer, living in the moment was the most precious thing in a man's life and I strove to focus on the 'here and now', trying to make this discipline my constant practice.

Step out of the time dimension
as much as possible in your everyday life.
Self observation is the cure...
The moment you realise that you are not present,
you are present.

Every morning, I forced myself not to be distracted from the moment and maintain this special chemistry of attention for at least part of the day. Unfortunately, as soon as I re-entered my slot in the usual work day routine, I would lose my resolve, falling prey to a thousand thoughts. Just like a levee giving way, as my state of vigilance slackened, worry, anxiety, and negative imagination all attacked me, reducing me to the size of a midget. Only occasionally, as if 'waking up' from a nightmare, I would find that I had become a kind of colander. A thousand wounds in my Being were letting my life seep out.

Through self observation,
a man enters the darkest corners of his Being.
Only then will there be a true transformation,
only then will he find the real meaning of his existence.

Through self observation and running, I discovered the connection that exists between body, emotions and thoughts. It is impossible to be gnawed by worry or ill humour if the physical part of your Being is pushed to a higher speed. The lowest states of Being can only exist by indulging in the densest, slowest levels of existence.

Our way of thinking and the quality of our emotions, in turn, inevitably produce an effect upon the physical being. A deliberate effort to lighten one's thoughts or transform an emotion can modify a condition with electronic speed and even affect physical features.

Thoughts, feelings and the physical condition were turning out to be a single universe made of concentric, interactive worlds, where the same events propagate their effects at enormously different times and speeds. I began to realize just how complex the work of understanding and change would have been if I had started with the more subtle and quicker parts of Being, rather than acting upon the physical body.

If you raise your body's vibration,
the entire world will be elevated to a frequency
where every strife, division, and war will disappear,
and only harmony, beauty, and truth will exist.
Erase limitations from within.
Put forth the command that
you are the very cause of all and everything,
and flood the universe with your inner light of life and power.

Running also forced me to pay attention to my breathing. Although it is the life function which is the most vital and with which we most closely identify, we are only rarely aware of it.

Breathing accompanies every activity of our lives, and follows the rhythm of our thoughts, modulating itself according to the intensity of our emotions and physical effort, connecting every fibre of our Being and our most vital centres. But we spend our lives breathing in a way which is shallow and superficial, rarely expressing any gratitude for it, and acknowledging the debt that we incurred with our very first breath.

"One day you will know how to transform the world and raise your level of responsibility, through the tools of 'dreaming': thought and breath."

"The world models itself according to your level of responsibility – He said, penetrating the whirlwind of my thoughts, while the magic of this discovery made me soar – *The depth of a man's breathing corresponds to his level of responsibility... and determines everything that he can own and do... You can possess only what you are responsible for."*

Through the words of the Dreamer, the balance that exists between having and being was revealing itself to be the fundamental principle that ruled the world. The implications of this discovery were so great that I was left breathless every time I witnessed another demonstration of its universality. The equation drawn between riches and responsibility, between financial power and Being, also indicated the limits of what could be bestowed or entrusted to a man and the measure of what he could possess, understand and contain. One day I would pass these lessons on to my students, demonstrating how all this applied to organizations, nations and entire civilizations.

Even in the animal world, a sort of 'ethology of having' assigned deadly jaws and claws to those animals with a more developed nervous system and progressively less powerful weapons to those lower down the scale. Nature would never give a turtle dove, which kills its enemy by pecking its feathers off, the claws or strength of a lion, which has the ethics of the most honourable hunter and lives in symbiosis, poised in a perfect reciprocal advantage, with its prey.

No animal, human Being or even organization can have weapons and in general, offensive power beyond their responsibility and capacity of control.

3 The lie

With every passing day, my speed and resistance increased, and with thus came a certain lightness of Being. In this way I learned to love that effort and bless its presence within myself. I continued to work in the other areas the Dreamer had indicated to me, trying to apply His principles to my own life as much as possible. More than a few times I misunderstood His lessons and often failed in my attempts to apply them. For a while I tried extreme sports in the belief that this might help me to develop courage and self-confidence.

"Do not seek certainties outside yourself or in the eyes of others. Do not feign courage – the Dreamer said to me one day – *Real courage is the victory over your own lie. Leave these sports and risky ventures to those who love their own fear and to those who depend upon it. These risks serve only to reinforce such fears. Someone, a liar like you, is now breathing through an iron lung, tragic emblem of a mendacious humanity."*

Instantly I thought of A.F., the Italian explorer I had met a few months before his accident. I remembered the Dreamer saying that he would be killed by his lie, by having risen to meet false challenges instead of facing his inner ones.

"If you want to expand your life, you need not expose yourself to extreme experiences... Expand your vision, ideas and thoughts through the power of earnestness and sincerity, and there will be no battle you will not win."

The reason why many people practice extreme sports and embark on very high risk ventures is because danger forces them into states of great intensity where they feel more alive, freed from time and the weight of the world. When one moment of distraction can mean the difference between life and death, it is no longer possible to do anything other than experiencing the instant. But this condition is artificial and creates a state of dependency. You escape from one form of hypnotism only to enslave yourself to another.

One day you won't need to challenge oceans
or practice daredevil flying in order to conquer your fears.
Once the lie is gone you will enter into
the 'powerful state of Nowness', simply and easily.

Because living in the 'here and now'
is the only natural, heroic, and immortal state of man.
Only in the Now one can be Immortal, and the Now is forever!
Remember! All happens here,
in this everlasting 'Instant', in this everlasting body.
All that you are Now paradoxically creates
all that you have always been and all that you always will be.
Focus all your attention on Now
and nothing will ever be impossible to you.
Now is the seed of the universe.
All possibilities lie in Now.

For the Dreamer, indulging in memories of the past or imagining what the future would bring was the root cause of all our problems.

Soon I began to see the fruits of my efforts. I developed a clearer vision and a vigilant spirit, which revealed previously invisible worlds and allowed me to make simple yet revolutionary discoveries. Seeing the ever increasing number of obese people and the way this phenomenon was expanding, not only in New York and the rest of America but also to a large part of the Western world, I asked the Dreamer for an explanation.

"The lie hides behind many masks – He said – *obesity is one of these. Behind the macabre expression of the jollity and ostentatious generosity so often found in fat people, is hidden their renunciation of life, their attempts at suicide."*

The monstrous transformation of their bodies is only the most crude reflection, the aggravated symptom of a psychological malnutrition. Stuffing oneself with vast quantities of 'junk food' and consuming food which is not nutritious or is excessively loaded with calories, is merely the effect of a diseased Being.

When I drew the Dreamer's attention to the fact that in America obese people now represented more than half of the population of the country, He said:

"It is the sign of a weakening of the will of an entire nation. A civilization which is addicted to food is one that is bent on self-destruction. Even its economy, like a shadow of its Being, reflects this dependency, this overshadowing of its will, and in just a short time it will weaken and be swallowed up by fitter predators, by

civilizations of greater integrity. Your physical destiny is intimately related to your mental, emotional, and financial destiny."

Along with my increased vitality, I felt a growing sense of community, an inclination to do things for others, people I perceived as trapped in a dead end existence. It was something I had never felt before; a kind of compassion for those creatures I saw as permanently drowned in anxiety.

"Stop indulging! – He screamed at me once, striking me to the core with his words of fire – *Your self-pity perversely borrows the human condition as a pretext to hide behind and perpetuate itself. Your vanity makes you believe that you are healed and ready to help others... The only thing you can really do to help the world is to wake up from your nightmare.Stop believing that the world needs your help. Stop believing that the world is a helpless victim. Stop believing that the world is a separate reality."*

Only much later would I understand the meaning of those words and open my eyes to the falseness hiding behind altruism and every form of charity fostered by institutions that live off people's sense of guilt.

"These are organizations that only exist to perpetuate themselves – snarled the Dreamer – *They specialise in obtaining funds and gathering resources which they then misspend and squander, barely managing to even support themselves. If you lift the smoke-screen surrounding philanthropy in its every form, you might discover that behind the suffragists and the Salvation Armies, behind medical and pharmaceutical aid and the distribution of food, hides the most atrocious organized crime and the worst acts against man..."*

"Don't waste your time in commiseration or sanctimony. No one can do anything for anybody. It's up to them to seize the opportunity. Everything happens for a reason, and a purpose, and it serves you. He who has not defeated the lie within himself, he who is unaware of the self-sabotage that continually goes on within him, cannot do anything for anyone."

"Man dies because he lies" was the motto the Dreamer coined at the conclusion of His discourse, as a summary of this essentially human drama: the lie. Man dies because he lies... and above all to himself.

4 Goodbye to New York

One day, I found myself singing in the shower. That was imprudent of me. The Dreamer had warned me that there were guards in our inner prisons watching over us and that it was the people closest to us, our nearest and dearest, who were the most watchful implacable jailers. That signal which I had carelessly sent out, that carefree manifestation of cheerfulness, gave Jennifer the proof she needed to realise that my bid for freedom had been underway for weeks. She connected it with my new eating habits, the fact that I had gone back to my correct weight and the improvement in my muscle tone and skin, in addition to my clothes and general appearance, and at this point she took action.

She tried everything she could to get me back inside my old boundaries, but my escape was already well underway. Other cages, other more insidious traps, certainly awaited me. But not these.

For weeks now we had not been bickering. Making accusations, shouting or sulking in order to make up again and faking attempts at still being in love, had all been expedients to fill the emptiness in our relationship and our lives; they were ways to keep us clinging to one another, locked in a hell of falsity and boredom. The attempt to recreate a family with Jennifer, after Luisa's death, was built upon the shifting sands of our immaturity; and it required continuous compromise to stop it from falling apart. Now, even this fake equilibrium had collapsed forever. Nothing worked any more. The menthol smoke of her St. Moritz cigarettes and the bright colour of her lipstick no longer had any part in the world I dreamed. It was in this atmosphere that on Columbus day, she packed up her belongings (or, to state it more precisely, she emptied the apartment of most of its contents) and went back to her parents' house in New Jersey. Goodbye, Jennifer. I would never see her again. At last I was starting a new chapter in my life.

When Giuseppona came home with the children and saw the bare apartment, she was concerned about one thing only. From a hidden corner in the kitchen, with a hand over her heart and a great sigh of relief, she retrieved her old Neapolitan coffee pot and kissed it with ostentatious veneration. It was the only object she could not have borne to part with, and she had wisely hidden it. She filled it with freshly ground coffee and put it on the stove, then, with the ironic solemnity of an ancient oracle, said, "Anyway, she just wasn't any good for you!" The choice of those words – the recurring epilogue of my adolescent heartbreaks – and her colloquialism, formed a comic epitaph, that united my family in one long, joyful burst of laughter. The lightness and fragrance of that moment, fused with the aroma of the coffee and I could never have asked for or imagined, a better or more auspicious new beginning.

The separation from Jennifer signified my simultaneous death and rebirth. It had required the elimination of just one atom of fear. I had believed I loved that woman, but what I had really loved was my suffering and pain which by this time, had become so familiar that they no longer hurt. I could never have made it alone.

No one can make it alone.

To abandon old ways of thinking, obsolete ideas, prejudices, superstitions and compromises like those which had tyrannically governed my existence, one needs a School, a system, a plan of escape. One needs to meet someone who has already made it. Somebody who, before us, has realized that he has been imprisoned by a hypnotic tale, a description of the world, and then escaped from it. I wish that every man could encounter the Dreamer and I offer all my gratitude to Him. Only those who are forced to face their own horror and can bare to contemplate their impotence and incompleteness, can succeed.

I am writing to tell you that the Dreamer exists and that He is the most real Being that I have ever encountered. His timeless, impeccable world, is more alive and concrete than ours and it is accessible. The way is hard but passable; it is a path towards beauty, truth and happiness; a new and swifter route to more fabulous Indies.

Something invisible and powerful, yet available to every man, had put into motion a marvellous mechanism.

The slightest change in one's Being
moves mountains in the world of events.

It was as though I heard a winch groaning, strained with the weight of the anchor pulling it out of the muck of a long imprisonment. At the other end of this voyage was not a small archipelago of islands but a huge psychological continent as yet unexplored. I held my breath between fright and joy, like a child about to ride on a rollercoaster. Once more I sent a thought of gratitude to the Dreamer and fervently hoped to see Him again soon.

That day, Giuseppona and I went shopping with the children for the most necessary supplies and in the evening we all went to dinner at Mama Leone's, happier and closer than we had been for some time.

With Jennifer gone, New York was leaving us too, and through a number of signs, I perceived that the changes that had taken place in my life were only the beginning and that there were many more ahead of me.

To depend upon a job, you have had to sing a song of pain for years,
you have had to give up your freedom,
sending out signals of your decline and impotence;
believing you were protecting yourself,
you reinforced your ability to forget and set limits upon yourself.
Now you have to go back to regain your freedom.
It is a long process of elimination, of simplification,
of lightening your Being.
Dance, dance, dance… and never stop!...
Celebrate your existence, and love yourself within!...
Observe yourself! Pay attention to your Being!...
You will see that everything that is real in your life will remain,
and everything which is illusory will leave you forever.

The Dreamer had called all this, the *Art of Dreaming.*

I was doing my utmost to follow His teachings. I was in perfect physical shape. A frugal diet, breathing exercises, the battle against sleep, and, above all, vigilance and self-observation, were producing extraordinary results. Simply turning my thoughts towards thc Dreamer gave me access to a new intelligence. At the end of the working day, if I had time, I would take the train to City Island to sail along Eastchester Bay. I'd listen to the voice of the ocean and the wind beating the jib of the Flying Dutchman, and I felt closer to Him. Self observation, an honest look at my states of Being, a higher sense of dignity, a new feeling of self confidence, were all bringing about changes in my life that only a few weeks earlier I would have considered impossible.

One morning, Mr. Keenan, the head of personnel at ACO, rushed into my office unannounced. He sat in the chair in front of my desk and looked at me for a long time in a knowing way without saying anything. He reminded me of a gambler who had just placed a bet and was waiting for the outcome. I took the result of his inspection to be a positive one, as gradually his expression changed and a smile spread over his face replacing his initial inquisitorial frown. ACO needed to set up a commercial network in the Middle East. This operation would take two, maybe three years of intense work and the operational base would be the foreign sales office of the Italian subsidiary, located in a small city in northwest Italy.

Mr. Keenan warned me right away that I should not harbour any illusions of settling down there.

«You will spend more time in the air and in hotels than at home with your children» he declared, in a prophetically ironic tone. At the end of this meeting he said that I should be ready to leave within a few days. Without waiting for any response, he pushed some documents for me to sign across the desk.

«When you've finished this assignment, I want you back here on the team – he said – with the hardball players.»

During that period, to reconnect with the Dreamer's teachings, I resumed my reading of the masterpieces of modern and classical thought and all the other books on philosophy I could find. I used to love them, but now they bored me to death. Often I would abandon them after just a few pages, and despite all my efforts, I could not discern a single spark of His intelligence or pragmatism in any philosophy, moral doctrine or religious thought. In no traditional wisdom or theories of ethics was I able to find even the most distant echo of anything I had experienced with Him. In vain I hunted through the books I had accumulated in my lifetime, for an idea, or *something* that came close to that precious substance, to that alchemy, which was always present when the Dreamer was there. I had wasted so many years on pointlessness! The books I had worshipped were revealing themselves to be masterpieces of stupidity and superficiality, written by people who were enveloped in the same insecurities and fears as their readers and in not one single page did I find even a pale reflection of the power that I had felt in His words.

Knowledge is an inalienable asset
which you have always had…
It is already within you.
Like happiness, prosperity, free will,
unity of Being and whatever you seek,
be it God or money,
knowledge cannot come from outside.
No one can give it to you…
It can only be 'remembered'.

The Dreamer's words reminded me of the story of the man who finds a treasure and then sells everything he has to buy the land where it is buried… It is the story of one who 're-members' a real object of value, and barters a sour description of the world, with all its limits, pain and ignorance for a real treasure that will neither rust nor decay, which cannot be stolen or lost… but can only be buried and forgotten.

5. Love doesn't depend

Back in Italy, I rented an apartment in Talponia, a subterranean residence conceived in the flank of a small hill just a short walk from the headquarters of ACO, the giant midget of the robotics industry. Until now I had only worked alone or as a member of a small team and almost always in a foreign country, but for the first time, I found myself working in an office complex, an industrial area with laboratories and factories, populated with thousands of workers. The central building was like the body of an animal. I could feel it breathing and sense the life pulsing in its gigantic arteries. In its turn, this creature had perceived my intrusion and, day after day, it attended to my assimilation. I flowed in its veins together with thousands of other cells, filtered by its immense organs and screened by its metabolic processes.

Just as Mr. Keenan had said, my new job kept me away from my home and children for the greater part of my time, requiring frequent trips and long periods spent in countries throughout the Middle East. Between one trip and the next, I had made various attempts to blend into the organisation, and many times I tried to participate in the rituals of the employees who lived within its folds.

I had tried to learn their habits, adopting their ways of speaking and trying to interpret their codes, but my efforts did not meet with much success.

The teachings received from the Dreamer and the vision He transmitted to me regarding the real conditions of working as an employee, assisted by the intermittent nature of my presence in Italy, allowed me to remain sufficiently alien to these environments and observe the life of that teeming population almost with the detachment of an entomologist. My observations led me to identify a kind of 'psychological pollution' within human organisations which I first heard the Dreamer mentioning, and which, up tonow, had eluded any form of scientific investigation. In fact I had never found any reference to this in any text. It is the result of an incessant flow of unpleasant emotions, fear, envy, jealousy, mean thoughts and futile discussions which poison the atmosphere of organizations, thereby producing sickness and incalculable damage to the minds and bodies of millions of men and women. Years later, right here at the ACO, I would investigate this phenomenon in greater depth. In the meantime, my discoveries in the area of 'psychological pollution' allowed me to develop reflections on the nature of organizations and the implications of subordinate work, which I had started in New York with the Dreamer.

Being an employee is neither the effect of a contract,
a position in an organisational hierarchy nor a social status...
It is the effect of belonging to a low level on the ladder of Being.

This had been my first, and one of the most disturbing lessons I had received from Him.

A man is dependent because of a low level of responsibility...
Being an employee is only the reflection
of an inner condition of slavery.

The revelation that employment was a modern form of slavery had rocked the foundations of my description of the world. His words had found a place in my consciousness that was almost physical and they remained lodged there like material which was difficult to metabolise, but at the same time impossible to expel.

Love doesn't depend...
Love and freedom are one...
One day you will realise that you are
the artisan and not the artefact,
you are the dreamer and not the dreamed;
the creator, not the creation...
Everything is at your service.
Then you will no longer be dependent!...
The world is such because you are such and not vice versa.

The revelation that employment was a modern form of slavery had rocked the foundations of my description of the world. His words had found a place in my consciousness that was almost physical and they remained lodged there like material difficult to metabolise, but at the same time impossible to expel.

Suddenly, the business world which I had so much desired to belong to, and which had captivated my imagination since childhood, was being revealed to me as nothing other than a huge prison camp, with its corporations like a vast network of penitentiaries as large as the planet itself. To escape and break free! That was the only reasonable thing for a man to do. A suitable file and a good escape plan were his only true assets. These reflections certainly did not help me adapt to my new environment. My fears about the future at that time took the form of a recurring vision of a crevasse ready to swallow me up.

I did nothing specific about my predicament, but for some time my morning run became less regular and I stopped re-reading His words.

6 You cannot both dream and be dependent

One day I received a small card from the Director of Human Resources accompanied by an instruction to stamp it every time I arrived or left work and whenever I needed to leave or return to the Main Building. It was a new rule that extended the existing procedures for monitoring employees to include directors, and those who like me, had spent most of their time working abroad, and up untill now had enjoyed a greater freedom of movement.

I made several attempts to comply with this new regulation, which miserably infringed on the last vestige of independence I had in my role as an employee. Numerous times I lined up along with the others, in one of the many queues that formed in the hall where the machines were and I noticed that everyone was submitting to this procedure as if it were the most natural thing in the world. Cards in hands, they chatted, smoked and laughed, while waiting in turn, to stamp them. But on each occasion when I reached the machine, I was overcome by a sudden feeling of intolerable shame so I would leave without stamping my card. With some modicum of dignity restored, the words of the Dreamer had come back to inspire me and I felt them resonating inside me, strong and alive, so for a while, my desire to live a life of freedom and happiness along with the vision of a successful existence, grew vivid again, like a memory of the future.

Be free, be independent. Be a rebel!
A rebel is not dependent on anyone…
and he respects his uniqueness.
His only purpose is to fulfil his 'dream'
This is what he dedicates his life to, and every ounce of his energy.
One cannot dream and be dependent on someone or something else.
One can dream, and serve. Serving does not mean depending…
Serving means governing your own life, and that of others…
it is the act of one who loves.
Only those who love can serve.
Those who do not love can only depend!

But it was only a short time before negative imagination took over again. Fearful thoughts of a future without this job made me go backwards, reducing me to a microscopic being. Fear took on a thousand masks and my concerns about the future were camouflaged as good sense and responsibility towards my family and my children, so after a few days I'd find myself back in that line in front of the timekeeping machine, with no other desire than to be like everyone else. I would have given anything to be able to escape my limbo, and go back once more to take my place among that multitude, sharing their thoughts, accepting their anxiety and even their pain… and to forget.

One morning, while I was facing the inner atrium from one of the top floors of ACO, I observed the spiral formed by the marble staircase going down to the centre of the lobby where an uninterrupted flow of men and women were populating that level, waiting in line to stamp their time cards before continuing into the lunch room. I had a sudden, absurd thought. I was absolutely sure that every one of those women and men had met the Dreamer. Even if only for an instant, all of them had at a certain moment in their lives, been given access to the world of the Dreamer. I realized that every cell of this crowd had encountered the School and turned it down. I saw them swarming about in this vortex. In the uniformity and mediocrity of their lives, I recognised my own life when I was far from the Dreamer.

Conformity is mediocrity

I felt an irresistible urge to go down there and question them, shake them and ask what had happened to their dreams, what had happened to the Dreamer. They would have thought me mad. These people had forgotten, choosing instead to yield and depend, to suffer, get old, and die. And I might be racing towards the same precipice.

You cannot dream and be dependant. The Dreamer's words echoed within me like a hymn of salvation. A spark of that intelligence was still reaching me.

7 A second hand future

My moments of lucidity became increasingly infrequent. As the luminous threads that tied me to the Dreamer relaxed their hold, or even disappeared entirely, I quickly rebuilt the world I had always known, in every minute detail. Nestled among some houses, in a small town by the lakes at the foot of an immense glacier topped mountain, I found an old villa for sale and bought it with my American savings. I dedicated myself to the task of restoring it and making it enough of a home so that I could leave Talponia and move there with the children.

Soon Gretchen arrived, a young divorcee I had met in my last few weeks in New York, bringing with her, her five year old son

Tony. Once again, I had made a home. After Luisella and the end of the affair with Jennifer, I was rebuilding my family for the third time. Without realising it, I was locking myself up in the depths of my old prisons. Gretchen was as different as you could imagine from Jennifer, a spoiled New Yorker princess. Being a ski champion, Gretchen had inherited the spirit and physical strength of the pioneering women who conquered the American West. She continually practiced sports and had muscles of steel. She was as down to earth, rough and provincial as Jennifer had been sophisticated, vain, and cosmopolitan. But even so, after a few weeks, this relationship also found its way into the old rut.

From all appearances I had changed my job, partner and even continents, yet in reality my life had returned to the rigid shape registered in the memory of its very fibre.

Our level of Being creates our Life

Day after day, little by little, I was reconstructing my old life, like a mechanical creature sealed in an unconscious eternity, condemned by genetic memory to repeat every gesture. Old habits, thoughts and emotions were meticulously recreating the same circumstances and events of my past. Disguised behind the mask of a new life and a clumsy attempt to camouflage it as a future, the past was meticulously reproducing itself, with merciless perfection.

A man cannot hide.
Every thought, emotion, or action,
is recorded indelibly in his Being,
and he himself is the ever-present guardian and executioner.
This is what determines his destiny.
A man can convince himself that he has escaped,
changing the external circumstances of his life,
but beyond the apparent differences of the situations,
he will always be placed on the same rung on the ladder of Being,
according to his degree of responsibility, integrity and love.

These were the Dreamer's memorable words at our first encounter, and since then I had read and re-read them countless times but the warning contained in this prophecy had not helped me avoid repeating the mistakes and pain of my life. I remembered an earlier conversation I had had with Him on this theme and I still consider this to be the cornerstone of my apprenticeship.

"Humanity's biggest illusion is the conviction of having a future – He had told me on that occasion – *In reality, an ordinary man does not have a future. Beyond appearances, he only and always encounters his past. Events, encounters, and circumstances repeat and recur in his life; they are always the same, only slightly disguised."*

"This is like saying that men are living a life that is used; a second hand existence" I said with a touch of incredulity in my voice to hide the uneasiness I felt at confronting His revelations.

"And yet everyone deceives himself into thinking that the events of his life are freshly minted, created just for him, and have never happened before" sighed the Dreamer.

"And therefore, what man calls reality is…" I started without being able to complete my sentence, seized by a sickening sense of absurdity.

The Dreamer looked at me without replying and nodded slowly, as though endorsing the fact that I'd reached the worst of all possible conclusions… the most unthinkable and unacceptable of all. I took a few steps in the direction He was indicating. I clinged absurdly to the hope that I had misunderstood His words and that, in some way, He would be the one to stop me and bring our conversation back within the confines of a reassuring rationality.

"So what we call reality… what we see and touch… would be… is indeed… a kind of… virtual reality?" I ventured, proceeding with reluctance and only after his continuous nods of assent which came like little prompts, and then waited. The Dreamer remained deep in thought for a few moments as if needing to find the right words to breach my resistance.

"What a man sees around himself... the reality outside himself, is the past – He pronounced firmly, and then, breaking the intense silence, added – *What you call the present is really just a* pre-recorded broadcast." Once I had heard these words, my world would never be the same again. In an extraordinary way, I was convinced that it was not only my own world that had changed but also everyone else's.

"What you see and touch, the events which you would swear are happening in this precise instant, were recorded in a past time. To happen, they had to have your assent in another dimension, in

the world of Being, in your states of Being" He said, as if this were something perfectly natural. He explained how events had already occurred and how what happens is the way it is because it has already happened.

"The events of one's life are the solidification of one's states of Being, made visible in time. While you are there and involved, you might believe they are happening right before your eyes, you might have the illusion that they are happening for the first time but in reality, they are the projections of your past repeating itself, with only slight variations."

I remember that, after the words of the Dreamer, I had imagined the events in the life of an ordinary man like an allegorical procession of masked characters, of tricksters bent on perpetrating the cruelest of jokes. I saw them coming round again and again, unremittingly the same, while under their false noses and moustaches they were stifling their laughs and sneering at man's blindness and inability to recognize them,

"What man calls the future is really just his past seen from behind – said the Dreamer, waking me from my reverie – *The only chance you have to take charge of your own life is in the 'here and now'... and it is only by managing the moment suspended between nothing and eternity that a man can 'act', and merit a real destiny, forming it and creating events on a higher plane."*

Later I was to have the opportunity to see for myself just how true this vision could be and how easy it was to forget and fall back into the hypnotic wheel of a false life and a repetitive destiny.

How many years I could have saved and how much pain I could have avoided if only I had known then how to receive the message of the Dreamer and open myself up to His vision which today seems so simple, natural and inevitable to me.

I forgot, I denied the 'dream' and for months did not think about it again. The doors of the old prison opened up to receive me. The days of my life with Gretchen and the children ran along in ruts which had already been formed. Between working trips to the Middle East and domestic life, I seemed destined to forget and be lost forever.

8 Dinner with the Sheik

At the reception desk in the Le Méridien Hotel in Kuwait City, I found an invitation from Sheik Yusuf. He was requesting my presence at a dinner that evening in the Behbehani Palace and a car would come for me in less than an hour.

I had just arrived there after a long journey and the idea of a ceremonial Arab dinner was not the most appealing prospect. But I could not refuse. The Behbehani family was one of the most powerful clans in the area and one of the financial groups that practically ran the country. In Kuwait, as in most Middle Eastern countries, business is kept strictly within the circle of only the grandest families. A map of the country's financial power would replicate the genealogical trees and the dynastic distance from the Emir, reflecting rights acquired as far back as medieval times.

In recent months I had had some contact with several members of the Behbehany family, and I had put together some business deals with companies in their group, but I had never met Sheik Yusuf. I knew he was the head of a vast financial empire built upon concessions and represented the products of the leading multinational corporations, with a well developed network of other interests and ventures outside Kuwait, especially in the United States.

The Behbehani palace, a gaudy structure built entirely of white Carrara marble, was constructed in the traditional form of a quadrangle, with a large internal courtyard from which one gained access to the various reception halls on the ground floor, and to the private family rooms on the upper floors.

A silent family servant dressed in a caftan led me to the dining hall. Around the long table, decorated in the most elaborate Middle Eastern style, I found a varied collection of representatives of the Islamic business community in traditional white *dish-dashia*, their brown arms lavishly adorned with jewellery. A few western directors from the big multinationals were also present. Naturally it was a dinner for men only, and without silverware, in any case Arab custom does not permit the use of knives. Meat and fish were served already cut into bite size pieces, while smaller dishes of fresh vegetables, cheeses, and creamed legumes were served alongside heavy platters of roast lamb and rice. The Sheik's eldest son served us personally, an honour reserved only for the most important guests. The discussion became animated right away, with Sheik Yusuf at its centre. He turned out to be a man of lively intelligence and the attentive head of a household, supervising even the smallest details. We drank tea and freshly squeezed fruit juices.

Kuwait is one of the 'dry countries' of the Middle East, respecting the traditional laws of the Koran, which forbid the consumption of all alcoholic drinks, at least officially. The dinner ended with some Lebanese sweets, made of nuts and honey, and coffee prepared over a fire according to nomadic traditions and served in small, extremely fine china cups. The spectacle of this thick, dark, dusty tasting liquid, masterfully poured from the brilliantly polished copper pots, always fascinated me. The coffee continued to be served, and the steaming rivulets continued to fill the cups, until each man swirled his around with a deft movement of the wrist, a gesture that meant that the guest was satisfied.

Only then did Sheik Behbehani, who had wanted me seated on his left, reveal his project; the creation of a new commercial enterprise in Kuwait. He asked me to transfer to Kuwait City to set up and direct this project. I would have an equity in the project and the status of Managing Partner.

The dream was becoming a reality: to create an international organization, assemble the men, recruit the resources and test myself against the challenges of a venture in such a difficult environment. At last I would be setting out to sail across the seven seas of business in my own ship. This was what I had always wanted, or at least what I had always believed I wanted. I asked for two weeks to reflect on my decision and took my leave. As I was returning to *Le Méridien* I was already in a state of apprehension.

As much as I tried to force a positive response, this proposal brought me no joy or sense of satisfaction. I kept thinking intensely about it all the way back, but the more I did, the more my resistance to the idea of transferring to Kuwait seemed to increase and proliferate. After only a few moments of initial enthusiasm, this prospect had fallen prey to my negative imagination and fears. As in the parable, the seed of opportunity had fallen on barren ground where it gradually dwindled and extinguished itself like the coals under the coffee pots at the end of that dinner.

Miles and miles of grey desert, wrinkled as the hide of a gigantic elephant, rushed by under the belly of the airplane taking me back to Italy, interrupted only occasionally by the perfect circle of intense green surrounding miraculous wells drilled to an incredible depth. I was sure that what was happening to me was the result of the promise I had made to the Dreamer and the work I had been doing on myself since my first encounter with Him. My desire for a freer, more responsible and richer life, had, like a rain dance, attracted this opportunity. And now what?

I was more convinced than ever that the smallest rise in one's state of Being can move mountains in the world of events, that *Our Being Creates Our Life*, but never would I have believed that such a radical change could happen in such a short a time. The cement and plaster in the house I bought in Chià was not yet dry; the grass on the lawn was barely starting to sprout from seed and the hedges to grow. That quiet, provincial life which had so often seemed intolerable to me after New York, suddenly acquired a new value in my eyes. Lakeside walks with the children, an ice cream by the banks of the river, racing over the snow with Gretchen, even the stifling atmosphere of a one-company town, revealed themselves to be attachments that without being aware of it, had put down deep roots in the space of just a few months. Brick by brick, one habit after another, I had constructed another house on a bridge, a stable home where the 'dream' had only allowed for a brief staging post before resuming the 'journey' and carrying me beyond.

I knew Kuwait City. I had been there many times for work, but had never stayed for very long. My impressions of it were limited to the lounges of its modern hotels, the dusty streets, the crowded Souks and whatever I had been able to see from the windows of a limousine, sealed into an air-conditioned bubble as though in a spacecraft travelling across the atmosphere of an inhospitable planet. On few occasions when I had ventured out, I had felt my skin stung by a million needles, grains of burning sand swept by the winds of the desert. The desert, like the sword of Damocles, is constantly threatening Kuwait City: an ocean of sand always ready to swallow up that islet which stubbornly claims a few miles of semi-civilization from its wild tempestuous dominion. Behind the opulence of its towers, the intensity of its traffic and the modernity of its buildings, Kuwait is not really a city state but an untiring challenge, a constant mortal combat between man and the desert. The ball of its history bounces back and forth between the modern age and a forgotten medieval period riddled with archaic habits and Koranic justice. A bizarre and dusty universe was opening up before me. A world as noisy as a bazaar, where cadillacs and camels, skyscrapers and tents, biblical poverty and financial power had found a miraculous coexistence.

9 Escape into sickness

My most gnawing doubts and anxieties manifested themselves at the idea of leaving my job at ACO. I was frightened and unsettled by the idea of resigning and moving to that country without the certainty of another job. However, I continued to lie to myself, neglecting all the evidence. I believed I was being sincere when I was angered by the apparent difficulties and when I had to face the many obstacles I continuously found before me. They seemed to be growing more and more insurmountable. I had not even begun the work of observing myself, of paying attention to my states and refining my Being, indicated by the Dreamer; nor had I yet acquired the degree of honesty I needed to recognize that, not just in this situation but always, fear was governing my life.

Today I feel compassion for that man who deceived himself into thinking he was reflecting and pondering the pros and cons, who continued to lie to himself day after day convincing himself that he was the one who made decisions which in reality his fear had already made for him long before. I refused to accept what the Dreamer had often accused me of:

"You are the only real obstacle, your own evolution's greatest enemy and the sole cause of your every failure. It will take many years of self observation and a great deal of hard work for you to realize that those negative circumstances which you see as objective, external and independent of your will, are in reality your own creation. The obstacles you encounter are the materialisation of an inner lament, the song of sorrow that always comes from the darkest parts of your Being."

In effect, I was searching for an excuse that would allow me to refuse without having to accept responsibility, holding onto the possibility that one day I might be able to pin the blame on circumstance or destiny. I grabbed any excuse I could to justify my refusal: the children, their school, the risks posed by living in that country. I also counted on Gretchen's firm opposition. Inside me, there was a determined 'no' in response to this change, to this derailment from my old ways. I searched everywhere for some unavoidable impediment, something to provide me with a pretext for blaming the world.

In the end, I found what I had been looking for. In the past, before having met the Dreamer, I had suffered from stones in my right kidney. Who, with peace of mind, could take such an important decision of transferring their family to Kuwait without first undergoing a full medical check up?

I persuaded myself that this was a matter of responsibility, for my children more than anything else. Notwithstanding my encounter with the Dreamer and all I had done to change the course of my destiny, I was about to fall back into the terrible rut of my past once more, so I made an appointment to have a kidney x-ray. This was the first step. Something inside me had already chosen the way of sickness. I went back to seek refuge in that dark part of existence where one does not fight or compete but only accuses, makes excuses and looks for sympathy from the world.

The shock would have stopped my heart if I had realised then that I was the originator, producer, director and actor in the film of my life, and, in particular, the creator of those images that I was about to project once more onto the movie screen of the world. As the Dreamer would one day say to me, *ignorance is a mother who gradually lets go of your hand, and only when you are ready.* If something had not happened to interrupt this terrible screenplay, the next few frames of my life would have been a close-up of the doctor's worried face announcing that the x-rays had revealed some shadows on my right kidney. He would have pointed these out on the luminous screen, small marks like fingerprints left from a light touch. I would have gone pale and then, back at home, I would have become desperate and for years blamed destiny, for my poor health which 'unfortunately' had prevented me from seizing this great opportunity. Everything was ready for this screening the following morning. The worst thing about the whole situation was that I was completely unaware of my conspiracy. With my last breath I would have defended the fact that I was acting in good faith and sworn that I wished for nothing more than a clean bill of health, confirming my perfect condition, and being able to leave for this new adventure.

Fortunately, I was still held to the Dreamer by a golden thread.

That evening I had an intense desire to see Him. I could not manage any more. I could not go on much longer without His help. It seemed as though an eternity had passed since our last encounter, and not finding any other way, I decided to write Him a letter, solemnly renewing my promise and asking to resume my 'journey'.

> There is a word that comes back to me at this time,
> presenting itself insistently to my conscience.
> It goes back to what you said during our last meeting.
> The word is 'dignity.'
> And this is the most painful part of my life,
> the part I have missed most,
> in every situation, in every event.
> I need it. I have to produce it, feel it, and distribute it.
> I know it has a cost. And I am ready to pay.
> I only ask, if I am in time and if I have the strength.
> Help me!
> '*Next to Me, in my world, one lives well,*
> *enjoying riches and good health...*'
> How many times you have invited me.
> But the guests are missing from your table.
> In a world ruled by lies, by men ready
> to betray and degrade,
> I see that there is only you watching over us,
> like the Cherubim with the flaming sword
> to gard the Tree of Life...
> I want to resume my 'journey',
> and revive my commitment to this task.
> I implore you to help me.
> For months I have been leading an itinerant life.
> I feel the need to reassemble the parts of my life
> that have been dispersed...

I was not so much writing as confessing, 'reading myself'. This effort at sincerity transformed me. The letter was received before it was even finished. It was meant for me, meant for the best part of me, for those few atoms of whatever was good, beautiful and true that still pulsed within the dark of my Being; in that part of me, among the inner multitude of dissidents and rebels, that had said yes to this great adventure. I had not yet finished it, when I burst into tears from a sudden, mysterious joy.

10 The spider and the prey

I found myself before Him. I had so wanted to see Him, but now all I felt was an infinite shame and an oppressive feeling of guilt. Shame and guilt held me in a dense world, where the force of gravity was much stronger than that of Earth. This was my interior world and these were the laws by which I, unconsciously, lived every day of my life. Only here, in the presence of the Dreamer, did I feel their weight and horror, making me hold my breath and keep my gaze transfixed on the floor of that room.

«Your every movement, thought, or word, announces your disposition to give way. Secretly you hope to fail, become sick, and give up fighting against this 'hostile' world. Like millions of men, you have seen the fight as outside of yourself. For this you abandon yourself to defeat, and hope you will get old and die... you have already done this many times before. It's time to stop... forever!» He said, and fell into silence, to let me taste to the height the bitterness of that truth. A cold sweat ran down my back.

«In the darkness of your ignorance, a man like you prepares his disasters, sets his own traps, reinforces his own prisons, packages all his pain, mishaps, accidents and ailments with great skill and attention to the smallest detail, so as to raise these labours to a fine art – said the Dreamer, sounding like a warrior throwing down a gauntlet before his adversary in a deadly duel – *a dark and unconscious art like that of a monstrous insect weaving his web in the oblivious depths of zoology. There, where man is tragically both spider and prey.»*

His words clawed at my soul, and I trembled and gasped as if I had been thrown into an icy shower after a long sleep. The Dreamer was unveiling to me how I could order a stone to appear in my right kidney and make it take the form I wished just as simply as I could have asked for harmony and success, and obtained them.

It was impossible for me to accept that I was the sole creator of my world as every attempt I made to understand was smashed to pieces against the rock of my skepticism. For the Dreamer, every obstacle we encounter is the materialisation of our inability to understand.

Man is his understanding

The measure of a man is his level of understanding which creates the world he deserves. Understanding is containment, a broadening of his vision and an elimination of excess and layers of debris. It is an act of will which cannot come from or be imposed by anything external.

A man doesn't have to look for paradise.
He doesn't have to do anything to deserve it.
The only discipline he has to master is the elimination of his hell,
his lack of understanding.

If the Dreamer had not spent all this time preparing me, had I not undergone a long period of apprenticeship, notwithstanding all my doubts and disobedience, I would never have been able to support the responsibility of such a revelation, it would have destroyed me.

I wondered what would have happened if 'official' science had announced such a discovery: that every man, as he is, is the only creator of all his disasters and that they must originate internally before they manifest themselves externally. The reognition of the degree to which the body and our own personal worlds are obedient; the discovery of the creative power, for good or bad, of our thinking, would be a much greater shock for civilization than the discovery made by Copernicus. In just the same way as his astronomical finding had cast man to the margins of the universe, outside the illusory world in which man had always placed himself at the centre, the Dreamer's vision had revolutionized his destiny, striking at his most deeply rooted prejudice; the conviction that there was an outside world to accuse and always someone or something to blame for the continuous defeat that was his life.

The world is such because you are such, the extreme synopsis of the Dreamer's philosophy and the culmination of His vision, contained such a powerful idea that it reversed the very direction of existence; no longer from the external to the internal but the contrary, from the internal towards the external, as in all healing.

The Christian *mea culpa,* the Roman faith in *homo faber*, *self knowledge* from the Ancient Greece and the voices of all the great schools of responsibility upon which empires and civilizations lasting thousands of years had been created, all echoed powerfully and solemnly together. And even though this vision had been presented to me many times, my thoughts went into a swirl when I saw my rationality and logic torn from their age old hinges and irremediably subverted.

It was then I realised that this time my encounter with the Dreamer was taking place in a part of His house that I did not know. It was not the room with the white tiled floor, nor the greenhouse with its great beams, the swimming pool in the middle and the elegant sculptures, but a large loft room furnished in a colonial style, with a ceiling inlaid with rare wood. He was sitting in the middle of a white couch made of finely plaited cane, so vast that it took up almost the whole wall. A black and white painting evoked the world of Steinbeck.

He paused again and seemed to be assessing my ability to take in what he was about to tell me. A special vibration in the air announced the crucial importance of that moment. We had arrived at another one of those crossroads of existence where you either continue onwards or lose everything. I was on the edge of a chasm and falling into it would mean that I would never see Him again. When He began speaking again, I drew a large breath to summon up some strength.

«Every stage requires one to exceed one's personal best! There are monstrous beings, millennial enemies who are as terrible and illusory as your fears, guarding the higher worlds, the highest bands of existence...»

His words were liquid fire that coursed through my veins devouring me.

«One day, you will have to confront them!»

I couldn't move a muscle and remained like that, quite still, for a long time. On every inch of my body I felt the pressure of an unknown force that restricted my every movement. Then, as though at some invisible command, I felt myself set free. I made my first cautious movements to emerge from that sheath of impotence and abandon it like a snake shedding his skin. Now I could raise my head and did so, slowly. I would not dare to allow my gaze wander freely, but I noticed that there was plenty of light this time and I could clearly see every detail of my surroundings. I was quite sure the source of that light was not the sun. The new day remained outside, clinging to the windows facing East, not yet deciding to make its way into the room. In some mysterious way, it seemed that the light in this room depended on me! I could increase it or decrease it, and did so several times, using only the 'dimmer' that was in my mind.

I was still trying out this curious power, when a thought invaded my mind with the force of a devastating truth. The universe depended on me! Just like this room, the world could have appeared full of light, but it remained in semi darkness because of my inability to make it glow. This revelation took my breath away.

Only later, when I could reflect upon things dispassionately, would I feel the full power of the Dreamer's words: *The world is such because you are such.* Man is an unhappy Being who, although surrounded by perfection and abundance, sees his world through a primitive visual apparatus, as if through the eyes of a frog, and is disappointed by what he sees.

11 The 'hide and seek' of existence

I looked up and met his sweet, yet severe gaze and detected what I thought was a shadow of apprehension mixed with pity. This frightened me more than His words and I felt like a sick man reading the severity of his condition in the eyes of his friend. Unexpectedly, I heard Him say:

«When you were a little boy you used to play 'hide and seek'...»

Immediately, the film of my life started to rewind. The sun had painted the crevices of the antique terrace liquid gold, leaving lizards open-mouthed in its path, shocked and motionless between a pot of basil and another containing a cascade of geraniums. We took turns to 'go under', our heads leaning on skinny arms against a wall, eyes closed and counting while the others scurried away to find a hiding place. *Ku –ku!* was the cry launched at those who were caught by surprise and discovered.

«This is how existence works... Ku-ku!» said the Dreamer, imitating precisely that sound of my infancy and delving effortlessly into the depths of my memories. I tried not to let go of those

refreshed images, holding on for just a little longer, trying to give names to my radiant boyhood friends on that sun-drenched terrace, but they were already disappearing, taking with them the enchanted perfume of childhood.

«Existence comes to find you, wherever you are hiding, and puts on the most horrible mask it can to reveal the state you are in. What are you afraid of? Of being poor? Of being abandoned? Of becoming ill and losing a house or a job? These are the masks that existence will wear to frighten you. Whatever a man's fear is, it will materialise in events that he will have to meet as he goes along his way. Like exams you have not passed, sooner or later you will have to confront these things again.»

I did not need to mentally review my experiences to recognise that the Dreamer was telling the truth. Yet I still resisted this idea. To view the world as a planetary mechanism for keeping mankind in a permanent state of fear and precariousness, in the grip of a constant threat, seemed to me a complete aberration.

«Only under threat can an ordinary man find the strength he needs to escape from the shadows, from the ghosts created by his childhood traumas and his guilt... A real man doesn't need these things... he lives in a perpetual 'state of certitude'» clarified the Dreamer, and emphasized the importance of this phrase with a special tone of voice.

I was perplexed.

I was hearing Him set forth a theory of planetary injustice which claimed that humanity was divided into two species: one happy and carefree, blessed by an unshakable certainty, and the other – a much larger part – prey to fear, trembling in constant expectation of problems and misfortunes. I asked Him about this, and found the Dreamer in a surprisingly understanding frame of mind.

In the world of the Dreamer, even asking a question required caution and attentiveness. In His presence, I was always mindful of what he might think or feel, of every small movement, intonation or glance. This transformed every single moment spent next to Him into the School's 'work'. But on the other hand, when I was away from the Dreamer, my concentration dissolved, my attention was drawn in a thousand different directions, and my entire Being became fragmented.

«Even the ordinary man feels secure; his certainties are his fears... his doubts are his reality. He loves them, and would not let them go for anything in the world. From his earliest childhood, he has fed himself with illusory fears, he has eaten the fruit of his negative imagination, of his reverse creativity. As a result of this, he mistakes shadows for real adversity, and lives and feels constantly under threat...»

The Dreamer explained that gradually one becomes inured to the painfulness of this condition and it becomes part of him. Pain and insecurity become natural parts of life, familiar pillars, which are so reassuring that for most men are impossible to abandon.

«*Feel safe* – He exhorted me – *There is no enemy outside. In reality, it is always you who threatens yourself. People never feel safe. Even when a man is rich, apparently with nothing to fear, he still feels doubt and a continual state of precarity. He lives in fear, uncertainty and pain... This is the only thing he knows how to do; he is indulging in an activity that rules his whole life.»*

«So there is no cure...»

«*There are no ways to make yourself feel safe* – the Dreamer told me – *there are no armour-plated doors, no strongboxes or bunkers, nor any precautions you can take.»*

And then, He recited:

Only a real dreamer can feel safe.
Dream is safety.
Doubt, fear, sufferings are illusions,
but ordinary man's sole reality.

I closed my eyes and allowed myself be lulled by the Dreamer's words... and felt that sense of security, of invulnerability, that only children feel, even though they are surrounded by nervous, fearful adults... I tried to go back, even further back, until I was merely a foetus in my mother's womb. And then I 're-membered' that wholeness, that innocence without the slightest separation, and I floated in the palpable certainty of amniotic fluid. The voice of the Dreamer recited the last few verses:

« ...To be safe, you must be without sin... without blame...»

In a flash it became clear to me that a man can only be attacked by enemies within himself. Liars, posers, cheaters, people who are full of sin, uncertainties and doubts... people who live in fear and have no way out. These are the same fears that open doors to thieves… I felt lost!... and I felt all of humanity lost with me, condemned to perpetual insecurity. Who could ever escape this? I was sliding into ever more distant and painful conditions of Being.

«Only a man who can wager everything on himself, only a man who 'desires,' asks for and does everything he can to change, can make it – said the Dreamer, interrupting my fall – *And even if to the average person he may appear rash, a risk taker or irresponsible, a man guided by integrity and conviction is always accompanied by a 'sense of salvation'. He alone knows that, in reality, he is not risking anything. In business, in the most apparently risky ventures, one who has these convictions cannot be attacked and cannot fail. Everything he touches flourishes and blooms; in any situation, even in the most desperate, he always find an answer and where events and circumstances always prove him right because he is his own solution.»*

He took up His verses again.

Feel safe permanently.
Be safe and feel immortal right now.

Then, whispering to me as if he were confiding a secret, He said:

«Even if the average man constantly feels threatened and is always afraid of someone or something, in reality, there is nothing and no one that can hurt him from the outside. The world is the projection and materialisation of our 'dreams'... or of our nightmares. The world can be either heaven or hell. Which one you choose to live in is up to you!»

The Dreamer stopped to give me time to make the appropriate observations in my ever present notebook, and then concluded:

«Be free from fear!... Fearlessness is the door to certainty and integrity, yet no amount of effort can make you fearless. Fearlessness comes by itself when you realize there is nothing to be afraid of.»

The Dreamer's revelation that no danger was external was bringing me to the edge of the frightening unknown. The prospect of having to live without fear, of enduring a condition which required one to be incessantly on guard, always making sure that even the tiniest grain of hell was filtered out, seemed to me to be even more menacing than our normal, precarious condition. To be fearful, to have doubts, to feel threatened by what happened in our lives... these were our only certainties, and, in the end, the quintessential conditions of what is considered the natural state of man. The idea of a humanity without fear was as repugnant as the prospect of discovering a new alien, extraterrestrial race, and a million light years away from my concept of mankind. This threat to our insecurity is more frightening than fear itself, just as the idea of immortality is harder to accept than the certainty of death. I was absolutely sure that any man would have been prepared to sacrifice his own life to defend, for himself and future generations, the right to experience fear and to suffer.

«Behind all pain, fear, doubt or uncertainty hides a destructive thought; and behind that destructive thought, is the cause of causes: the idea of the inevitability of death – reaffirmed the Dreamer, before continuing – *this is the real killer of humanity... the origin of every one of man's misadventures, of every war and crime in the civilizations he has created. Awareness of this seed of death in man would cancel physical death from his existence forever. Death, the stockade of limitation, protects the ordinary man from the disconcerting concept of the infinite.»*

The Dreamer explained to me that the sense of death that a man bears inside seems to originate at the moment of his birth although in reality its origins go back much further. As he comes into the world, the human Being's first sensation is that of suffocating and of being overcome. In our so-called civilised societies, life starts with one of the most brutal rituals, which the Dreamer defined as, '*a veritable welcome to Hell'*. Delivered in pain, welcomed by the blinding lights of an operating theatre, by the doctors' excited voices and the mother's screams, before being spanked and placed on a cold steel surface, the newborn receives fear as his first impression of the world, and from that moment onwards he is compelled to seek pain as his true mother.

«From that moment on, nothing will ever be as familiar as that bittersweet taste of pain» affirmed the Dreamer. The whole life of an ordinary man is ruled by that first moment, by the first taste of that liquid fire that he has felt entering his lungs in the terrifying transition from aquatic creature to air-breathing Being.

12 The bottle

Time passed in total silence and I tried to fill it by examining the notes I had laboriously taken down. I felt an irrepressible desire to know more growing within me. What is the secret of the fear and anxiety we carry inside? Why are millions of lives, like mine, so particularly unhappy? The Dreamer seeming to draw these questions from the air, broke His silence. But the words He uttered were completely unexpected.

«In New York, he always lived with a bottle of water at hand» He said loudly, in an accusing tone, as if reporting this fact to someone standing behind me.

I felt mortally embarrassed. The Dreamer accompanied His words by gesturing, pointing both His forefingers at me insistently, with a strange movement from upwards down, as if he were drawing my attention to an invisible witness. This way of excluding me from the direct conversation by placing an invisible observer between us, was painfully disconcerting. Suddenly, the false protections, compromises and masks created in stratified layers throughout my life, jumped into line one behind the other, like layers of dead skin. I lost control of the muscles in my face and felt a thousand expressions take shape in a fast forward film of grotesque grimaces. The machine had gone mad along with its management programme as if the Dreamer had opened the floodgates, and it was in that space of freedom that the memory of those years took over and the images started to flow.

From the start, those memories felt to me like fragments from someone else's life. I had been advised by doctors to drink a lot to prevent the formation of kidney stones, and over time, keeping a bottle of water near me, to hand became a habit. The bottle became a kind of prosthesis, an extra limb I could not dare to do without. One of the first effects of my encounter with the Dreamer – along with the commencement of my morning runs, through the application of His principles to my life – was the dumping of so much psychological clutter and, with it, the bottle.

«Your sickness was never kidney stones, but dependence. The stones are only a symptom, indications that point the way to the real sickness, to find a way to healing.»

He said that when we don't listen to these signals and fail to go back to the real cause, the sickness becomes more acute and the signals more insistent and painful.

On His instruction, I stopped drinking, or no more than a small amount, and the problems with my kidneys became a distant memory. Seeing all these images go past on the screen of my mind, I wondered why He had dug up this particular episode from my life. A hidden mechanism within me suddenly clicked and I was catapulted into a memory out of time, vertical to the plane of those recollections, in the eternity of one of my states of Being. I went into the distressing memories of those years. I 'remembered' that the loss of that slavery and the escape from the tyranny of fear that had made a bottle of water my inseparable companion, had not brought me any joy or relief. On the contrary! Penetrating into just one atom of that past, I discovered that, for me, this new freedom had the taste of an irremediable loss, like the loss of a dear person or the occurrence of a financial crack. Now I clearly remembered that the most difficult thing to bear had been dealing with the emptiness left by the healing. The loss, albeit only temporary, of the fear and worry of becoming ill, felt to me like the fall of some kind of vital protection, the abandonment of old, familiar handrails.

13 The real poors

The voice of the Dreamer startled me, bringing me back to my chronicler's task.

«To remove a problem or sickness from a man who is not ready, is like switching off his alarm system or removing the automatic braking system. If he is not ready, the consequences are unpredictable and He might find himself in a much worse condition than before. This is why a man cannot be helped from the outside. Once a sickness or preoccupation of any kind is removed from him, he needs to immediately replace it with another, often more serious, sickness or preoccupation, in order to reinstate the conditions that correspond to his Being, as though he were a perfect homeostatic machine.»

The Dreamer was revealing the secret of a kind of behaviour that was common to the mass of humanity. A psychological mechanism found throughout the planet that has been evident to us since the beginning of time yet whose function remains a mystery to this day. Man finds it hard to abandon his sufferings, fears and uncertainties which are things he has in abundance. He is attached to these burdens as if they were his most treasured possessions, and they prevent him from going beyond. The Dreamer explained that the reason for this was that humanity perceived them as protective shields.

"...sell what you have, give it to the poor and you will have a reward in heaven; then, come and follow me. Having heard this, the young man left saddened, as he had riches aplently."

Finally, in this parable of the rich young man, I discerned, as if through a filigreed screen, the light of the intelligence that had created it, and the treasure held for twenty centuries in those extraordinary words revealed itself in all its splendour.

The explanation of what had happened at Veronica's suddenly came to me, astonishing me. What the Dreamer had really asked the men and women at that dinner had not been to give up their riches, but rather to give up their poverty, and in reality he was showing them how to rise to a higher plane of existence. *Put someone else in your place*, He had said. This was the meaning of the parable of the rich young man, "...sell what you have, and give it to the poor". These were the poor referred to in the Gospels. Give all you have to those who are aspiring to take your place. You will then see that everything you possess, the things to which you are most attached in life, are the trappings of poverty compared to what is to come.

As a result of a particular mechanism which the Dreamer described to me in detail, everything that does not evolve in our universe, degrades over time. In our own lives, too, at any given moment, there are only two directions in which one can go: upwards, or downwards. The Dreamer called this '*the Law of Evolution*' and explained that it was universally the case in individuals, as well as in organizations, nations, and entire civilizations. Without an upward impulse, without the special energy of aspiring to be more, life curves back upon itself and degrades.

As an example, he made me consider the case of the Church, which, in certain periods of history, had not been able to find the energy to rise to a higher level. It had turned in upon itself and fallen progressively until it took a direction that was almost opposite to the original one. In this way it had negated itself, becoming an idol-worshipping, superstitious and even criminal institution with the inventions of thc Inquisition, *auto-da-fé* and the crusades, while continuing paradoxically to call itself and believe itself to be 'Christian'.

In the Gospel the rich who are condemned to stay on this side of the eye of the needle, outside the Kingdom of Heaven, were not the moneyed rich of the ancient world, but men loaded down by the detritus of negative emotions, attachments and feelings of guilt; drawn under by their weighty fear of both living and dying.

I could clearly see the disastrous result of such an inverted interpretation of this message, which for centuries had encouraged millions of people to seek privation and foster a victim mentality. I thought of the attitude of the Church, which by sympathising with, justifying, and, at times, even exalting poverty, had unknowingly perpetuated it, making it even more difficult to eradicate it from man's consciousness, and therefore, from society itself.

14 Fear is degraded love

«Fear is a drug that has always circulated in the veins of your existence. It is not the fear of something. It is simply fear – He said – *By now you are addicted to it. The conditions a man encounters in the world of events serve to reveal what he has tried to avoid and not recognise inside himself. For those who do not have a School, evil and chance are misfortunes. For those who do have a School, they become tools to recapture one's lost integrity and gain understanding. At the same time, they are symptoms, alarm bells signalling one's true condition. Contrary to what a man thinks, fear comes first; and then we choose what to fear.»*

Early in the life of an average man, doubts, fear and pain define his limits: a hypnotic and unreal space in which he feels safe, as if he were in a giant bunker which was half refuge and half prison.

«Abandoning fear is the first step towards integrity, towards a unity of Being. You can't build anything upon fear, nor can you use your intelligence with it. Fearlessness is the first rule for the warrior. Fear makes you dependent on a job and drives you seek refuge in sickness, as you have done in your past.»

The voice of the Dreamer assumed the tone of a severe exhortation when He ordered:

«Turn fear into opportunity!... Man has only two sentiments... fear, and love. These are not opposites... they are the same but on different levels of Being... Fear is degraded love and love is fear that has been overcome.»

He gave me just enough time to take my notes, and then checked to see if I had done so before going on.

«Fear is the death within you. A hero is a man without fear or inner death. Hero, from Eros, love, a-mors, meaning immortal. He who has no death within will not find it outside. The hero is a step on the ladder of humanity that is not earned in the clash of battle, but in solitude, by conquering himself. The battles serve only to make visible what the hero has already conquered invisibly. His invincibility and invulnerability are simply the demonstration that something has happened within his Being, the litmus test of his victory over death.»

The Dreamer finished this speech with a long pause. I used the time to complete and tidy up my notes. I sensed the special value of the material I had collected and the importance of the Dreamer's revelations which shone a brilliant light upon the most secret mechanisms and darkest areas of our psychology; on everything that made us a lying, fearful and mortal species.

When the Dreamer resumed, He went straight to the question of Kuwait, to the concerns I had about leaving my job and transferring to another place.

«Going to Kuwait is important for you. Externally, it is the start of a new business opportunity while internally it represents the first step towards conquering a state of apnea, a limited condition of Being in which you have wallowed for too long.»

«An 'entrepreneur' is already a man on the path towards the 'dream' – He said, in a vibrant voice, His tone was sweet – *The man who is capable of gambling his reputation and means to change things, to break out of existing situations and create better ones... is a rebel. Bringing other men together, taking responsibility for them, transmitting enthusiasm to them, making them share his own dream... these can be said to be the qualities of the entrepreneur, but in reality they are the qualities of Being; allowing access to higher steps on the ladder of human responsibility.»*

I felt the anguish grow uncontrollably inside me along with an unmistakable twinge in my kidney, my entire Being was cast in shadow and my inner world had grown dark. There is no other feeling like this, which lies exactly halfway between physical and psychological pain. Instinctively, I put my hand on the right side of my lower back.

I would have liked to draw His attention to my fear of a recurring ailment which I had hoped had gone for ever, and I would also liked to have told him about the medical examination I was about to undergo.

«*Stop being such a liar* – He said, brusquely – *You are a member of the worst possible species, of those men who lie to themselves: hypocrites... Sickness does not exist. The body never becomes ill. It can only send signals in the form of symptoms, to let you know what is missing from your Being... Sickness does not exist, what does exist is healing.*»

Then, with deliberate slowness, He continued:

«*All healing is a release from fear. Once you are free from the real cause, the symptoms disappear too.*»

I fell into complete disarray. The pronouncement that sickness, just like health, depended totally on me and that dependence and fear were responsible for my kidney stones, threw me into thoughts that rippled like circles in water, expanding until I became lost in them.

«*Up until now, you have lived the life of a parasite* – He said roughly, hauling me out of a perilous slide into self pity – *let me diagnose your sickness: irresponsibility. A man with sick kidneys is fearful, and that makes him dependent. Kidney disease means that you have communication problems, first and foremost with yourself, and then with those around you.*»

At that moment these statements seemed rather obscure to me and I responded with some scepticism. It would only be many months later that I'd discover that some of our ancestral cultures already knew that the planets, which form our solar system are analogically associated with the organs in our bodies. Classical antiquity associated the liver with Jupiter, the heart with Mars, the spleen with Saturn and the lungs with Venus. In this last case I saw confirmation of the fact that breathing is connected to our emotions, to love, in Latin '*a-mors*', meaning the absence of death.

Through breathing and its associated organs, we can control our emotions and we can fight fear. In the beliefs of the classical world we also find confirmation of what the Dreamer had just told me: that the kidneys were associated with Mercury, the winged messenger of the gods, and therefore had to do with communication. But this discovery would only come later. For the moment, I ostentatiously clung to my doubts and enquired:

«Why then is communication so easy for me and what has caused me to always work in fields where this activity is most intense?»

«Exactly this – stated the Dreamer, cutting me short – *People who have kidney problems are attracted to activities involving communication, and they immerse themselves in this activity precisely in order to achieve a balance with what they are lacking... this lack of connection, of understanding... of communion.»*

Then, with the tone of someone turning to a more serious subject, He said:

«Your fears have made a monstrous idol of the company that pays you, that reflects your dependence upon it... you have transferred your 'dream' outside of yourself... you have bartered it for a salary and a false sense of security, reducing yourself to a state of slavery. Those who depend are already in the sewer up to their necks.»

«The truth is, that like millions of others, you had decided to eliminate yourself» He concluded with a final thrust at these words.

I felt a fierce feeling of rebellion, a resentment bordering on hate which due to its suddenness and violence, terrified me. His words had touched a raw nerve and exposed that most hidden and vulnerable part of me, in the dark, blindly guiding my life. Suddenly just as quickly as they had come, those feelings of resentment and rebellion disappeared completely like ghosts of my Being. Behind them, deeper inside me, I found acceptance and gratitude. Something in me, more true and sincere than anything else, knew that meeting the Dreamer was meeting one's healing.

«Go to Kuwait – He ordered, in a fatherly tone and with unexpected gentleness – *Take that job and live the life of an entrepreneur... start taking the first breaths of a sweeter air... it will help you break down the barriers that keep you from accessing higher states of responsibility... Remove your inner obstacles to*

growth and all your personal, economic and social problems will dissolve. Fear and dependency are the same thing. One is dependent because one is fearful; and one is fearful because one is dependent. There is no war more holy than fighting and conquering this limitation... defeating fear and casting it out from your Being...»

Here He stopped and I had the impression that He was deciding whether or not to impart one last piece of information. His image was already beginning to lose definition when He said:

«In Kuwait, you will meet men and women who are precious cells of the Project.»

15 The solution comes from above

The next day, I cancelled my x-ray appointment and accepted Yusuf Behbehani's proposal. Doctor L., the director of human resources at ACO, was very surprised to receive my resignation, expressed in just a few, formal lines, and he asked to see me. I had already met him on several occasions, and the impression I had was of a severe, rather condescending man but this time our meeting was different. His life unfolded before me, *d'emblée*, as if his past and future had become compressed into that moment. I 'saw' his relationship with wife, children and the existence itself. Mr L. represented the personification of a corporate life lived horizontally, a career which was apparently successful, but was actually driven by the same fears, dependency and unhappiness as in my own life.

Once I had made my decision, everything became crystal clear and I had a sharpness of vision I had never had before. In the eyes of my ex-boss, I 'saw' the reflection of all my own insecurities and the insignificance of my life as an employee, the stifling reality of this description of the world. 'Seeing it' and feeling free was one single sensation. I was free because I could 'see' and I could 'see' because I was free. Recognising myself in this man and observing my own image reflected in his every word and gesture was like placing one foot on a step and going upwards. He could never have been my boss again. Raising myself one fraction of an inch had been enough to 'understand,' in just one instant, every aspect of that man's existence: his studies, his career and his relationships.

His private and professional life, his apparent successes and failures and everything he believed he knew and possessed was suddenly contained, and I was free. I felt my old chains breaking throughout my Being. Man's devotion to privation and the general veneration of all suffering, our attachment to lies and our unshakable faith in the inevitability of death, then appeared to me as absurd as idol worship. The encounter with Dr. L was a duel within me between the old and the new. Had I hesitated for just an instant, I would have been thrown off balance and sucked back down into the pit of dependency. But as in a medieval combat, my victory had been recorded in the world of the invisible and I was filled with the wild, nervous joy of someone who has just successfully beaten a mortal challenge.

When we parted, at the door of his office, I had the impression that Doctor L.'s eyes expressed satisfaction at my having passed this test. Our time together had given him a whiff of freedom and for a few moments he too had been able to venture forth from the prison of his role. It suddenly dawned on me that all of humanity feels joy, in unison, when just a single cell heals itself and announces the formation of a new species.

I realised that for all those years the ACO Corporation had represented not only a job and a source of income but also protection, the tangible representation of the dependent condition and it was time to turn over a new leaf.

In just a few days, I closed up the house and sent the children to stay with their maternal grandparents for a few weeks. I was ready to transfer to Kuwait City, that city state floating in a sea of oil, which was already a frontier of world business and one of the major financial centres on the planet.

As always I had Giuseppona as my ally, her eyes gleaming with excitement. Once again, she was ready. With the enthusiasm of a child, she was accepting this new adventure and the prospect of living in the Middle East for years.

«Hurry, my boy! – she said, hugging me. The bags had been put in the car and Giorgia and Luca were already inside, ready to leave – Find us a nice house… I can't wait to see the desert… I think it will be like a beach, a little bigger than Licola… And, I've always wanted to meet an Arab prince…»

Giuseppona's good humour was irrepressible and contagious. Thanks to her, this goodbye was life-enhancing for the children. Our promise to get together again soon made me stronger and even more determined as I went towards this crucial turning point.

The Dreamer was always reminding me that the 'dream' was the most real thing that existed and that the art of dreaming was an elevation of the Being that allowed one access to the world of solutions.

«*In the world of events, in the world of opposites, you can never meet with solutions. The solution is not on the same plane as the problem. The solution comes from above, and not in time! You have to know how to get into the world of solutions. When you elevate your Being, everything that had appeared nebulous becomes clear and problems that had seemed as intractable as mountains become slight bumps…*»

These words made me reflect on a vital question, on a fact which is right under our noses and yet continues to elude us, and our every attempt to understand it: throughout the entire history of the world, problems have never been solved! At most, they have been transferred geographically or in time, postponed to be resolved in the future or shifted to some other country. The changes throughout the history of humanity and the solutions found to its immense problems over time are therefore only superficial. Today these problems are exactly as they were thousands of years ago. Man was unable to solve them back then with bare hands and stone axes, and is still unable to solve them today, despite being armed with the most advanced technology.

«But we have certainly made many improvements, we are better off today…»

«*Always talking about how things have improved and believing it, is one of man's most harmful and ingrained habits. Common language is full of references to 'evolution' and 'progress', but everything remains as it was. Improvement is impossible* – concluded the Dreamer harshly – *Believing that you can improve and evolve is a part of the old humanity's cache of superstitions. It is a bigoted blind faith.*»

For thousands of years, nothing has happened. Planetary problems, from poverty to crime, conflict, and war, have remained the same from the stone age to the digital age.

«*'Improving' is the password for those bent on keeping things the way they are, for those who indulge in an obsolete and lethargic way of thinking.*»

Believing that the world can be changed from outside is the fideistic belief of a humanity without the strength to face the roots of its evil. A revolution in thinking is required. An overturning. To change reality, you need to change the 'dream'. Only the individual can do this.

Time bends and man and all his civilizations bend and deteriorate in cycles which always return to where they started, to their past, while maintaining the illusion that they are advancing towards a future. Therefore, the solution, in the life of a man as in the history of an entire civilization, can never exist within time, but on another plane, in 'vertical time', a time without time, in a raising of the quality of thought that can only take place in this very instant.

«Only by managing the instant suspended between nothing and eternity, can humanity shape its destiny and create events of a higher order.»

As had happened before at every stage in my life when I was guided by the Dreamer, from that moment on everything adopted ideal proportions, falling into place like pieces in a perfect jigsaw puzzle. Once taken, the decision resolved situations that had been stagnating for too long, and in which I had been indulging myself.

«First things first! As soon as you put the most important thing, the 'dream', your evolution, before all other things... when you remember Me... a sense of discrimination will emerge... you will know what to do and what not to do... When you start to observe yourself and know yourself, everything that is right will start to happen and whatever is not part of the 'dream', whatever is not useful, or is damaging or superfluous, will start to dissolve.»

I could feel the truth of these words at all times and I touched it with my hands. Everything which was part of the past simply disintegrated, without any effort, and without any regret or attempt to hold onto it on my part. Like Noah, I could only take with me the seeds of my new world.

On the surface, I was abandoning the security of a job, a stable family life and a house for a business venture in a far off land. Only the years spent with the Dreamer, the long work of self observation, and His presence, made me see that what I was really renouncing was the lie and dependency that still pushed me to believe in the certainty of a 'secure job', in protection and help from the outside world.

Gretchen was the epitome of that outside world, she was its representative and loyal custodian, always careful to feed and perpetuate its way of thinking, feeling and perceiving life. As I had expected, when the moment came, she could not bring herself to leave the Alps for the sands of the Middle East. That woman and all she represented, could not follow me in the direction I was going. Exactly what had happened with Jennifer was repeating itself. Every time I said 'yes' to the Dreamer it meant death to a world of falseness, compromise and hypocrisy. For Him my certainties were old rubbish which I had to trade in as soon as I could for something of real value but still invisible to me.

These changes, which were so radical and apparently sudden, were actually just the result of a fraction of an inch of understanding, achieved by years and years of effort. Notwithstanding this, it was to take years of more preparation and several more falls from grace into error to be able to advance and absorb His words more fully and profoundly.

As I gave more of my space to the principles of the Dreamer, Gretchen could only dissolve with the rest of the insincerities and ghosts of my past life. She went back to New York, her letters became more and more infrequent and we never saw each other again. The idols I had worshipped, the things I had most firmly believed in, were crumbling around me. All my old priorities were being overturned. My career, family, money, an entire set of values were all taking a new shape. Something extraordinary was coming into my life, and in a simple way, something gentle, sincere and true was creating space for itself.

V. Goodbye to New York

CHAPTER VI

To Kuwait City

1 This is economy!

I leaned back in my chair, stretching my legs under the long mahogany table. It had been an intense day, full of commitments, and every day had been like this for months. We had been working in a kind of joyous disorder; the offices cluttered with boxes of new equipment and furniture that had arrived from Europe. The twin towers of the Al Awadi Center, where I had established our new headquarters, were silent at that time of night, while the monotonous hum of the air-conditioning was reassuring, like the purr of a huge mechanical cat. Outside in the darkness, Kuwait City was a handful of diamonds sparkling among the coils of the Ring Roads, the city's concentric beltways. The country's sole highway drew a line of lights towards the wells, several miles to the North-West. The huge extraction pumps were panting, their heads like those of great saurians emerging from mineral oceans millions of years old.

It was evening now, but the temperature outside was still unbearable with the heat surpassing every record that day. The Emir had issued a decree for all work-related activities to be suspended if the temperature rose above 40 C. I smiled at the thought that from that day on, no official thermometers would ever register a temperature above 40, thus offering an elegant solution to the humanitarian issue and the problem of costs due to work stoppages.

With the relocation of the offices and technical assistance departments to the business unit in Al Awadi Towers, the company I had started in Kuwait was now fully operational and already proving to be one of the most productive activities of the many businesses in the Behbehani holdings. I had chosen the most qualified managers and technicians, from every corner of Europe and the United States, for this enterprise, and as the ongoing development of the sector demanded, other people were appearing in this exciting climate, the kind of climate which always accompanies epic deeds and the conquest of new frontiers. I had signed a contract with each of them, requiring that they stay in the Middle East for at least three years. It had not been easy to find and select them, but persuading them to come to Kuwait City had been even more difficult. This small army of expatriates had a thousand problems and endless needs: from obtaining visas to finding accommodation and getting their families settled. I spent days and nights organizing and planning all that was necessary to make the enterprise run smoothly, and ensuring the well-being of all those men for whom I was responsible. Now that I was in charge, I wanted to do everything I could for them; all that I would have wanted for myself if I had been in their position. But in spite of all my efforts, I never managed to satisfy them.

With all their different languages, nationalities and professions, I had assembled a little tower of Babel, a multiform body, happily heterogeneous, and it continued to grow every day, following the design of a perfect gestation. Each element and each man fused naturally, falling into place along the weft of that densely woven fabric, and I soon came to feel that this team was an extension of myself.

To put yourself at the service of these men,
working for their well-being,
means constantly remembering the principles of the dream...
The change in you will make them more alive, responsible, free.
The leader's integrity is the solution.
This is economy!

Now, alone with my thoughts, I reviewed His words in my mind. Fragrances from my childhood permeated the air and I felt light and festive. In my mind I could see all the men and women who were working for me. I saw their faces again as I listened to the Dreamer's timeless words:

"Looking after them, serving them and loving them is the task of a leader. Even the most distant cell in an organisation must be tended in order for it to evolve and progress rapidly."

2 Forgetting the 'dream'

During those months of construction, I was so intensely absorbed in my new life that I forgot the Dreamer's advice and lost the wonder of the game. For increasingly long periods of time I lived in a kind of constriction, without breathing the pure air of His teachings, and I forgot my search. Worries and anxieties, which I mistook for the signs and irrepressible effects of responsibility, caged me to such an extent that I came to believe that everything depended on my decisions and strategic choices.

«*Everything is already done* – the Dreamer repeatedly tried to warn me, foretelling the disastrous path on which I was taking my first steps – *Everything is already done. You only have to reap the harvest...*»

But these words fell on stony ground, or rather they shattered against the ramparts of my presumptuousness. I felt sure that my management of the operations, along with their growing success, was the natural result of abilities and talents that I had always possessed. The thousands of situations in a business, with all their snares and ambushes, and the struggles to prove oneself and succeed, kept me ever more painfully tense, worried and sad.

One evening we were driving along the corniche, on our way to dinner at Riccardo's, the most improbable traffic was flowing past: Bentleys and Ferraris pressed forward beside old Mercedes and pick-ups, bedizened like camels on parade and I had difficulty hearing what the Dreamer was saying to me. Suddenly every sound ceased and as if at an invisible command, the cars drew up to the pavement, or stopped in the middle of the road. Prayer rugs were unrolled towards Al-ka'aba to welcome the genuflections of hundreds of drivers who had been transformed, as if by magic, into a throng of worshippers. Under a sky now thick with stars, the seafront had become a huge mosque. In that silence, the Dreamer's voice reached me with an indescribable intensity.

«*These men are on the very same path as you. They genuflect five times a day and pray to attain the same goal as yours. But the paradise they believe in will never come. Paradise is a state of Being... The afterlife is this world, without limits. Religion with its mass rituals is illusion...*»

Later that evening, having waited for the right moment, I asked Him to tell me more. He explained to me that religions, ideologies and science are bridges we must cross, transcend, and then abandon. Once their task is done, we have to free ourselves from them; but due to our indulgence, they turn into prisons of dogma and superstition, mortal traps. For humanity as it is, aggressive and conflictual, for people who would destroy themselves and others if left to their own devises, religion is an instrument of social control, of prevention and containment of criminality; tasks it shares with law courts, sheriffs and prisons.

«Remember your goal – He concluded – *If you truly want to turn your destiny into a great adventure, remember the principles of the 'dream'... Man's indulgence in negative emotions and destructive thoughts is the true cause of all his troubles. Be alert! Don't allow even one atom of pain to enter. Use whatever means you must, but close each of your mortal wounds immediately!»*

Despite the Dreamer's presence and His recommendations, I inevitably found myself retracing the same old lines of an unhappy existence. On that occasion as well, the Dreamer had to end our meeting with a threat.

«Let your revolution begin! – He commanded – *or one day you'll find yourself genuflecting with this crowd hoping to propitiate a divinity outside yourself.»* Then in a whisper, fierce as the hiss of a huge predator, He added:

«Change! Or I'll have to replace you with someone who is more prepared.»

The pressure at work increased every day as the company grew and its operations expanded. At night I would wake up with my heart beating tumultuously, keeping me awake for a long time. Providentially, every so often, like a ray of sun coming through the bars of a prison, the memory of the Dreamer would come and give me respite. A breach opened up in that wall of forgetfulness, and for a few moments, I was able to connect with Him again. I no longer wanted to abandon that place in the Being, that timeless island where there were no worries, uncertainties or dread. But that state passed in the blink of an eye. Soon the fears and doubts – that had receded for a short time – returned even more strongly than before. I could feel myself suffocating, before nausea took over, and my mind was again at the mercy of an army of dark thoughts.

That evening, silence and solitude appeased my reflections, and I opened my notebook 'at random'. The Dreamer's words appeared, vivid and powerful:

«Every man is the sole artificer of his assigned reality. The world is a large screen on which we project the ghosts of our life... Outside ourselves, there's no force, beit known or unknown, natural or supernatural, that can influence our destiny... Whatever the events of our life may be, they cannot manifest themselves without our consent... Do not believe that this world exists outside of yourself. Try to realize that all that you believe to be coming from 'out there' starts instead in yourself and nowhere else. Your recognition of an inner cause responsible for all that happens outside yourself makes evil, sufferings and death totally disappear from the earth.»

I raised my eyes, struck and suddenly enchanted by the darkness framed in the marble arabesques of the three-mullioned Moorish windows. I realized how different my life was now from what it had been in the past and I experienced an intense moment of gratitude for how much I had received and for all that was happening in my existence. A single drop from a superior world is enough to dissolve all calamities of a life.

I scrutinized that environment and its every detail with a new clarity. I surveyed the opulent, showy, Middle Eastern elegance of the conference room and through the half-open door, I glanced at the haphazard stacks of boxes strewn across the rich carpets. The following day my men would unpack and assemble the equipment and furniture and I imagined their smiling faces. At that moment I sensed that I was not alone and my heart was beating wildly as I slowly turned my chair towards that presence.

3 Worry is an animal instinct

He was there, a few steps away from me. Elegantly dressed in His timeless style, the Dreamer sat slightly turned away, with His legs crossed. His look was that of someone who was perfectly at ease, and He seemed engrossed in reading a small, finely bound book. He did not look at me nor did He show any sign of having noticed me. How long had He been there?

I did not have time to get over my surprise before He had already started His theme - without preamble, as usual.

«Men like you, identified with the description of the world, worry because they've forgotten the wonder of Being» He said, never taking His eyes off the book. A pause followed, as if He were musing on His own statement. Then, without bothering to hide His disgust at the very thought of it, He added:

«Worry is an animal instinct!»

I had not seen Him for months and finding Him before me again so unexpectedly and so close that I could touch Him, gave me contrasting feelings. Once I'd overcome my surprise, I felt the sudden, tumultuous joy of someone wandering in the desert who sees in the distance the miracle of a palm tree grove. But that joy was quickly clouded by unpleasant emotions and I felt a long-stifled regret emerging. For many long months, He had left me to face this task alone, and it was beyond my strength. How many times had I regretted having listened to Him. How many times had I endured desperation, feeling myself trapped, without the strength to go forward, without the possibility of going back. I had yearned for the wretched security of a salary, longing to take refuge again in that dark womb of slavery. Even blind suffering, the dull pain of my life before the Dreamer, had come to seem preferable to that exhausting climb. I tried to contain myself, but I could not avoid an aggressive reaction, almost an open challenge.

«If worry is an animal instinct – I snapped, feeling my facial muscles grow rigid, losing control of my expressions – then what is one supposed to do? If we don't worry, if we don't think about it, then who does?»

The Dreamer didn't react. He continued to read His little book which was open in the palm of His left hand. Now that I'd uttered those words, I wanted to go back, rewind the tape of time and erase them. But it was too late. The violence and arrogance in my tone turned back against me; I felt crushed under the weight of a huge boulder. At least I had managed to avoid saying 'I'. Absurdly, this gave me some slight relief. The silence continued, growing deeper and more painful. In the meantime I remained quite still, watching Him read. When He stopped, I was seized with anxiety, sensing an imminent and unknown danger. Unhurriedly, He closed the small book keeping His middle finger between the pages, like a bookmark, and raised His eyes until He rested them on me with an intensity that I was unable to bear. For a moment I perceived the huge expanse that separated us and a dizzying sweep of light years measured the distance between our two Beings.

«You still belong to a world that believes it acts and make choices... a world where people make plans and programmes... and where the breath of existence passes unnoticed» He said, scolding me as a strict father might. Then, becoming imperceptibly more gentle, He said:

«The only planning a man can do is to develop himself and nourish his own 'dream'. All the rest will be added... Abandoning an atom of fear moves mountains, and projects you like a giant into the world of events.»

«How is it possible to avoid worrying about the future?» I asked with trepidation, dreading the painfulness of the Dreamer's intervention. Then, encouraged by a gleam of benevolence, I added:

«How can we live without plans, without making programmes?» I spoke gently and respectfully, trying somehow to remedy the coarseness of my first remarks.

«Planning is a form of exorcism, an escape from reality – responded the Dreamer – *Man calms his fear of the future with the false security of expectations, through rituals made up of plans and programmes. Faced with apparent uncontrollability and the unexpectedness of existence, men like you have always resorted to rules and formulae, they're deluded into bending the universe through the deforming lens of rationality, replacing it with a more reassuring description of the world. But none of this has been able to alleviate the sensation of their* own *precariousness or sense of peril»* He concluded, as if observing the bottom line of a bitter balance sheet.

«But what can we do to foresee what is about to happen; how can we protect ourselves without making plans?»

«Making plans is like digging a well and expecting it to contain the immensity of the ocean. This shield of weakness, this armour of illusion that makes you feel protected, the frail mental screen that you've placed between yourself and reality, rips open, and suddenly a man is confronting an abyss, the immensity of life as it is, and not as it has been described to him.»

Long-held beliefs and practices in organizations, theories of decision-making, business strategies, models, managerial grids and skills; and the entire arsenal of theories and technology learnt during the study of economics and business in Italy, the States or Great Britain, were collapsing on top of me like stone idols.

«But in order for a manager to make decisions, will he still have to plan his operations and those of his colleagues; will he still have to set out objectives to be accomplished?» I asked, a moment later, in a feeble attempt to save at least a few of the convictions on which I had founded my life and the illusion of being able to manage my company in Kuwait.

«Don't hide behind the mask of a role! – thundered the Dreamer, in a tone that had become aggressive again – *Don't say "a manager", say: "what can 'I' do?" Deliberately use this little 'I' and take responsibility! The universe listens to you. Always!... and it weighs you even when you ask a question.»*

An old wound opened inside and I felt the searing pain of resentment and humiliation, as though a Barnabite's stick had struck the palm of my hand. In an instant I was back inside the walls of my old parochial school set like a white pearl in the bowels of Naples. And I felt the healing. When those images disappeared I found myself again before the Dreamer, innocent once more. Now at last was I able to listen to Him.

«A true leader plans and makes programmes just as all the others do, but without believing in them. His planning is a performance that respects the actions and roles of an invisible theatrical script. Every moment is an act of creation... every moment is new – finished the Dreamer – *There's never been a moment before, or a moment after... Nor will there ever be!... All that you see... and all that you don't, is created in this very moment... Everything happens now, in this eternal instant, in the omnipotence, in the infinite space of your Being.»*

The Dreamer accompanied these words by pulling an invisible thread between His finger and thumb from the sky, tracing a vertical line through the air to the world.

«The moment is the territory of the 'dream'... An ordinary man's plan happens in time and space... sooner or later it plummets and fails.»

«But isn't 'dreaming' also a kind of plan?» I asked with the comfort of surrender, growing more and more fascinated by His vision.

«The 'dream' is a plan that happens without time... in eternity, in vertical time... I am this moment... This moment contains

all that I will find and gather through time... crumbs, fragments of me. This is why a dreamer neither makes plans, nor worries. He allows the 'dream' to express itself in all its freedom, all its beauty... he knows the results will come naturally, through his level of faultlessness and integrity. Deep within you is a unified field of limitless possibilities. It is here that your dream takes place. It is here that whoever or whatever is necessary to create prosperity and success in your life, appears. It is here that your purpose in life becomes very clear to you.»

Then in the tone of someone presenting a mathematical proof, He continued:

«In all companies and in every organisational pyramid, the lower the level of responsibility, the greater necessity there is for planning. The more it descends towards those who play minor roles, the more it becomes necessary to plan every minute detail, to set and execute precise objectives. There, all rituals in a decision-making process are scrupulously followed, but by means of these men and women nothing happens.»

The air was still vibrating with these words when the lights of the conference room, where we had remained, dimmed. Slowly a screen came down and covered the back wall and I had the impression that the walls and the ceiling were disappearing. I felt some sharp jerks as the armchair shifted, as if it were now on a moving platform, or some extraordinary, invisible vehicle.

4 Escape is only for a few

Images began to flow across the screen. I saw human masses groping in the corridors of organisations, crowding the 'open spaces' or caged in cubicles, which were like insects' cells.

«These are shadows – He said to me – *Nothing has been done so far to change this humanity, and ferry it towards a new species. Only an 'Individual Revolution' will reverse the way that millions of men and women think and feel, trapped in their hypnotic sleep.»*

The 'Individual Revolution'.

Those two words would come to be of decisive importance in my life, but at that moment, they meant nothing to me; even though they were an announcement of the Project, for which the Dreamer had been preparing me for years. But it was too early then, because He still had to reveal its magnificence to me.

I visited the lowest levels of organisations with the Dreamer, and with Him, I penetrated those thick, slow worlds, swarming with prisoners. With bated breath, I witnessed the succession of those images. I watched men and objects floating in the greenish liquid of an immense aquarium, poorly illuminated by livid neon lights. I had lived there for so many years, yet it was only now that I realised how painful the experience had been and how difficult the condition was for those creatures, condemned every day to breath the air which they themselves polluted.

All of a sudden, the glass that contained that sick universe became reflective, and in it I saw the images of two decrepit figures, both grey and bent. I noted their wrinkled skin, split like burnt earth, while the creases in their faces were so deep they seemed like scars. Something in their appearance was disturbingly familiar.

I scrutinised them, forcing myself to discover what could be the cause of that worrying sensation, and when I recognised them, I was horrified: those two old people were... the Dreamer and myself! Terrified, I turned to Him... I saw that He was perfectly in control and His harsh face was younger than ever. He gave me an encouraging smile that cheered me, but my soul remained seized by a mute desperation.

I saw a boundless number of young people waiting in line, in whose eyes, one could still perceive a flash of light. Like a human ribbon, they flowed past a fierce examiner who, one by one, discarded them, or assigned them work. Like Minos with his coiled tail, he indicated to each one a situation of pain, a 'permanent position' in the infernal circles of the organisations. With emotion I observed their pallor, their gazes that were not completely dead. I knew they were condemned to unhappiness.

«Being chosen is below dignity – said the Dreamer – A *man 'dreams' his work and chooses it according to his intent, his partiality.»*

He noticed my compassion for their destiny, and plucked the question I wanted to ask Him from the air, anticipating me:

«Evolution of the masses is impossible! No revolution or ideology can succeed... Escape is only for a few... Only the individual can make it...» My expression remained painfully absorbed. I felt myself to be the representative of a species who at

the bar listens to the announcement of an unfavourable and final sentence.

«What you're looking at is not humanity – He said, revealing my incomprehension – *The crowd that you see is not outside of you!»*

I thought the Dreamer, Himself, was making me confront my falsehood, unmasking my false altruism and my presumption of being able to do something for others and I was mortified. But the Dreamer's lesson was a long way from being over. With a turn of the screw He made His examination even more ruthless and thorough.

«That multitude you see is your own degradation. Those men disheartened by pain and the dread of competition, are the scattered fragments of your Being, the reflected image of the desperation you bear inside.» Through me the Dreamer was scourging the Pharisee in the temple. I felt some disfigured part of me being turned out, laid bare and exposed to the world. My mortification turned into a more honest feeling, an irresistible shame that seared me from head to toe.

«You can only do for yourself! – He said gruffly, wanting to shake me out of that state – *They are you!... Your own change will transform all mankind... If you want this suffering to stop, and mankind to change, heal yourself!»* I reeled at those words, at the announcement of such responsibility. It was as though an armoured door was sealing off every means of escape behind me. I could not blame or commiserate with anyone and a vice gripped my stomach. In my desperate search for a refuge, I hid amid the pages of my notebook. I bent to the notes trying to gather my churning thoughts and concentrate on what He was saying. According to the Dreamer, the only possibility for humanity, the only way to progress, is to construct an integral man.

«This is the only salvation for the masses» He declared.

He continued, claiming that man is still a Being in transition, with an incomplete psychology. The evolution of the species is a journey towards integrity; it has to be performed from the inside to the outside through a process of unification that cannot be imposed on it. This is why all the old systems have failed. Wars and revolutions do not succeed. With my mind in turmoil, I was taking notes, compulsively underlining the Dreamer's statements many times.

«Man's next evolutionary passage cannot take place in a historical future, but in a 'timeless time', a vertical future» He said. As if I were peering through a sudden rip in a curtain, suddenly I could clearly see the evolutionary sense of human organizations, and the reason for all their apparently foolish pain. A man's aspiration to transcend himself and his millenary search to give meaning to his existence, was moving from the traditional grounds of religion and politics to that of economics, enterprises, factories, industries, laboratories and offices. Man's exodus towards integrity was taking place in those organizations, just as it was on spacecraft launched towards other worlds. Enterprises and organisations, and the endless network of temples and oracles of business, were replacing convents and churches, changing into places of aspiration and evolution.

«Future organisations will be Schools of the Being» prophesied the Dreamer, coining one of His epigraphs destined to be engraved in the skies. Then He pronounced words that would always remain imprinted on my mind:

«Business will be the religion of the planet, the religion of religions. It's in Business, more than in convents, mosques or ashrams, that men are engaged in a titanic effort aimed at the highest levels of responsibility. It's in Business that adversity and difficulty are being converted into a propellant to be used on the journey towards freedom. It's in the skyscrapers of multinationals and the temples of finance, more than in synagogues and monasteries, that men are attempting the impossible: reversing their vision... changing their destiny.»

The immensity of that vision made me tremble, and just listening to that prediction demanded a responsibility that I still did not possess. In its design one could sense, decades early, the revolution that would heave the entire economic system off its ethical cornerstones, and demand an end to the old 'rational capitalism'. The Dreamer's message held the secret for the School's success: all companies, big or small, will one day become schools of aspiration and responsibility. At their summit there will be visionaries, both philosophers and men of action, aware that economic success and longevity of their company is at one with the evolution of each of their men. To know this long before any other university, would create an unbeatable competitive advantage.

At that time I could not know that. It was as if the Dreamer, along with the task of creating a car industry, had entrusted me with the complete designs to build the engine of the future. His message contained the life breath of ESE, The European School of Economics's planetary philosophy, the uniqueness of the Work it would take forward, the grandeur of its scope: preparing visionaries, philosophers of action.

«Dreaming is the development of an internal world, which prevents you from being merely a function of life, a mechanical puppet of the external world of appearances. The object of the School is freedom: freedom from conflict, suffering, division and death.

The 'dream' is something you place between yourself and life... The ordinary man thinks that life is the cause and he is the effect. Only work on the Being, the work of a School of overturning, can subvert this disastrous vision of the world.

The work of a true School is a labour of excavation... a work that will eliminate dross, stratifications and pollution... in search of something that we once possessed, that made us integral, happy, immortal: will.

The School and Will are a single thing. The School is Will outside us. Will is the School within us.

When the 'true will' emerges, you'll no longer need the School. When Will is unearthed we'll be masters of ourselves. And to be masters of ourselves means being masters of the universe.

Underneath all and everything there is 'something precious' that is rightfully ours. It is our contact with this 'very thing' that will lead us to possess all and everything.»

5 Make programmes but don't believe them

Here we started to rise again. With Him I climbed the paths that led to the richest and most brilliant sectors in business. The Dreamer showed me that behind the biggest multinationals, the world's financial and industrial giants, beyond every human achievement, there is invariably an individual and his dream.

Climbing up the pyramids of decision-making to the summits, up there, where the organisation reaches its utmost velocity, He showed me the immobility which had given rise to that action, and the invisibility that had produced that brilliant idea. As for the founder, the visionary man, the bright madman, the pragmatic utopian, he, and he alone had allowed that world to exist and, like a termite queen, still nourished it.

«His only operation is caring for his integrity – He revealed – *What makes him special is his capacity for alertness, a spirit of vigilance that doesn't allow any doubt, or shadow of a compromise to make a rift in his determination; nor does it allow even a single opaque atom to enter and pollute the 'dream'.»*

Because of a leader's psychological swiftness, programmes and plans are too slow and rigid to be valid instruments. At the point where decision-making requires a sixth sense: intuition, and a seventh sense: the 'dream', there is, in reality, nothing to decide.

«A true leader makes programmes, but without believing them – He claimed – *His aspiration guides him, and he believes only in his faultlessness...»*

«He has no objectives outside himself – He continued – *because the objective is himself... his freedom!»*

Having reached that level of integrity, it will be his vision that creates the way, his step that creates the path. He will have no need to choose a direction, because he is the direction; the inventor of the dream that is unfolding and taking shape in the world of events.

«Commit yourself to integrity – the Dreamer ordered me, enunciating these words slowly and clearly to underline their importance – *Inner commitment is investment. It is your commitment that makes things happen! It is the incorruptibility of the leader that attracts all opportunities and necessary resources... The solemn promise that he has made to himself to honour the Game to the very end. The success of each of his actions in the external world is only a reflection of his integrity.»*

The accomplishment of enterprises at the edge of the impossible, the creation of immense wealth, the foundation of economic empires, these are only an extension of his Being; an authentication of his degree of interior freedom and level of responsibility. If a man maintains the integrity of his commitment, success is inevitable, it is the natural product of integrity.

«A true leader knows that true business is only internal! He's the incorruptible guardian of his own promise. This is what he must keep intact» said the Dreamer in conclusion. Then he fell silent.

Images of financial empires and boundless fortunes succeeded each other for a few seconds on the screen. As they dissolved, a deep silence permeated the meeting room. His stern eyes were scrutinising me, observing the effect of those revelations. I felt my being literally turned upside-down. In the inner shop, prices and merchandise had been tossed into the air and were now being rearranged. New priorities were marking the right price on the right merchandise, while a new order was assigning placement on the shelves, relegating old beliefs and dusty principles to the storeroom.

I closed my eyes and wished with all my heart for that operation to end. When He began to speak again, He took up the question of immobility. For the leader the most powerful action at his disposal is doing through 'not doing', acting without acting. The Dreamer defined it as 'an effortless action': a poetic, dreamy state of suspension...

«*For the leader, solitude and immobility are accumulators of power* – He concluded – *the state in which he senses and attracts precious messages from the Will is now buried in man... Be serious, be sincere and you will feel it strong and clear... and you will know.*»

At those words my imagination veered away. I visualised endless masses of dependent people. From above, I watched thousands of men and women; their constant comings and goings. The images were vivid and real. I focused my mind on them and saw pathetic beings with their restless behaviour, their fluttering, mechanical gestures, moving as in a comical sequence of silent film. The Dreamer interrupted my reveries at this point; He penetrated my reflections and guided them. After so many years spent in organizations, only now, with Him, did I realise that the more agitated their movements, the more worried, and busy people appear to be; the more insignificant their positions, and the lowest levels of responsibility and compensation.

«*From the motionless void, I move the 'wheel' of the entire universe... and the beings that are on its circumference, on the spokes, on the hub*» solemnly recited the Dreamer.

«*That void at the centre of the hub is the true creator of the 'wheel'... and it's on that invisibility there rests the hierarchical pyramid of beings that constitute it*» He finished, and fell silent.

Who was this being subverting my life?

I felt my jumbled thoughts come into harmony within me; emotions and scattered parts of my being gathered together. A torrent of energy increased, carrying away doubts, worries, and everything that was dead inside me. With Him economy and business exceeded their limits to become poetry, and went beyond, a universal art. I wanted to maintain that state of understanding: the clarity and lucidity of that moment; that sensation of being able to contain everything and anything. It was then that He showed me how to live strategically and spoke to me about the *art of acting.*

«A leader has to know how to act all the roles to perfection – He said – *He can fake absent-mindedness, ignorance and even negativity if his role requires it, but he doesn't have to believe it!»* He cautioned. The urgency of his tone implied that this was a matter of life or death.

«He can get angry and violent, he can change his face into a mask of aggressiveness, but inwardly he doesn't need to feel even slightly affected.»

This performance of negativity He called the '*right negative attitude'*.

He added that, through *acting* a leader may programme, make plans and pretend to project into the distant future.

«But without believing them!» He repeated in the same peremptory tone.

A free man, a real man, knows that every moment requires a strategy; every instant has its statute, and he imposes a script that must be performed flawlessly. The detachment of those who are conscious of acting, allows them to choose between different courses of action and possible roles, such as choosing which mask to put on in order to perfectly align themselves with circumstances and the events that they confront.

«Only a real man can act! – He announced firmly – *An ordinary man, identified with his role, conditioned by his fears, hypnotised by the description of the world, has forgotten the art of acting, the power of acting, and knows only falsehood.»*

Many times, at crucial points in His speech, I had tried to shield myself from those subversive ideas. To me, the leader's acting skills seemed very close to lying, to opportunism.

«Acting consciously doesn't mean lying – roared the Dreamer – *Acting means living strategically!»* It was clear that the Dreamer had free access to my every thought. My surrender to this clarity dispersed the shadows before they even gathered.

«Living strategically is the action of a warrior who intentionally and flawlessly performs the acts that the situation

requires. Externally he responds to the need of the role... at the same time, internally, he takes possession of the responsibility and power that hides behind that mask. Only those who live strategically can make it!»

He waited for this statement to produce its effect, scrutinising me like a doctor who had just injected an antidote into a drug-addict and when He started to speak again, his voice was serious, somewhere between a warning and the solemn announcement of some vital knowledge:

«When you worry, when you plan and think negatively, when you forget what you've endured until now, you reduce yourself to the dimensions of an insect and the world gets the upper hand. Thousands of frames of film in the universe record your defeat, and not only will you not get any more, but whatever you think you already have will be taken away.»

The Dreamer was giving me some final advice before throwing me back into the jaws of the world. His voice became lower, until it turned into a whisper. He was about to tell me something that would become the cornerstone of all that I would build in my life and the first principle for all prosperity.

«The 'dream' is the most real thing that exists!... The 'dream' is reality without time... Only a man who dreams can create wealth.»

According to the Dreamer the 'dream' is the sublimated world, the real cause of all that you see and touch.

«The 'dream' is vertical planning that only a visionary can know... The 'after' doesn't exist if not in the imagination... Inwardly, every instant is a shop that opens and closes, and at every moment one gains and looses. Every moment is a success or a failure. Everything takes place now, in this eternal instant.»

6 The Diary

«A diary stuffed with appointments, like yours, with no room left – the Dreamer began, indicating one of the pages that was densely covered in names, times and telephone numbers – *is a declaration of suicide. It means affirming one's own death... The more dead a man is, the more he fills his day with engagements.»*

It was like a punch in the stomach. That pain I knew so well by now was a sure sign that the Dreamer's new attack on my system of beliefs was effective. I tried to flee from the speed of those powerful, direct words. Feelings of aversion, and violent thoughts against the Dreamer joined forces into an uncontrollable *crescendo* inside me. I rebelled against being classed as a dead man just because I had an active and busy existence.

«But it's impossible to live in the context of a 'modern society' without having obligations, appointments or meetings» I said, resentful. I emphasized the words 'modern society' sarcastically, as if to demarcate the difference between our worlds. I was certain that everything that the Dreamer was claiming had no practical sense. Once He said to me: "*Let the game continue, let the comedy unfold... allow collaborators and professionals to do what their role demands. The company is a theatrical representation... with masks and characters who follow a script... Don't believe it! Don't lose your way!... don't forget it's a game.*"

I was sure the Dreamer had no idea what it meant to manage an international company with hundreds of collaborators, and to feel the shareholders breathing down one's neck every day.

«So – I said, in exasperation – I don't understand!... What can an appointment book possibly have to do with being dead or alive?...» I hardly managed to pronounce these words as a lump of emotion sealed my throat.

«Every appointment you make, every meeting you arrange – said the Dreamer, apparently without noticing my secret cry for help which was hidden by my aggressiveness – *serves to strengthen your illusion of being alive, to corroborate yourself in your foolish convictions. First of all being able to plan. Planning and believing it is like dying. One can only plan what is dead...*

The true plan is in this moment, in the 'here and now'...

A leader can have armies of collaborators who make plans and programme future operations in every detail, but his own decisions will always be the fruit of the moment. Until that moment he doesn't know, nor does he act until the moment reveals its eternity. Only then will he know what he needs to know.

Everything will be at your disposition once you have learned to live the moment in its entirety. Plans and programmes arise naturally, without effort, when you cease believing in them.»

His gaze turned to steel and, still looking at me intently, He moved His head first to the left, then to the right, as if He were evaluating my countenance. I began to feel uneasy. There was a silent and impending menace in His movements, like those of a predator who hides his ferocious intent.

«For men like you, a little book that says how busy you are helps you to forget» He said in a low voice.

At once my mild worry became terror. I had to find a way out of that state, whatever the cost. The moment required a lightness of touch I didn't have; I should have simply been able to ask Him to explain that bizarre and perhaps even comic vision. How can a pocket diary help anyone to forget? But I felt wrapped in a psychological cocoon from which I was unable to free myself. That meeting with the Dreamer was exposing a mortal duel between the part of me that refused to yield, and the other part, thirsty and parched, that was ready to drink His words.

I could hardly summon the breath to ask:

«Forget what?»

Slowly the Dreamer moved a few millimetres closer to me.

«Forget yourself» He murmured.

My dread had grown into an irrational, devastating fear. In time, I would come to recognise the fundamental stages of my evolution in moments like this; when the Dreamer, penetrating the armour of my unshakeable certainties, managed to deposit a little of His precious substance like a bee pollinating a flower. This is how I came closer to the 'dream'.

«The world is the unfolding in time of all that we dream... An appointment is always with yourself... or better, with a part of you as yet unknown to you. Men and events rise and dissolve following a script already written in the Being...

When you plan and believe it... you are moving away from the 'real world'... The more you convince yourself that appointments and meetings happen as you have programmed them, the more you strengthen your sense of death... And this is how you come to meet dead people who make plans and schedules just as you do. And others under the illusion that they are making choices and taking decisions. They never recognize their true powerlessness.»

Here the Dreamer paused, and I believed that His work of demolition was finished. I desperately needed to draw breath. But the Dreamer never left a job half done. He calibrated his timing with great precision, and then delivered the punch-line of that extraordinary lesson.

«One day your agenda will be like that of a free man, a man who truly acts and does so because he knows that he always has the solution within him... that he himself is the solution. You'll act out the meetings and roles and let the world be free to happen... in the best possible way. The world will become your masterpiece without effort or constraint. Only then will your agenda be that of a true leader... and it will contain only blank pages.»

7 "Hello, who am I?"

The day had begun on an early morning high note. From the terrace of the house in Samia I had already answered several different telephone calls. The Dreamer was at my side and watching me in silence while I, involved in ongoing events, lost in the content of the conversations, issued orders, raised my voice, grew angry, and in a couple of cases, actually lost my temper.

Every so often I turned to glance at the Dreamer, hoping to discern a look of complicity from Him, or to receive a nod of solidarity for the mass of work I'd had to deal with since early that morning, owing to the thankless task of managing a team of bunglers who needed to have everything repeated a hundred times. How could they be so dim-witted to misunderstand the simplest and clearest orders?

«When you speak on the telephone you shouldn't say: "Hello, who is it?" But "Hello, who am I?"» the Dreamer remarked, just as I was ending a lengthy telephone conversation. I thought I hadn't understood what he was saying. He had spoken very softly, as He tended to do when He wanted to tell me something particularly important, something for which I should instantly abandon every other preoccupation to give full attention to Him. I went on alert. One look sufficed for me to recognize that the Dreamer was in predator mode. I shivered and could feel the adrenaline pumping. With all the calmness I could muster, I asked Him to repeat what He had just said; but my voice was already frayed by the apprehension I was feeling.

«The others are YOU!» He shouted in a terrible voice. In my interior world, in the hell of the self into which self-pity and

complaining had flung me, the Dreamer was no longer a polite guest seated at my table, he was no longer a passenger but a terrifying captain roaring out orders in a raging storm while the ship yawed on the very brink of a watery doom. I was stiff with terror and jerked back in fear. The telephone receiver almost crashed against the table skipping from one hand to the other like a mischievous, live and slippery being.

I must have looked comical and the Dreamer couldn't help laughing at me. Even behind His most severe mask, His apparently uncontrolled anger, a vast calm sea persisted; His pitiless gaze concealed a sphinx-like serenity that dismayed me even more than His threats. He remained this way for a moment, then His face resumed its fierce predator's glower.

«The others are you!» He repeated. Now His voice sounded calm again but I was not reassured.

«The world is as it is because you are as you are, not vice versa. Don't run away... The visible helps you to recognize the invisible. Other people help to show you what you don't want to see in yourself... What is it in me that projects all this? This is the question that a respectable person asks himself! I have been listening to you. You're indecisive, prolix... The confusion is in you, not in the others» the Dreamer retorted, leaning slightly across the table.

«The world manifests itself as doubtful, chaotic, irresponsible, and this certifies what you are, where you are. In every phone call, whoever is on the other end invariably asks: "Am I disturbing you?"»

Now that He had drawn my attention to it, I realized this was true. But I still didn't grasp why He felt this detail was important. "Am I disturbing you?" was a circumstantial question, one that I had always heard absent-mindedly, nothing more than a common courtesy, a sign of respect for another person's privacy, for someone of higher office.

«They say *"Am I disturbing you?" because they sense that you're unprepared. The world, the other people, reflect you... they're a mirror replicating the image of an indolent man, one who talks to himself. "Am I disturbing you?" is your lack of responsibility! "Am I disturbing you?" means that you're not clear! "Am I disturbing you!" is how the world denounces you!»*

Driin! The telephone rang again.

I picked up the receiver and mechanically asked:

«Who is it?»

I didn't even have time to finish that customary question before the Dreamer's voice rang out even more terribly than before.

«You should say "Hello, who am I?" not "who is it?"» He was furious now.

«"Who am I?" – the Dreamer insisted, still shouting – *That's how someone answers who has understood that it is himself on the other end!»* I was simultaneously listening to the Dreamer while trying to maintain some semblance of normality in the conversation I had just initiated.

«"Hello, who am I?" means remembering that you're meeting your confusion» continued the Dreamer, overriding my conversation, heedless of who might be on the other end of the line and what they might be hearing. I listened to the Dreamer's voice and answered my interlocutor in monosyllables, trying to shorten the conversation and end it by whatever means possible.

«The world wants to be ruled! Whoever calls needs to be contained... needs clarity... But after a few remarks from you, he discovers that you don't have any direction... You're wounded, saturated...»

«Let yourself go, let lightness prevail, enter some other zone of understanding! – the Dreamer urged me with unexpected benevolence, returning to His normal tone of voice – *An attentive man knows that, hidden beneath the crust of determination and false securities, there's always the same wound, the same grief... he knows that there's nothing he can undertake or do as long as that wound remains untreated, unhealed. And even if he tried to escape, were he to retreat into a cave like a hermit, or into the ascetic life of a convent, far from any telephone or engagement... that wound, that grief, would painfully return to denounce his lack of preparation.»*

«But you, like all ordinary men, don't feel that pain anymore, or else you pretend it's nothing.» In His voice was the echo of a failure without remedy, the pain of a cosmic defeat.

The telephone rang again. At this point I had no idea what to do. I did not want to offend the Dreamer, nor did I feel I possessed the freedom, the lightness of touch, or the essential understanding of the game that would enable me to respond according to His instructions. The ringing continued. The Dreamer with a nod encouraged me to answer and accompanied His gesture with these words:

«Think what a blessing it is!... The world calls to tell us who we are and what we lack... It's like having the Delphic oracle nearby and the ability to question it at will.» Then, half joking, He added:

«Everyone answering the telephone seems to ask who is calling... but in actual fact they already know... You already know who it is on the other end... because it's you who is calling yourself...»

Something in me flew open; a sensation of rightness pervaded me, as if a displaced psychic vertebrae had readjusted and returned to its place. The telephone kept ringing, but I was writing too feverishly to stop and answer it. I was about to capture and possess those words, words that contained a force capable of changing a life and transforming a man's destiny.

«The world is a pure reflection of your Being... See that you don't forget that! – cautioned the Dreamer – *The world telephones to tell you who you are... to let you know what you've always tried to avoid knowing about yourself! It's you and only you who decides who must be on the other end... It's you and you alone who decides what will be said to you... For the moment, on the other end of the line you find humanity waiting to reflect your fragility. It's you who is asking for help, for healing...»*

I listened and wrote down everything the Dreamer said to me with the absolute certainty that things would be exactly as He stated. Now everything was perfectly clear. The scattered pieces of many of the Dreamer's teachings were finding their place in a perfect composition. I wanted to record every detail of my comprehension of that moment so that I could retrieve it, whole and intact, whenever I needed it, and I also wished to be able to pass it on one day.

«A living man invites life – the Dreamer asserted, exploiting the breach that had opened within me – *Your self-pity emboldens failure. Like attracts Like. Understanding attracts understanding. Do you want to change the people on the other end of the line? Do you want to change their words, their tone, the news they bear?... Change yourself! Become the solution and the world will be changed forever.»*

He gave me a few seconds to take a breath. He waited until I had added even that part of His speech to my notes, then He continued.

«Answering "Hello, who am I?" is the attitude of a man who knows and remembers that he is the only one responsible for all that happens in his own life... A telephone call allows you to understand what you have so far refused to see or face.»

At that moment the telephone rang again. Before answering it, I waited a few seconds to hear the Dreamer's advice:

«Clarity... Give clarity to the world... and on the other end of the line there will be good news.»

«Hello, who am I?» I said, smiling at the thought of the effect this bizarre question would have on my interlocutor. From that moment on, picking up the receiver would not initiate a common conversation, but a prophetic and adventurous journey of discovery like the ancient pilgrimages to Delphi; as intoxicating as the vapours coiling up from the cracks in the temple's floor, attending the officiating Pythia.

The telephone rang again.

«Become the solution inside yourself – commanded the Dreamer giving me a nod of permission to answer – *Be free!... There's no problem to solve outside... no wicked entity to defend yourself against, no enemy to fight. To give an answer to the world you have to become the solution... Enter into sincerity, simplicity, lightness, and the brightness of the Being... If you're able to watch the 'game' from above, you'll discover that the world on the other end of the line is offering you all its gratitude and devotion.*

Then one day you'll discover that the real work of a man, the only work, is to repair the world. You'll realize that you, only you, are the cause of every lunacy, every defeat that happens in the world; and you, only you, can heal, protect, save and love it, if you know how to heal, protect, save and love yourself inside.»

The telephone was still ringing.

«Hello, who am I?» I answered, lifting the receiver. I felt a welling of gratitude within me and I could hardly resist a sudden, disrespectful yearning to embrace Him.

8 Tripping up mechanical habits

Several times a day the Muezzin's call summoned the faithful to prayer. As in the ancient *polis*, that summons seemed to determine the perimeter of invisible walls. There were no bands of religious police patrolling the souk, unlike in Saudia Arabia where saving one's soul is a government affair, and where one can hear cudgels battering shops' shutters to ensure that every profane activity has been suspended and that everyone has gone to the mosque. Here however, verses of the Koran wailed from the slender minarets bringing every activity to a halt with a peremptory call to one of the daily rituals of genuflection towards Mecca.

It would seem that Muslims possess a profound interior orientation that allows them to keep the direction of their Sacred City constantly in mind. For them, Mecca is the pole star in their spiritual navigation and in every office, hotel room, or public place, there is an arrow pointing exactly towards Mecca. Five times a day, throughout the Islamic world, millions of prayer rugs are deployed in that direction, to receive the kneeling worshippers. On the stroke of the appointed hour, all other activities take second place. Those who find themselves in heavy traffic pull over to the side of the road, stop, unroll their prayer mats, and genuflect.

Once, on a return flight from Europe, I found a last-minute seat on a Saudi plane with a stopover in Jeddah. I discovered too late that it was a hajj flight direct to Mecca and I was the only 'infidel' on board. At a certain point this became embarrassing when all the other passengers took off their clothes after departure and donned the white garb of Islamic pilgrims. Then, despite the forcible calls to order and superhuman efforts by the onboard staff to get them to take their seats, they took turns praying, occupying the aisles of the Tristar and genuflecting towards Mecca. How could they know in which direction it lay? I mused about flights of mystical birds, flocks gifted with an arcane instinct, that bore them inevitably back to their small black sun, at the centre of Al-Ka'aba.

More than once it happened that, in the middle of a negotiation or business meeting, my Islamic counterparts would stop everything and withdraw in prayer. I noticed too, that those few minutes of interruption somehow rejuvenated them, but I did not know how. I tried to investigate the innermost reason for that religious practice, the hidden understanding behind this ritual, but no one could give me an explanation that went beyond a bigoted and superstitious vision. In the course of one of my meetings with the Dreamer, however, I seized the opportunity of asking Him. The explanation He gave me was of extraordinary importance to my preparation. I noted it carefully.

« ...*Throughout the millennia, the traditions of wisdom have devised and transmitted every kind of 'trick' to contrast with the rigidity and repetitiveness towards which men inevitably tend* – He said – *Genuflections towards Mecca five times a day, the fasting ritual of Ramadan in the ninth month of the Islamic lunar year; indeed, the current rituals of every religious tradition, these could all be characterized as 'tripping mechanical behaviour'. Their function is to nourish mankind's drowsy intelligence and latent understanding, by the interruption of routine; pushing men to deviate from the rut of deep-rooted habits.*»

The Dreamer went on to explain that there are norms of physical, mental and spiritual hygiene, common knowledge of which has been lost. They now survive, hidden, in the form of religious beliefs, empty rituals, or as superstitious practices. If we bothered to pay the slightest attention to our movements, we would discover how mechanical and repetitive our lives are. Every morning we set out with scrupulous rigour on a series of actions which are always the same: we get out of bed with the same foot, we start shaving from the same side, we clean our teeth repeating the same number of movements, in the same direction, and always with the same facial expression. We have settled habits, we express received ideas with the same gestures, words and inflections we have always used. Even our emotions are predictable, like conditioned reflexes of the soul. In the ordinary man, the will is buried. His behaviour is the reflection of a mechanical intelligence and could be studied more profitably by sciences like ethology or robotics than by psychology.

«*Even when he's sure of making a decision or of freely expressing his will* – continued the Dreamer – *with a minimal degree of self-observation, he would notice that he was constantly guided by mechanical processes, that he ran along an old mental rut marked by prejudices and commonplaces, emulating others out of habit.*»

I was simultaneously staggered and fascinated by the Dreamer's ideas and by His style of explication, expounding the harshest truths of the human condition without inflicting injury, reaching back to the original source of His authority and wisdom. Behind the severity of His aspect and words, there was an invisible and constant smile, an infinite compassion that mitigated His systematic and ruthless demolition of ideas, beliefs and illusions rooted in the being. I wanted to know more about 'tripping up our mechanical habits', but the Dreamer seemed to have closed the subject. I only managed, by insisting, to obtain a few more words, which I noted down faithfully; they somehow allowed me to insert this new concept into the larger framework of the Dreamer's philosophical system.

«Every intentional effort, even the smallest, made to modify a repetitive action, a mechanical reaction or to break a habit, is a victory over our monotony, the tripping up of repetitive habits and recurrences of our life.»

The Dreamer added that this 'work' allowed a man to escape the laws of fortuity, to ward off accidents and even the chances of finding himself involved in disasters and natural calamities.

Ever since, I have tried to remind myself of this as often as possible; and I have begun to observe, and contrast within myself, the hardened automatisms, rusty and creaking mechanical reactions, recurrences, habits and routines of every kind. Only he who has tried to do this can understand the difficulties involved and realise how little of our life remains outside the tyranny of automatisms and unconscious repetition. But it is worth the effort. The development of attention and a watchful spirit, extend one's validity way beyond the sheer intentional modification of one of our routines, customs or reactions. In this inner game of cops and robbers, the ability to lay an ambush for our habits, to become the implacable hunter of all the obsolete responses in us; the attention to our movements and awareness of our reactions, is a work on the Being which has an unequalled reflection on the quality of thinking and feeling in our lives.

9 Winning ourselves

My meetings with the Dreamer became fewer, as events and external circumstances grew even more suffocating. I felt inadequate and dissatisfied. The world had become enlarged, and towered over me menacingly. Its 'hypnotic strength' became more pervasive and overwhelming as the months passed by and the company in Kuwait grew in importance.

"Sustain a good mood and stop taking yourself so seriously – the Dreamer had exhorted, on many occasions coming to rescue me on the brink of desperation – *Use self-irony. It's a powerful antidote against every form of fixity and identification.*"

In the Dreamer's language, 'identifying oneself' with the world, demonstrated our fall into a state of diminished freedom, a psychological shrinkage.

"You become the effect and the world becomes the cause. You become small, and the world grows huge and swallows you up." At His words, the scene of Alice at risk of drowning in her own tears flashed across my mind.

The Dreamer had taught me an entire series of devices and strategies designed to protect myself from identification, and avoid being swallowed up by the hypnotic blob of events called 'reality'. One such method required me at a certain point to stop every activity, intentionally choosing moments, which are apparently the least suitable, the most intense and crucial. Motionless, in the corner of a room, I tried to fight the pressure that time exercised on every square centimeter of my Being.

At those moments, I physically felt the world's tyranny trying to seize me again, forcing me back into the vortex of anxieties and worries of my life, thus eliminating the small void I was creating in the *continuum* of its mechanically preordained events. When I put His advice into practice, my ability to stay detached, to remain independent of events, and in command of circumstances, grew quite noticeably. Life and business lost their usual gravity. Thus, freed from their hypnotic attraction, I was able to rediscover the importance of the game.

On other occasions, to defend myself, I chose, among other stratagems to make faces in the mirror. Watching my mocking grimaces, I never let myself forget what was at stake in the game. A mortal match was underway.

Those intentional efforts opened up a connection with the great schools of antiquity. Like sounds released through the tuning fork of time, their teachings vibrated in unison with each atom of my body. I remember these flashes of lucidity as moments of rare grace.

During that period, the Dreamer introduced a new and memorable expression into my lexicon: *'winning oneself'*. I distinctly remember the first time He spoke of it to me. We were in the penthouse of *Le Méridien*, seated near the large swimming-pool of the roof garden. He was wearing a white linen suit, lizard moccasins, and dark glasses. Each small detail and gesture defined Him as a refined westerner with a deep knowledge of the Arab world. We were talking while looking out through the glass at the slender minarets, expanse of terraces and dusty buildings of Kuwait City, which descended to the cobalt waters of the Gulf like the domes of Water towers. I was confiding my difficulties to Him, those I had encountered as an entrepreneur, and the obstacles I was continuing to meet along the way. I asked him how one can possess the keys to leadership and I wanted to know the magic formula for fearlessness, invulnerability, victory, glory.

«A leader is first and foremost a manager of the Being – stated the Dreamer *– he knows how to recognize and circumvent every negativity in himself. He knows that to win all the battles he first needs to 'win himself'.*

'Winning oneself' means not allowing negative emotions rule us and get the upper hand; it means winning over the destructibility of our thoughts. It doesn't permit self-sabotage. It means overcoming our limits, triumphing over every obstacle crated from doubts, fears, and every other shadow in our Being...»

«'Winning oneself' means unearthing the will, swimming against the tide towards integrity. There is nothing else to do in life! – He stated apodictically – *The tests existence throws at him, obstacles and every difficulty a man meets on his way, all represent so many opportunities to calm the quarrelsome crowd he carries inside him, and ferry them towards singleness of soul, unity of Being.»*

He smiled at my bewildered expression as I noted down his words, and waited a while before adding anything else. Then He leaned gently across the table. As frequently happened with Him in such situations, I entered a state of anxiety. I foresaw the proximity of some vital information; the announcement of one of those fragments of His philosophy which were themselves capable of speeding up my comprehension. I left my small notebook open on my knee, and straightened up, partly to show Him I was ready, but also to relieve slightly the increasing tension I felt while he moved almost imperceptibly closer to me.

«Winning oneself – He whispered – *means not letting even the smallest expression of negativity to seep in, and never allowing even the slightest inner debasement or grimace of pain.»*

He waited. He was monitoring my reaction to this revelation with the faintest of smiles. Then, modulating His voice, He recited these lines:

When time attacks you, swallow time
When pain attacks you, swallow pain
When doubt attacks you, swallow doubt
When fear attacks you, swallow fear.

I perceived how often the Dreamer would express a concept or evoke an image, reiterating them; bringing them up time and time again. On this occasion it seemed clear to me that His use of reiteration was not, as I had believed until now, only a pedagogical device, but also a form of rhythmical poetry based on parallelism, the reassertion of a concept or image from different angles. As I was experiencing it myself directly, now, He was able to overcome psychological barriers and penetrate the hard stratifications of my interior geology. The Dreamer started to speak again, and I put aside those reflections.

«'Winning oneself' means not depending on the world – said the Dreamer – *It means being creators, masters of oneself, of one's own states of Being, and thereby masters of the world.»* He added that this ability to remain detached is completely natural, the birthright of everyone.

He fell silent, looking at me intently.

Under His gaze, memories flowed out of obscurity, like a convoy of rafts and into my mind. The images grew increasingly vivid, until an episode from my childhood reemerged. Once more I saw myself as a child, in Carmela's room, having one of my frequent tantrums. Surrounded by apprehensive adults, I was screaming and shedding floods of tears. Not even Giuseppona was able to calm me down. Although I gave every appearance of desperation, I was furtively observing my audience. As soon as they turned their attention away, and so that I could be certain that no one was looking at me, I peeped at myself in the mirrored doors of the large armoire, and secretly laughed maliciously, happy at having the freedom to perform. I regained possession of that long forgotten fragment of my childhood, and savoured again the secret power of that time: the power of entering and leaving that state at will, without parents and adults, who were blind to my talent, ever suspecting my capacity to remain detached. From that position, I sensed that I was able to control and tyrannize them, without remorse.

«But one day the child will stop performing. And the mask he once put on at will, will have become a permanent smirk that tyrannically rules his life – the Dreamer remarked, entering the flow of memory at that point – *and the child will 'truly' become the naughty, touchy, weak being whose role he's been interpreting, a fragile adult who can only be dependent on someone or something, such as a drug or a job, appointing the whole world as his boss.»*

«Freedom – He seethed – *is going to cost you the masks you've been wearing for so many years.»*

10 The 'dream' is the most real thing there is

In the years I spent in Kuwait and the Middle East, I grew inured to the wonder of the Dreamer. Gratitude for my well-being, health and success; and the possibility of turning to His mysterious and inexhaustible wisdom at every difficulty was gradually replaced by a creeping antagonism, a repressed rebellion against His authority.

From the thousands of wounds the world had inflicted on me, I was losing energy; and with it, my faith in myself, wish to live, and capacity for joy. Even the sense of the miraculous that the Dreamer had brought into my life was evaporating, like a precious essence left open to the air. My entire world was beginning to blur. Like a reflection of my loss of vitality, even my collaborators no longer put the energy and enthusiasm into their work that they had at one time. My role as boss, which had come to mean solving an incessant storm of problems that constantly besieged me, was killing me.

He who does not rule himself cannot rule others

Our meetings were becoming more infrequent. I still transcribed his words and thought about them, but for a long time a deep rift had been separating the 'dream' in me from what I believed to be reality. Now I know that mankind's ancient drama, the escape from Eden, did not happen just at the dawn of time, nor did it take place all at once.

The unexpected always requires a long preparation

The story of Adam cast out of Paradise, so incomprehensible and ingeniously absurd – was reproducing itself and unfolding before my eyes. A sentient being had bartered paradise for fear and pain. How could that be possible? Who would ever exchange life for death? Yet mankind has done it, and continues to do it. I was testing it on my own flesh. The bite of the apple is to believe that the external world is the cause; that the world outside us has a will that possesses and controls us. The proscenium lights come on, the curtain rises on the theatre of the absurd, and mortal players replicate that drama not only with every moment of death but with each deferment of the here and now. *To have a fault, to sin,* in its Greek etymology, means *to deviate;* my sin was also by its structure a deviation, a moving away from the highest part of me. Atoms of forgetfulness, disobedience and division multiplied and entered paradise, polluting it.

A little at a time, I banished the Dreamer's philosophy to a fictional Utopian world that seemed out of touch. His vision and words still fascinated me and I continued to feel the power of their breath, but deep inside, I convinced myself that His mindset was merely theoretical. Practical considerations were an entirely different matter: someone with my responsibilities had to face thousands of difficulties each day: a company to manage, hundreds of men and women who depended on it and my own family to support. Living in a beautiful villa in Samia, the most exclusive quarter in Kuwait City, with servants and a driver, and surrounded by enthusiastic employees, I forgot the hell in which the Dreamer had found me two years before and the wonder he had brought me since then.

Sometimes I even thought the Dreamer had conceived His theories and principles with the specific goal of complicating my life and deliberately increasing my difficulties.

"The dream is the most real thing there is – He had taught me – *bind yourself to the dream by a steel cable, and don't allow*

anyone or anything to separate you from it. A man without a dream is a fragment lost in the universe."

But for months now I had been nurturing a division between His world and my quotidian reality. And now I was losing the little bit of integrity that I had gained thanks to the Dreamer, the imperceptible shift in my being that had moved mountains in my life. The unforgivable sin, the fault of all faults, is to believe that the world creates us. We commit this at every moment in our hearts, when we make the world our god: a grieved god, an ignorant god. From the book of Genesis to the story of Frankenstein, from the tale of Alice, who was frightened of drowning in a pool of her own tears, to Blade Runner, man has forever continued to tell himself the eternal story of the creator who becomes the victim of his creature. Hypnotic suggestion leads us think that the world is getting the upper hand, and we believe this to be real. We set this belief above everything, we idolize it.

"The world, when you see it, is already made" He once told me, explaining that this is the reason it is called 'created'. It comes after. It is the effect! There is a cause that has come before. Only very few individuals can recognise that the world has neither direction nor a will of its own.

"Will belongs only to the individual... it rules the world. When the will is absent, the world automatically takes control."

This was troubling news! Recognizing that the world, the mass, cannot have a will, is like noticing mid-flight that there's no pilot on board so you have to learn to use the controls immediately, and take charge of the whole plane.

"And so your worrying is completely useless – the Dreamer concluded – *It only perpetuates your dependence on the world."*

"Dependence on the world? What does that mean?" I asked Him, more than ever feeling his philosophy clash with everything I still wanted to believe.

"It means that when you 'forget', you get smaller and the world becomes your boss – He answered dryly – *Without will, men are reduced to psychological dwarves who trot around their universe with their tails between their legs, bent under the weight of guilty feelings, terrified to death of ghosts that they themselves have created."*

He added that beings reduced to this condition can do nothing more than accuse, complain, make excuses, and pity themselves. And this continues to be the human condition on earth, a condition into which I was flinging myself headfirst. As in Pirandello's Enrico IV, I found myself imprisoned in a role that I had only needed to perform.

"Becoming a businessman and taking on the more extensive role of an entrepreneur, doesn't make you a free man. Identifying yourself with that role only means that you've moved to another prison. You've merely entered a new cell. Freedom means being free from identification with the world; it means forever silencing the song of pain that has ruled your entire life."

In my heart, I had already smashed the talking cricket with my wooden mallet and I was determined to suppress His troublesome voice in me. With the passing of the months, my contact with the Dreamer became increasingly rare and difficult, until it almost disappeared. By then I was having to count on my own strength for ever longer periods of time. I toiled and struggled to pursue solutions that in time, revealed themselves only to be more problems, forming a perverse, never-ending circle. My solar batteries, charged by the Dreamer's energy, grew weak. Everything was apparently going on as before, but that energy, the precious lymph, the irreplaceable vital liquid that had entered my life with the Dreamer, was gushing out from a hundred wounds in my Being.

I no longer trained, and neglected my body, blaming fatigue, wrinkles, and other signs of ageing and physical decline on my heavy workload and lack of sleep. In actuality, having left the 'dream', I was going backwards along the road I had travelled with the Dreamer.

Even the confidence of partners and loyalty, at times, admiration of my collaborators; things that I believed I merited because of my personal abilities, were none other than a reflection of my relationship with the Dreamer. These relations became blurred, and in some cases disappeared altogether. I blamed others for this change. They seemed to be profiteers, ungrateful and greedy. Meanwhile, problems and antagonisms were constantly becoming more menacing, and failures ever more frequent. In most instances, at least at the beginning, I felt a certain sweetness in falling behind.

Initially, I perceived the new infrequency of my meetings and contact with the Dreamer, who had almost disappeared from my life, as leaving me in a lighter and more carefree condition. My dress became less austere and my habits less restrained. I began to accept invitations to society functions more often; to embassy receptions and parties in private villas. I became a *habitué* of restaurants and the most crowded clubs of the city. The Dreamer had always suggested understatement and the importance of not being too accessible by participating in only a few official events and carefully choosing and strategically preparing for those occasions. On the eve of important meetings, the discipline shown me by the Dreamer had required to intensify the work on myself through heightened attention to food, physical exercise and reading. The strengthening of a state of alert awareness was aimed at not leaving even the smallest loophole open in the world and not allowing anything that would pollute that wealth, that precious substance that I had accumulated over months and months of 'work.'

In freeing myself from most of this, I felt the relief of a Spartan who joyfully welcomes the news of war only to interrupt his intolerably tough peacetime routine, made up of extreme exercises and unbearable strain.

Meanwhile, the threat of war was gathering over Kuwait, like clouds swollen with rain, with every day bringing new incidents on the border with Iraq. The political and business worlds were showing signs of nervousness and uncertainty about the future of the tiny sheikdom, while some of our international suppliers were insisting on contractual precautions before filling our orders; and on a couple of occasions, some western managers who had already signed contracts backed out at the last minute and decided against moving here.

I minimized these symptoms and wholly dedicated myself to developing the company. I renewed my efforts, and decided to launch a new line of products by means of an advertising campaign, for which I approached a local agency of DBDO International. The director, a young Lebanese man with a background in European culture, promised to entrust the project to a new manager who was English, and whom he believed to be the most suitable for the job. Within a few days she would come to meet with me to present her ideas, in the office at Al Awadi.

This was how I came to meet Heleonore. I do not remember much about the ideas she proposed for the publicity campaign, but her smile, vitality, and Andalusian beauty made an indelible impression on me. I remembered the Dreamer's words, and hoped that she was one of the precious cells that I had been appointed to meet in Kuwait. I concentrated all the things I yearned for into a single wish, and expressed it strongly in my heart:

"God, let her be the one."

11 Heleonore

After that first meeting I saw her almost every day. Swims together, tennis matches at the Hyatt Club, a meeting in the giant bubble at Water Towers, from where we admired the lights of the gulf, dinner at the Versailles: these were snapshots of my swift courtship. Heleonore became my best collaborator, the friend and confidante of my two children. She came gently and inexorably into our life, occupying every corner of it a little more each day. No invasion had ever been less opposed.

Giuseppona said not a word, but I knew she disapproved. I didn't connect her attitude to my growing distance from the Dreamer, to my disobedience, but thought it was a form of jealousy; a temporary and understandable reaction to a threat to her role. Actually, however, Giuseppona sensed that I was entering a sea of troubles. She was born in Cuma, a place far more ancient than Rome and the very cradle of Neapolis, and in her DNA she carried the prophetic spirit and Sybilline language of that civilization. Her primordial understanding, unpolluted by instruction and without mental superstructures or cerebral schemes, had the lucidity of the essence, the strength of simplicity and sincerity, the purity of someone who knew without knowing.

I was trying once again. Since Luisa's death, I had never given up believing I could start a true and happy family again. I still felt certain that the familiar disaster of my previous relations with Jennifer and Gretchen could be blamed on external conditions. I had, as they say, been unlucky in love. That was all. Sooner or later I would meet the right woman, and then everything would turn out for the best. I was still deluding myself that a happy destiny lay before me if I stayed the same; that circumstances and events from the past could be different in my life without my having to change.

The external world is the materialization of your psychology...
It's you who have given consent to each of your problems,
to each difficulty in your life...

One day, when you've come to know yourself,
you will understand why the world is as it is.

With Heleonore's arrival, the Dreamer's voice receded even further into the distance. Every morning, Jamil collected fresh dates for us from the palm trees in the sandy garden, and served us a breakfast of fresh cheese, tiny black olives, and tabbouleh intensely redolent of mint and parsley. These months were passionate but not happy, tinged as they were with an inexpressible, subtle suffering: the same feeling that used to darken my joy at playing hooky from school, making it hard for me to swallow mouthfuls of the sandwich that Giuseppona had tucked into my school bag.

It seemed to me that the world was hindering our union, but in reality it was I who was unable to forgive myself for having transgressed an invisible code that, in my wounded conscience, marked me as an outlaw in the eyes of the world.

The Dreamer had been preparing me to be a king, and yet again I had chosen mediocrity. Only by forgetting his ideas, ignoring His words, and distancing them from my life was I able to meet a woman who would lead me back into the chasms of my past, the ghettoes of dependency.

I can't say that I missed His teachings during those first months. My own presumption had filled that space more than amply. I did have, however, a dark feeling of uneasiness like a superstitious premonition, a prophecy of an impending misfortune. All the clutter of emotions, negative fancies, and feelings of guilt that I believed I had by now left behind were again taking over my life.

The notion of being able to construct our happiness without taking into account anything more than our selfishness faded away in the night, like the moon of that Islamic sky under which Heleonore and I had become outcasts. We were outlaws, not just in the Dreamer's sight, but under the laws of Kuwait as well. The risks we ran were not to be underestimated in a country that had appointed the Koran as the absolute law that governed every aspect of existence; a country with a Pharisaic morality that was as inflexible in public as it was licentious in private.

Day after day my connections with the country, work and Yusuf Behebani himself were slackening, while life in Italy, the house in Piedmont, surrounded by lakes, at the foot of the Alps, called out to us ever more irresistibly.

We were overwhelmed by an exaltation that caused us to paint our situation, along with everything else we had in Kuwait, in the darkest possible hues. Enchanted, we exaggerated the appeal of all that we believed to be awaiting us in Italy. Heleonore was delighted at the idea of going to live in the house at Chià, and together we planned how to make it more comfortable, and how to complete the reconstruction and organization of the family. In my imagination, it would be wonderful to return to Italy. The children would go back to 'normality'. Even Soshila, the female cocker that I smuggled into Kuwait, brought back from a recent trip from Italy, hid in my jacket pocket, could live like a real dog.

12 The adoption

In Kuwait, a misocynous country, dogs are avoided by Muslims as impure animals, indeed they are almost nonexistent. Soshila – our cocker puppy – only had to brush against a servant for the latter to rush off for ablutions and other rituals of purification.

I paid dearly for the pleasure of seeing Giorgia and Luca's joy when I let the puppy's little muzzle peek out of my jacket pocket as the Dreamer was particularly harsh on that occasion. He made it clear to me that the decision to present a gift to children by introducing an animal hated by that culture hid an egocentricity as dangerous as it was unconscious.

"A man of integrity, no matter at what latitude he finds himself, respects the customs, habits, and religious beliefs, whatever they may be, of the people who are his hosts. The heart's understanding guides his choices. Beyond time and geography, his ethics will, without effort, always allow him to feel at home, in lawfulness and morality" the Dreamer told me.

Although I did not understand, I faithfully wrote down His discourse, with particular attention to the exact words with which He closed His discussion:

"Introducing that dog is the manifestation of a hidden vanity, of a division both in yourself and from the others who banish you to the last steps on the ladder of Being. When you recognise it in yourself, you'll be able to heal it. For now, until you understand, make an effort 'not to create a scandal'."

I had to wait for a favorable moment before I could grasp the sense of that lesson which at the time, to be truthful, seemed excessively severe to me. One day, opening the Gospel by chance, I came upon the parable in which Jesus asks Peter to pay the tribute due to Caesar, and 'not create a scandal'. He would find the appropriate coins in a freshly caught fish. The explanation was already there, folded away in my Being. Now it stood out brightly, as if a curtain had been lifted.

Not only did the episode of the puppy become clear, but also apparently distant situations, connected by the thread of the same psychological mechanism. It was as clear as vanity and egocentricity: this wish to be at the centre and 'create scandal,' was the secret incentive and most profound explanation of the most varied and least comprehensible behaviour of countless men and women, from passion for extreme sports and the most perilous adventures, to humanitarian and charitable undertakings, such as the adoption of children of another race or colour. It's only through vanity and egocentricity that some can face oceans in a frail and tiny craft, erect cathedrals or found religions. I understood that the opposite polarity of 'creating a scandal' is the behaviour of those who are silent, who have no need to create unfavorable waves, antagonisms or pointless aversions. There are those, who in silence and without ostentation, take upon themselves the weight of burdens and responsibilities that ordinary people would not put one finger to.

I remembered a couple of friends - he is a gynaecologist and she is a university teacher - who, out of humanitarianism, wanted to adopt a baby from Ecuador. They faced the long trip to that country many times, overcoming every difficulty; hiring intermediaries and finally succeeding in paying the mother herself.

"They would never have made even the slightest effort for a child from their own country. A white child would have passed unnoticed as they would have believed he was truly a son – was the Dreamer's comment when I told him this story – *It would have been the equivalent of praying or fasting in solitude, making sure that no one would ever know anything about it."*

The dark baby would instead have 'created a scandal'. It would have provoked aversions, divisions and rancor, and it would have prompted them to descend into apparently external quarrels, which were, in actual fact, creatures of their own repressed violence, realized by their own unconscious racism and sense of guilt which that adoption was intended to soothe or in some way hide from themselves.

I told the Dreamer that indeed, many years later, I had met those friends of mine again and they had grown extremely embittered and aged. They told me that their child, and even they themselves, every day had to endure thousands of anxieties and abuses, large and small, every day because of people's intolerance and a backwards environment. This was so prevalent that other parents with the same problem had had to set up an association that 'fought' for the defense of their rights and the affirmation of the principles that had inspired their 'act of love'.

Finally I admitted to the Dreamer that some time later, disappointed and unhappier than before, they had reached the decision to separate and finally divorce.

"The adoption your friends decided on was not an act of love, as they wanted to believe, but an attempt to fill the emptiness of their relationship. Nothing is external. Nothing, not even the adoption of a baby, can eliminate inner deaths, fear, solitude and suffering."

I asked Him why that couple had been attacked, why their act and that of other couples like them had provoked so much aversion and ostracism.

"The world's attacks are a blessing; they always come to heal us. The world has to intervene from the outside, to denounce that lack, that sickness you believe you don't have."

He explained to me that if they had been more sincere they would have known that the baby had adopted them, and not vice versa; that in reality it was he who was their benefactor. That little one had come to take on all their malaise, and loneliness, attempting to heal them from their fears, guilt, and sterility. According to the Dreamer, had they recognized all this, they would have had no need to adopt the baby and endure the conflicts and hostility.

"The world knows!" concluded the Dreamer.

Listening to Him and knowing that couple, I could now 'see' that in adopting a 'different' baby they had been moved by motivations that they would never have been able to suspect or confess, even to themselves. In truth, what could have been more gratifying over a lifetime than seeing in the eyes of others, admiration for their extraordinary generosity?

Even as I write, I know that if we are to discover that falseness, egoism, and vanity lurk behind our acts of humanity, it will require a long labour of self-scrutiny and observation. I am conscious of the severity of this judgement, and I assume full responsibility for it. As a cell of humanity, I have discovered in myself that it is this very ignorance, apparently negligible and insignificant, that degrades us and makes us prey to the fear of living as well as dying. It is this shadow on our Being, ignored, the unwittingness of this inner criminality, that is projected onto the screen of the world where it materializes all the horrors, atrocities, and violence.

As the signs of an approaching war became more intense and acute, I did not need to make excuses for leaving Kuwait, at least, that was what we chose to believe. Once we had decided to return to Italy, we sought and found new confirmation to justify our resolve. We had considered the decision for a long time; now we acted upon it in a few hours.

Sheik Yusuf Behebani seemed neither surprised nor overly displeased. I liquidated my assets in the enterprise, and by mutual agreement we appointed my second-in-command to replace me as manager. Roger's eyes glowed with satisfaction at his unexpected nomination to the position the Dreamer had created for me; I could read my condemnation in his gaze. It was too late to go back. I preferred to stifle and snuff out that glimmer of lucidity.

Heleonore also left her job at DBDO International, and the entire family, including the cocker Soshila, departed from Kuwait City. A brief stop in Cyprus, some days in Athens, as if in a decompression cabin, and then back to Italy.

CHAPTER VII

Return to Italy

1 The clause

I was awoken by a troublesome thought. I rubbed my eyes many times, but the nightmare kept pressing on me. I was in a bare room, full of rubble. Under the light of a dangling light-bulb, the wall revealed gashes of cut stone and bricks that had yet to be plastered. For a few slow seconds, I couldn't believe that this house had taken the place of our elegant villa in Samia. I gazed at the base of the walls and saw clusters of coloured electrical wires sprouting from the small plastic pipes fixed with lime to the surface of the wall. Heleonore was sleeping next to me. I shuddered. Her presence convinced me with a pang that everything was real.

This was the house in Chià, the one that we had dreamed of so much.

When I review the course of events and return to the roots of what had thrown me into the tangle of the past again, I think about one fact in particular. For years I had kept it secret, something for which I couldn't forgive myself , until the day I found the courage to confess it to the Dreamer. Before I left for Kuwait, the Dreamer had urged me:

"Make a clean break! Cut all ties forever! Don't take even one atom of the old world with you."

And while He was saying these things to me, I could already feel death in my heart. In leaving the ACO Corporation, and signing the agreement that put an end to my employer-employee relationship, I had asked for and been granted permission to add a clause that I kept secret. It was the assurance that within two years, if I decided to return, I would be able to resume my old job again.

How many times had I thought of the involuntary will that had set that trap, the sly calculation that had dictated that clause, leaving doors open that would swallow me back into the past again.

The Scythian chieftains, those mysterious inhabitants of the Euro-Asian steppe, the fierce people sleeping in the ice, ruminated for a long time around a fire as to whether they should set out towards the south, or launch a war of conquest to the west. This decision could take days or months; but once taken, it was irreversible. As they installed their families and everything they possessed on carts, they burned everything behind them: bridges, houses, crops and all that they were unable to take with them.

How different my attitude at going towards the new had been!

«You are led by fear – was the Dreamer's comment at my confession – *You've spent your life conforming to the crowd... years and years of dependence... without finding the courage to respect your 'dream,' your uniqueness.»*

«Ulysses ordered his crew to tie him to the mainmast so as not to abandon the ship. He wanted to hear the sirens' song but didn't want to forget his promise, his 'dream' – He continued – *The ropes bind him to his principles. It's the act of a 'man of the School,' an impeccable man who, like all heroes, knows himself!»*

«Don't fear obedience. Align yourself with the principles of the School – He said, His voice was gentle – *Obeying the School doesn't mean being dependent. It means following what is most pure, most truthful in yourself. One day, when you are closer to a greater honesty and sincerity, you'll see that there's never been a gap. The School that appears to be outside you, will merge with the School that is inside you: you will have a will.»*

The work at ACO and the house in Chià were only two of the bridges that I hadn't had the courage to burn; only two of the sirens whose song I had been unable to resist. Their call would have proved fatal. The distance between myself and the Dreamer's world grew enormously until it become too vast to be crossed.

2 An unpleasant awakening

Ever since the day of our arrival, we had woken up to the depressing sight of the weed-choked garden and the crooked geometry of the scaffolding that clung to one of the house's outer walls. Only a few weeks had gone by since I left Kuwait, but the time I had spent there as head of a business and international team already seemed remote.

Even Heleonore had difficulty recognising me as the man she had followed with so much trust. The Dreamer had shown me the path to prosperity, He had cured my body and spirit, and overturned my despairing description of the world by opening my mind to an intelligent and courageous vision. With Him I had tasted freedom: freedom from pain, doubt and fear. With Him I'd had access to an energy capable of transforming my life and tearing me away from my inexorable destiny but I had repaid Him by abandoning all that He had entrusted to me. And I had even hidden my relationship with Heleonore from Him. From afar, the Dreamer's words still echoed, but the golden thread, which connected me to Him, seemed to have been broken forever.

Vision and reality are one and the same thing

Only now was I realizing what Heleonore really loved in me… the Dreamer's philosophy, His strength, those words that, like Rostand's pathetic character in Cyrano, I still parroted, pretending they were mine. My presumption, my inability to feel gratitude for all that I had received, separated me from the Dreamer. And now I was even losing her, the woman who had followed me with so much trust. Once the solemn promise made to the 'dream' had been forgotten, my life revealed the crude patches of its condition.

I was slowing myself down, putting the brakes on my Being. All the ghosts of my past swarmed back, restoring me to the conditions of my earlier life in New York, before I'd met the Dreamer. Even physically, I was again taking on the features and attitudes of the man I had been. In my face and body, the effects of a psychological decay were spreading visibly. The dynamic man that the Dreamer had awoken in me, the self-confident head of a business, determined, elegant and loved by his staff, was sadly withering. I wandered around the house fretting. I spent my time making calculations for the restorations, arguing with the workmen about the placement of a fireplace or a floor, getting into trouble with a neighbour over a boundary dispute, or dealing with the downspout of a roof gutter.

I had tried to make friends with my neighbours, presenting them with some electrical gadget, gifts brought from Kuwait, and inviting them to my house. But my efforts never managed to placate their hostility. Even in that small village, hidden in a Neozoic wrinkle, Heleonore and I were outlaws. It was as if everyone knew our transgression, as if our arrival had been preceded by a greater excommunication, by a general order not to welcome us. And to this order the entire town had responded with the rapidity and precision of a hypnotic obedience, and this made our life difficult. Indeed everything, from Giorgia and Luca's introduction in school, to the municipal permits required for the reconstruction of the house, encountered unbelievable obstacles.

I complained and moaned, blaming everything on bureaucracy, events, people and circumstances, without understanding that the change had only been apparent. By leaving that door open behind me, I had already decided my failure, planned my defeat.

The greatest enemy of man is himself!
You're the best example of how impossible it is for a man
to abandon the prison of ordinariness,
to rise up in arms against his own limits,
to overturn the description of the world.
The pain you're feeling and your faith in suffering are proof of it...
It may seem as though your life is withered and numbed,
as if its roots were infected,
but the truth is that you've never dreamt of
anything that differs from this poverty,
painfulness or imprisonment.

Giuseppona had lost her humour and the proverbial chattiness, which, in whatever country we moved to, had always filled our house like a song. I no longer heard those funny monologues of hers, true theatrical pieces that went from grumbling to *rondeau* to epic: a poetical commentary on all familiar facts, present and past. Since I had been on earth, Giuseppona had been the symbol of energy and a warrior's courage, the indomitable Indian chief who had watched over me and my children. Now she was growing old and beginning to stoop and that comic coquetry of hers, that vanity she revealed in choosing the most bizarre and improbable clothes, had been stifled. At night I could hear her coughing painfully from her little room. Each cough broke my heart and chilled me like a presage of misfortune. Until I saw what I thought to be impossible: Giuseppona in bed and a doctor by her side. I never would have believed it. With her motto 'stay clear of doctors', she had made an iron law, an unbreakable rule in life. The failing light in those months sadly evoked the time of Luisella's illness and darkened my spirit. Even Giorgia and Luca had lost their vitality, and to keep them away from that wretched atmosphere, I enrolled them in after-school classes where they stayed until late into the evening.

3 Ignorance is always close at hand

Some time before, the Dreamer had warned me with these words:

"Until you've discovered your buried will, until you've reached complete freedom, your integrity, the past will always lie in wait to take you back to the old things.

Ignorance is always close at hand... If you cease to be alert and forget the 'dream', it will snatch you again in an instant, and along with you every achievement and understanding, despite being tirelessly pursued, will diminish.

It's not important how much work you've done. Until you've achieved the totality of your Being, you'll always be poised on the abyss of your ignorance...

The totality of the Being means being the master of oneself, and it's the result of a long 'work of the school'... until that moment a man is a tightrope walker suspended between nothingness and eternity."

I reacted to these assertions in an exaggerated way. I remember that I talked on the subject in terms of its 'serious injustice' and even appealed to universal principles of fairness. Actually, I was just defending myself many years in advance, and I was justifying my disobedience even before it materialised. The uneasiness I felt, that discomfort that chose the words and determined their tone and ardour, was revealing my forthcoming disaster. My fall already lay before me, in the womb of the invisible, recorded and ready in every detail, like a plant in its seed.

"Injustice doesn't exist!" He declared, apodictically closing the argument. He knew that any other explanation would have been useless. I was not ready. It was still too soon for me to accept the idea that in every man's life there has never been anything more just or providential, than what he has considered unjust. I would soon undergo a harsh lesson on the subject of injustice: when painful, dramatic circumstances would put me in a position to understand.

Many years after those warnings that I had mistaken for 'pedagogical exaggerations' of the Dreamer, I was experiencing firsthand how much pointless suffering arises from forgetting. My anachronistic return had thrown me into the *Erebus* of existence, back to the place I had managed to escape from. When will is absent, doubt, fear and limits, the description of the world, get the upper hand. Now I was floundering in the turbid waters of a past that had continued to flow beside me, like a contaminated stream, an unlucky parallel life.

Once I had abandoned Kuwait without the Dreamer's approval, the luminous steel cable that connected me to the 'dream' became very thin and I started to fall back into the hellish circles of my existence.

4 Return to the past

My existence was taking on water.

The money I had made from my share of the assignment in the company in Kuwait, was quickly running out and I soon needed to look for a job.

As in a Middle Eastern fairy tale, once the magic object has been lost, that world the Dreamer had made me recognise began to disappear and slip through my fingers, like sand. The receptions with tables sparkling with silver, the elegant outline of Water Towers, the spectacle of the desert plunging into the cobalt of the sea, the house in Samia, the trips around the world, the entrepreneurial challenges and the men and women that I had chosen were all swept away by a cosmic wind. I never saw them again; as if they belonged to a parallel universe, without passages or any form of communication with mine. That opening, no bigger than the eye of a needle, through which miraculously I had followed the Dreamer, had closed forever. The Project had abandoned me, and like Esau, I had swapped the birthright of a kingdom for a miserable dish of lentils.

It was in those conditions that I decided to contact the ACO Corporation, just before the expiration date of the clause that allowed me to return to work for them again. On the occasion of the interview that followed, I entered a number of offices to visit acquaintances and former colleagues. I was about to be sucked into an infernal vortex again.

In the ACO Corporation everything was the same as it had been before my departure for Kuwait. The company ghosts still fluttered exactly where I had left them, behind their microscopic desks, in corridors or around the automatic coffee dispenser, with their usual talk, thoughts and attitudes. As they saw me pass, they winked and exchanged a look of complicity. On meeting me, sad smiles were etched on their faces. Rather than looking at me, they peeped at me from their insuperable enclosures, through the bars of their invisible cages. They were obviously satisfied to have me as an inmate again. By returning to my place of work, I was bringing them a breath of artificial life, like a mouthful of oxygen to a sick man. What could possibly have made them feel better? I was the indisputable proof of their deeply rooted belief: the living, decisive demonstration that escape from their circle of existence was impossible, even dangerous. I suppose that their feelings about me were involuntary and confused. Malice, sarcasm, a mean-spirited joy at my failure to escape, mixed into an emotional slime. The case of the recaptured inmate swept from their minds the slightest. My return brought them relief, and also a deeper acceptance of the insurmountable; the sweet relief of surrender we feel when faced with what appears to us to be irremediable, ineluctable. Once the scraping of my solitary file against the bars had been stopped, the silence of the 'prison' returned, along with its sinister and reassuring order.

A kind of oblivion accompanied my reinstatement as an employee and mitigated what would otherwise have been an unbearable pain. Another day or so, and my reintegration into that world would have been complete and irreversible.

Before this could happen, with my last flashes of lucidity, I tried in some way to find the Dreamer again. I returned to London and looked for him in St James' and at the Savoy. I returned to the bench on Roosevelt Island, and the *Café de la France*, in Marrakech.

Bit by bit, I combed the places where I had been with Him and went down the same streets that had seen me at His side. But without success.

The Dreamer had abandoned me.

In the breathlessness that accompanied that conclusion, and the pain of that loss, I even thought that He had never really existed, or only in my imagination.

5 Psychological pollution

My request to return to work took them by surprise. The management in the ACO Corporation welcomed it, but more to respect the promise set out in the contract, than through any real necessity. The bosses did not know where to put me or what they could entrust to me. I was expecting to get a responsible job, but they only managed to find one in the Department of International Marketing. I was neither assigned a role, nor did I receive any instructions as to what my responsibilities were, so I was in limbo: with neither colleagues nor boss and without a secretary. My only furniture was a desk, and a telephone that never rang.

In the first few months I tried to maintain a state of awareness and made every effort not to let a complaint slip, or show even the slightest hint of an accusation; nevertheless, poisons of the being disguised as envy, jealousy, rage or frustration, constantly rose up in me. ACO was a factory of negative thoughts and emotions. Any mishap or a colleague's error was sufficient to bring all the old dross to the surface.

However, the Dreamer's work had not been useless. A filter of attention allowed me to observe those states of Being, to circumscribe them and control their manifestation.

The only thing that gave me life was His words, which I read again in my notebook. My isolation helped me find the Dreamer's traces again, and keep His teachings alive in me.

Disobeying the principles of the dream means self-sabotage,
and killing oneself inside.
The external life does nothing other than
reflect that inner suicide.

For lengthy periods of time, I managed not to breathe the atmosphere of ACO, keeping myself at a distance; but it was a desperate undertaking, like trying to survive in an aquatic world without gills. I knew that without the Dreamer I would not be able to resist for much longer.

I remember the exhausting efforts towards self-observation and awareness I made during those months, to avoid being overwhelmed by the river of negativity that surrounded me on every side, and I noted how those muddy waters rose every day gathering psychological debris and other toxic material. They gushed along floors and corridors, bursting out and converging on the banks of factories and offices, before finally flowing into the open, into the outlying parks, and reaching the small town, flooding its streets and entering the homes and lives of its people.

That period of isolation allowed me to study at close hand, but with a necessarily minimal engagement, a phenomenon that the Dreamer called the 'psychological pollution' of organisations. Returning to ACO meant having, at my disposal for months, one of the most sophisticated and complete scientific laboratories for this kind of observation.

My study and first tests on the phenomena relating to the expression of worries, thoughts, doubts and fears and, generally, to the production and manifestation of every kind of emotional clutter, go back to that time. Scientist as well as guinea pig, I discovered that destructive thoughts, negative emotions, not only polluted me, but, once shown, emitted an invisible substance which although unknown to our physics was capable of polluting the environment, people and all those who came into contact with it. I was intrigued by the discovery of their contagious nature and capacity to spread from person to person at the highest speed, at times showing the real characteristics of an epidemic. This is how hundreds and thousands of people can be polluted by the same suggestion, fancies and the same negative emotions, and driven to mechanical, collective and very often violent reactions, like conditioned psychological reflexes.

According to the Dreamer, happiness, love, joy, gratitude, serenity, and all superior states of Being in general, are emotions that mankind, as it is, is unable to feel.

Positive emotions, in order to arise,
require long preparation and work on ourselves.
It takes years of self-observation
to eliminate the layers of ignorance, coarseness,
and everything that impedes these states of Being.

Perhaps I had always believed that. In any case, now I could no longer pretend to ignore a discovery of such importance: human organisations are mortally sad, true industries of pain. Factories and offices, and even before them, schools and universities, seem to have been designed and organized to produce and nourish apparently useless suffering. Huge quantities of energy are wasted through divisions and conflicts between groups and individuals, useless and unpleasant emotions, states of anguish, anxiety and conditions of worry, uncertainty and irritability. I could confirm a paradoxical truth: while raw materials, at the end of the day, come out of the factories, and of any industrial process, enriched and transformed, men and women are likely to leave poorer and disheartened.

Observing this from the inside, I came to ask myself why in organisations, there stubbornly seems to exist, beyond every scientific and entrepreneurial effort, a 'perverse' mechanism that constantly produces and feeds a condition of disagreement, a painful situation of tension and conflict, for all those who work there. Absurdly, everything pointed to the fact that this was their very *raison d'être*, their true production and at the same time their mysterious cause.

6 In the belly of the whale

While reflecting on all of this from my current station and pretending to be absorbed in the study of the documents strewn artfully across my desk, I sensed in ACO, the organism that was hosting me, an effort at assimilation that constantly pushed me to belong, while trying to snuff out that spark of life which still allowed me 'to see'. It was as if an iron law, unknown but powerful and ineluctable, a kind of gravitational force, a psychological entropy, would not permit the anomaly of a witness, an observer, for too long. Attention, that state of awareness, which I forced myself to maintain, alienated me and made me a cell of a universe ruled by other laws. The antibodies would soon take effect. They would find me and absorb me, or even reject me, as the physical body does with a foreign object. A lack of awareness, a grimace, a muted complaint or even a hint of envy, jealousy or antagonism, would be enough to ensure my inclusion in that world of sadness, where my condition as an observer had placed me.

Surely, an instinctive intelligence was supervising all of this. I distinctly felt the sensation of being inside a huge living organism, like Jonah in the belly of the whale; or in an immense prison so evolved it could read the prisoners' thoughts and knew beforehand if one of them was planning to escape.

One day, I observed the hall, crowded at that time with the transhumance of ravenous and salivating beings moving towards the canteen block. I had the menacing vision of a hypnotic organisation, of a human termites' nest full of tyrannically busy beings, just like those archaic and blind insects, so similar to us. It was then that I made the sensational discovery that she, the ACO, was the living being, that highly organised organism which contained us. All of us, managers, office workers and workmen, were only organs, glands, organic corpuscles that flowed in her arteries without an actual will or an individual destiny. I was horrified to see them stuck to that world led by the mysterious influence of negative emotions and I multiplied my efforts.

I turned to every kind of stratagem in order to avoid being discovered and metabolised. I erected psychological barriers by writing pages and pages of the Dreamer's sentences and then rereading them all in one breath, without stopping. Once I came to the end of my strength, I ended up reciting the prayers I had learnt as a child. I murmured them, one after the other. Instinctively, I felt that this kept the doors closed; it prevented, at least temporarily, the flow of those poisonous ideas from penetrating me. In the most difficult moments when I felt each of my defenses toppling, I would clutch at the Dreamer's teaching; remembering. I would stop for a while to stare at a point, a technique the Dreamer had taught me years ago, in an attempt to gather the scattered fragments of my Being.

As yet there appeared to be no one inside ACO who noticed my attempts to escape, or the stratagems I constantly invented, beyond all rationality, to try and maintain a state of concentration and detachment. Up until that moment I had managed to resist, to play my part even better than I had hoped, but I had no illusions. I knew I had little time, perhaps only a few days; before the alarm at my attempt to remain outside the condition of all the other dependents would ring. My condition as an 'outlaw' would be discovered and I would suffer the fate of a white ant that has spent too much time away from the influence of the queen.

Without the Dreamer's help I had no chance of succeeding.

7 The accident

That morning I was busy following the reconstruction work on the house in Chiá when I heard a screeching of brakes on the road. The premonition of a misfortune, darkly awaited, froze the air. I crossed the garden in the direction of the sound and ran through the gate into the road. Even in that short time, my fear grew immeasurably; it turned into dread and then a boundless horror.

In Kuwait, Luca had missed riding his bicycle. Back in Italy, he had been given one as a present and, with it as his inseparable companion, he had been tearing up and down the streets of the town like a little rocket. Now I could see him. That body lying abandoned on the other side of the road… was him! I spent the night at my son's bedside in a hospital room. Anxiety, fear and pain, became physically unbearable; until, having reached their peak, they disappeared, like the effect of an anaesthetic. I thought of the Dreamer and something came undone inside. I felt the lightness of an aerostat freed from its ballast sacks.

I had not met him for months and I did not know how to get in touch with Him again. So I decided to make a final attempt: I wrote a letter to Him, as I had done many years before; a letter that was a testament to what was false in me, the final deed of a man who has decided to renounce forever, hypocrisy, accusation, and all that has guided his life until that moment. There was no-one else to blame. Now I realised I was the sole cause of each of my misfortunes.

The world cannot move a hair without our consent.
The world is as you dream it.

That same evening, when Heleonore came to take my place, I began to put in order my thoughts and the sensations I felt in those moments. They took the form of a letter dedicated to the Dreamer. That task kept me occupied for many days without my being able to see any end to it. Each time that I thought I was close to finishing it, I noticed, on reading the letter again, how inadequate it was, and far from the result I had desired.

Apparently, it was me who had written the letter but in actual fact, it was the letter that revealed me. In it, I could see the reflection of my image and with a little sincerity, I 'saw' the embarrassing expressions of a false ego peeping out from a sentence here or there, denouncing vanity, falsehood and the absence of gratitude. Then I left what I had written and started again from scratch. The very same sentences that up until a little while before had seemed right to me, now, as I read them again, appeared unsatisfactory, arrogant, or meaningless. Often, some minutes later, looking over what I had written, I had the sensation I was reading the work of someone else, a stranger, so I replaced some words, discarding entire phrases and concepts, and did the job again, challenging my resistance each time, with an incomprehension I was unable to remove.

A voice inside was constantly asking me to stop, criticizing and even making fun of me, due to the absurdity of such an effort. Finally it said "You won't even know where to send this letter!" I considered this harassing thought the most important signal that I was doing something good and useful.

Up until that moment, I had been learning to distrust myself, that is, what I had believed to be me until that moment. It was then that I started to know the dark, slothful part of my being that had driven my existence. It was finally emerging.

After a day and night of frustrated efforts, and disappointed by the reading of the umpteenth version, I realised that whichever way I looked at it, that letter could do no more than reflect who I was. The old could not write the new! There was no way of keeping the old rubbish and past monstrosities out of that letter. There was no idea, expressive style, structure, or choice of words, behind which I could hide my horrifying deformity. The thought of Luca, the circumstances of the accident and the tiredness, overwhelmed me.

Years later, I felt again the terrible sensation that there were two of us in the same body, and I was terrified by the thought of being trapped forever in ambiguity, with no way out. I would have given anything to no longer cohabitate with this foreigner and leave behind that clot of doubts, fears, compromises and hypocrisy, which held me prisoner.

The certainty that even this last desperate attempt to make contact with Him was in vain, that the Dreamer would not come and save me, threw me into such a profound depression that I could no longer control myself. I hastily gathered the pages of the final version that still cluttered the table, screwed them up into a ball and violently threw them away. With a desperate, impotent gesture, I hurled myself against the wall and hammered it with my fists until my hands and wrists began to bleed. Then, with no strength left, I slowly fell to my knees crying.

At that moment, at the height of my desperation, with no more defenses or protection, I knew the accident that had involved the being dearest to me was payment for my disobedience, I cried for Luca to be saved. I offered myself in his place. My grief was numbing and as it disappeared just the pain's pain remained. I picked up my pen and paper again and wrote the letter unhesitantly.

8 The letter. A King Midas in reverse

To the Dreamer,

This letter is me.
This empty page is the reflection of my emptiness.
For a long time I've felt sickened by all that I see in me,
by all the signals that show a lowering of my strength,
a return to the past.
I dig and dig inside but I can't find anything of value,
not even the consciousness of having no value.
A state of unhappiness, insecurity, fear, makes me
a stranger to You and my own life.
I try to find any stratagem to escape from it,
but the effect only lasts for an instant.
My will is still deeply buried!
The work of observing myself
leads me to greater disappointment.
Wherever I look

I always see the same grimace of unpleasantness.
The mirror of the world, of others,
has never been brighter, clearer.
Some parts are like a 'magnifying glass'
and show me every detail with ruthlessness.
Others, less lucid, denser and more distant,
need more time to send their image to me.
But all the world knows.
I defend myself, I try to shield myself…
I try to be brave, but I'm exhausted.
My back is against the wall.
The limits of my Being suffocate me.
I know you've given me so many chances
and I've only taken the crumbs.
I suffer because of this… the thought
of what could have been, of what could have been done…
"Mending the world means healing oneself."
These words of yours are working inside of me.
I'm more humiliated by the thought of having been
an obstacle to Your plan, than by my own failure.
My presumption, my assumption that I was knowledgeable,
has caused me to miss the target.
I've jeopardized the evolution of
thousands of men and women
who are in your dream, and waiting to make the passage.
I've compromised their 'journey' towards integrity.
I know that the opportunity is still great, even now,
even in these conditions.
I know that everything can be conquered again
and carried further beyond.
The price terrifies me.
The fact is that in all those years in which
you've given me the chance to be close to You,
to have direct contact with Your ideas, with Your words,
they still haven't become flesh of my flesh.
I write them down, I go over them in my mind,
but I don't apply them to my life.
Today less than ever, do I know who I am.
As You've said: I've never known!
But many times in the past, and for long periods,

I've been able to delude myself and confuse my selfishness,
fear and the worry of saving myself, with aspiration.
I believed I had some ability.
Now I know that everything around me
takes on the aspect of the lie that still rules my life.
I'm a King Midas in reverse.
All that I see and touch turns to dross rather than gold.
I'd like to express my gratitude,
to say thank you for all that You've done for me,
for having derailed my life from its terrible tracks,
for having given me a new destiny;
gratitude for having shown me the road to dignity,
even if because of my limitations
I've only been able to drink a few drops of it.
Gratitude for making me experience the absence of fear,
Doubt and pain… for making me see,
beyond the apparent invincibility of death,
a fragment of eternity, its ineffable glow.

9 "Dance, for heaven' s sake, daaance!"

I came in on tiptoe and saw Him busy reading, His head leant back against the headboard. The bed seemed taut and untouched, and the ashen colour of His long hair stood out against the white linen pillows, so impeccably ironed and starched. He looked like a Renaissance prince. I held my breath in the absurd hope that He would not notice my condition. I felt ill at ease, yet I would not have wished to have been anywhere else in the world.

Something extraordinary had happened in me and a change had brought me to Him, one more time. Gratitude had been the key to access. While these thoughts turned over in me, I felt the thinness of the thread that connected me to Him.

«I have come to offer you a short cut – He started in a decisive tone, without preamble – *As long as you're ruled by fear, doubt and conflictual thoughts, you'll have to depend on someone or something outside of you. Until you're able to free yourself from them, you'll replace dependence on something with dependence on something else, but this is neither freedom nor evolution.»*

He scrutinised me and a shadow darkened His face.

«Everything denounces your falsehood. You're a fake. Hypocrisy still rules your existence. And now, at your son's bedside, you'd like to know why life seems to torment you...»

Here He stopped, and during that pause He rose from the bed.

That unexpected reference to Luca made me start, and I suddenly felt all the pain of that difficult episode in my life.

Meanwhile I was following His movements with a growing anxiety. The Dreamer was looking at me threateningly and coming towards me without turning away. Then He leaned forward, His face coming imperceptibly closer to mine, shortening the psychological distance between us. Every molecule in the air was vibrating, as though anticipating a vital communication. I saw Him move His head several times rapidly, from one side to the other, like a boxer looking for an opening in his opponent's guard. His face took on the ferocious expression of someone who is about to strike a blow. Fear cut off my breathing and I had to gasp for air. An eternity passed as the silence grew even more profound.

Then, almost hissing in a voice as fierce as that of a mortal enemy, He whispered:

«The world is as you dream it.»

I could hardly swallow and wanted to flee, but was unable to move a muscle.

«Change the dream and the world will change» He said. I nodded slowly to show that I had understood, that He could pull me out of that dense and heavy corner of the universe,into which He had forced me. At that point, He gave me the most incredible order that one could imagine. So unexpected and inappropriate that, at the beginning, I couldn't believe He was serious.

«Dance! Dance!... Dance!!!» He ordered me several times, each time, raising the tone of His voice until it became a powerful cry.

«Dance! Dance!» He shouted, seeing me paralysed with surprise.

«Dance... Dance, for God's sake... DAAAANCE!» He continued to shout until it was horribly clear beyond any possible doubt, that He was literally ordering me to dance, there, at that moment. Fear and bewilderment turned into a sudden, irrepressible rebellion, born from years of shame and an endless repugnance. Lured by the obvious absurdity of the Dreamer's demand, my usual

hypocrisy seized on an easy opportunity to show off paternal feelings and demonstrate pain for my son. In the inner struggle that was tearing me apart, the old won and I gave vent to that clot of falseness that I was.

«Dance?» I asked, pretending to be checking that I had fully understood, but meanwhile loading that question with all the violence of someone who, for once, believes he is wholly in the right and has the entire world on his side.

«Are you saying I should dance while my son is in danger of losing his life?» I asked in a challenging tone. I had just enough time to see Him lunge forward with the speed of a tiger.

«It's not your son who is in danger of losing his life, but you! – He said – *And not just now, but forever.»*

10 "You're alive and sincere only when you're threatened!"

Shaking, He hurled himself at me with His fists clenched, His eyes were bursting out of their sockets, while the veins in His forehead were swollen with rage like a furious flood. I tried to protect myself by raising my arms, but I could not complete that action and my face was left undefended. I was crippled with fear, and unable to avert my gaze from those threatening eyes that, all this time, from a few centimetres away, remained constantly fixed on mine. Motionless, helpless, I saw them shining like burning coals. Only then did I recognize, with a shudder of terror, a flash of arcane cruelty crossing His eyes, and when at last I was able to interpret it as ferocity, there was no time left for me to be horrified.

Twice He feinted at my face, alternating His punches as He would have done against a punch bag. Then He searched my eyes, to ascertain my reaction. I was terrified.

«Don't move those eyes!» He thundered, scanning my pupils as if He were searching for a dangerous, foreign object. It was something that I had never seen before in encounters between men.

«Don't move theeeem!» He threatened several times, shouting and horribly extending the vowel, noticing my inability to obey His order. There we remained, eye to eye, predator and prey, for a time which seemed endless to me. Then in a hiss, more horrible than His shouts, He said:

«This monstrosity must leave forever!»

I did not know to whom, or what in me He was talking to. A moment before I would have fainted, He drew back His head with calculated slowness, but continued to stare at me with the implacable menace of His eyes. When He started to talk again, His tone had returned to normal, and for this reason the effect was even more devastating.

«*I have no limits!* – He said with cold ferocity – *I am here to either heal you forever or lose you!…*»

Surprisingly, He displayed a radiant smile, as if a difficult experiment had succeeded, or he had won an impossible bet. There was nothing human about that being; or rather, nothing that I had considered human until that moment. With no basis for comparison, I reeled back, dismayed. I would have preferred His angry outburst a hundred times to that inhuman, anachronistic smile of His.

«*You, like millions of men, are alive and sincere only when threatened. Only when you meet someone or something more violent than you, do you appear human... For a moment I became your mirror, and you recoiled before your reflected image, as you've always done in life. You were frightened by your own violence, and horrified because you didn't know yourself*» He said, in His usual tone. His face was serene again and suddenly calm.

«*Men like you join the pacifists to the bitter end; they fill the ranks of all the Salvation Armies on the planet; they become apostles of humanitarianism and defenders of non-violence, never knowing that they themselves are violent and, unconscious propagators of struggles and oppositions.*

Mankind creates charitable institutions, humanitarian organizations and philanthropic movements that are the incarnate reflection of its falseness and degradation... Altruism and humanitarianism become ways for men to hide their own violence; and most frequently take on the shape of their separation and distance from others. Benevolence, generosity, and love become degraded and coarsened, materialising into a mendicant soul; in the most complete misunderstanding of the real meaning of 'do unto others', in the final and most extreme degeneration of charity.»

Now it was no longer to me that the Dreamer spoke. Mankind – just as it is was – had become the target of His invective, a decayed humanity that had lost all sense of connection and even memory of what it really was to be a human being. This widening of the audience lowered the pressure I was feeling, and allowed me to breathe. I felt relieved and bewilderment mixed with the happiness of someone who miraculously survives a mortal accident without a scratch. The taste of an unknown freedom became imperceptibly stronger and stronger, until it filled my soul. It was a birth; and that was my first breath. It entered my lungs, which were brand new too, and a molten flame filled every corner of them. But that respite did not last for long. The Dreamer took me in His jaws, pitilessly, like a wild beast that stops for a moment to lick the still palpitating prey, before resuming its ferocious meal.

«Evil is not to be violent, but to be unaware of one's violence. Violence is the reverberation of a conflicting mentality, the effect of self-sabotage, of killing oneself inside.»

When He started talking again His discourse had the solemnity of a sermon. I thought how rarely modern mankind had been struck by words that were so mercilessly sincere, so unbearably lucid, and so irreverent. Who could have pronounced them?

«The first task is to build oneself! Ignorance of the self invites all the misfortunes and troubles that you can observe in the lives of human beings... unconsciously, the victim creates the conditions to attract his aggressor... For a long time, in the darkness of his Being, he has been spinning the terrible web to capture his very executioner.»

11 Healing can only happen from within

The discussion was becoming quicker and started to focus on Luca's accident. With the Dreamer I was exploring, at its roots, the phenomenon of causality, trying to understand why life seemed to show such a deep hatred of me. I imagined I was following Him along the course of a mythical river back to the remote source whence it had burst forth and I knew that this search, turn after turn, would lead to me. I experienced the pain even before He started.

«The accident isn't about the child, but your world... it's the effect of your sinfulness» He said, going on to assert that when a man has made an inner promise, and set out on the path towards the unity of Being and integrity, he pays for every deviation, blemish, 'sin.'

Here He paused in His discourse and scrutinised me for a long time.

«A good past is like having good capital... Your past is like a biblical calamity – He noted with bitterness – *It's a ship with a cargo of debts, and until you've paid them all, you'll have to endure countless sufferings and face the cruelest of Antagonists...»*

«When you become conscious of this, you will feel gratitude for all the sufferings and you will bless every pain and apparent injustice... One day you will know how they came to elevate and improve you, and how necessary they have been for your evolution... Difficulties and sufferings are tests on your path to integrity. When a man realizes this, life itself becomes his teacher. Every crisis, fall and difficulty is perfect, irreplaceable.»

Noticing the difficulty I had in accepting that explanation and assuming full responsibility for every event in my life, He resorted to a sharp reprimand:

«If My words don't change you, life will. What you can't understand through my words, you'll have to understand through the errors you make in life.»

He told me that between these two 'options', there is only one difference: 'Understanding through one's errors' is a hard road, much slower and more painful. He concluded:

«After My words, comes life with its rules and instruments of healing.»

The Dreamer explained to me that humanity as it is, sealed in a hypnotic dream, can only live permanently under the threat of ruthless antagonists. Through His words, as had happened on many other occasions with Him, I had a vision: the planet appeared like an old oil mill with huge stone wheels constantly grinding the disobedient and those who stubbornly refused to understand. I saw the never-ending series of ills that have always afflicted the world and felt the splitting and crushing of their bones under the press; I acknowledged the necessity of the holocaust, of that endless horror, of wars, calamities and inhuman tragedies that have always tormented the planet, and followed the winding course of our millenary story until, beyond the crust of an ignorant description, as if through a tear in the canvas, I 'saw' that those misfortunes were the bitter medicine for a degraded mankind, for those individuals, nations and entire civilisations, who have no other way to recover.

«Life is not a machine of transformation, as you imagine it to be – intervened the Dreamer, correcting me – *but a machine for*

truth. Events and circumstances don't come to heal us; they're symptoms to make us see what we are…»

«True healing can only happen from inside. There are no political, religious, or philosophical systems that can transform society from the outside. Only an individual revolution, a psychological rebirth, a healing of the Being, man by man and cell by cell, can lead us towards planetary well-being, and a more intelligent, true and happy civilisation.»

12 In praise of injustice

It was in those circumstances that I listened to the Dreamer's apology, reporting it in my notes under the title 'In praise of Injustice'. While I was taking it down, my hand flew quickly over the pages to keep up with Him, and I felt concepts and mental schemes crumble under the battering ram of His words. With one hand I wrote, and with the other I invisibly clutched my old thoughts and usual beliefs. I was dangling from them over an abyss, suspended by my last shreds of rationality.

«It will take many years for mass humanity to swallow this bitter pill and accept the evidence of such a simple truth» He said, and fell silent.

I knew this preamble and that silence gave me the opportunity to prepare myself for what He was about to tell me. But this only managed to heighten my anxiety. I tried to gain a little equanimity, and in those few seconds, I desperately tried to gather myself and collect the skeins of my scattered thoughts; but that improvised construction wouldn't stay up, that fictive unity collapsed each time I attempted to assemble it. Until I resigned myself to my lack of preparation, and listened.

«The victim is always guilty!» He proclaimed.

I had already heard this paradoxical assertion of the Dreamer's during the dinner at Veronica's, but this did nothing to mitigate the bombshell effect of that declaration and the shock of its unbearable absurdity.

«Injustice is the highest form of justice, the most impartial! – confirmed the Dreamer – *What the ordinary man calls injustice is a resource of existence which allows him access to a state of*

completeness and higher levels of comprehension. Injustice is 'compassion' made manifest.»

I could not believe it. In quick succession images exploded in my mind: Luca, crumpled under the wall, the ambulance's arrival, the dash to the hospital, the doctors' anxiety concerning my child, and I felt a sense of uncontrollable rebellion. The Dreamer read my thoughts.

«Your son's accident is no accident at all... 'happenstance' doesn't exist... An accident is a true act of will... the act of an unconscious will... Unpleqsant events and disasters befall us in order to make us complete... Injustice comes to men in the form of opportunities for improving their own lives, to awaken in each one the 'dream' of being one day free. Injustice is the road towards self-knowledge and true completeness. No justice could be more just than injustice itself» the Dreamer said, and as I wrote down His words, I continued to shake my head as tears rolled down my cheeks. His voice softened.

«I'm ready to explain it to you scientifically – He said with patient sympathy, His voice softening – *There is in every man, even the most degraded, a involuntary will... an unconscious conscience... a brutalised beauty...a smattering of unity that shouts at its recovery...»*

«Evil is always at the service of good. Evil doesn't exist!... That which is apparently negative... every adversity or what the horizontal man calls 'injustice'... is in actual fact, a blessing – He said in conclusion – *The most unjust events, actions and circumstances come to raise the Being to higher levels of completeness, integrity and freedom...»*

He explained to me that even the symptoms of a disease are the precious signs of the body that denounce a degradation of the being and a loss of understanding. But man no longer knows how to read them and confuses the cause with the effect. This is why every intervention to suppress the symptom, the practice of all institutional medicine, ignores the true disease and makes it worse. One eliminates the symptom along with the opportunity of achieving a true, complete recovery...

«No evil exists outside us, only visible signs of recovery, bright indications of a true salvation that is in ourselves.»

«Even the most serious diseases?»

«Even apparently incurable illnesses are only symptoms or signs that point the way towards recovery. They show the fault concealed behind every fall and reveal the self-sabotage, the thousands of inner deaths that are the true cause of physical death. If one wants to recognise them, it's essential to follow the path back to the true cause!... One day science will discover that there aren't so many diseases. Behind their apparent multiplicity, beyond the complexity of their symptoms, there's only one disease... which is a thought, a feral seed...»

«The cause of all ills… is therefore… our psychology?»

«No! Even our psychology is still a symptom by which we return to the true cause, to the cause of all causes, to the evil behind the evil: the idea of the inevitability of death. The elimination of this superstition and discussion of this 'self-fulfilling prophecy', this prophecy that comes true on its own, will resolve psychology and psychology will resolve all ills.»

«Man has made death his limit, but in actual fact even this is only a sign, a symptom of healing... and, paradoxically, the clearest evidence of our immortality – He said, adding – *Death is the clearest and most tangible sign of our omnipotence, and man's ability to realise the impossible: the destruction of his body. At the root of every disparity between men, every injustice or lack of freedom, lies the true difference from which all others originate: the degree of inner responsibility. Being, understanding, responsibility and destiny are one and the same thing.»*

«Man is his understanding – reaffirmed the Dreamer – *Men belong to different levels of comprehension. This is the true difference between them!»*

Even though human beings appear similar; the differences between them are like an eternity. Like zoological species at different stages of evolution, their beings belong to evolutionary periods that are often immeasurably distant from one another.

«But what about… – I asked, hesitantly – all man's assertions, his most noble declarations… and the struggles, wars and revolutions made in the name of liberty and justice?…»

«They've all been in vain and have left everything as it was!» said the Dreamer, stressing these words, and imposing order on my confused thoughts.

«Wars, revolutions and every other attempt to give human beings equality, justice and peace have failed because they're based

on the belief that there was an evil to fight and external obstacles to eliminate.

Wealth, privilege and social disparities are only effects and the reflection of a much deeper difference. It's in the Being, in our breathing and feelings that everything happens.

Our level of Being creates our life.

Mankind 'as it is' needs evil! A man can only listen by means of pain... To feel alive he needs suffering... an Antagonist... time...

So long as this condition continues, pain and all that man calls injustice will remain the sole driving force of the world and the only impetus capable of pushing human beings towards superior states of Being.»

13 The world is created by our thoughts

«Your son hasn't died because there's still a thread that connects him to Me!»

Like a small flame, which grows piercing the obscurity and making its own space, the Dreamer's conclusion penetrated the fog of my concerns for my son's well-being. What I saw emerge was unbearable and I would have fainted if the Dreamer's voice had not come to shake me with its ironic severity.

«Now, at your son's bedside you ask yourself why... you ask yourself why he has had an accident... You'd like to know why your life is so disastrous...»

To avoid His gaze, I averted my eyes; I looked at the cinders burning in the fireplace and pretended to be absorbed, following the reflection of the flames on the golden weft of His gilet.

«Take one segment of your life, a millimetre of your existence and you'll find a map of your destructive thoughts and polluted emotional states there... Doubt and fear have decided the events of your life up until now.

Those who live in hell can only create hell! Your doubt becomes fear and fear forms stones in your kidneys... or plots accidents and disasters in the world of events.

The world is such because you are such.

The world is one of your inventions... The accident is the world's attempt to let you see your lack of attention and love and show you the right way. But you don't listen to yourself!»

Therefore, thought creates… even that which is most destructive and sick!

«The horror is to have moved God outside us!» He said, and announced that when man has repossessed his dignity, his will and right to be his own master, religions will disappear.

«Once upon a time man didn't have any religions – He stated – *They appear when, due to a decline in religiosity, man becomes degraded and transfers divinity outside himself.»*

I felt the unbearable weight of this responsibility, and my abilities wavered before a vision so different from all common interpretation, before such a pitiless explanation of the human condition and the machines that perpetuate it.

Along with me, all of humanity was on trial, there in the criminals' cage; bound by that sentence that proclaimed a general, iron law of causality that left us with no means of escape. Complaining, accusing, self-justifying and lying, now appeared to form part of the ancestral cry of zoological beings still at the dawn of evolution, groping through the darkness of their consciences.

At the centre of the Dreamer's vision was the overturning of the relationship that we believe exists between states and events. The Dreamer's voice and the teaching of Lupelius' 'School for Gods' were merging into one sole concept that upset and overturned the ordinary vision of the world. Man's most deeply rooted belief is that the external world is the cause. This is the architrave on which its hallucinated cosmology rests: the superstition that states are the effects of events. Like the flat and inverted image of reality that falls on the eye's retina, so does man perceive the overturned relationship that exists between his moods, emotions and external events. Our first education, from the earliest age, has convinced us that fear is the result of having met something terrifying, and that pain is the reaction to something painful. The Dreamer explained by way of example the necessity of a 'second education', a psychological revolution that in human history assumes the titanic dimensions of a flight from Tartarus, from the abysses of zoology.

Man is 'depth blind'. He does not perceive depth. Our natural system of sight is lacking the ability to see beyond the two dimensions. As a matter of fact images fall on our retina flat and upside down, but during the course of a slow evolution man has learned to elaborate and integrate visual information, inverting it and giving it depth, thus adding a third dimension. In the same way he will have to reverse his concept of the world by 180 degrees, adding a third dimension, drawing a vertical line to his psychology. This will allow him to 'see' that it is states of the Being that anticipate and determine the nature and quality of all the events and circumstances of his life.

«States and Events are one and the same thing – the Dreamer asserted, summing up in this formula the most important element of His vision – *States and events are a single thing!... The time that passes between them creates the illusion in man that there is no connection between his states of being and the happenings of his life.»*

At this point the Dreamer stopped and waited. I had the impression that He was gathering some assent as yet invisible to me before continuing. Then He said:

«If man could lift the curtain of time, or compress time, he would discover that states are already events. A man's emotional states are events seeking a chance to happen.»

At these words the earth suddenly split open, and a rift opened inside me setting asunder my personal universe from top to bottom, separating forever the old from the new; everything that I had believed up until then, from the new ideas and principles that the Dreamer was instilling in me. I was alone at the edge of that crevass.

The old system and its exhausted ideas, eroded by the millennia, were crumbling. The certainties on which man bases his life, the very causes to which he has always attributed his unhappiness, and all that leads him to complain and accuse the world, were exhibiting all their unreal properties. The fatalism which makes him believe he is a helpless being, at the mercy of uncontrollable events, the victimisation and self-pity that unfailingly leads him to find the causes of each of his misfortunes outside himself, were collapsing like dusty idols. There is in man a tragic difficulty to perceive the cause-effect relationship that exists between his states of Being and the events of his life.

14 Past is Dust

«Thinking is Destiny... Mankind thinks and feels negatively! – pronounced the Dreamer in the tone of an irrevocable judgement – *This is enough to explain the interminable succession of disasters*

that man persists in passing down, and that he calls History; and it explains why, through the millennia, our civilisation has been constantly marked by such a terrible destiny.»

«But if we don't remember our history, how can we learn from it?» I objected, attempting to save some shreds of the old vision. Already close to tears, a trembling in my voice suggested the defeat of all my beliefs.

The Dreamer remained silent and I tried to put a veil of rationality over the panic I felt growing incontrollably inside, and said:

«In the future how can we avoid repeating the errors of the past?»

«Past is Dust! – declared the Dreamer in a laconic tone, sweeping away my imaginary fears at once – *Man's history is the tale of a criminal vision, the materialisation of its vilest part... Remembering this endless series of crimes, as all schools in the world insist on doing, can only pollute us...»*

He stated that it was the millenary attempt of the lowest part in man to survive and perpetuate the past, repeating it and putting it before him like a false future. It is not the experience or memory of past errors that can transform humanity, changing its history and destiny. Only the individual can do it, through his own transformation.

I understood the absurdity of relating to children a story of horrors, not ruled by will but by chance and criminality. Wars and revolutions, crusades and persecutions and the rise and fall of empires, seemed like dirt that had escaped a cosmic broom. We have to cancel that criminal past, and with it, the memory of all the criminals and small-big men which the old mankind has turned into legends and passed down as benefactors and heroes.

The Dreamer's stark message only seemed to be predicting an inevitable and dire fate. That knife probing our wounds was really a scalpel of light. Behind His pitiless analyses, which relegated man to the darkness of an infernal world, below the grave, the Dreamer was revealing how to free oneself from guilt, pain, ignorance… and death. His words were drawing a glowing map to guide our return to a state of innocence, integrity and power. Finally, this was the short-cut, the passage…

The words that followed comforted me. They held the suggestion of a solution.

«We should not remember the past, we should remember the above! It's necessary to develop a 'vertical memory' perpendicular to the plane of History... It's necessary to elevate the Being of man... The world isn't created... the world is projected...»

I felt the strength of that authority run through every fibre of my body; the same authority that – through the millennia, in the darkest moments of its history – had flung codes and gospels, fairy tales and parables at man, as if they were rafts or life-jackets. I understood the tragedy of our incurable hardness of hearing, the deep sleep that has clouded us. This is why angels have always been depicted with trumpets and drums, like a band of clamorous musicians.

«Once I told you that if you had been alert, conscious and attentive to everything you make in your Being, then your wife's death wouldn't have been necessary. You wouldn't have made the world reveal it to you with such violence. To recover you've chosen time, and time is pain... You are not living here and now and your absence makes way for all the disasters programmed by your lack of attention.»

The *grandeur*, the universality of that vision redeemed man from the condition of an automaton, a bio-chemical puppet moved by the threads of a prevaricator fate, making him responsible for every event in his life. I was grateful for the gift the Dreamer was giving me. A new, dazzling truth was replacing my old ideas: *Nothing is external*. Everything depends on you. There is nothing a man can receive from the outside: neither success, nor money, nor health. This was the millenary voice, the same voice that had echoed through the old schools of responsibility, breeding grounds for heroes and demi-gods, where a healed humanity has always been forged. *Our world, with all its events, is created by our thoughts.* Even destructive thoughts create; for we are also purveyors of negativity. Instead of reacting to the world that we ourselves have created, we should learn to follow the fresh trail of all events and return to the states that generated them; and then circumscribe and delete them.

15 Will and chance

«*Awareness is light* – continued the Dreamer – *Knowing what happens inside us allows us to intervene in the moment, which is the only real time, and project a new world free from chance.*»

Where this awareness exists, where this light penetrates, casualness has no *raison d'être*. Accidents and illnesses, in order to enter our life and take on reality, must have our approval; they can happen only when this light has grown dim.

Once again, in a more and more convincing and incontestable way, the Dreamer was setting before me the evidence that chance does not exist. *The unexpected always requires a long preparation.*

«*A man cannot hide. Everything in his life is regulated by Law and Order*» He enunciated.

«And what about accidents?»

«*They exist for man as he is!... for the degraded creature which he has become... for that being who, by burying his will, has become a caricature of himself*» He answered; and added that, for a humanity that does not possess will, life's events and circumstances are regulated by the outside, by the description of the world.

Through the Dreamer's words I realised that an unhappy life, scourged by difficulties and problems, cannot be blamed on chance, but rather a lack of vigilance or absence of attention to all that happens inside us. It was like driving with a blindfold. Man, as he is, has become a somnambulist who passes by crossroads and streets in a deep sleep. I realised that survival for common mankind is a daily miracle. A frisson of fear ran through my body. I do not know how to express the horror and compassion I experienced at the precariousness of lives like ours, groping about in the most desolate parts of our psychology with a complete absence of a guide-will.

Then, the solemn words of a universal epigraph vibrated in thc air and I gathered them meticulously:

«*You are completely in charge of your life. You are completely responsible for your destiny. You must recognize that pain, sickness and poverty are not accidents but products of your inner conflicts. It is you, and you only, who makes them up.*»

According to the Dreamer, a casual acceptance is always the sign of a healing, it is always a payment, but an involuntary one. When will is not present the world gets the upper hand and man is prey to chance and fortuity. The states of Being governed by the will determine the events that we encounter. The voluntary payment, given in advance, is the choice of a cured mankind. The deferred payment, involuntary, is the choice of a fallen mankind that uses chance to pay, suffering time as its only currency. The degradation of this understanding, in any latitude and at any time, has generated a never-ending series of methods, of attempts to pay in advance, their common denominator being self-punishment. The attempt to avoid future disasters and desire to cancel them from one's destiny, has been accompanied in the history of all civilisations by sacrifice and expiation through self-inflicted sufferings.

I started thinking of small sacrifices, penitents' vows and martyrdoms offered to sanctuaries and churches; I also thought about self-flagellation and hair shirts. I thought again, armed with this new intelligence, about ancient tribal rites and animal sacrifices, and men immolated and offered through the millennia to visible and invisible divinities. Behind the apparent differences in rituals and choice of method, I recognised the degradation of a forgotten wisdom. Behind those manifestations it was still possible to perceive the distant reverberations of the original understanding, splinters of the awareness that the true cause of all that happens is inside us. As the Dreamer told me, they are a vague memory of the payment made in advance, as it is perceived by a mankind that knows no other way to achieve inner forgiveness.

According to the Dreamer, the payment made in advance is the transformation of oneself. It is therefore, the synthesis of man's highest functions: attention, knowledge of oneself, the transformation of negative emotions and freedom from inner ballast. At the lowest levels of mankind, this intelligence degrades and the advance payment changes from work on the inner self into self-punishment.

I remembered processions I had seen as a child, the bearers sweating blood and tears under the weight of a statue, the Madonna or a saint. I had watched them wide-eyed. Before starting through another stretch of town, they would rearrange the cloth on their wounded shoulders to protect them from the crushing weight of the bars. They traversed alleyways and neighbourhoods, pushing their way through two wings of a ragged crowd that made the sign of the cross and went down on bended knee. I saw again their faces, purple from the effort, and the saints with their eyes turned to heaven and the swaying halos of gilded brass nailed to the nape of their necks. Giuseppona towered over me protecting me from that fever of bodies. "They're going to paradise" she told me once, and I swore to myself that I would never want to go to a place where those scary-looking people lived, even if they called it Paradise. I did not realise that I was observing a living allegory of the payment. It would be the Dreamer who would one day explain to me that this is the attempt to pay in advance, to suffer and use the pain to avert future sufferings, to exorcise calamities and disasters planned by one's own lack of attention, that are already on their way to meet us in the world of events. A poverty-stricken mankind, crushed by the weight of its superstitions, can pay only in the specie of suffering and chance.

«Casualness is always payment or the sign of a healing, but involuntary» repeated the Dreamer, several times stressing the fact that it was still a payment, an evil at the service of good, and never a punishment. He did not want His vision to enter in any way that infinite list of rules that goes from lex talionis – an eye for an eye – to Karma, even going as far as the Dantesque law of retaliation, invented by man to give himself an explanation for his own misfortunes. He made sure that I had written down this point in my notes.

For the Dreamer, when the will inside does not work the world outside is allowed to take charge. When we apply will to each of our choices we are eliminating the possibility of *chance* to govern and lead us to an involuntary payment. Through will we can guide our destiny.

«Chance is a degraded, forgotten, buried will – continued the Dreamer – *Paradoxically, chance is an 'involuntary will' that has taken the place of true will.»*

I remembered that the Gospel speaks of 'men of good will' and the Dreamer confirmed that, that expression meant men who had returned to the spring, who had returned to win back the forgotten, buried will, the 'good' will.

«Man has bartered will for chance. Those who realise this are seeking a School that is able to win back lost integrity» He said, and stated that this is the true reason for the existence of any real school: the return to the unity of Being, to one's integrity. This purpose is still encoded in the very root of the word uni-versity:

versus unum; but these institutions have long forgotten their *raison d'être*.

«Only a few realise the necessity for a special School, and fewer still have the qualities to be able to meet it.»

For a split second, the thought crossed my mind that I was among this number, part of this happy few, but I did not have time to enjoy the slightest particle of presumption before the Dreamer was already rummaging inside me to flush out the thief that I had allowed to enter my thoughts.

«No! You're not one of the few!» He said. His tone was grave, halfway between disappointment and a scornful reprimand.

«It's I who have chosen you!»

As He pronounced these words, the Dreamer adopted one of his hardest expressions, like a warrior that prepares himself by lowering the helmet visor. I froze. I regretted that thought a thousand times and wanted to stop what He was about to say; but it was too late.

«I've chosen you because you are the last, as an example to show that if you can make it any man can!» He said piercing me without remission.

«Mankind can reform, regenerate, revive... it can regain the buried will. There's no need for a mass revolution. The true transformation of humanity happens through the transformation of one single individual who achieves his own integrity, the totality of himself.

A man is beset by a mishap, like the accident to your son, to make him understand that he's still a part of the band of men who only pay if they're forced to... by chance.

If you don't know how to give direction to your suffering, you'll always be part of that superstitious crowd that you saw as a child, of a mankind that tries to avert events through the propitiation of an external divinity which, in its imagination, controls its life. If you aren't in a procession, then it will happen in a stadium, amid the bawling crowd, drawn together by a fanaticism for sport.»

He told me that another popular way of payment is through roles. An infallible law wonderfully puts everyone in the right place. Those who do the most thankless jobs, in hospitals, laws courts and prisons, believe they work to help others; they believe they have chosen that job, passed a selection or won a competition to occupy that role; they believe they have paid for this, but in actual fact they are still paying.

«Those roles are instalment payments – said the Dreamer with His dry humour, ironically maintaining His severe expression – *The role that a man steps into is his expiation and, one day, it will become his coffin.»*

«A new mankind will replace the involuntary payment, the involuntary purification, with a payment made in advance – He foretold – *Healing will come before the disease and the solution will come before the problems.»*

«Love yourself with all your strength, in every circumstance and in every condition... constantly. Things happen as a natural consequence and are all regulated by our will.»

He gave me some seconds to finish my notes which covered pages and pages of my notebook, then, as if making an appeal to all the heroes listening, He said:

«We have to bring a fragment of eternity to those, like you, who live in the infernal circles of organisations.» I hoped that extraordinary mission had been entrusted to me; but He said nothing about it.

«You must start again from where you left off. I can't avoid it for you! – He said, suddenly referring to my condition, now that I was working again at ACO Corporation – *What hasn't been overcome has to be repeated again!»*

The news that the Dreamer was taking me on board and that the 'journey' would continue gave me a burst of energy and I felt the ecstasy of those who take a deep breath of fresh air after holding their breath for a long time.

Following that meeting with the Dreamer, my son Luca started to improve; and after a short convalescence he recovered completely. The sky above Chià became free and lighter as if a suffocating fog had passed beyond. In the following days I carefully listened for signals that would show me the next step and I promised myself that no matter what changes in the path the Dreamer might indicate, this time I would not forget. I imagined that the new work would require the entire family to move to a distant country. In actual fact, my base in Italy only moved a few kilometres away, but the field of action was to be found on the other side of the world. The 'unexpected' letter from a head-hunter in Via Larga invited me to a selection. Only three weeks after that meeting with the Dreamer,

I found myself at the head of markets for the Far East in the Foreign Commercial Division of a multinational colossus. This time I burned my bridges and sealed behind me every possible passage or way of communication with my past.

CHAPTER VIII

To Shangai with the Dreamer

1 Perfection never repeats itself

From the Plaza Concert on the Bund, the Dreamer and I watched the busy boat traffic plough up and down the Huangpu. At that point the immense river flows between the two souls of Shanghai: one from the European colonial period with its monumental architecture; the other incarnated by the new districts of Pudong with its futuristic skyline. From here, as far as the eye can see, the city is a huge construction site full of skyscrapers built in a visionary style, conceived for a megalopolis of the future.

I had not met the Dreamer since my return from Kuwait and the move to my new job in the Far East. In these months, I had endlessly read and reread the notes made during my long apprenticeship, and in all the different circumstances of my life I had steadfastly tried to maintain the principles He had taught me. I was so much looking forward to this moment, yet at the same time I feared our meeting. Two arguments, closely bound together, were still unresolved and remained open like unhealed wounds: the hasty way in which I had left Kuwait and my relationship with Heleonore. They were thorny matters that I could no longer avoid.

That afternoon had been busy and the Dreamer's teachings had been among the most extraordinary of my entire apprenticeship. At His side, listening to Him, I had crossed the age-old gardens of Yu Yuan, and later I walked with Him through the web of little streets around the Buddhist temple, in the old market district. In His presence, amid the dense crowds of that huge city, I felt the same wonder and sense of protection as years before when, clinging to

Giuseppona's hand, I'd descended the maze of swarming streets that scarred Naples' body like infected wounds.

The Dreamer seemed to know Shanghai and China as if He had lived there for a long time. He explained its history and mindset by examining its details and commenting on the smallest events of everyday life. A craftsman at work, the clothes of a passer-by, or the negotiations that were tightly woven together in the miniscule shops, became deep rifts through which I viewed the roots of a civilisation that had been the cradle of Confucianism. The secret of that social glue, capable of keeping together more than a billion people, and the wisdom encapsulated in six virtues, was revealed to me by the Dreamer with the same authority as the understanding which had created it.

We came upon a young artist absorbed in decorating microscopic glass vases. She painted them from the inside, patiently, and with incredible ability. Stopping in front of the bench the Dreamer observed her movements for a moment without making any comment. Then, slowly, He moved His gaze from the girl's hands to me. Time appeared to expand. That moment became an eternity and I lost myself in those eyes, which penetrated me like none had ever done before. My mother Carmela's tenderness, Giuseppe's severity, a friend's affection and a master's venerability were all concentrated in that single glance that ravished my soul. He was that youthful artisan; He was the decorator of the vessel I had become. He was showing the 'work' the process of interior transformation that every man must perform, that no one in the world can accomplish in his place, and becoming the maker of his own existence. In that split second, I was the creature who had come face to face with his creator, with no more screens, masks or roles, and in that moment, I sensed the magnitude of that Being. I listened to His timeless, limitless breath, letting it invade me, and for a moment I experienced His total freedom, as dizziness took the place of my thoughts.

The first photogram of which I became conscious, after that moment, was of being seated at a corner table in a public establishment, an ancient teahouse. From what I could see from the window, its structure seemed entirely made of wood, and was erected on piles in the middle of a lake. Thinking about the Dreamer, I looked anxiously around in search of Him. I found Him there, seated next to me. Relieved, I noted that the establishment was patronised exclusively by Chinese. The customers, their faces and clothes and the furnishings, seemed to have emerged from a woodcut of the colonial period when Shanghai, then a village of fishermen, was beginning its ascent towards becoming one of the biggest ports in the world. The Dreamer's voice, which reached me through the customers' frantic chatter, was at first faint and distant, but gradually grew clearer and clearer, and from the first words I heard, it seemed as though He was continuing a discourse that He had already begun.

«...Therefore each of mankind's problems... from the criminality of affluent societies to the endemic poverty of entire regions of the planet, is only the symptom of a mental illness.»

The Dreamer's assertion catapulted me out of my state of torpor, and those words were merely the prelude to a statement that I would one day recognize as one of the cornerstones of His system of thought. I straightened up slowly, almost furtively, and prepared myself to listen even more carefully. From the explanation that followed, it emerged that, from the dawn of time, man's misfortunes were only the materialisation of his incompleteness, the reflection of his fragmented Being. That rupture in psychology goes back to humanity's remotest infancy...

I was completely awake, painfully lucid, when He stated:

«The world is such because you are such. The world, the reality we believe to be outside us, is the physical echo of our psychology and Being.»

The mere suggestion was mind-boggling.

In the meantime, two young waitresses, in traditional costume, arrived to set our table for tea. The Dreamer suspended His discourse to oversee that operation which He seemed to consider of great importance. For several long minutes He remained absorbed in regarding every particular of that meticulous ritual. I was anxious. I couldn't wait for Him to continue. The secret of the millenary misfortunes afflicting man, and perhaps the root of my own unhappiness, was about to be revealed to me, and I was astounded and disappointed by the fact that He could break off an argument of such importance for something so insignificant. Naturally I did not voice my thoughts, but I continued to dwell on them, still believing then that thoughts were invisible and that a man could hide them.

«Nothing exists that is too small or insignificant!» He surprised me. His statement sounded like a reprimand. He was talking without looking at me, apparently still intent on the details of

the tea ceremony. I felt as if I had been caught red-handed, and I blushed with embarrassment.

«Make sure every one of your actions is faultless! – He said *– Impeccability means not performing a single unnecessary action.»*

Then, while He was choosing the different kinds of tea we were going to sample from an endless list, He added:

«When something is done well, it's done forever! The entire universe knows about it and it's no longer necessary for you to repeat it... Only imperfection repeats itself. Perfection never repeats itself because it is constantly being transcended. A perfect chrysalis has to cease being a perfect chrysalis apparently dying in order to become a butterfly, a Being of a superior order.»

He went on to tell me that, through awareness, regulating inner mechanisms and the most minute workings of one's own machine, a man can repair the world and change its history.

«The evolution of the universe depends on the evolution of the individual, on his transformation. The individual and the universal are one and the same – He asserted – *This understanding is at the origin of civilisation and every form of art... It has to return and become the central element of every man's education.»*

He added that the theatre, sacred dances, and all the rituals invented by mankind have originated from this realisation: *everything is connected.* The smallest movement in verticality and the world of the will, causes the greatest changes in the world of events.

«The universe is in our brain... it's a seed within man which develops however he chooses – He recited, adding – *This is why, if a man intentionally acts upon the smallest thing, or makes even the simplest thing perfect...»*

«Like making tea?» I forced myself to ask politely, in an attempt to gain forgiveness for my former musings, which were still unhappy but remained unexpressed.

«Or at least learning how to serve it faultlessly» thc Dreamer suggested in a mock-serious tone, raising the stakes of His game again. As He spoke I noted the two girls exchanging glances with one another and smiling. It seemed to me that they were showing a respectful complicity, a reverent understanding towards the Dreamer. The thought that they were both 'students' crossed my mind in a flash and left me astonished.

«With the faultlessness of that gesture a man could have adjusted his personal universe forever... he could have emerged from a casual level of existence, where everything is already decided, from birth until death, and he could have changed his destiny... The world is the reflection, a resonance of the Being...»

Precious as tiny gold nuggets, I carefully recorded every word of that teaching in my notebook and described the particular circumstances, which gave rise to it.

2 Man's reason is armed

By now our table had been covered with an exquisitely embroidered snow-white cloth and sumptuously laid. Fine china and lacquer trays arrived with delicacies of every kind. When this part of the ritual had been completed and He deemed that His orders had been perfectly followed, He returned to the subject that had been intentionally put aside.

He gestured with His chin to attract my attention to what was around us and said:

«All that you see and touch, all that man calls reality, is psychology... solidified. Man's thoughts materialise and become the 'world'. Facts are thoughts.»

His voice became deep and its hoarse tone betrayed how painful His next revelation would be.

«Man's gravest sicknesses, the cause of all his ills, individual and social, is inner division, his conflictual psychology.»

At these words, a kaleidoscope of images burst forth in me, assuming the voice of myths, which man has created and recounted to himself for thousands of years. Against this fictive background, more than any other, the great scene of the birth of the goddess of reason stood out: Athena leaping forward, shining with weapons, from the hollow walls of Jupiter's cranium: the daughter born out of his headache or nightmare.

«It's a warning-myth» said the Dreamer, plunging into the whirlpool of these thoughts and seizing that image.

«Man's reason is armed!»

The pause that followed made me hold my breath.

«This is the most lucid diagnosis a civilisation has ever been able to make of its illness.»

«So, then, Ancient Greece… knew what would happen to it!» I exclaimed, excited by that discovery.

The Dreamer's answer was not immediate. My nervous joy at His announcement had peaked, and now it was rapidly turning into anxiety. I felt the weight of that revelation intensify as I realised its magnitude. It was painful for me to touch the limit, to discover my inability to contain the beauty and grasp the intelligence of that discovery.

«No! Greece didn't know how to listen to its wise men or its oracles. Recognising one's own evil, one's own guilt, is already a recovery.»

While I noted down the Dreamer's answer, trying to imagine Jupiter giving birth to Athena from his own brain, I became aware of the astonishing fact that I had never seen any representation of this myth; not one trace of that terribly symbolic birth in the entire history of art.

«Man doesn't want to see his foolishness or recognise the destructivity of his thinking – explained the Dreamer – *For centuries mankind has been warned; feeling the shadow of this prophecy loom over human destiny. Not being able to accept it, not knowing what to do or how to avoid it, humanity has tried to delete and ignore it. The recognition of the dark side within a man is the solution, the healing, the true salvation.»*

He announced that if the crowds could recognise the cause of their misfortunes, they would emerge from the state of slavery in which they live. But this is impossible. Only the individual can gain access to this awareness. The masses do not want to have knowledge of themselves, nor do they look for it. They fear all that is new and unknown. The slavery in which mankind lives, the countless misfortunes, are founded on the fear of the unknown that disturbs and blinds it. Political leaders throughout the ages have fed and reinforced this phobia of new things. The crowd cannot dream. When a civilisation no longer knows how to listen to the 'dream' that has created it, to the voices of its solar men, it falls into decline. Their absence heralds the fall of cultures and civilisations; it coincides with moments of collective madness capable of destroying all that has been created throughout the centuries by individuals who dream, by poets of action.

«The mass is a ghost – concluded the Dreamer – *a mechanism influenced by everything and anything… It doesn't have*

faith, it doesn't have a real will... it can't create... It can only destroy. This is the true role of the crowd... Only those who possess a will and integrity can dream and give form to the impossible...»

All that the Dreamer had told me could be applied to companies and modern organisations. I understood that they have a limited lifespan, not because they have financial difficulties, or problems associated with technology and markets, but because they lack responsible, integral men: men who love.

At His signal numerous kinds of tea started to arrive; He had ordered them one by one following olfactory and gustatory laws as old as China itself. He happily breathed in the aromatic spirals that rose up from the various teapots and He himself poured delicate servings into our tiny cups.

After our long walk and the emotion at those discoveries, I did justice to the table, and sampled the various delicacies. The Dreamer fascinated me by relating the legendary origins of certain pastries, and describing recipes and ways of preparation whose traditions dated back to the Ming Dynasty. As always, He was a very kind host but He did not touch any food.

«Man crosses oceans, scales the highest peaks, and risks his life in the most dangerous enterprises – the Dreamer began – *He retreats into temples, ashrams and mosques... he gathers to pray or unites in sex... he chooses the path of penitence or that of libertinism... a monk's cell or the challenges of business... always attempting to unify himself within... in his endless search for completeness.»*

All laic religions, from psychoanalysis to communism, are merely the twentieth-century version of the same search...

Even they, like religious confessions, could be considered experiments, born from the endless attempts man has made, throughout the ages and in all civilizations, to regain his integrity: that special state of certainty which is his birthright and that he still, ancestrally, remembers as the lost paradise.

«Man's history is a journey of return... the parable of the Prodigal Son is its unsurpassed metaphor – stated the Dreamer – *But all religions have forgotten their 'raison d'être'. In degradation, they've become their own opposite: machines for promoting not only death, but the idea of its ineluctability... Rather than healing, religions nourish division and conflictuality; cultivating intolerance, wars of principle, and every kind of superstition...»*

Even Christianity, the Dreamer remembered, in the hands of men with a conflictual psychology, bit by bit ended up turning itself into the Saint Inquisition, without even changing its name. And still today, the blows of the battering ram of evangelical paradoxes, strong enough to crumble the mental structure of the old mankind, come to nothing; and the gentle power of its fables and wisdom of its economic laws, have been reduced to tales for catechism, kid's stuff. Its teaching is entrusted to unconscious preceptors who teach themselves and are, absurdly, the very perpetrators of that hypnotic sleep which the Gospel came to strike down. My notes already covered pages and pages of my notebook when I heard Him announce:

«One needs to nourish in children the idea of immortality, physical immortality.»

Behind the apparent calm tone with which He pronounced these words, I felt the power and heroic strength of a call for planetary insurrection. A flash tore through the darkness of the centuries and I saw a banner flutter at the uproar of thousands of battles waged against superstitions, ghosts and idolatries.

«One needs to bring this idea to all schools, of every order and level, and into the universities... with the prudence of those who know that by entering into a discussion about death, you become the enemy of every ideology and religion» finished the Dreamer in a premonitory tone.

3 The animal that lies

At that moment things became clear to me. Like pieces of a puzzle, each part of His extraordinary teaching found its place, and became in my eyes another coherent element of a breathtaking vision. Finally, the millenary story of disasters, atrocities and misfortunes found an explanation. The absurdity of thousands of conflicts, the tragic paradox of the impoverished multitude in a universe of boundless riches, the atrocity of letting millions of children die who could have been saved at the drop of a hat, finally found a true explanation; a cause beyond time, geography, ethics and faith. Man, as he is, is mentally ill! And his societies and institutions are the materialisation of his divided psychology and conflictual logic, the mirror image of his belief in death.

I asked myself how and when this mental damage had occurred. I would have given anything to know! It would have been the most sensational discovery in history and certainly the most useful. My fantasy took flight. I imagined I was on a scientific expedition going back over the path of the millennia, in search of the event that had reduced man to the conditions in which he finds himself; a kind of journey on the moon in search of Orlando's lost wits.

«The Judaeo-Christian tradition has called that fatal tumble 'the fall from Paradise' – the Dreamer remarked, with a hint of affable humour in His voice – *and has branded it the sin of sins, the 'original sin' the unforgivable sin.»*

I had a hundred questions to ask the Dreamer. It was wonderful to draw on His inexhaustible knowledge, on that special authority which does not belong to those who interpret or make suppositions, but to those who know. The symbolism of the bite of the apple, the snake, the fig leaf, had always intrigued me. Above all I had always felt a kind of intellectual discomfort before such an authoritative tradition; one that had stood for four thousand years, but had created so much tragedy from such an insignificant fact. And why had that been called a mortal sin?

«The bite of the apple is not an insignificant fact – the Dreamer explained to me – *but the decisive metaphor of that tumble in man's Being that renounces his nature and turns the creator into the creature. Biting the apple means believing in a world outside us, one which contains and rules us and gives consistency to the fantasy of an otherness... For man it's the beginning of dependence and his entire tragic history.»*

The Dreamer recalled Adam's first words which will resonate forever as the self-denunciation, the stigma of a disgraced Being: "I hid myself… I was afraid… it was not me… it was the woman whom you gave me…" I felt I was the only witness to a universal disaster, a tragedy without remedy. The drama of our degradation was being performed there, in that moment. I was the first one to behold the appearance on the world's scene of that being which the Dreamer wonderfully defined as 'the animal that lies'.

«Adam's words mark the birth of dependence and are the manifesto of common, untruthful, irresponsible mankind – said the Dreamer – *the oldest of which 'you' can find a trace.»*

His skilful use of that 'you' *en passant*, unfolded before me a vision of traditions more dizzyingly ancient than Genesis. I imagined treasures of inaccessible or lost knowledge, of which I would never have known anything, and of which the Dreamer was now the immortal custodian. Once again I was confronted with the mystery of that Being that could cross time and civilisations, and knew the secret of lost schools, shining in vain like buried jewels. Harried by these continual discoveries, while the Dreamer's words were bursting inside me, creating earthquakes in my Being, I frantically continued to take notes with my trembling hand. Noting my excessive pallor, the Dreamer intervened to give me a little relief, and half in jest, alluding to my working condition, gently joked with me saying:

«It's in Adam's words, those first words uttered by a wretched human cast out of paradise, that the employee mentality finds its roots, as the epitomy of dependence and identification with the external world!»

The language, which according to the Dreamer is the synthesis of man's thought and breathing, in Adam reveals the existence of psychological fragmentation, of a crack in the Being. If Adam were at one with God, how could he desire and believe himself capable of becoming more than Him? It is clear that even before Eve, before the temptation of the serpent, Adam's psychology was already divided. First he lost his integrity, then the serpent appeared.

«Lying, hiding, accusing, justifying oneself, self-commiserating: these have been, and always will be the verbal and, even earlier, the psychological stigma, of a man expelled from Paradise; a Being who has betrayed himself, who has lost his own integrity.»

With the bite of the apple, Adam exchanges life for death, freedom for dependence, integrity for division. Immortality, the individual's birthright, has been replaced with a fragmented, unconscious, mortal eternity and reduced to a zoological perpetuation founded on sexual copulation and viviparous reproduction… While the Dreamer was speaking, I felt that rarest of sensations; that spine-tingling thrill that prefigures a discovery of understanding.

«Adam's sin is mortal because it is a 'fall in time' – concluded the Dreamer – *a fall into a hypnotic state: into the 'belief' that one can die...»*

«But man cannot die, he can only kill himself» He said, with the wary attitude and caution of someone imparting an unbearable secret. The sentence that followed, its anachronistic humour, added *phatos* to that already intensely dramatic statement:

«Death is always a suicide!»

«It's time for man to return home, to awaken from his sleep and take what is his by right... lost immortality.»

I felt that vision transform me with its intelligence, entering my organs and pervading my molecules, cells and atoms. And whilst He was talking to me about the evil of evils, the ancestral origins of man's division and his 'sin', He healed me and I was overcome by an unprecedented sense of gratitude.

4 "Become a free man!"

My thoughts whirled around the extraordinary things I had heard from the Dreamer that afternoon. I tried unsuccessfully to put those ideas in order, to harness them, or at least to dwell on one of them, but they kept on forming a continuous motion, one after the other. Detached from me like leaves falling from a tree, no longer mine, they pursued each other, swirling together in the whirlwind created by the Dreamer's breath. The teahouse where we were was now becoming crowded as new customers arrived, and the hum of the wings of a hundred conversations made the air vibrate pleasantly.

I started with surprise when I heard His voice whisper in my ear:

«The planet's religion is division!... The divinity that mankind venerates above all else is always the same one: fear!»

The force of those words came through the dense swarm of voices, and in this silence, in this space, each of my thoughts was hushed and His words, sharp as scalpels, dug and penetrated deep into me.

«Dependence is fear!... Even you have made fear your idol... This is why you depend and you still earn a living hidden behind a job...»

I had known that sooner or later that moment would come, and I was also prepared for the fact it would not be pleasant; but the Dreamer's tone and the words He used to start His discourse, forewarned me of an even more stormy passage. I took out my notebook and pretended to busy myself with its pages, to hide, as I did whenever the Dreamer's severity reached the limit of endurance.

«I have come to liberate you! – He said with a hiss – *I entered your life because one day you dreamed of being free...»*

His voice became a vibration that rummaged through every corner of my being, chasing my fears, wherever they might lurk. Then He concluded:

«But years have passed, and you still find yourself in slavery!» I felt an inner wound open at such a direct reference. The hint of disappointment in His words annoyed and embittered me, as if He had committed an undeserved wrong, an injustice against me.

«In order to escape your condition, to emerge from the prison of roles, you have to overturn your vision» He said, moving His chair slightly back. I understood the signal. The moment of departure was near. My face must have shown a painful perplexity. The Dreamer waited a few seconds, as if to choose the words that would help me to understand better, before saying:

«Free means free from the world...»

«Where can one start?» I asked determinedly.

«It's a demanding task that will take years and years... even if you started at this very moment, your entire life wouldn't be enough...»

At those words I saw myself facing walls without footholds, I imagined insurmountable distances, remote targets eons of time away from me. I felt discouragement take over and engulf me.

The Dreamer continued without apparently detecting my inner feelings:

«Free means free from fears, doubts, anxieties and negative emotions... free from prejudices, preconceptions, from a wretched description of the world... Free from every limit... free from falsehood and work which is still a punishment for men like you, the perverse effect of a biblical curse... The belief that there's a reality outside you has made the world your boss... Hypnotised by the mirror's reflection, you still search for security in the eyes of others.»

Those words showed the absurdity of my attempt to swim in the Dreamer's turbulent waters with the gills of a primordial, incomplete being. Each phrase was a mortal attack on my past, on my falsity. I knew that when the Dreamer chose to floor me with such violent statements, my life improved and was cleared of so much clutter, making way for states of certainty, clarity, determination.

I endured every blow hoping it would be the last. Come on, stop!… Or at least, give me some breathing space, for God's sake! Just listening to those words required a strength that I did not always possess. My level of responsibility fluctuated: it came and went, increased and diminished, without my being able to control it. Those words were alive! I could feel them pressing unbearably against my limits until they overwhelmed my prejudices, anachronistic beliefs and obsolete ideas… and every fibre of my Being vibrated.

«Free from roles… from fear… Free from identification with the world…»

Those words were rebounding off my chest. Suddenly they exploded in a whirl of lights, sounds, images… My head was in flames.

The Dreamer was showing me a message from the future, a powerful and extraordinary prophecy about man's destiny that I was unable to bear or contain. The idea of a mankind freed from every need, cast out of its nature – or at least from what I had believed was its nature up until that moment, but what in reality was its hell – seemed mad to me. I could have simply put it aside, thrown it away, but it was too late. The Dreamer's vision was already excavating inside me, devouring dead material and old descriptions. I could not assimilate it, but neither could I expel it. I knew that the Dreamer was showing me the path upon which everyone, "*heroes and demi-gods first, others later*" will have to walk… and then will finally arrive. Even if it takes thousands of years. And as He was talking to me about it, I knew that this incredible exodus of mankind had already started. The most courageous individuals had already taken the first step, questioning the invincibility of death and no longer accepting its inevitability. The Individual Revolution was knocking at the door…

I filled pages and pages of notes, without stopping, until I had cramp in my hand. When I came to the bottom of the last page in my notebook, I feverishly continued to write on the back of the teahouse's menu. It no longer mattered whether or not what He was saying to me made sense, or was acceptable. The only thing that counted was to keep writing, to record everything. I knew I could not leave out a word, or change a stress mark… One day, I would reread those notes and understand the preciousness of the substance that then the Dreamer was giving me in abundance and I had been completely unprepared to receive. Or perhaps I would merely pass it on to new generations of researchers.

The Dreamer stood up, carefully moving His chair away, and headed towards the exit. I reluctantly followed Him and we left the teahouse. I realized how easily I could develop an attachment to anything; I could have willingly camped in a place like that, a teahouse. Indeed a strange melancholy overshadowed me while I quickened my pace to catch up with the Dreamer who was already striding over the wooden bridge. Several taxis waited nearby. Without being able to ask anything further, I found myself seated in an old limousine ready to take me to the Hotel. When the door was closed and I saw Him on the other side of the window I feared that might be the last time I would see Him. But the Dreamer reassured me saying:

«We'll meet there tomorrow, at the same time.»

While the taxi went through the streets of Shanghai and crossed the flyovers of that huge city, I was still pondering His words, and trying to bring order to my confused thoughts when I arrived at my hotel. That day every one of my convictions had been shattered, and I had come to the devastating conclusion that – after that meeting with the Dreamer – my old mental schemes, like the walls of a defeated city, had been reduced to rubble.

5 The Budda's father

I was several hours early for the appointment. Some western tourists, a few believers, entered and left the Temple of Yufo Si where the White Jade Buddha is kept. That was where the Dreamer said we would meet. I whiled away the time strolling around the maze of streets of the old market. Passing again in front of the broad door, I searched for His face among the crowd, each time hoping to see Him appear.

When I noticed Him, He was still a long way off. He was walking in my direction accompanied by three old men, quite tall and of austere aspect. One of them, with sparse hair and a pair of gold glasses, gave Him a packet, offering it to Him with both hands, with a bowed head. I then saw them part with bows and signs of deference.

Only when He was alone, did I go to meet Him. A quick glance was our sole greeting. In silence, He continued along the street that ran beside the wall of the enclosure and I followed Him. After all that I had heard Him say about religions, I was surprised when He turned towards the temple's entrance and started to climb the steps, but I followed and entered with Him. A group of monks was eating at a table in the corner. We burned the customary sticks of incense at the huge bonfire that was lit in the centre of the patio, and gathered before the imposing statue of the god. There were few visitors and after some time we were left alone.

«Long but never belong!» He announced, and with that memorable and pithy epigram, He gave me the most complete and profound response to the hesitation I had experienced outside the temple.

«Respect all of men's cults and religions – He said – *but don't belong to any of them!»*

I was still reflecting upon these words when I heard Him say in a low voice:

«At my side, you will be able to change your vision... and with it your destiny.»

The flames of thousands of candles assented, swaying together, gleaming amid the god's ornaments. With the Dreamer, the School was always present. I took my notebook from my bag and started taking notes.

«Growing old, falling ill and dying are part of the world's description – He continued, speaking in my ear – *They've been accepted as natural and inevitable events, and no one has ever rebelled against them. It's the result of a system of beliefs and expectations which have become universal…»*

«Whatever we expect to happen, happens – He stated firmly, and added – *Falling ill, growing old, and dying are bad mental habits.»*

Those words, pronounced there, before that idol, surrounded by papier-mache divinities, emblems of all of man's superstitions and prejudices, broke open the walls of my Being with their paradoxical assertion. For the Dreamer, as for Lupelius, falling ill, growing old and dying were 'bad habits' from which man had to free himself. I started to write and went forward for a few minutes without stopping. He waited until I had finished my notes, then He continued, stating that only a 'work of the School' would allow man to dispel that witchcraft and emerge from the hypnotic sleep in which he had been confined for centuries. The advent of a new education – which He called 'second education' – would allow man to abandon the mortal rut of repetitiveness.

The time had nearly come, He told me, when dying would no longer be fashionable; man would start to change his beliefs and rebel against the idea of death and its inevitability. He left me to meditate upon these assertions until with a nod indicated it was time to go. We turned leaving the Buddha behind us and headed towards the exit. Before reaching the door, the Dreamer imperceptibly bent His head towards my ear as if to tell me a secret. In a whisper and with that gesture I once more found the fragrance of those Sundays I'd experienced as a child; the complicity I'd shared with my brother and sister, the church of S. Antonio Abate that smelled of wax and incense, and that irreverent, unbearable joyfulness which endlessly fed our sniggers and infantile chatter. The Dreamer knew all the keys to my soul.

Feigning to confide a deep secret, He said to me:

«In Buddha's story, the father is the one who is truly enlightened.»

When we were outside the temple I asked Him to tell me the story of that king. Thus I learned that Buddha's father wanted to protect his son from every message of degradation, from the concept of limitation. He personally ensured that the young prince was constantly surrounded by joy, beauty and wealth. and continually changed the members of the court and the servants who attended to his son. He himself wore make-up and dyed his hair and beard to prevent sickness, old-age and death from entering the young Buddha's vision.

«Even today this remains one of the most instructive stories that has ever been passed on – was the Dreamer's gloss – *The Buddha's father understood the importance of the world's description, and he knew the strength of beliefs.»*

He was able to conceive a School of immortals and training in immortality. There the young Buddha was trained to live forever. The Dreamer concluded that the king, having dreamed of a world where sickness and old-age were banished, and having made every kind of effort to protect his son from it, should be celebrated as one of the fathers of mankind and one of the most courageous schemers in the entire history of man.

«It isn't by chance that tradition made him a king, a regal/real man – He said – *In the Olympus of great heroes, his myth deserves a place beside that of Prometheus.»*

6 What depends is not real

It was dusk. From the river-bank along the Bund we saw Shanghai change into an ocean of lights. The Dreamer had just begun one of the most painful arguments, which he had touched upon in the temple, and then left, but I knew that this time He would conclude it.

I drew a deep breath and prepared myself for the painfulness of His intervention.

The lack of integrity, the incomplete psychology, the division and conflictuality that man bears inside, had been the guiding thread of His teachings in Shanghai. Man is mentally sick and the world is a reverberation of his folly. Now the Dreamer was leading me to discover the roots of dependence.

«Only a man who is complete can be free» said the Dreamer. I listened to Him but I did not dare look at Him. I pretended to be busy observing the quivering reflections of the lights that revealed the expanse of the river, which was otherwise invisible.

«A man divided within himself can do nothing but depend!»

These words instantaneously joined the wonderful declarations I had heard from Him many years before, during our first meeting.

«To be employed is only a visible manifestation of depending… this condition isn't the effect of a role, the consequence of a contract… and neither is it born from belonging to a social category… Dependency is the absence of will… it denounces a state of fear, the belonging to an infernal circle of the Being…»

For the Dreamer, everything began when one started to consider time as merchandise and thought to buy men's time rather than what they produced: ideas, goods, services. He stressed that the formation of a huge army of millions and millions of 'dependent' workers, labourers and clerks, willing to sell their own time at a fixed price, so much an hour or a month, is an entirely modern phenomenon, without precedent in the universal history of civilisations.

I connected the Dreamer's discourse to the aversion, even repugnance, that Classical Greece and Rome nourished for every form of work, be it physical or intellectual. In the Age of Homer, *Thetes*, the farm worker who had to sell work done by his own hand to make a living, was considered to have the worst of human conditions. For the Greeks, who were so attached to freedom, depending on someone else for daily survival was an intolerable servitude. According to Aristotle, citizenship should be refused to all those who needed to work for a living. The exercise of political virtue was impracticable and impossible for those who led the life of a hired worker, or who were tradesmen with retributive work that prevented elevation and comfort of the soul.

I felt an irresistible animosity, followed by a mental barrier, rising up in me. I thought that perhaps this vision might have been appropriate in 4th century Greece, but it was not even remotely applicable to a society in the third millennium. This sliver of rationality helped to foster my resentment as I braced myself for the attack that I felt was imminent and which I could already sense flickering behind the Dreamer's words. Without being able to contain myself any further, I burst out:

«Everyone could do without work, if they were able to enjoy the privileges of an aristocrat…»

But the Dreamer turned my vision inside out.

«It's the level of freedom attained within – He stated severely – *It is the victory over fear that makes man belong to the class of gods, men who love and dream, and not those who have to work for a living… Man should only devote himself to maintaining a high state of Being, a condition of serenity, and he should never stop dreaming; then, everything will be given to him.*

«Only a 'mankind' educated in beauty, truth and well-being… Only a dreaming, intuitive, contemplative mankind, can bear the power of not-doing, the responsibility of golden laziness. The old

mankind wants to continue to work... humanity wouldn't know what to do if it stopped... It wants to be dependent, it has already decided to live under the aegis of fear... it has elected doubt as its natural patrimony and master – the Dreamer commented, betraying a hint of bitterness, as if He were observing the distressing and irreversible effect of a cosmic defeat – *It commits suicide by busying itself, by fretting, by bothering and worrying over it... becoming a slave of time...*»

7 Vision and reality are one

«Vision and reality are one. The world is your vision. Change yourself and the world will change for ever!... This is the greatest help you can give the world.»

«But even if I change – I asked, in the tone of a concession – what will become of all the horror, unhappiness and pain in which the world is living? What will stop its wars?»

«The world is you! – exclaimed the Dreamer, impatient – *The world is at war because you are at war... A dreamer only believes in himself and his flawlessness, and he projects the world he desires. The reality in which he lives is the exact representation of his portable paradise.»*

«But reality...»

«Reality is like a stick of chewing gum; it takes on the shape of your teeth!»

«But what I see and touch...»

«The world you see and touch is not objective nor will it ever be... It reflects you...

Learn to be brilliant, elegant, magnificent and grand; learn how to use injustice and anger; learn how to act the role that circumstances demand: comic, ironic, sharp, dreaming and playful, sober and sincere, quiet and detached.

Become a champion of freedom. Use your work to help mankind free itself from tyrannies and oppressions of every kind: political, religious, social, intellectual and emotional... and you'll see an earthly paradise rising before your very eyes.»

Each time I thought about it or reread this dialogue, I remembered Abbott's geometric tale of the encounter in Flatland between the plane geometrical figure and the sphere, a flat creature and a three-dimensional Being.

The Dreamer's discourse, which included strata and levels, and which asserted the existence of as many universes and personal realities as there are men, could not be included in a flat vision, in the bi-dimensional perception of an inhabitant of Flatland.

8 The clerical species

According to the Dreamer, the absence of a role can be borne only by those who have reached the highest level of responsibility in the Being.

«One day, when you've surpassed them and know how to play them perfectly, will you also be free. This conquest can take a few moments or an entire lifetime. It depends on you!»

He added that the ordinary man cannot bear the responsibility of such freedom.

«Only the man who has caught a glimpse of eternity, can make it! – He concluded – *Below the level of an integral man, existence imprisons you in the steadiness of a role.»*

For the Dreamer the roles we play in life measure and demonstrate our level of responsibility. At the dawn of the industrial revolution, the 'sapiens' species found itself at the crossroads of its evolution. In the offices and factories of the world somatic, psychological and behavioural changes were occurring to such an extent that a new species emerged.

The Dreamer defined it as '*The clerical species'*.

«Its main characteristic is the ability to stoically accept the unbearable painfulness of dependency» He announced in a humorous yet dry tone. He added that in time this branch of mankind grew until it came to represent the dominant group; the most widespread on the planet. He stated that similar changes take place in animals after domestication. With meditated slowness, He started to list them: the relaxation of the muscles, adiposity, the flabbiness of the stomach, the shortening of the cranial base and limbs, the pallor of the skin, premature aging, softening…

Whilst making this list, He started to scrutinise me from head to toe, feigning a growing wonder at the discovery in me of all the characteristics found in the 'clerical species'. He continued with that pantomime until He asked me in all seriousness if He could use me as a live specimen for His theory.

Looking at my face, drawn into a grimace of offence and shame, the Dreamer could not help but laugh out loud. It was only then I realised that He had been pulling my leg.

It was as if I had been encased in plaster and my facial muscles were so tense and rigid that I was unable to join Him in one of those rarely witnessed fits of laughter.

«A man who observes himself, who laughs at himself, is free! – the Dreamer would comment on this episode some time later – *If you're confused, observe the confusion in you and you'll be free. Self-observation is self-correction.»*

On that occasion He told me that the ordinary man's true religion is actually his identification with the external world. Mankind is in the conditions in which it finds itself because it lacks the capacity to observe itself.

«If you were capable of observing your hell, it would disappear, your healing would be immediate and it would be communicated to the whole world.»

Looking back now at that reaction of mine, I can see the fragility of the man I was, and how far I still had to go to be among those who had just begun the journey towards integrity. The sick portrayed in the New Testament, those who were blind, lame, deaf, leprous, were living metaphors of a psychologically handicapped mankind but at least one that was aware of its own incompleteness, and ready to enter a place of healing. These were the very few men and women who had asked to gain access to integrity.

It was painful to discover and admit that I still had not reached that condition; that I was like Nicodemus, a man caught in the world of appearances, attached to institutions and dusty temples, to useless rituals, incapable of abandoning the false certainties of the establishment for the great individual adventure.

Certainly, I did not belong to that humanity endowed with faith, endowed with what the Dreamer called the 'dream.' The Dreamer was, and represented for many long years, a threat to my vision of the world, to my beliefs and to all that I wanted my life to be.

Now I understand that healing means going to the roots of that sinfulness, the true cause of all of man's miseries and each of our misfortunes.

«You are the origin and end of each event. Control it at the source. This world of adversity and suffering has been made by you, and only you can change it. Healing is an inside-out process, it goes from within to its manifestation outside. It can only happen if you want it to» finished the Dreamer who then pointed out to me that the miracles of the New Testament were in fact 'certifications'. Not even He could heal, if healing had not already taken place inside us. "Go, it's your 'will' that has healed you!"

9 "Do only what you love!"

«Working is the reflection of an incomplete psychology. The role that a man occupies in the world is the clearest symptom of incompleteness, the simplest way of returning to the cause of each of his ills. You can only do what you are. When this becomes clear to you and becomes your flesh and blood, you'll also know how to intervene.

To change oneself means intervening at every moment in one's own way of thinking and feeling; it means bringing light to one's life. The better you know yourself, the higher your role will be. The more inwardly responsible you are, the less you depend. This allows one to cast off the inherent suffering of each role and transform the work-effort into a dream. Work will be sublimated until it disappears from human activities.»

For millennia, work has been the reflection of a curse… the effect of a fall. Through the study and observation of his self, a man shortens the distance between himself and the world that he has projected, thus healing the incompleteness of his own states of Being and, as a consequence, his reality.

The Dreamer pointed out to me that in all cultures and throughout time, work has always been connoted as effort until it has become the very synonymous with constraint and strain. In the very language of those ancient civilisations, the biblical definitions of pain – embodied in man's work and woman's childbirth – mingled and revealed their common origin. In the coining of the French word 'travail,' in the Anglo-Saxon term 'labour', this understanding is recorded and sealed forever. The same is true in Spanish; and also in ancient dialects: the direct heirs and invisible bearers of the Greek vision.

«It's time to transform work into a 'dream'!» announced the Dreamer forcefully. His words rang out like a war cry capable of rousing souls and calling together endless armies under the banner of the same crusade.

«Use all your strength, time, energy, and everything you have, to realise what you truly want!»

The Dreamer's exhortation was directed at a planetary audience, at millions of men like me who had forgotten the magical flight, the 'dream'.

«The Art of Dreaming means loving oneself inside – He told me – *it takes years of self-observation and awareness to rediscover will and regain lost integrity»* He stated that for the young it is easier to rediscover what they truly want. Will, the 'dream' in the young, is not yet completely buried.

«A true school removes all that opposes the dream. Rather than impose false, useless notions, a true school frees the young from fears, superstitions and the hypnotic sleep that confines them to the ghetto of a dependent mankind.»

My father, in his way, had tried to entrust my education to a school that could nourish my being; he had searched among religious institutions; but the Barnabites, at that time, already trapped by the description of the world, had ceased to prepare responsible men, a decisional aristocracy. Even they had forgotten.

«Those who love what they do, don't depend. Those who love don't offer their time for a salary... Only those bereft of love can be recruited, paid. A man who loves is priceless.»

«Among the great illusions of those who work – He said – *there's that of collecting a retribution. In actual fact, what is considered a reward, wage or salary, is only a modest, partial compensation for damages incurred by the condition of dependence.»*

In my notebook I underlined those words several times, being aware that they flung us many light years away from all that we were used to believe and think. The 'good' pain of a wound, healing, is accompanied by the awareness of that physical and moral degradation which men and women suffer; or rather inflict on themselves, working without creativity or love in psychologically polluted environments.

In its overall scheme the Dreamer's vision anticipated the advent of a more responsible, liberated and happier mankind, set free from dependence, devoted only to what it loves. He predicted that this would inevitably be accompanied by a more evolved economy, by a progressive and persistent reduction in work-effort, and a decline in traditional education.

Economy is not founded on work, but happiness.
Happiness is economy.

The schools of the old mankind are founded on the opposite concept. They are the offshoot of an entire civilisation's mental attitude that still sees work as pain, as a punishment; of a society that at one time used slaves and today needs to educate an army of losers, men and women capable of accepting the unbearable painfulness of dependency.

«At seven years of age the Spartans ceased being dependent, they were placed in a school of courage, where they were shaped into heroes, brilliant, invincible warriors; today at the same age children are organised into the sad army of adults.

Their transformation can be observed. The enjoyment of the game, the fresh emotions, enthusiasm, adaptability and courage, are gradually replaced with the learning of apparently human emotions: envy, jealousy, rancour, anxiety and fear and the acquisition of unhealthy habits; whining, excessive chattering, hiding and lying; along with practicing those facial distortions which are the masks of their degradation.

The encroachment of the child's freedom and clipping the wings of its dream, is an immorality that present-day mankind is incapable of seeing, and for which it pays with the thousands of social ills that afflict it, and an economy founded on disaster.»

There was a long pause. The great Huangpu had been absorbed into the night, and only the river traffic, still busy at that time, with its lights flying back and forth, allowed us to detect the river's presence. Standing under a lamp on the Bund's riverside, I completed my notes on this unforgettable lesson noting down the words that concluded it.

«Like the rattling of the train, that we no longer notice after a while, the painfulness of dependence becomes part of existence for us, a natural constant and, absurdly, a reassuring presence in life. Abandoning it would be, for an adult, an impossible undertaking.»

10 The terrible and wonderful direction…

Meanwhile, that stretch of the Bund had taken on the pleasantly lazy air of an elegant boulevard from another time, with its tall lamps, wooden and cast-iron benches, and the hectic presence of a multi-coloured, cosmopolitan crowd. We reached the Peace Hotel on foot, its restaurant offering a superb view of the riverside and the Oriental Pearl TV Tower. The architecture and ambiance from the turn of the last century and the notes of a jazz orchestra on the ground floor, like a time machine, took us back a hundred years. Everything was perfect, but I remained taciturn and thoughtful. The hard words I had heard the Dreamer say that evening had only been a prelude. I knew that the most thorny part of the meeting was yet to come.

The manager welcomed us like guests of honour, and accompanied us personally to our table, which was attended by two impeccable waiters. The maitre seemed to know the Dreamer very well. His behaviour, the information he provided on the evening's proceedings and the goings-on in the restaurant and Hotel, together with other signs acquired at the entrance, made me aware that the Dreamer was more than a respected guest.

I was nervous. I wanted that conversation to continue, for the *maître* to stay, so as to delay for as long as possible the moment in which I would be left alone with Him. The Dreamer's expression was terribly serious when He commenced the argument with these words:

«Every aspect of a man's life and each of his decisions and choices, corresponds to his level of inner responsibility... This is what determines his role in the world and what gives him the destiny he deserves. In Kuwait, conditions were being created for your passage to a higher level of existence… but for a man like you, still a victim of doubts and fears, the opportunity appeared as a mortal threat…»

«Apparently you've abandoned it. You believe that you've chosen a simpler way, a more peaceful life; the truth is that you were unprepared to receive the opportunity I gave you! – He said and His gaze became even more serious – *Your level of responsibility could not contain that prosperity. Freedom frightens people like you. For the umpteenth time the world of dependency has swallowed you and*

cast you out into the darkest circles of existence, to repeat the disasters of your past.»

«If you already knew that I'd given up, why...» I said without being able to finish the question. A knot of tears shrank my throat.

«It's the only way to make you understand that nothing can be given! A man has to pay for everything he receives. And the payment takes place in his Being. A man can only have what his vision holds, he can only possess what he's responsible for.»

The lesson that followed was a milestone in my apprenticeship.

«Nothing is external – He reasserted, His voice sounding hoarse and serious – *An unprepared man, even if he's temporarily favoured by an event or external circumstances, can be driven back into his former poverty, if his new status exceeds his level of Being.»*

The richness, well-being and quality of a man's life – like that of a nation or an entire civilisation – does not depend on the availability and abundance of means and material resources, but on the breadth of his Being. The way of feeling, thinking and acting, the height of aspirations and the depth of ideas; what he believes in and what he dreams, decides the destiny of men.

«Be a King and the kingdom will come – He announced, and I could feel the force of those words in my every fibre – *The grandeur of the Being always precedes the birth of a kingdom.»*

«Kuwait was an acid test for measuring your responsibility, to make you experience first-hand how fear in a man creates hell in the world of events. It's fear that makes you depend on a job, woman or drug... It's fear that makes you believe that a salary can protect you and give you security.

Those who don't know themselves, those who are not masters of their states, can do nothing either for themselves or for others. A man can only choose himself! Your falling in love is still a way of running from your responsibility. The woman whom you think you love is also a refraction of your propensity for dependence.»

I should have known by now that the immediate and total aversion I felt for the Dreamer's ideas was the surest sign of their efficacy in upsetting my mental schemes, in discarding obsolete and ruinous plans. And yet I always resisted, every time. I rebelled against the intolerable pressure that I felt with Him, which crushed every square centimetre of my Being.

The Dreamer was always right. With Him, or by remembering His words, it was impossible to fail, make a mistake, harm oneself or to go astray. One cannot imagine how unbearable the wisdom of the Talking Cricket is for a Pinocchio who has decided to remain wooden, driven by external, invisible strings.

That evening, His words became even more subversive and it was too revolutionary for me to bear their weight and immense energy. The acceptance and understanding of ideas of a superior order, is always a painful operation for those who are not ready and do not want to understand. Just to be able to listen to them requires an increase in psychological space, a quickening of thought, a change in deeply rooted beliefs and habits, and every time I found myself completely unprepared to receive them and make them my own. Every time the Dreamer's philosophy came and appeared to me not only contrary to everything I had always believed, but also blasphemous, a true transgression of the natural laws consecrated by history and religion. The Dreamer's ideas opened before me the vortex of an overturning of the world's vision, and revealed an adventurous passage towards a new species that no longer had anything in common with the old humanity.

In moments of grace, when comprehension was finally able to open a chink in my Being, I recognised that the direction shown by the Dreamer was absurd and necessary, terrible and wonderful, difficult and joyful, like the flight of the salmon that return up the river to their origin. Behind His paradoxical language, a psychological revolution of the individual, towered above, brilliant as an Exodus, as visionary and epic as the exploits of Spartacus.

11 To fall in love

The Dreamer resumed His discourse by referring to my relationship with Heleonore and my multiple attempts to build a family. The tone of His first words confirmed my fear that what He was about to tell me would not be pleasant, and even less easy to accept.

Welcoming the Dreamer's philosophy and making a place for His ideas, had never been easy; but now that He was touching upon the thorniest subject, I felt the bastions of my obstinacy strengthen and my ancient defenses rise up, even more unforgiving. I was afraid that He would ask me to leave her. My apprenticeship was at a crucial stage.

In the dark forest of my worries, the words that followed sounded even harsher and more threatening, like a hunting horn stirring its prey in the depths of a lair:

«Fear and your inclination to depend on people, make you clutch at everything you meet, which is precisely what has happened with this woman. And you're lying to yourself if you believe you are in love with her...»

The Dreamer spoke to me for a long time. Some atoms of comprehension penetrated and changed my attitude. Even the tone of His discourse became imperceptibly sweeter, yet the initial severity in His voice still remained.

Pointing out the true meaning of that distortion of the being, which men call 'falling in love' and uncovering the mortal trap that hides it, He said in a lapidary way:

«Every time you fall in love, you are, in fact... taking a fall.»
He gave a quick wink and in an advisor's tone, added:

«And behind every *fall, there's a fault.»*

I learned from the Dreamer that the declaration of this threat, the signal for the fall, which lies in wait behind every infatuation, is traceable in the most diverse cultures. Idiomatic expressions like 'to fall in love' or '*tomber amoureux*', are used by millions of men and women without any of them being able to listen to that cry of alarm. They wave a danger sign under our noses without anyone noticing. The Dreamer pushed forward and penetrated even deeper with His exploration, stating that falling in love with someone or something is not a warning but is already a fall or descent, with respect to the condition of loving.

«Nothing is external – He repeated – *the world, the others are yourself distributed in time. Loving someone is loving a fragment of oneself... it means becoming smaller... it means becoming fragmented.»*

According to the Dreamer, loving someone more than oneself is like trying to fit the ocean into a glass, or claiming to absorb all the water in the sea with a handful of sand.

«Love (a-mors) means without death. To love means loving oneself inside and removing every form of self-sabotage from oneself.» He added that this can only be accomplished deliberately.

For the Dreamer, 'loving oneself inside' must be the expression of a true act of will.

«Only integrity can love – He said firmly – *and only the totality of the Being in all its splendour can contain love.»*

«Isn't it possible for a man who has attained integrity to have a companion, children, a profession, a social life, relationships, friends?» I asked, worried by that prospect for which I felt completely unprepared.

«Yes – affirmed the Dreamer – *but never forget that whatever happens outside you... is only a theatrical representation, a film version of your Being, which because of its grandeur can only live inside yourself... The other... the others... the world... are your reflection... a glass of water... A handful of sand...»*

According to the Dreamer, love of oneself is the only possible love. To love oneself is the highest art. To love someone beyond oneself is a form of idolatry, which finds the peak of its expression in sexuality.

«In his choice of a partner, as in a hundred moments in which he has to give meaning to his life, a man is constantly influenced by sex» observed the Dreamer. The calm tone of this prelude added intensity to the escalation of His discourse, and acutely sharpened my attention.

«Humanity has placed sex at the centre of its existence without ever guessing that it's only a distant glimpse of a forgotten ecstasy: the unity of Being!»

The Dreamer continued, saying that sex, like food and sleep, requires attentive management, a capacity for governance that humanity has forgotten. Sexual activity, which should serve as a discipline, a technology to help humanity attain unity of Being, has been distorted. Those who have entered other areas of being use sexuality to propel them towards integrity.

He continued, stating that this understanding has been lost. The sexual function has been degraded into an ephemeral activity that leaves us even more dissatisfied, even more incomplete, even further from that condition of the fullness of Being which is every man's lost birthright.

Never before, not even for a moment, had I thought of sex in the way that the Dreamer was describing me, and one which left me breathless. Images quickly alternated in my mind, like a sequence of photograms in fast motion. I saw humanity relentlessly occupied with copulation, toiling in the bedroom. I observed this planetary human obsession with the detachment of an ethologist who studies the sexual behaviour of a zoological species with its courtship rituals and reproductive procedures. For a moment, I perceived the precise state of degradation into which we had fallen, and the distortion that our functions and organs, born to receive messages, glimpses of the unity of Being, had undergone. In the Dreamer's vision, sex is the golden thread that allows us to retrace the path in search of our lost integrity.

A fragmented humanity has distorted its function, turning a relationship with a partner into dependence, and sexuality into a pretext for oblivion and further dependency. I felt completely alone, like an alien being, the only witness allowed to bear the vision of that panting search for integrity and completeness which is always doomed to failure, since it is not guided by will and understanding. A search condemned to perpetual fruitlessness as it's the impossible attempt of a being who expects to find love outside himself, before loving his inner self.

I saw those desperate couplings brighten then fade quickly, like the blinking of an eye; insignificant as sneezes, ending each time in a new disappointment, in another 'little death'. And I saw that human expectation of happiness, that yearning for wholeness, each time destined to be betrayed and failing… endlessly. In my mind's eye, I saw the images of frozen tundra and the mortal trek of reindeers following the musk scent, which drives them wildly over great distances. I saw their vain search for it outside themselves. They are fated never to know that the essence that inebriates them is produced by their own glands.

«Man looks outside himself for freedom, happiness and love – He said, entering my thoughts at this point and suspending that flow of images – *but the journey of the prodigal son isn't external… it's an inner adventure, the journey back to the unity of Being.»*

«Man constantly sets forth on this quest: the re-conquest of his integrity; he has sexual intercourse with a woman, who is a part of himself, created from one of his ribs, in order to regain that state of inner unity, his lost paradise.»

Then, in the tone of an irrevocable judgment, He said:

«In the algebra of the Being, two halves don't make a whole, but a squared incompleteness! A true dreamer expresses himself in totality. He doesn't have room for an incomplete world.»

12 "I am you!"

«But if everything that happens is one of my creations, one of my projections, then You… Who are You?»

«I am you! – He said unexpectedly, coining an expression that would be branded in my mind – *I happen inside you.»*

The world was disappearing from under my feet. Everything had changed and it would never be the same again. Noting my expression of loss, the Dreamer came closer and said:

«You see me outside you because I am in you… All that you see and touch, from insects to galaxies, is in you… or you would not be able to see or touch it.»

I felt dizzy and my temples pulsated with my heartbeat. Something unusual was happening… something was growing, making its way through me, forcing itself out from the inside, like a being whose gestation has been rapidly accelerated.

«Everything is connected. Nothing is separate. If you could only change one atom of yourself, your slightest thought, habit, attitude, inflection of voice… this change would explode in your entire Being and your universe would change for ever…»

«But changing this atom in the Being – He added – *is like swallowing oceans or moving mountains in the world of events.»*

There was a note of sadness in His voice, for the pain of that discussion which touched the very root of man's condition, and the reason for his unhappiness.

If changing an atom of ourselves required the strength to move a mountain, I stepped back from the precipice at the thought of how many years it would take for humanity to change. To reduce that distance to humanly conceivable proportions, I objected that, at least in my history, there had been plenty of stirrings and sudden shifts. Certainly more than one atom had changed in my life since I had met Him. In actual fact, in the last few years, I had changed job, partner and country many times; and I had moved my work and family from one continent to another many times, before arriving in Kuwait, and then finally here, Shanghai.

«Those are only apparent changes – the Dreamer answered – *Nothing ever really changes in an ordinary man's existence. His past becomes his future and everything in his life exposes his incompleteness.»* His voice became resolute and stern again.

«He fears every change that would force him to abandon the comfortable and mortal rut of repetitiveness.

Beyond the illusion of change, even in your life, everything repeats itself; everything is always the same. Your attempts to have a family, the women you've chosen, just like the roles you've occupied, the houses you've lived in, the friends you've had, have nevertheless always been a reflection of your rigidity... signs, above any other, of the narrow strip of existence to which you've confined your life.

There are worlds parallel to yours, which only the dream can enter. If you have nothing that at present satisfies you, it is because of the state of your Being. You will never get what you want as long as your Being remains as it is. You have to change yourself to get new understanding, new meaning, new life, and consequently to attract events of a higher order. Changing yourself means, first of all, 'getting rid of yourself'. In order to be born 'at a higher level' you have to die 'at a lower one'.»

I was floundering. The Dreamer noticed my difficulty and waited. His words were sheaves of light aimed at unknown areas of my being; arrows that were piercing my organs with an unbearable painfulness.

My past, which I had unwisely recalled, was suffocating me. Luisa's death and all the unhappiness of my relationships; the arguments, misunderstandings and betrayals of an entire life, were again coming to the surface, each one with its own bitterness.

Luisa had been the outburst and unawareness of my twenties, and had burned fast like a candle lighted at both ends. Jennifer, I recognised now, was the very personification of my vanity, possessiveness and fear of life. Gretchen had been the projection of my aggressiveness, of the betrayal that had always been there, hidden behind each of my glances, actions and words. It was true. Each of those women had been the reflection of my condition.

The Dreamer took me away from this thought.

«Those women came to make physically visible, to denounce, what you've never wanted to *discover in yourself.»* His tone was extraordinarily tender, and I was pained at the thought of what I would discover hidden behind my latest love, behind my most recent 'fall'.

13 Universe means towards oness

We remained silent for some minutes. From our table, we enjoyed an extraordinary view of the river. The steel outline of the Oriental Pearl TV Tower stood out like a bright comet against the background of the night and the fine dusty lights of distant Pudong. In the meantime, the restaurant in the Peace Hotel became crowded. Its *démodé* atmosphere was heightened by the dress of the clientele; they were mostly couples who seemed to have emerged from a photo taken at the beginning of the century.

The Dreamer was now introducing a final argument; it was one of the most important of that meeting. He paused to let the waiters take away the plates. Once again the Dreamer's meal was untouched and I realised that, left breathless by His words and busy taking notes, I too had hardly touched the food.

«The Project is carved with immortal characters in the very word 'universe'» the Dreamer began, and demonstrated how for innumerable generations men have uttered the word 'universe' without realising its immense power, which an eponymous intelligence has hidden in its etymology, like an invincible sword in its sheath.

Universe: uni-verso, 'versus unum' in Latin means towards oneness.

Throughout time, the sense of existence, direction of the world, events and men, had been shown, stated and placed there under our noses. That cosmic message, as ancient as the stars, as powerful as the energy encapsulated in millions of suns, as simple as the truth, had crossed eons of time, and yet only very few had understood it.

The same powerful message of integrity has passed through all religious and sapiential traditions of civilisations from every period; they have been born from that irrepressible impulse towards unity of the Being which still makes them tremble. In the Dreamer's *excursus* I saw the connective tissue of men and nations, the thick plot of ideas, philosophies and visions connected by a golden thread that united them beyond time and space, beyond every difference in culture, race and geography.

«Monk, from monos*, is a single man advancing towards the One, a man in search of his integrity»* He stated. The shadow of a

smile, which in Him often forewarned of a witticism, was on His face when He added:

«It's a Being under construction. Outside his cell could be inscribed the words, 'work in progress'... The habit and the discipline he has chosen serve his intention of becoming an 'individual'...»

He explained to me that 'individual' derives from indivisible and shows man's direction towards unity. It is a condition of extreme rarity. Only very few, through strenuous work on themselves, accomplish it and become true individuals. The reference was too obvious for me not to grasp and feel the pain of the unfavourable comparison made with me. There had been and there were determined men, tireless seekers of their own integrity.

And I, where was I? Fruitlessly, I would look for my face among that small army of courageous Beings, of brilliant madmen, who in every epoch have searched and made superhuman efforts to emerge from the ordinary condition. And I, what had I done to leave the rut of my existence, to deserve an individual destiny, a great personal adventure?

I made a quick examination of my conscience and I immediately laid a pitiful veil over my life. Then, the magnificence of the secret hidden behind two humble fables, passed on almost unobserved for two thousand years, exploded in my mind with all its brilliance, two tremendously powerful stories, immortal metaphors disguised as simple tales: the parable of the shepherd who leaves ninety-nine sheep to go in search of one that is lost; and the other of the woman who, having lost a coin, and left with only nine, sweeps and searches in every corner, and does not tire of looking until she finds it. Those rudimentary fables were showing themselves to be the millenary keepers of a message of integrity. In them, there still exists the memory of the 'project,' and the secret of man's ceaseless tension towards that universal asymptote which is the unity of Being. This is the great arrival, the target to hit, and the very reason for our existence on this planet.

«Not even a single grain of hell can enter into paradise – summarised the Dreamer powerfully – *For a vertical man to lose even an atom of his own integrity means losing everything. And he can't live in peace until he has regained his own completeness.»*

He added that 'saint', in its deepest meaning, beyond ecclesiastical Christian dogmatism, means sane, healed. A saint is in actual fact an integral, whole man, who has chosen completeness or unity of the Being, as the aim of his life; he is a man aware of his states and emotions, as he knows that the smallest deferment from the totality of himself throws him into the hells of ordinariness.

All the sacred iconography I could remember crossed my mind and I felt the wonder I'd experienced as a child watching the saints' heads encircled by a crown of light. I always saw them banished to the fragrant half-light of candles, in lifeless churches, or in the aseptic rooms of museums and galleries, and remembered them as men of the past, pathetic, anachronistic. Only now, could I see all the ignorance and absurdity of a collective imagery that has projected its own suffering, its own defeat on saints - and of a crowd that absurdly believes in miracles 'outside itself'.

«'Outside oneself' is the true madness, the ill of ills from which humanity will have to heal.»

In reality, saints were men and women who had simply dared to 'believe in themselves', ordinary people who, aware of their incompleteness, had made the journey back towards a lost integrity.

14 The King is the Earth, the Earth is the King

«This is economy!» stated the Dreamer unexpectedly, breaking those memory-imbued thoughts, before they could become melancholic. For some moments, suspended in the air, there was only the vision of an army of victorious men and women, with no haloes or palm fronds, against the background of a timeless epic. Then, even that final image disappeared, blown away by the breeze of new words.

«Without individuals, without their will in action, there isn't profit or progress, there isn't business or wealth. They're the salt of the earth. Great political empires and financial fortunes crumble and disintegrate without them.»

Suddenly, the Dreamer's words gave me the solution to the enigma that has tormented scholars and researchers of economics, and which research centres in universities and business schools all over the world have been uselessly trying to solve. Enterprises die young on this planet. Their existence becomes more and more precarious and their average lifetime is progressively reduced until they last for only ephemeral periods. Even economic and financial giants do not live for long; one only has to think of half the enterprises, which twenty years ago were considered among the five hundred largest in the world, but now no longer exist.

Now I knew that these corporations were the projection of incomplete leaders and the only true reason for their premature disappearance was the absence of integral men and women. A single one would have been enough to avert the loss of vast patrimonies of knowledge, men and means; or the dissolution of entire civilisations. I wondered where Rome would have been without Scipio, and later, Caesar; and what would have become of the Catholic Church, the largest multinational in the world, without managers of the calibre of Agostino or Francesco d'Assisi? Sane, integral men… who was preparing them? And where were they?

Again, the Dreamer's voice came to release me from the limbo of those reflections.

«The King is the Earth, the Earth is the King – He intoned, linking my thoughts to the 'dream' again – *An organisational pyramid is connected to its leader's breath. A golden thread binds his image and personal destiny to that of his organisation and men. His physical self coincides with its economy, as it did for the ancient sovereigns.»*

The Dreamer related this to classical Chinese traditions, and I hung on his every word as He told me that, in moments of great difficulty, when the empire had to face a famine or an enemy invasion, the Chinese emperor, the son of heaven, would retreat to the Palace's inner rooms to meet the doors of all things. Motionless, facing south, with his superhuman virtues, he ensured that the whole empire remain in accordance with the Decree of Heaven. He knew that the difficulties he himself faced revealed a decline in his integrity and that the battle would first be won inside.

When the dikes give way and the floods come,
and the barbarian hordes and attacks rain down
from every corner of the world,
it means that the 'portable paradise' given to the leader
has been lost,
and only the regain of his own integrity
can reverse that catastrophy.

For that man, with that level of responsibility, there was no separation between his own integrity and that of the empire. Winning himself and re-integrating the unity of his Being, was the real victory. Only then would the solution, the effect and measure of his level of flawlessness, manifest itself in the form of an allied army, or the enemy's collapse from inner strife, bad weather, or famine.

With the Dreamer, I felt the living and throbbing understanding that has always run through the history of civilisations, from the oldest traditions to the modern history of business. From the Chinese Empire to that of Robert Maxwell, from Walt Disney to the realm of King Arthur, the same, immutable law resonates through the centuries:

When the King becomes ill, the Earth becomes ill.
Because the King is the Earth, the Earth is the King.

Even Louis XIV's famous mot now appeared to me in the light of a new understanding. "L'Etat c'est moi" was not the cry of a despot, the assertion of a sovereign without limits, as we have believed for centuries, but the awareness of a man with a perfect connection between his personal destiny and that of millions of men, of an entire empire.

«A leader, a businessman, a man with responsibility knows that his financial destiny, the longevity and success of his undertakings, and even his physical health are directly connected to his level of integrity. There's only one condition through which to move from a divided world to a unified one! There's only one thing we have to abandon...»

The short pause that followed seemed endless to me.

«Suffering»

«That shouldn't be too difficult – I quickly replied – Who wouldn't accept that?»

«And yet for the ordinary man this is truly impossible – insisted the Dreamer – *Take you, for example. You'd like to renounce suffering, but this would involve renouncing a world composed of struggles, conflicts and divisions: this is your world, the only world you know. Only those who know themselves can discover that "nothing is outside oneself"... that they're alone in the universe, that they're the only ones responsible for the situations in which they find themselves and all that happens to them.»*

Here the Dreamer straightened up, slowly moving His neck upwards, as if to rise a little closer to the sky. Then He said:

«In order to attract something wonderful, to give concreteness to something, a man has to rise in his Being and move closer to that condition of unity and integrity, which is his birthright... It's the truest, most concrete part of each of us: the 'dream'.»

The Dreamer closed His eyes and recited these words that I faithfully wrote down in my notebook:

«The 'dream' is the most real thing that exists... All that we see and touch, and all that we don't, from atoms to the most distant galaxies, is only the reflection of our dream...»

15 Reality is 'dream' plus time

«Our future aim is to become one. The goal is the unity of Being. When this unification has taken place inside us and we've reached a state of integrity, only then do the conditions exist for one 'to be touched by the dream. Reality is the 'dream' plus time.»

I recorded this aphorism in my notes in the form of an equation, with the symbols:

$$D + T = R$$

I would one day communicate this form to my students, transferring the understanding of this vision and the secret of the immense energy encapsulated in its formula.

Everything comes from the 'dream'. All that we see and touch, each visible thing is born in the womb of the invisible. Time reveals it. This is the culmination and heart of the Dreamer's thought. It is the architrave of His coherent, spherical, iron-willed philosophy which has nourished the roots of the future university and has forged its motto: *Visibilia ex Invisibilibus.*

«Dream... dream... never stop dreaming... Dream!... Fly!... and never stop – He urged me forcefully – *Reality will follow.»*

And with this exhortation the Dreamer concluded His second day with me in Shanghai.

The Dreamer and I were alone in the restaurant now, and even the jazz orchestra in the foyer had stopped playing. From our window, the Oriental Pearl TV Tower appeared like an immense sparkling missile on its launch pad, ready to devour space.

«Dream... never stop dreaming... reality will follow!»

«In world history, why have there been so few men with a dream?»

«To be 'touched by the dream', a man has to have reached the unity of Being – answered the Dreamer, and I remember that this expression infiltrated my entire Being – *Only an individual who is integral and indivisible can dream intentionally and realise that the 'dream' is the most real thing that exists.»*

«And what about those who don't dream?» I asked, becoming aware of all those who would never be accepted in the dreamers' exclusive club.

«All men dream, all of them have the power to create their own world, but only a few are aware of it and know how powerful their dream is... that it has the strength to enrich everything around them or feed the world's nightmare. Only very few, through will and their own flawlessness, can dream a perfect world and give it concreteness. It's the condition of the warrior, of the hero, of the man who loves.»

The 'dream' in the Dreamer's vision, as the most real thing that exists, occupies the top rung on the ladder of reality, in fact it is the very condition of concreteness.

I felt as though my mind was under siege. A hundred questions were piling on top of one another, and they crowded forward demanding answers, but before I could open my mouth, the Dreamer interrupted me with a decisive gesture of the hand.

«You can't find will in the world – He said like someone imparting some decisive information – *Will only exists in you... but it's buried. You need to uncover it!»*

He said nothing else, but granted me a few minutes to finish my notes and reflect upon this final assertion. Then, He defined flawlessness as the ability to head unequivocally in the direction of one's dream, without ever relenting, without 'sinning'.

«A man who has his dream constantly present can't be corrupted... Everything in his life is flawlessly focused on his great adventure.»

I noted that this condition seemed rather widespread.

«Apparently, every man tries – I argued with the strategic intention of pushing Him to say more on such an impassioned subject – Everyone, or at least most, try to improve their life, make plans, have projects; most are busy trying to reach some objective.»

The Dreamer then clarified the difference between dreaming and planning. Men who nourish a 'dream' do not have doubts, they do not feel uncertain or fearful. Every time they turn their mind to the 'dream', they feel their enthusiasm is renewed and they enter a state of freedom. Because the 'dream' is connected to will, it is the 'true' will. On the contrary, those who plan, those who resolve to attain an objective, suffer anxiety every time they think about it, and they fall prey to fears and doubts.

«Fear and doubt are the dream's cancer» He stated laconically coining another of His powerful and ruthless maxims. He paused and I took advantage of this time to put my notes in order, notes which already covered pages and pages of my notebook. I had been busy attending to this for a while suddenly I started at the sound of His voice.

«People work, plan and accumulate with a strength and an energy that you could describe as tenacity. But it's only fear... Volleys of adrenalin, like electrical storms, constantly dart across the dark universe of their cells. These men and women seem to be very busy, confirmed idealists or determined businessmen, but in actual fact they're loyal to death and their names appear on her payroll.»

My writing devoured the blank pages and I felt the preciousness of the substance which His words, His presence, produced. I felt them enrich the air and travel untiring to the most distant corners of the planet, to the most hidden folds in every man's Being, softening his wounds and driving away his shadows. I was upset. An irrational emotion, a kind of weeping, softly pushed against the walls of my being and made each of its fibres tremble. I lifted my head from the notes and saw His face come imperceptibly closer to mine.

«Work for an ideal. Put yourself at the service of the humanity that dreams, that aspires, that asks!» said the Dreamer. I would never be able to forget or avoid the words that followed.

«Constantly strive to perfect yourself. Always try to increase your understanding. Pay for your existence in advance. Helping others in their efforts if there is a sincere request.

It's you who must do this work from the inside. I can no longer do it in your place. I've tried the impossible... I went against the inflexibility of your destiny, which had already condemned you... to give you a chance, to let you emerge from your condition.

Only a man who loves can be free and only a free man can love. Freedom and love are two faces of the same reality.»

The unforgettable lessons on dependence, falling in love, and the last one on the unity of being, which had started at the Peace Hotel, were finding their epilogue, along the Bund's riverside, in those words which were now echoing in my bosom, powerful as the cry of a great revolution.

«One day ask to become the Dreamer – He advised me with resolute sweetness, and added – *Of all possible destinies, it's the greatest... Ask to become the inventor, the creator of your universe... Then the world will obey everything you order it to do, and it will give you all that you desire...»*

At these words I closed my eyes. It seemed to me that the sky over Shanghai was crossed by the brightest and most auspicious comet. I was certain that my wish would be granted; asking sincerely would be enough! Now or never, I thought. I would never have a second chance. But I felt paralysed.

The Dreamer, and with Him the entire world, seemed to wait, suspended by the thin thread of my intention. Never before had I clearly perceived that everything depended on me, and that even the Dreamer Himself existed for me.

Years of work, my long apprenticeship, and all my special efforts had led me there, to that crucial crossroads. And now finally, the great undertaking for which He had been preparing me for so long would begin, or it would remain in the limbo of possible worlds. It was time to fly. On the edge of that abyss of no return, I hesitated. I felt His glance on me, the Dreamer's hidden trepidation. Then I knew with absolute certainty that He was the only Being in the world who had ever truly loved me. I felt tears rise up irresistibly and my eyes swell in the attempt to gather and stem them. Then the world became clouded and I had to stop writing.

16 To be touched by the 'dream'

Since I had met Him, the Dreamer had constantly forced me to extend my vision, to change my attitudes and with them my destiny.

Attitudes and events are inseparable.
The attitude is the event.

Strategically, He had used every occasion, and had created events, meetings and circumstances to hasten my passage to one of the highest areas of existence. Immersed in the role of an international entrepreneur and with the opportunity of leading a company in Kuwait, the Dreamer had pursued that evolutionary design which had its strength and beginning in my promise. What had happened in Kuwait had marked a sharp break. It had been a true fall into the lowest states of my Being. At the edge of the abyss everything became a pretext to draw back, in order not to plummet: Heleonore, the children, an illness, the house…

But now, I could neither hide it nor lie to myself anymore. In Kuwait, for the umpteenth time, I had run away before the passage to a superior level of responsibility, of understanding! I had betrayed the highest part of me. Heleonore had only been a pretext.

«*The next step is always unknown and invisible* – He said – *The passage to the superior states is always a leap into the unknown. In order to do it, you must 'die' to your imaginary past, to everything you believe you have been until now.*»

«*Moving even one millimetre in the Being, is a mortal jump, a cosmic somersault that only a few can perform* – said the Dreamer, entering my thoughts and gathering the true essence of my condition – *The true difference between two men is the breadth of their 'dream'. A man who thinks only of himself, moreover a false self, and is constantly worried about his survival since he doesn't know himself, can't be 'touched by the dream'.*»

It was only years later, on Mount Olympus, during a trip to Macedonia, that I discovered that the Ancient Greeks had coined the term "idiotes" for man in his present condition, for the selfish. The idiot, for the Greeks, was the opposite of the demiurge, the leader, of those who does things for others.

«Behind the apparent search for an advantage or profit, an entrepreneur, more deeply than he himself can ever know, is at the service of a project; he's already a man who does for other men and he knows that their improvement is his success. His life is devoted to it. He has no choice. Like the captain of an ancient sailing ship, he knows he will have to return with the ship or sink with it.»

With the Dreamer I was discovering that only the 'dream' can make us free; it can break down our every limit. Only the 'dream' can change poverty into prosperity, difficulties into understanding, fear into love. Only the "dream" can allow us to cross the threshold of the lost paradise.

«Paradise isn't another world or afterlife... Paradise is this world... without limits – He said to me – *To be touched by the 'dream' means receiving the gift of a great personal adventure, it means coming face to face with one's own uniqueness.»*

«Those men devoted to a description of the world founded on scarcity and fear, can't be touched by the 'dream'... because the dream is freedom and they have been looked after by prophets of misfortune, by priests and devotees of dependence since childhood. Each has been educated in imprisonment. This is why millions of men depend on others for their survival. One can always recognize them, for they are marked by a total absence of gratitude and an inability to love.»

«Giving is self-giving... To give one needs to have and to have one needs to be.»

He was about to continue, and His lips were already half open perhaps to talk to me about the Project, when He stopped to observe me better. I felt His glance penetrate deep into my soul, and the expression I saw on His face, as if at the discovery of my hopeless inadequacy for the task which awaited me, made me feel like a tramp who had come to seek admission to the most aristocratic of clubs.

«Do you know what the difference is between us?» He asked in a dry, rough tone.

I remained silent, caught offguard by such a direct approach by the Dreamer. After years of absolute restraint, it now seemed to point candidly to the subject of His mysterious nature.

Who really was the Dreamer?

He waited until it became clear that I would not provide an answer, and said:

«The difference between us is that my atoms dance, drunk on immortality – "on the everlasting nectar of immortality" were His exact words – *whereas you're attracted and ruled by all that is mortal... I've conquered death, and you've invested everything in the belief of its inevitability.»*

I was floundering, and I would have been overcome, had the Dreamer not come to my rescue. It was then that I heard Him repeat those three unforgettable words.

«I am you!» He said, and the appeal of this expression was so powerful that it devoured sidereal distances between our beings. Again I found myself closer to Him than ever before. When it seemed to Him that I had at least absorbed the initial impact of His words, He added:

«I have been you and you will be Me. Eons of time and an abyss in conscience divide us. Go faster! By sending you to Kuwait, I gave you a drop and you mistook it for the ocean. Now that I want to give you the ocean, you're holding back.»

I closed my eyes, I felt the unbearable speed at which He was pushing me and I feared I might not survive it. While He continued to speak, I hid in a corner of my being and waited there for the storm to pass. Relentlessly He followed me there, drawing me out. His change of tone was sudden and His voice exploded so powerfully in my chest that I was pervaded by an arcane terror.

«Make a decision once and for all!» He thundered. In His voice, I heard the ruthless determination and heroic ferocity of a commander shouting orders in the thick of a mortal battle.

«Work day and night towards your improvement! Never forget your promise!»

«What promise have I forgotten?»

«The promise to change! – He said – *A promise you've made not only to yourself but to all the other shining, visionary beings, who will undertake this passage.»*

«How can I change?»

«Dream a new 'dream'. Dream a new world!... The world is as you dream it. The world is as you want it!... You've wanted it to be violent, false, mortal. The world will be different when you change!»

«Your continuing regret of the past always carries you back to the old things...» He said after a long pause.

« *Abandon it!* – He ordered – *It's time to devote yourself full time to the Project.»*

I promised with the utmost sincerity and solemnity that I would not break my word, and that nothing would come before my evolution. The Dreamer stared at me for a long time. I withstood that examination. I was anxious for the result, until a flash of stern benevolence in His glance gave me a little relief.

«Promising doesn't make any sense. The promise of an ordinary man is already a lie. Change your attitude, now!... *This is the true action. The facts, circumstances and events of life will change in time. Leave your work and move to London. There, you'll meet men and women who are ready to work with you. They'll be the pillars of a great revolution: an individual, psychological, planetary revolution that will change at its foundations the way of thinking and feeling of humanity, which for now is incapable of facing the challenges awaiting it.»*

CHAPTER IX

The Game

1 Believing is seeing

The Dreamer's influence had begun to produce surprising results in my life. Within a few days, and without hesitation, I had sold the house in Chià, left my work at the ACO Corporation and moved the family to an elegant Georgian villa in leafy Hampstead on the outskirts of London.

Seven Oaks had been the residence of a prominent businessman. The architecture, objects, furniture, paintings and antique statues were symbols of a genuine, powerful aristocracy of entrepreneurship. Seven Oaks also revealed itself to be a potent alchemical laboratory. Such a house could only develop and change me, reawakening in me a clarity, a courageous attitude and the strength to 'do', to accomplish great things.

There, in that residence, guided by the Dreamer, I would devote all my energy to excising the lie from my life once and for all. There the last notes of my old song of pain, composed of doubts and anxieties, would fade out. Now I could devote myself to the strong discipline that the Dreamer called the 'Art of Dreaming': the art of believing in oneself, the art of balancing opposites, and changing adversities and antagonisms into events of a superior order.

With the Dreamer at my side, I felt secure and invulnerable. Beside Him, the most radical changes, even the apparently most risky, like those taking place at that very time, simply entered my life and gently reshuffled its order. That leap into the unknown, instead of turning my existence upside down, gathered the scattered fragments of my life with a strong hand, and firmly fastened them together.

Heleonore and my children faced those changes without difficulty. They felt protected and my own determination gave them security.

And yet I still did not fully possess the strength and conviction with which I had seemed to make those decisions. My own trust and self-confidence, which knew neither hesitation nor doubt when I was with the Dreamer, became shaky as soon as I deviated from His teachings. Everything that happened within the Dreamer's sphere, that gestation of the Being, which ruled events, facts and circumstances, and made the world obedient, compliant and malleable as clay, was still incomprehensible to me.

Months passed. Far from the Dreamer, the dream began to crumble and the past seized power once more. As the Dreamer's principles began to cool in me, the air outside turned to dense fog and ice. In my universe even the slightest movement became difficult, painful. Every aspect of my existence, through its many symptoms, revealed my constant backsliding, looking at the past, my doubts and my regrets.

As had happened earlier, when I'd returned from Kuwait, the more I yielded, the more I felt the need to programme and make plans. My calculations led me to the conclusion that our lifestyle was going to eat up my savings very quickly.

The pace of life beside Him was unsustainable. I had trouble keeping up. According to the Dreamer there were no limits and nothing was too costly.

Everything is at our door.
The limit is within us.

Yet I reached a point when that life seemed too risky to me. The fear of having no money prompted me to open a new account in a London bank where I deposited a good part of the proceeds from the sale of the house in Chià, promising myself I would only touch that money 'in an emergency'. I said nothing of this to the Dreamer. The certainty of being able to count on that sum if things took a turn for the worse comforted me at the low points when anxiety invaded me and took control of my life. That account became a psychological prosthetic, a replacement for self-belief and courage, and that decision represented a way for me to feign responsibility, just as I had done years before by inserting the re-entry clause in my contract with the ACO Corporation. This recurrence was an unmistakable sign of my descent into the deadly pattern of repetitiveness. When the symptoms of my imminent fall became more obvious, I confessed everything to the Dreamer, and closed that account before the past could swallow me up, without possibility of return.

"Everyone believes in something... to believe it's not difficult... but to reawaken the will, choose one's intention, and follow it unswervingly is only for a few... To bind oneself to believe is actually higher than just believing..."

At the conclusion of His discourse the Dreamer coined one of his most admirable paradoxes, but also among the most hidden.

"This is 'believing without believing' which is the very act for creation, a state of Being which is only possible for a man who knows the Art of Acting and has achieved the unity of Being."

"Remarkable men in every epoch have only found capital to accomplish their impossible endeavours once they have eliminated every kind of doubt from their beings. The real capital is inside us, and the resources we find are the material reflection of an inner prosperity that we know how to keep alive whatever the circumstances might be.

Don't ever separate yourself from the principles of the 'dream'. Always keep them alive. Don't let them grow cold in you, and you'll see that everything turns to your advantage; even history, the most coarse and superficial part of existence, will prove you right."

His ideas inspired me deeply, but they were not easy to put into practice! The Dreamer's philosophy revealed itself to be unbending and severe, a path reserved for the very few, when the moment came to apply it. All the same, along the ridge defined by His vision, like a vast geological divide, the entire human mass was separated into two parts: one, made up of weak and incomplete men, influenced by everything and anything, who follow and depend, even when they believe themselves to be leaders; and the other, composed of a handful of vertical men, the very few integral beings, blessed with an unshakeable belief and determination. It was they who sustained the world. According to the Dreamer, the life of a country, of an entire nation, is apparently led by those who govern, but in reality their destiny is decided by the integrity of a few individuals. If they did not exist, then the fate of vast regions of the planet and even of entire civilisations would have already been sealed.

Behind the men who seem to accomplish things, behind the appointed leaders of world organisations, political and humanitarian institutions, big businesses and financial empires, behind magnates, tycoons and leaders, there are simple, sincere, sober men who, motionlessly, invisibly lead through 'not doing'.

"When a man who believes in himself, apparently takes a step into the unknown, only then, unfailingly, does he see the ground appear beneath his feet, to prove that his shining madness is right... Believe in order to see, never vice versa!"

But at that time the requisite qualities for joining this club of remarkable men were still beyond me. With growing doubts and fear, I did and redid the accounts, always coming to the same conclusion: the money from the sale of the house in Chià would only last for a few months. I had no idea what I would do in the future. I had no plans, no work. The old world had abandoned me and the new one had yet to show its face.

2 "Change your Liiife!"

One episode, at the beginning of that new adventure, was particularly significant and decisive. While I was still searching for a house in London I was able to show Him a number of different possibilities. Worried, led by the fear of having insufficient means, and uncertain as to what the future had in store, even unpretentious houses seemed too expensive for me. Thus, at that meeting I warmly supported the choice of a flat that was not too big, but was, in my opinion, adequate, well-furnished and situated in a little street between Marylebone Road and Regent's Park. I will never forget His reaction. It remains among the most invaluable of His teachings.

His words struck me like a jet of icy water.

«You can only choose yourself, your limits, your mediocrity – was His reaction to my proposal. His tone was scornful – *Years go by, but your life doesn't change. The world is such because you are such... Enter the Dreamer's vision and stop believing yourself to be*

a miserable being. Whatever conditions may rule a man's existence, they correspond perfectly to his expectations.»

I remember attempting a defense. I maintained that my choices had to be attributed to the conditions in which He had put me. In this particular case, I judged that it was simply wise to make decisions and assume commitments that also took into consideration possible, future difficulties. My choices would have been very different, if only I had been able to count on adequate resources…

«Everything has to be earned. The difficulties I put in your way are hidden blessings. In actual fact they're milestones towards integrity and understanding.»

I thought He was being facetious. I believed that after years of 'work' with the Dreamer I had already managed to bear every possible shock to my system; that I was ready to accept the overturning of every ordinary idea or belief; and that I knew how to persist despite obstacles and disappointments. But I was wrong.

«You no longer have time for self-indulgence. Transcend, constantly transcend every achievement, every apparent success. Don't remain even for one instant in the old rut and old beliefs. Transcend yourself. Evil is yesterday's good, not yet transcended.»

My facial muscles contracted and I no longer knew what kind of expression to assume. I wanted to rebel, to shout all my aversion at that vision that left no room for justifications, accusations, complaints or regrets… The frustration and impotence formed a solid lump that constricted my throat and I could only utter an inarticulate sound. I tried to recompose myself, I tried to order my ideas so as to say something that made sense, but…

«Change your liiife!» shouted the Dreamer with all the power of His voice. I saw the veins in His temples and neck swell like a raging torrent; I was afraid. His cry vibrated in the air, and remained suspended between us for a deafening eternity. The vision of a warrior roaring through his horn instantly flashed before me. I did not have time to record this image before the Dreamer commenced His thundering invective.

«You're still projecting your past. Selling the house in Chià means nothing if along with it you haven't given up your scarcity and suffering. Be careful not to carry the past with you, with its usual miseries… Remember… the Past is Dust.

Don't go into the world proposing yourself to others... You are already showing too many signs of need... Carry My *presence...* My *words... Carry Meeee.»*

At this new cry, even more unbearable, a boundless terror exploded inside me. I felt its chemistry flood every corner of my Being and consume the huge distances that existed within me. At that cry, which still absurdly persisted, all my inner barriers started to crumble and fall into ruin, like the walls of Jericho under the sound pressure of Joshua's horn. I felt healthy, united, as never before.

As suddenly as it had appeared, that storm fell silent and the Dreamer returned to His usual attitude, as if nothing had happened. There was a pause and in those few seconds I hoped against hope that it had passed. With difficulty, I was trying to gather myself again, when I saw Him slowly place His forefingers vertically around the corners of His mouth. I noted that that gesture took an infinite amount of time to complete, like a slow motion sequence. I followed each frame of His movement, which seemed to be part of an unknown warrior ritual, with apprehension, then with worry, and finally with a growing anxiety. His eccentricity, the extreme slowness with which He completed it, weighted that gesture with an inexplicably threatening... terrifying significance. I could hardly breathe, and my emotions were in complete turmoil.

When at last I understood that He was simulating a megaphone, I braced myself for another of those roars that could actually brand the very essence of His teachings into one's flesh. But now the Dreamer did not shout. He brought His face a little closer and then, in an almost inaudible voice, He hissed:

«The house you are looking for in London is not for you, but for the Dreamer! Remember that! If you bring yourself, then whatever comes to you will be weak and sparse like your world... Set aside your worries and come closer to Me. You'll find that no obstacles exist but that you, with your unshakeable belief in limitations, are the one true obstacle.»

From that day forth, the estate agents started to offer completely different solutions. As always, the Dreamer was right. Once I changed my attitude, the world followed like a shadow. I no longer looked for a house for myself, but one worthy of the Dreamer. When I found Seven Oaks, I recognised it. That was the house where I would continue the 'work,' and within a few days

Heleonore had organised everything, and we moved in with the children.

I couldn't have known it at the time, but that residence, so far beyond every reasonable parameter, had been created to fling me into the abyss. Surely this was a strategy of the Dreamer's, meant to accelerate my learning process, but I was still unable to make sense of that *mise en scène*. Without His help I could never have imagined embarking on such a passage. Seven Oaks represented the breaking of a barrier; the instrument for destroying an interior geology composed of poverty and ignorance, which had been stratified over the years. It was a charge of dynamite, set to breach the bastions that defended a nightmare: my identification with a poor, limited, unhappy world.

3 The Payment

«Money is not real. What is real is a man's vision, his ideas. Resources and money are only a natural consequence of them... they fall into line and assume the proportions of his 'dream'...»

«But if you truly believe that your problem is lack of money – He said with a seraphic sarcasm – *then go to the bank and ask for a loan!»*

«If only I could» I lied with vehemence. My stomach was gripped in a knot at the thought of meeting a Cerberus, an ogre banker, trying to secure an impossible loan. Inwardly, I blamed the Dreamer for having placed me in this difficult situation. My worry turned into aggression and I burst out:

«And then what? On what grounds would they give me a loan?»

«The world knows!... The Bank knows! – He stated – *The Bank, like the world, isn't outside you. It can only give you what you already 'possess'.»*

With a quick theatrical movement of the head, He looked left and right, to make sure we were alone and that no one could hear the secret He was about to confide. Then, in a low voice, He said:

«In the universe there is nothing that can be given to you. A man can only receive what he has already paid for.» His improvised pantomime had caught me by surprise, and He resumed His usual severity before I had time to rearrange my facial muscles.

«Payment can take place in time or out of time!» He enunciated. The long pause that followed magnified the significance of this declaration and forewarned me of the importance of what He was about to say.

«If there's a difference between men, it's in the way they themselves have chosen to pay…»

«A man who believes in himself has already paid for all that he possesses. His true and sole occupation is keeping himself whole and allowing nothing and no one to impair his integrity. He knows that it's his indivisibility that creates wealth. He knows that his financial destiny depends on his level of integrity.

Every effort you make to drown out the chant of sorrow you keep inside will produce financial power. Every time you travel in the opposite direction from the multitude, you'll create wealth in the world of events.

Nothing is external.

Self-observation, the ability to circumscribe a negative emotion, a pain, a doubt, is money that comes to you.

The world of events is too slow to recognise who has paid beforehand, who has already settled his accounts in the invisible. It takes time to record those credits, but its administration is infallible.»

Here, He stopped to look at me intently. In His eyes I read the gravity of the revelation He was about to make, and I could sense that it would be painful.

«You, like millions of men who love to be dependent, have chosen to pay in the currency of time: pain!» He said bitterly.

«Credit and debt are one and the same thing but divided by time… The future knows! Obtaining credit is only the signal lit that shows the payment has already taken place. If the loan has been accepted, it means you've already paid for it.»

I was dumbfounded. The Dreamer was imparting a secret that no economist had ever been able to discover, much less encapsulate into such an important rule that could include the courage, creativity and sense of certainty of a statesman and visionary businessman; a theory about the brilliant madness of entrepreneurs, industrial and political leaders whose choices and decisions, often crucial to so many men‘s futures, often appear reckless if not foolish in the eyes of ordinary men.

«But why have great financial and industrial empires collapsed, even with courageous men at the top?» I tried to object. The Dreamer was accelerating and I was struggling to keep up with Him.

«In life as in business, there's only one way to lose: stop believing in yourself!»

In the Institute of Economics in Naples, with my beloved teacher, Palomba and on the path first marked out by Professor Amoroso, I had taken the first steps towards the territory of the 'dream', the universal ideas that rouse man, inspire humanity and constitute powerful forces in economy and society. But those teachings paled in the light of what I was learning from the Dreamer.

«How can a man control events and phenomena like market progress, exchange quotations, political climates, legislative frameworks and international relations?»

«There exists an art of dreaming, the art of believing and creating, an ability to elevate the being to higher levels of responsibility in order to attract new ideas and greater possibilities of doing and having.

Economics, politics, and even history obey the laws of the Being. A mind trained in limitation, in the finite, can't understand it. You only have to know that the universe which surrounds you is a grain of sand when compared to your Being.

The more you are, the more you have. A man who believes in himself gains all the resources with which to face every undertaking, even those which are impossible. A man's economy corresponds perfectly to his level of integrity. The more you are, the more you have, and never vice versa.»

He paused for a moment, allowing me to reflect upon His answer. The more you are, the more you have. The more you are, the more you have, I repeated to myself… but that concept, so simple and yet so powerful, escaped me. I was unable to absorb it, to make it part of me.

Finally, a thought made its way through… Quality creates quantity. This was the great secret. Qualitative economy would lead a future humanity, and bring solutions to all its problems: a planetary healing. The quality of a man's thoughts creates his economy, visible wealth and prosperity. Only qualitative economics can produce true, inalienable, permanent wealth. It was wonderful. The Dreamer's philosophy was heralding a new economic model;

He was giving me the formula for a totally unknown teaching in schools of economics and the world of business.

«The economy will never be led by economists – He said, penetrating my thoughts in turmoil – *In the near future every organisation, from the smallest company to the largest multinational, will be an ideological company, a School of Being.»*

«Its success, longevity, its very destiny will depend on its philosophy. At the top of every organisation there will be philosophers of action, poets and visionaries, pragmatic utopians, capable of penetrating the being and nourishing its roots. The smallest widening of the vision, an elevation in comprehension, can move mountains in the world of economy and finance.»

4 We are the bow, the arrow and the target

Every day since moving to Seven Oaks I had gone jogging. I only had to cross the road to find myself in Hampstead Heath where I could run along small paths, around lakes, and down the grassy slopes of Parliament Hill. That morning I had run with fury, without sparing myself, to expel the anxiety and doubts that increasingly assailed me and tried to take root. I had not seen the Dreamer for months. I had left my job, sold my house in Chià, and moved to London, but in all that time I had received no message from Him. Without a role or any work commitments, without meetings and plans, I did not know how to give meaning to my life. Up until then I had never recognised with such clarity how important my relationship with others and the outside world, in all its kaleidoscopic manifestations, was to me. Moreover, the anxiety and worries that at that time I identified with the very idea of responsibility, the contrast and frictions, which I considered the natural, inevitable effects of relationships with others, had become a drug whose deprivation was producing the effects of a true withdrawal.

Pain is all that men know...
It gives meaning to their existence.
It makes them believe they're alive.

I had reflected upon these words for a long time, and for months I had experienced firsthand how paradoxical the human condition was.

In states of serenity and joy, in the absence of every pain, man feels annihilated. Once, the Dreamer told me that a state of joy cannot be experienced by mankind as it is, even a moment of happiness is unbearable.

"Joy, serenity, gratitude and love, are states of Being that mankind, in its present condition, can't feel. If they could enter in an ordinary man's life, he would see them as hell in his own hell. Happiness can only belong to those who know the Art of Dreaming. Only a man who loves, a man who dreams, can bear the energy which the absence of pain generates."

At the end of my run, I turned down Courtney Avenue at full speed. In the last few metres I quickened my pace, I often did this. The thought of a hot shower gave me extra stamina and put new strength in my legs.

Suddenly I felt His presence. It was an unmistakable feeling. He was there. The Dreamer had come! I glanced at my clothes, at my sweat-soaked tracksuit and my muddy shoes. I decided to go around the house and enter from the back, through the garden entrance. From there I could slip into the bedroom, get washed and make myself presentable. In truth, the thought of meeting the Dreamer, especially as I had not seen Him for some time, caused conflicting emotions in me. Seeing Him, hearing His voice, or even recalling His words, was an acceleration of the Being, a compression of time which set me anxiously to 'work'. I loved and detested the unexpected effort of having to reconstruct my body's scattered fragments, which in the absence of the Dreamer, had become dismembered. It was always a rude awakening that compelled me to recognise that through forgetfulness we lose our identity and become the crowd, the multitude.

I did not even have time to put my foot on the bottom step of the staircase that led to my room, before His unmistakable voice froze me on the spot.

«You're regretting the past!» He opened in a loud voice, giving our meeting an abrupt start.

The Dreamer was synthesising all the troubles of the last few months and reading me inside in those few words. I felt caught red-handed.

Oh yes! For months I had been regretting the past! Like the Jews of the Exodus, ready to barter their freedom, I preferred the security of old constraints to this solitude and life without meaning. I needed to worship the golden calf, the idol of the world; I needed to return to my usual confusion. If only I had been able to, I would have returned to the familiar womb of irresponsibility, of dependence. I would have preferred the small villa in Chià a thousand times to that rich London residence which I was unprepared to keep, and which made me feel small and unreal.

In moments of clarity I understood that the Dreamer was pushing me towards limits that I would never have crossed; He was putting me in situations I would never have experienced. Beside Him, I was constantly tiptoeing on the edge of an abyss, like a tightrope walker without a net. Below ran my life like the river Styx, a swamp of putrid water, thick with malaise and vulgarity.

From our very first meeting, the Dreamer had warned me against the perils of this desert; against the ambushes of invisible predators that I would meet while crossing it. I remembered the words He said to me the night before my departure for London:

"AIM... I AM... We are our objective... we are the bow, the arrow and the target... The aim, which seems to be always outside us, is in actual fact the anagram, the other profile of I am. This takes us back to the moment, to the compression of time, to the elimination of every distance from our selves. The supreme art is our changing, which can only take place in this instant.

An ordinary man's existence, hectic and busy as it might appear, is only a continuous indulgence in meaningless repetition. Our life's goal is to create an original masterpiece: ourselves... It's a journey that everyone, sooner or later, in one lifetime or a hundred, will have to face. There's no other objective and nothing in the world is more exciting..."

Slowly I took off my shoes and left them there, where I was. Barefoot, I followed the direction of the Dreamer's voice and, silently, peeped out from behind the sitting room door.

5 "I have come to set you free!"

Fatigued from the run, I leaned against the door-jamb, panting slightly. This irritated the Dreamer.

«Stand up straight! Don't lean on anything! – He ordered *–Don't let anyone see you tired or worn out.»*

With an imperious gesture, He silenced me before I could even open my mouth to explain.

«Don't blame the run... Even if you had run a whole marathon, you would have no right to look anguished or exhausted. Always tell yourself: I could have run even further!...»

Those words were like a whip, sweeping my thoughts away along with the lie about being tired. When He saw me straighten up and move away from the doorjamb, He began His discourse:

«You're regretting the past» He repeated and the hint of scorn in His voice wounded me cruelly.

« Regret takes you back to the laws of your past and cancels out all your years of 'work'. On the road to integrity, there's no room for regret. Once you've set out on the 'journey' you can't turn back!»

Then His tone changed.

«You're looking for labels – He said, displaying the exaggerated patience that adults show when talking to a child – *There's no handrail, so you don't know what to hold on to. This suspended state makes you more afraid of the fear you've always borne inside.»*

The Dreamer was talking to me from one of the sitting room's armchairs, next to the open fire. A silver buckle on His coat gleamed in the firelight. That glow penetrated the folds of my being and shook me, opening me up to a new understanding. Like all ordinary men, I too loved pain more than my own life. The Dreamer would explain to me that rather than face the horror of entering what he does not know, man's true fear is that of losing what is most familiar to him: pain and suffering. This phobia creates an insurmountable barrier to the manifestation of will, to what we truly, genuinely possess, and is also what makes us belong to the dark sea of nonentity.

After physical birth, with the cutting of the umbilical cord, the child is attached to two new parents: doubt and pain. Only encountering the School will allow for a new birth and the severing of this terrible cord. It is a return to our true parents: the dream and the will. The absence of doubt and fear is a state of ecstasy and freedom, which only an integral man can bear.

«This is what I'm offering you. Freedom is very costly, but that doesn't make it unobtainable.»

«You're still looking in the shadows of the past for some old mask to put on» He said, and in His voice was the compassion that one feels for a poor, defenseless being. He added in the same tone:

«You miss having a role to play... A man can't be led by the past or by the experiences he has lived. What's past is dust. On the way to integrity he has to entrust himself to new senses: intuition, and a seventh sense, the 'dream'. Roles are prisons... their bars are invisible but more solid than steel...»

«But I've listened to you... I've quit my job, I've sold my house. What else should I do?» I burst out, venting the rage I'd accumulated in all those months of waiting. I felt blame and resentment bubble to the surface because I was ensnared in that new adventure, realising that it made no sense no matter how I tried to get around it.

«If you don't understand, leaving your work, or changing countries, is no use... nor will it make you free» He answered with rough sweetness, disregarding my emotions for the moment. Years later I would recognise that once again the Dreamer had come just in time to save me.

«Before he can break out of the prison of his roles, a man must feel disappointment for the sterile repetitiveness of the events and circumstances of his own life.»

There was a long pause.

I was still standing at the entrance to the sitting room, listening to Him. Still dirty and sweating from my long run, I felt uncomfortable. I wanted to wash and change into something clean. The moment seemed right, and I asked if I could leave. The Dreamer was engrossed. I interpreted an imperceptible movement of His head as an assent and I left. A shower and a clean shirt changed my attitude.

When I returned, I came in with cat-like steps and sat down in the other armchair near the fireplace, at a respectful distance from the Dreamer. I had my notebook. I took in a huge mouthful of air and then I felt ready to begin, knowing it would be a demanding session. The Dreamer's tone had changed:

«No one builds a house on a bridge. A bridge isn't meant to be a dwelling-place – He remarked – *Roles, like bridges, are there to take you to another place; they're made to be surpassed. Humans*

spend too much time on them, and instead of crossing them and going beyond, they stay there, trapped. On the path to integrity every moment must be new... every instant serves to transcend the previous moment... every breath must be an act of gratitude devoted to elevating the being towards new areas of freedom.»

«How can one live in a world, free of roles?» I asked.

«Roles are masks to be worn deliberately, while performing. To 'play' a role means not to believe it!»

He explained that the first step in the direction He was showing me was to understand fully the way roles function. In the Dreamer's vision, roles are ordered hierarchically according to complexity and the level of responsibility they demand. He was categorical on one point: a man cannot in any way move to a higher role if his own Being does not first contain all the hierarchical pyramid below. From His explanation of roles, I gleaned an image of containers of different sizes, stacked one on top of another like Chinese boxes.

«Freedom from a role only comes when you've learnt to act it perfectly» clarified the Dreamer, citing the example of an orchestra conductor, who has to know the possibilities and difficulties of every single instrument.

«When we perform a role intentionally, and act it perfectly, it not only frees us, but also frees the world from that coarseness, that violence – He said – *When you identify yourself with it, when you believe it, you not only become a slave of the world, but you cling to it as if it were the real thing, your only certainty. To believe in a role, no matter what it may be, means lying to yourself.»*

I couldn't estimate accurately, but my rough calculations suggested that ten lifetimes would not be enough to accomplish such a feat.

«Exactly – confirmed the Dreamer – *This is why no one, following an ordinary path, will ever free himself from his roles... nor would he want to!»*

«Why is it that no one wants to set himself free from his roles? – I asked – Who wouldn't be happy to get rid of the commitments and responsibilities of being a father, husband or manager?» I suggested that only a sense of responsibility prevents us from abandoning them.

«On the contrary – the Dreamer dryly retorted – *for an ordinary man, abandoning a role is like asking him to give up his*

life... like abandoning a life vest in an infinite sea. Men are more attached to their roles, and even more to the sufferings that are an integral part of them, than they are to their own breath.»

A long pause followed. I remained silent.

«Roles are shields. Men hide behind them pretending to be busy, but in reality they are defending their own irresponsibility. Take you, for example!» He pointed out in the tone of someone embarking upon a conclusive demonstration.

Now the Dreamer's sights were trained on me. His announcement came as no surprise, but that did not make it any less painful. After years in proximity to the Dreamer, a painful pressure in my stomach always forewarned me that His discourse was about to shift from a general plane to a personal one.

6 Playing roles

«This is what you have to change... what you are feeling now – He said, noticing my grimace of pain – *Look at yourself! You continue to believe that I caused it by my words; but in fact that pain has always stagnated inside you, like a swamp of dead water! This is the symptom of an unhealed wound, and it's the cause of all your troubles... Contain that pain... Understand it... Love it. Don't run away from it!»*

I was still trying to understand and recover from His last remarks. The Dreamer had already linked it to His initial discourse, resuming it from where He had left off.

«By identifying with the roles, you've forgotten the Game – He said – *There's no performance or theatricality. An event, a situation, or a meeting sets off mechanical reactions in you, like the compressed spring of a mousetrap. Mental images, thoughts, emotions, sensations adapt to mechanically pre-arranged schemes, facial muscles contract and take on certain expressions certain words appear on the lips, and you become a hostage, until new conditions and meetings catapult you into another cage...»*

He explained to me that this happens when a role is imposed by the outside world. However, when we perform it consciously we cannot be enslaved by it; we become free of it, and thus we also free the world.

«A role must be played without believing it which is only possible for those who have acquired an understanding and a command of themselves: a result that requires order, discipline, and a considerable work of self-observation.»

He stressed that, in order to make it a part of our life, every role requires us to learn a specific language: gestures, behaviour, attitudes, and an entire range of facial and verbal expressions. Having a role presupposes the acceptance of entire blocks of ideas and complete packages of beliefs through which one thinks and feels. Learning to play a role is a complicated matter. Often a man can spend his entire life learning to play just one role without his will and responsibility ever maturing sufficiently for him to be able to surpass it and go beyond.

He told me that every man, through the necessities of his ordinary existence, learns and plays a limited number of roles, five or six at the most. In order to adapt himself to circumstances, he passes from one to the other like an automaton, without purpose, conditioned by changes in his external situation. Contrary to what he believes, he has no freedom to decide.

«Freedom means playing whatever role 'on purpose', without ever being imprisoned by it – He emphasized – *in an ordinary man, this ability, which is negligible to start with, becomes less and less with age, until it disappears completely. The consequence is that when conditions occur that are only slightly different from the usual few roles he knows, a man can no longer choose the right mask to put on.»*

I realised that this is why we constantly feel out of place, ill at ease and threatened. By not knowing which mask to put on, or including it in our repertoire, we reveal our limits, as in the Pavlov's experiment where a dog unable to decide between the circle and the ellipsis, goes mad. Thus every faculty, mental, physical and emotional, functions randomly; thoughts, emotions and actions combine together by way of a spastic relationship, and the human Being becomes a biological puppet. We feel naked in our terrible shame and would like to run away. Yet these are the moments when, peeping through the paper-thin gap between our skin and the mask, it is possible for us to observe ourselves and recognise our essence, our truest part.

«Those who recognise that they have a limited repertoire of roles and are aware of the tyranny that those ties can impose on their action, have already taken the first steps towards freedom.»

But the ordinary man, plunged into a hypnotic sleep and lulled by a song of pain, will keep on lying to himself. No matter how terrible his life may be, he will continue to indulge in it, and will never ever find enough energy to escape.

«The role is a pleasant game, if it's performed with total awareness. Identifying oneself with it, forgetting the Game, is fatal.»

The Dreamer got up and went over to the window. He remained silent for some minutes, looking out at the garden in Seven Oaks, the impeccable lawn and lush plants in the last rays of the sun. When He started His discourse again the tone of His voice was unusually tender.

«Roles are rungs on a ladder. Don't linger on any of them. Use them – He urged – *Use them to step on and go beyond!»*

According to the Dreamer, every role is the materialisation of a certain way of thinking. To abandon one role and move on to the next one, means that it has already been overcome in one's being; every step taken and left behind means a progression towards healing.

«Learn to raise the quality of the Being, and each role will be dismissed as quickly as a cast-off item of clothing – He concluded – *This is called 'using' a role and freeing oneself from it once and for all.»*

This new expression struck me. The Dreamer noted my perplexity, and He explained to me that 'using' a role means taking possession of the essence and responsibility behind every role; it means freeing oneself from it forever, once it is no longer needed.

«Thus will you free the world from the thankless task of showing you the hells you bear inside, from the appalling task of reflecting your every deficiency, pain, and death.»

7 The path back

«All that is outside us, the world that we see and touch, the people, circumstances and events that we encounter, are a revelation of the Being; a confirmation of our way of thinking... The

roles in which we're still trapped show us the wounds we have not yet healed.»

He paused for a long time. Rather than understanding and laying claim to the energy of that moment, I took refuge in the pages of my notebook, pretending to reread and amend them. Those corners into which the Dreamer was pressing me were painful. Once again I tried to flee. I made a mute request for more time… still more time…

The Dreamer apparently diverted His attention and I, who had savoured true life with Him for a few moments, returned to take my place among the inanimate objects of the room, I was finally at ease, a shadow among the world's shadows.

«Events serve to go back to, and make visibles the states that generated them... Only a School of Being knows their symbolic language and can trace the path back, through labyrinths, deserts and inner hells, to the innermost states, the true source of every happening.»

The shadows of the encroaching evening settled against the great windows of Seven Oaks, ready to enter and take possession of the sitting room where we were. The Dreamer's face glowed with reflected flames while He carefully placed new logs on the embers. It was a perfect moment, and in the semi-darkness, I could no longer see to write. I rested my head against the back of the armchair and closed my eyes to concentrate better.

«Straighten up – the Dreamer ordered dryly – *you are actually capable of falling asleep there, in front of Me…»*

It felt like an unexpected blow from a rod. A mass of thoughts and feelings, self-commiseration, blame and resentment, erupted violently and mingled in my being, until they formed just one sense, the most burning and unbearable of them all: the sense of injustice. In that moment, with a sudden jump, like an insect's, I found myself in the Dreamer's place. I observed myself. I saw life watching death die. There were only a few infinite moments of impressive clarity; then I found myself again alert, with my eyes wide open and my back perfectly erect. For an instant, a tingling sensation vibrated just beneath my skin before it disappeared. I promised myself I would never lower my guard again.

I am recounting this episode to give an idea of the strategies to which the Dreamer tirelessly resorted in order to take me to those zones in the Being where His teaching, His energy, became my very essence. When this happened, I knew I only had a few moments to strengthen the staves of my container, the oak ribs, which creaked and threatened to yield under the pressure of that new, strong new wine.

8 "You are not ready!"

I felt my resistance rise and my blood pulsate under the pressure of His words.

«For too many years you've renounced your will and placed your life in the world's hands The outer world has been the only reality for you, and you've made a divinity of it... a stone idol that has tyrannically ruled your existence.

In reality, the world is only a reflection... Thoughts, emotions and attitudes take shape in the world of events and respond to each of your wishes.

For too many years you've thought the world was real, that it had a will of its own. You've made it the lord and master of your life. For too many years you've relinquished power to a shadow that you yourself have projected.»

The moment I had dreaded had come… It was time to let go of my former handholds, to let the old things die… I could feel the enormous gap of an overturned world opening up under my feet.

«Things do not change and cannot change... Only you can change.»

Here He stopped. That pause expanded hugely inside me. A vague disquiet, then a sense of fear, widened its circles until it touched the edges of my Being. There was apparently nothing to justify my alarm, and yet I discerned in His words, and above all in the charged silence, that something unforeseeable was taking shape. I tried to calm myself, but it was impossible. Finally, as if making a difficult resolution, the Dreamer announced the following phase of the 'work' that would allow for the next passage. That moment marked the beginning of the quest, the journey that would valiantly engage every moment of my life. In the tone of someone communicating a carefully considered decision, He said:

«It has taken years of preparation for you to realise the fragmentation of your Being... years and years to make you

recognise the hypnotic sleep that tyrannically rules every man's existence.

I've brought order to your life... I've freed you from commitments and programmes so that you can devote yourself to putting together the principles of an educational system that will show the way to emerge from the hells of ordinariness.»

The Dreamer paused, remaining absorbed for a long time. Then in a resolute tone, He announced:

«There are men and women whom you should meet...»

«Who are they?... Where are they?... Why should I meet them?» I urged apprehensively.

«There is no finality – the Dreamer responded with unexpected gentleness – *This is what makes the 'game of encounters' interesting, unique and effective. You'll have to meet hundreds of people for no other reason... than to recognise in each of those men and women a fragment of yourself... If you remember Me, your promise, every meeting will be an opportunity for you to compare yourself with an unknown, unresolved part of yourself.»*

«Hundreds of meetings?... But that's going to take years!...» I exclaimed, terrified at the prospect.

«The amount of time this takes will depend on you... The 'game of encounters' will last as long as your incomprehension, and will be as arduous as your resistance.

Through the 'game of encounters', you'll realise that the world is one of your creatures and the others are your reflection... And even if this result takes years of work, at least you will weaken the old belief inside you that the world has the power to hoist you up or knock you down, that others can love you or fight against you, and that there's a hostile will outside you, which controls and rules your life.»

«The world exists because you exist. The world is alive because you are alive – declaimed the Dreamer, and continued – *The world is your shadow... Man would like to find in it the understanding that he feels inside... and so he spends his existence searching for life among ghosts... He believes in a reality outside himself... He wastes his time excavating shadows!... But, through this wasted archeology and your eagerness to be identified with them, they become even more real for you, and the outer world becomes a fetish... an idol to worship, fear and propitiate. Because*

you've forgotten your true will, you've given up your creator's right...»

Then He articulated these words:

«Don't forget... the others are you outside yourself... the others are the reflection of all you don't want to see, feel and touch inside yourself.»

«So… I, and those closest to you – I asked Him – What do we mean to you?»

Once I'd pronounced these words, my heart beat faster, and I understood that I had dared to go beyond the limits of what I was able to hear and contain. His gaze weighed upon me for several infinite moments, perhaps to evaluate my ability to withstand what He was about to tell me.

Then I remembered His words: *Nothing is external... Nothing is external*… Their force hurled me into the solitude of a universe of which I was the sole inhabitant, creator, lord and absolute master. I was frozen and dismayed, and would have given anything to go back and withdraw that question. The walls of my Being quaked under the pressure of that crucial moment.

«All of you are Me – He said – *fragments of Me... seemingly in exile.»*

9 The short cut

I was despondent. The Dreamer had set me such an impossible task that I felt drained of all energy before even starting.

« ...The 'game of encounters' will allow you to compress time... You'll learn more about yourself in the game than an ordinary man could do in ten lifetimes...» He said in an exhortative tone, but the prospect of meeting so many illustrious strangers, of working for months or years to this end, continued to seem absurd to me. Was there no other way?

«For you the world is too real. Only the 'game' will free you from this petrified, rigid description, and allow you access to a more fluid, more liquid vision of the world. The world is an emotion» He said, and then waited for the precious substance of this overview to penetrate my Being.

«The meetings will help you to measure your level of responsibility, they'll teach you to know yourself completely, and

you'll realise that every man or woman you meet is an unknown part of you, an opportunity to see one of your wounds or hidden illnesses which you will then be able to heal.»

«How will I choose them? What will I talk about?» I persisted, without even trying to hide my apprehension. I hoped with all my strength that I would be spared that task.

«What you talk about doesn't matter at all – the Dreamer cut in – *You ask this question because you still believe the others are outside you. But the others are states of Being which materialise in the world of events... The others are time.»*

«And the man who gives his own life for others? Who meets them in order to help and heal them? Missionaries?»

«Even the missionary meets himself, his doubts, his fears, his division. He mixes with those who are superstitious in order to conquer his own superstition. He enters the world of suffering to heal his wounds and return to the source, the true cause. And even if he's unaware of it and believes that he does things on behalf of others, it's really the others who are doing things for him, taking care of him. Once he has understood which states in himself have made his mission possible, he'll be healed; he won't need to be a missionary any longer. He'll put someone else in his place and go beyond.»

I was in turmoil. The Dreamer's answer had turned me inside out and I was still trying to compose myself when I noticed that He had left the argument and was responding to my initial question.

«As for whom you'll meet, for now all you need to know is that I myself will decide on them and point them out to you. The important thing for you is to learn to 'see'. If you 'see', you'll make that man or woman's history your own and in an instant you'll gain the benefit of years and years of experiences, efforts, sacrifices, successes and falls. 'Seeing' them means recognising them inside yourself like wounds to be closed or organs to be healed. 'Seeing' means forgiving yourself inside. Then every meeting becomes a step on which to rise above and go beyond.»

My growing interest in what the Dreamer was telling me had not escaped His notice, and this story of meetings started to take the form of an unknown and mysterious martial art. The world, with its continents and cities, and the endless kaleidoscope of human activities, like figures constantly reshaped from soft clay; seemed like a vast combat in which millions of invisible duels were constantly taking place. Their outcomes would decide who should lead and who should follow.

«Wherever they meet, for a few moments or years, in the desert or in a business, two men inevitably form a pyramid. Placing themselves on different rungs of an invisible ladder, they respect an inner, mathematical order, a planetary hierarchy made up of brightness, orbits, mass and distances from their sun.»

I continued to take notes and line after line, my resistance disappeared, I changed my attitude. From the discourse that followed, life emerged as a path traced along a system of roles of increasing complexity, until it reached the summit, the place where every role has been surpassed.

«Mankind, as it is, doesn't seek healing and doesn't want it. It's forced to proceed mechanically, under the pressure of unknown forces... Suffering and pain are the driving forces of its evolution. And even if it seems that most men have exchanged their own progress for the apparent security of a career, or for the mirage of financial wealth or artistic success; even the most ordinary man can't escape an involuntary, mechanical, imperceptible healing process. The work in organisations, the drudgery of roles, the antagonisms, suffering and problems, which life unfailingly presents him, together form a necessary discipline that betters him and projects him towards the highest zones of freedom...»

«It's a very slow system – concluded the Dreamer – *and it might take more than a lifetime to advance even a millimetre in the verticality of Being...»*

On the other hand, the 'game' – as the Dreamer would subsequently describe – is the quickest way to scale the pyramid of human roles and transcend them at electronic speed. At the end He summarised the most important information for my benefit and concluded:

«You're still trapped in what you believe you are. What you'll see in the meetings isn't what you truly are, but what you are not: the man whom you've believed yourself to be. I would say that the study of yourself, self-observation, is light. When the light comes, the shadows disappear and all that is true and real in you remains, and all that you are not or that you've believed yourself to be, vanishes...»

Our meeting was coming to an end. I felt my heart tighten as it used to when Padre Nuzzo called me to the blackboard, and, having left my bench, along with the anonymous irresponsibility and the warm complicity of the group, I could count on no one but myself.

My new adventure was about to begin. I wanted to know more about the people I would meet, the arguments I would counter, but…

«In the 'game' there's nothing to plan. You'll have to invent instantly, and purposefully act out the roles and language of existences you've never lived. The moment will tell you the strategy, the words to use and all that you have to know in order to 'satisfy' the encounter.»

He then told me about special men and women who, in their own environment are true masters. Like highly specialised, perfect machines, they have reached an absolute flawlessness within their world-role… I had written pages and pages of notes without once lifting my head from the book, and re-reading them made me find all the strength and determination which I now felt beside Him.

It started to become clear that behind every encounter and beyond the apparent superficiality of a relationship, something special existed: encountering a multitude of different human types marked the path towards a healing which the Dreamer called 'integrity'.

«The others reveal you, measure you and perfectly reflect your level of responsibility.»

Apparently, men meet each other so as to make decisions and conclude business arrangements; but they are unaware of what truly happens in their relationships. Meeting oneself is a pretext. The true relationship takes place at another level. Beyond the surface, when two men meet, the stakes are much higher.

«Every man you meet is a door. He can bar access or become a step from which to climb beyond. Every encounter measures you and determines your position on the ladder of human responsibility» the Dreamer informed me with the tone of someone advising extreme caution on the eve of a risky undertaking, and added:

«Remember! The others are you!… In the 'game' you will meet no one but yourself… Within a few seconds, you'll have to learn which part of yourself is before you, and understand immediately what the aim of that encounter is, which mask to put on,

and which role that the other, whether it be a man or woman, wants you to interpret.

The difference between the two of you in the 'game' is that you know how to act, while the other acts without knowing. There's an infinite distance, a difference of eternities between the two, a difference which will allow you to climb vertically at vertiginous speed, the pyramid of human roles, conquering positions which in the horizontal world would take years and entire generations to reach.»

Here the Dreamer spoke to me about the 'short cut', a vertical way which compresses time and carries us quickly to the most real thing in us: the 'dream'.

10 Compressing time

The Dreamer taught me to perceive a world where a challenge constantly rules and where there is no space for hesitation. Two men meet each other, without any identifying symbols or devices, naked in the desert. Inevitably, one decides the direction and the other follows. Like two animals in a wild region, and by means of a zoological language, they ascertain each other's race, strength, territory and rank. A reaction, a habit, a pose, the expression of an emotion, a look, a word or the slightest grimace, reveals the position that each one occupies on the evolutionary ladder. That level of comprehension is recorded in the universe and decides the events in our life: what we know, do, have and finally what our financial destiny holds.

His tone became imperceptibly more familiar and He said:

«When two men meet each other, inevitably, one contains and the other is contained...»

«What does 'containing' a person mean?» I asked.

«It means being responsible for his entire world, his roles, his life and all the lives that depend on him. It means knowing the solution to every difficulty and the answer to every request. If you don't succeed, you'll have to go down the ordinary routes: those of time and experience. It will take years and years before that lost opportunity presents itself again in order for you to enter higher zones of the Being, towards understanding and integrity. In any

case, you'll have to repeat that examination, if you're lucky enough to have another opportunity.»

I felt my vision physically expand and I prepared myself to listen even more intently as the Dreamer got ready to communicate another piece of that teaching which was to change my life.

«It's a difficult and dangerous game – He admonished – *a look, a word, the slightest movement or thought can betray you and make you fall into a mortal trap! A man without the School is helpless. He goes through the 'game of encounters' but he doesn't know the rules; he doesn't have the slightest awareness of his true place in the game, or that he is in one at all. Those who 'see' the game lead it, those who don't see become a victim of it.»*

«How will I know if I've passed the test, what will be the result of such an encounter?» I asked in a loud voice, as if I could already see Him disappearing over the horizon.

«Things in a man's life come together in the most unique way and reflect his level of understanding and flawlessness. If you 'contain' the other, you won't make any mistake, but will feel immense joy at having brought light and healing, to another corner of your Being. When this happens in a man, the whole universe knows.»

«How do they know about an encounter if it's taken place in private and without witnesses?» I asked.

«Men and things all share a single connective tissue. A sensitive planetary system joins all of humanity's cells. Alone, in the corner of a room, a man can communicate his condition, his own level of responsibility and his intention, to the whole universe. There's no way to cheat, nor is there any room for interpretation.»

11 Others reveal you

The Dreamer had promised me that we would see each other the following week at the Spaniard's Inn, the old pub in Hampstead. In the meantime, I spent the days and hours contemplating what He had said about the 'game'. The thought that assailed me most was that of finding myself committed, for who knows how long, to carrying forward what still appeared to me to be the most eccentric of tasks: meeting hundreds of people so as to discover… that they did not exist.

«I didn't say the others don't exist» the Dreamer rudely corrected me during our meeting, with a grimace of commiseration that wounded me like a blade.

«I said the others don't exist outside you!... When this is clear to you, you'll know what the others are for...»

Thinking 'by analogy', I knew for certain that the Dreamer was offering me a unique opportunity, and that the 'game of encounters' would reveal itself as an irreplaceable evolutionary instrument. And yet, I was besieged by a crowd of doubts and worries from which I was unable to free myself.

Apart from the complexity and effort of organising so many meetings, a question that assailed me more than any other was: how would I bear the cost, if the 'game of encounters' occupied all my time, if it required me to travel and stay for lengthy periods in Great Britain and other parts of the world?

In addition, there was another aspect that I found particularly worrisome: the idea that those meetings were in fact real duels. Once, He said to me *"There isn't one moment when your life isn't at risk"*. The memory of these words reinforced this belief, and my anxiety about competing grew, along with reluctance at the thought of encountering those unknown personages, without knowing why. I glimpsed a ruthlessness in the 'game' that, as if seen through filigree, clouded its image and painted it in dark colours. And finally, it seemed to me that its ends were these: either you send forth a message of strength, courage, and dignity so as to be promoted to the next level or your adversary will condemn you to fetters and the dregs of existence, and you'll leave the spoils of a defeated warrior behind on the battlefield of life.

At first, I did not dare say anything to the Dreamer about this. I still didn't know whether this sensation came from my dread of being unequal to the task, or from a humanitarian apprehension, as I didn't know who was going to be 'defeated' in the encounter.

These were the thoughts that accompanied me as I walked to the old inn. The atmosphere I found inside could not have changed much since the days when artists and poets like Shelley, Keats and Byron had patronised it. I was early, and the Dreamer had not yet arrived. Looking around, I tried to discover which place He would strategically choose and I decided on a table in the quietest corner. On the wall, a trophy of a harquebus evoked a legendary brigand's exploits.

I was still brooding over my fantasies of competition and defeat, and the Dreamer's arrival caught me off guard, but before I could do a thing, I felt myself caged in embarrassment similar to the confusion experienced by those caught unprepared or unaware by their superior. The sight of the Dreamer caused me to 'remember' the correct attitude and I quickly tried to adopt a more dignified air and gather myself before He came too near, but while He was still at the door, He beckoned me to follow Him. I left the table I had chosen for us and went out with Him by the ground floor. I felt annoyed by the crowded room, the noisiness of the clients, the stench of beer and the rancid air. For the private conversation I had in mind, the table on the first floor would have been more appropriate; but the Dreamer went directly to one right in the middle of the room, where the buzz of conversation was most intense, and invited me to take a seat.

He did not let the condition in which He had found me go unnoticed; He remarked on it in passing, admonishing me in a facetious, almost mocking tone.

I thought I might take advantage of His good spirit, but cautiously. I had learned at my own expense and all too frequently how suddenly the Dreamer's attitude could change, and how terrible His anger could be. A word, an accent or the slightest movement, untimely or inappropriate, was enough for Him to explode. I wanted to ask Him the question that summed up my state of mind and occupied my thoughts about the 'game': what happens to the players who lose?

My physical proximity to the Dreamer made everything clear. I realised that what I truly wanted to ask Him was what would happen if I came out defeated after the first encounter.

«Don't get the wrong idea – He said, anticipating me – *I've already told you... In the 'game' there are neither winners nor losers.»*

Those words were clear and distinct, as if the shouting had suddenly been suspended, and we'd been left alone in the pub. His voice did not cross the crowd; it did not need to rise above the clamour, but came to me from inside. By making His way back through those thoughts, He came to their root, to the old beliefs and prejudices from which they had sprung, and added:

«Your vision is still the fruit of an inner separation, a description of the world that rules only through oppositions and

antagonisms... In actuality, the duel only takes place within yourself. One's relationship with the other is only the most superficial and visible aspect of what really takes place in an encounter. And even if you fear that the other will take all that you've accumulated from years of preparation, it is really in you, and only in you, that destinies are decided.»

He continued, taking up a principal argument. 'Containing' a man did not simply mean including him in one's own responsibility, but electing him.

«An encounter with a man of superior responsibility always leads to a quickening – He asserted – *even if we're unaware of it.»*

«Meeting a man who 'contains' you is a blessing. He who takes a step beyond doesn't abandon the other to his destiny. On the contrary, he becomes responsible for him. He knows that his own evolution also leads to the other's evolution. The advancement of a man, the healing of just one cell, quickens the progress of all mankind...

Think of how much study and how many opportunities the others can offer in order for you to realise that there's no limit to success; because the true victory is winning oneself, through the harmonisation of opposites inside us, at this very moment.

Without this understanding or inner awareness, men meet each other in a somnambulistic state, meaning they're troubled by worries, clouded by doubts and fears and lost in daily discord. They meet so as to pursue objectives and insignificant, external, vain advantages.»

Light-heartedly, He stressed that no matter how much they devote themselves to doing, to discussing business or making apparently important decisions, from an evolved man's point of view, they appear to be little more than uncivilized individuals busy negotiating and haggling over glass beads, bric-a-brac and trash.

«They've lost the true objective – He announced, again using a harsh and serious tone – *They're not aware of the game... they've forgotten... they're no longer acting; they've become the very role itself!»*

With a glance, He made sure I was open to understand, then He concluded with this comment:

«On the road to flawlessness, in a responsible man's world, there's only space to conquer oneself: one's mediocrity, one's lie and one's identification with the world.»

12 Intentional role-playing. The Art of Acting

«There's a right mask for every occasion – He said – *The principal skill you have to develop in the 'game of encounters' is the art of disguise.»*

I could tell from His tone and expression that He was about to undertake a crucial part of His teaching. From the ancient manuscript 'The School for Gods', and my research on the life and thoughts of Lupelius, I had learned of his legendary skill in disguising himself. In his School the art of disguise was an integral part of a warrior's preparation. According to Lupelius, roles were psychological clothes he wore and made his disciples wear, teaching them how to 'become' that role, how to explore it and know every corner of it and secret, but without forgetting the game or ever becoming ensnared by it.

The Dreamer's gruff approach quickly communicated the importance of this element in my preparation for the 'game'.

«'The Art of Acting' is a warrior's ability to live strategically – He stated – *This is the skill that allows him to be 'on cue', to assume the most correct attitude for each circumstance.»* I recognised Lupelius' teaching in the Dreamer's words. Their voices blended together and their images were superimposed on top of one another in my mind, becoming one.

«Learn to live strategically and act purposefully, and you'll always know which image to present in each situation. Only those who act can evoke the thousands of peculiarities which make each encounter unique, different from all those which have gone before, and those yet to come, in the entire history of the world...»

He paused, then His voice echoed, even more imperious and intense.

«Learn to act – He said – *Only those who act can rule their own life and those of others, winning and being free!»*

I felt an instinctive repugnance for those rules. All that I had been taught forced me to see things from a completely different point of view. A man was free if He could 'be himself', if he did not have to act and pretend to be someone else, and I said this to Him. At the end of my reasoning, I still harboured the belief that meeting others through playing a role or wearing a mask, was a false, insincere way of managing a relationship.

Most people would have found my objections proper. Ordinary people would have seen them as appropriate for someone who has both good manners and unbreakable ethical principles; who knows how to defend them courageously, even to a superior. In the Dreamer's world, however, my words set off every alarm system, as if a thief had entered.

«*Quiet!*» the Dreamer berated me, with a sudden burst of anger. He didn't let me finish.

«*Being oneself... being oneself...* – He repeated, mocking my presumptuousness – *Someone like you who has lived in falsehood, imprisoned in roles throughout his whole life, wouldn't even know where to begin to be oneself*» I could hear repugnance and an open contempt in His voice. The Dreamer was not responding to my words but mirroring my arrogance, my division. Behind those arguments, and much more deeply than I could see, my resistance was changing.

My remorse had to be absolute and immediate, if the Dreamer was to continue, resuming His usual tone as though nothing had ever happened. Once again, I noticed His ability to enter and emerge from a state of Being, changing tone, language, gestures, facial expressions and reactions... He could do it all without leaving residue, without leaving a trail.

«*Living strategically isn't opportunism and it doesn't mean lying; it's the warrior's ability to adopt the appearance and perform the actions that the situation requires, and which the world is ready to receive. Only those who live strategically can survive... Acting is freedom.*»

Acting a role 'perfectly' means having overcome that role in life, it means 'understanding', and having access to higher zones of responsibility. The theatre, in the beginning, was a school of Being, a school of freedom, where disciple/actors learned to act and go beyond roles, acquiring the ability to move from one character to another without becoming trapped in them. Therefore acting means learning to free one's Being from destructive thoughts and negative emotions. And the theatre's cathartic, purifying action – which predominantly affected the actors – extended to the chorus, the public, the city and the entire nation, binding and unifying it, creating the conditions for its freedom and prosperity. This purpose has given the theatre the central role it has always had in every culture, and it still fascinates man and gives meaning to its magic.

The Classical Age in Greece discovered the centrality of the Being; it knew that the secret of economic prosperity, civil harmony, maturity and the longevity of its institutions was to be found in the elevation of every man's being and the enrichment of every cell in the city. This vision conceived and produced a civilisation of the Being, an emotional, timeless civilisation. Art, beauty, music, sport and the search for truth, were all pillars of the polis and the great governors of its life.

With the authority of a direct testimony, a mysterious being without geography or time, the Dreamer told me that the most ancient civilizations, far older than Greece and Rome, in founding a city, even before laying out its walls, first chose the place on which to construct two public buildings: the theatre, to cleanse the emotions, and the baths, to cleanse the body. They were the two vital glands of purification, the kidneys of that society. As in a living being, these two organs were entrusted with the essential task of filtering and purifying the city's vital lymph, with purifying and enriching every cell.

«The theatre isn't a physical place, but a state of Being, a psychological space where the greatest of man's faculties come into harmony... where the word, which is a union of thought and breath, comes together with the gesture.»

I was travelling in a time machine in search of vanished worlds and buried civilizations, and in His presence I could still feel their pulse, their breath.

13 The 'Game of Encounters'

So, with the Dreamer, I entered upon one of the most arduous periods of my apprenticeship. Like a warrior father, He bestowed upon me an armour and shield, and the weapons I would carry, entrusting them to me with this advice:

«Be aware, be attentive to every moment and each of your falls. Observe yourself! Fill every part of yourself with the memory of your promise. For those who don't remember the 'dream', the real, mysterious and invisible strength which rules the world, is a fragment lost in the universe.»

The 'game' kept me intensely busy for the next two years and throughout this time I did nothing but meet the men and women whom the Dreamer had specified, or placed in my path, according to strategic choices that only He knew. Today I recognise that each encounter was the fruit of a precise choice, a piece of a lucid, conscious and provident design. With each encounter followed an admirable pedagogical progression. Those encounters, besides helping me to discover and heal the most hidden wounds of my Being, created the indispensable presuppositions in the world of events on which the new university would be founded and developed.

Seven Oaks was the focal point of memorable meetings, a cenacle that brought together the world's intellect: men and women at the peak of culture, business, politics and art. Seven Oaks was a paean that summoned together all those who would be so essential in realising the great undertaking. The beauty and style of that house, which for months had appeared to consist of expensive extras and unnecessary details, became the tenets of the whole strategy; the unique setting that enclosed and imprinted irreplaceable characters on its entire history. Seven Oaks was the compass for those components of entrepreneurial vigour, style of life, responsibility and leadership which would accompany as constant components, the birth and development of a new campus of the university and trace the lines of its teachings. Seven Oaks was a house, an ally, headquarters, coffer, and invaluable custodian of my familiar joys. My children matured there, as did my affection for Heleonore.

The 'game of encounters' occupied a fundamental part in the general management of my apprenticeship, and moments of discomfort were not unusual in those two years, when His discipline and austerity became too severe for my level of tolerance. The Dreamer was a 'master of blame'. He employed blame and accusation to eradicate the song of sorrow from the labyrinth of my being. That keening pain had always afflicted me and killed me inside. Nothing escaped Him, and the smallest inobservance or deviation from the Project, made His terrible anger erupt. Then He knew how to enter the very folds, the most hidden sores of my Being and heal them with a red-hot iron. I wish that every man who wants to leave the rut of his own destiny could meet the Dreamer and have such an attentive and ruthless guardian. Every step at His side bore the breath of eternity. Now, as I write about Him, I recognise that His every movement was exclusively, remarkably designed for me; and, through me, dedicated to the evolution of every man who has realised his own state of slavery. Beside Him, the whole of existence has been revealed as a School of Being, a School for Gods; open to those who want to change and make a true masterpiece of their lives.

Moreover during those first months, the 'game of encounters' appeared to be an extravagance, which thoroughly tested my determination. Before the Dreamer's revelations, I would never have imagined that one could meet the 'others' without a 'practical' goal.

«Once, you asked me how I would choose the people you would meet» He said. He was returning to a question of mine, one to which He had never considered giving an answer.

«Their principal characteristic is that they have to be impeccable and ruthless. One day, you'll know that no meeting can take place outside you. The men and women you meet will prove to be fragments of yourself, like the pieces of a mosaic, and you must join them. Each of them represents one of your possible lives... In the ocean of mankind, each of them is a drop that reflects an aspect of your psychology... Remember: the others are only mirrors. There is no one to blame, or condemn. A man always and only meets himself!»

Following His advice and using Seven Oaks as a base, I travelled constantly. On numerous occasions I had to leave England, and very often the old continent, and found myself in the most varied situations, approaching diverse people of every social position, age, intelligence, family origin and business capacity, with the sole, absurd, wonderful aim of observing, 'reading' and 'knowing' myself.

Thus, I passed in review, a vast range of human beings: artists, directors, industrialists, consultants, healers of mankind and Fathers of the Church; politicians, entrepreneurs, philosophers and professors, doctors, great lawyers and bankers, Nobel Prize winners and vagabonds; men at the peak of their success and men who had fallen into disgrace; financial gurus and impoverished entrepreneurs; in their houses or offices, in the street or on their yachts, in luxury hotels or modest guesthouses, at work or on holiday. Hundreds of meetings, each one requiring a certain attitude, language, behaviour, dress or 'punctuality'. Each one challenged the limits of my vision and rigidity of my mental schemes; each one laid bare a hidden sickness, discovered a soft point in my Being, trained an inner quality or cauterised a small sore in my soul, allowing me to observe myself in the most diverse circumstances, before all possible mirrors.

I remember the attention the Dreamer gave to each small detail, especially on the eve of a particularly important meeting. His directions were no different from those of a director on set before shooting, or a coach before a decisive match. Everything passed through the sieve of His attention: my dress, the arguments I would broach, even the diction of certain key words I would use.

«Take care of yourself; be completely aware! Look after every corner of your life meticulously – the Dreamer told me – *Look within!... be aware of all that enters and leaves your Being... Our Being creates Our Life... The Being creates the world... A truly attentive man knows that through the smallest gesture he is fixing the universe.»*

14 The new paradigm

Once, after a long and patient work, I finally made my way to meet with the founder of a multinational, a leader in the field of fashion and the luxury-goods industry. The pretext for our meeting was the acquisition of a piece of property from his estate. The negotiation, which I had started in London weeks before, had reached its final stages, and it was necessary for us to meet. The name of that French entrepreneur was in the long list of figures, 'masters' of business in their own field, whom the Dreamer had asked me to contact.

It was during a period in which I was valiantly challenging my bad relationship with money. According to the Dreamer, it was essential for me to learn to negotiate from the 'hardest' businessmen without fear or subjection. On the eve of my departure for that meeting, which was to take place in Paris in the *sancta sanctorum* of one the most famous labels in the world, I was exasperated by my awareness of having no precise idea of what I would say. I felt my anxiety increasing, and with it a kind of resentment towards the Dreamer, who was 'guilty' of putting me in such stressful situations.

I asked Him if I could meet Him, secretly hoping that He would excuse me from this trip and let me cancel that meeting, which was already arranged at Rue de la Paix. We had only been together a few minutes before my mood erupted in an aggressive question, which I was unable to control.

«But what is the point of negotiating over a building or a company? – I burst out, trying to hide my discomfort behind irreproachable good sense – what purpose is there in talking about the details of acquiring a luxury car or a private plane, if you haven't got the money to buy them?»

«If you know how to act 'flawlessly' – the Dreamer answered, with unusual courtesy, ignoring the aggression I had just exhibited – *if you appear credible as he's questioning you, then it means the money is already in your pocket.»*

I did not understand. For me 'acting serious' was something completely different. I was certain that if I really had the money to buy that property in Paris, I would not be worried and would know what to say and do.

«You're quite wrong – retorted the Dreamer sharply – *your first education accustomed you to believing that if you had the money and sufficient means, you could do all that you wished and so feel secure; that you would be rich, happy, respected. Having-Doing-Being is the dominant paradigm, the epitome of a degraded mankind's mythology, and the cause of all its ills and misfortunes.»*

Having pronounced these words, He lifted His head and looked at me intently. Then, without turning away, He extended the index and middle fingers of His right hand and closed them together, tapping His right ear, slowly and repeatedly. The Dreamer was advising me on account of my difficulty to understand; He was demanding my complete and undivided attention. That strange mimicry disturbed me and beneath the gloss of normality of that movement, I felt the command and authority of a tragic gesture, a hint of theatrical magic, which so increased my heart rate that I had to take deep breaths to avoid falling into a state of agitation.

«This mindset is common to millions of human beings –He said – *you have to overturn it! The paradigm of a new mankind is: Being-Doing-Having. The more you are, the more you do, the more you have. Having and Being are the same thing but on different planes of existence.»*

The discovery that Being is already Having, and that the being leads the having and is its veritable cause, had the effect of an explosion that flung my life's ideas and beliefs into the air forever. This was one of those shocks to my thinking that was powerful enough to alter my destiny. The Dreamer's discussion became charged, probing. I took out my book and there, in the street, I started to make notes. While my hand flowed quickly over the pages, capturing each of His words, I memorised and repeated the phrases in my mind, which I did not have time to write down. I was afraid of losing even a single atom of that precious material, as it would have been irretrievable.

Returning to the initial discourse, He said that the meeting I was about to have in Paris would be the same as visiting an elegant clothes boutique or a famous jeweler's. The important thing was not to buy the clothes we tried on, or the precious jewels they showed us, but to be 'recognised' by the being, by the invisible essence of that boutique… He explained to me that the important thing was that that world… that band of existence said 'yes' to us.

«It's true, you won't come out with that expensive watch on your wrist, and that garment won't end up in your wardrobe, but you'll have trained your capacity for possessing them... Style is conscience... Train your being... Every effort you make to enter richer bands of existence will help defeat your sense of lacking funds. Become accustomed to wealth, raise your vision and dream the impossible, create a 'prosperity consciousness' that is the true origin of all wealth and the conditions by which to maintain it.»

«Money is an inner matter – the Dreamer said on that occasion – *It is made inside. Dream, constantly visualise harmony and success, and you'll obtain it. Money will only be a natural consequence of it. Then it will come without effort... Then you won't have any fear of losing it... Money has to come by itself, naturally, from your inner prosperity... then you'll feel it grow and crackle in your pocket, like popcorn...»*

This time, since I had to meet a master of style who was also a businessman, the Dreamer stressed that my clothes should fit the occasion.

«Taste is consciousness» He said to me, as we walked together along Via dei Condotti and I listened to His instructions for that meeting, which the Dreamer considered to be of extraordinary importance. I had to choose a suit, and, while we walked past the most prestigious designer showrooms in the world, the Dreamer made me observe the beauty, elegance, style and attention to every detail, which had made those boutiques, establishments, and their founders the planetary epitome of the art of living.

«One only appears to enter these shops with the aim of buying an object or an item of clothing – said the Dreamer – *that's only an alibi. What you are really buying is conscience.»*

We went into the most elegant boutiques and with Him I visited jewelers, exclusive shops, and the most important property agencies. They showed us houses, collections of clothes, the most expensive objects; and each time the Dreamer made me note that the activities, which had made them become the best in the world, all had a common denominator: attention. Attention to the smallest particular, from the furnishings to the quality of the people who worked there, their cheerfulness, shining appearance and love they showed for their work.

«What you see concentrated in this street is the materialisation of a level of human awareness – He said, and ended with a piece of advice – *whenever you buy something, even the smallest thing, you must accept nothing less than this level of care, attention, love.»*

I assured Him that I asked for nothing more, and noted that it would be a pleasure for anyone to be served in those shops, surrounded by that beauty, by that richness. It was then that I received one of His most memorable lessons.

«Like attracts like – enunciated the Dreamer – *a man always meets himself and chooses himself. Everything corresponds perfectly to his level of awareness.»*

«And money? – I asked – isn't the money that decides what one can have and what one cannot have?»

«Awareness is money! – asserted the Dreamer – *It is Being that decides having. A man can only have the money that he is capable of dreaming, visualising, imagining... When you've worked on your Being, when you've simplified, enriched, and sublimated every corner of it, prosperity and beauty, will correspond to you. This is called 'prosperity consciousness.' Money, in order for you to have all this, will come by itself, as if by chance, as a simple consequence of your elevation.»*

«Objects have a soul – continued the Dreamer – *We appear to choose them, but in fact, they, the objects themselves choose their possessors. Things know with whom they should go and whom they can abandon... You can only possess what you're responsible for... Don't be distracted by scarcity. Give all your attention to the 'dream,' to the inalienable goods, which are every man's birthright:*

integrity, beauty, happiness, understanding, love and truth. Design beauty, elegance and taste inside yourself.»

In the meantime, our shopping trip continued and I began to relax. The meeting in Paris no longer worried me and I was a child at a huge fairground. I noted that wherever He entered, the world yielded. An atmosphere of lightness spread everywhere. The Dreamer enriched the air with generosity, power, and everyone felt it. Beside Him the world celebrated and offered the best of itself.

«Those who are masters of themselves rule the world. The world recognises them and is happy to serve them. Each of these retailers is in actual fact a guardian of the invisible» the Dreamer revealed to me, coming closer to my ear while a group of assistants went off in every direction in order to satisfy His requests.

«When you've overcome your limits and inner obstacles... when you've eliminated doubt and fear, which still separate you from it, the entire world will learn of your passage towards that zone of existence. The world knows everything about you!»

A river of people flowed past us. From a strip of sky, caught between the cornices of the patrician buildings and the greenery of the terraces, a ray of sunlight, narrow as a laser, chose us from among all the others. The Dreamer raised His head to welcome it, and I followed Him. With half-closed eyes, I stood there with Him, for a few eternal moments, with folded wings, like butterflies pierced by a golden needle.

15 The Replay

I soon discovered that the most interesting part in the 'game of encounters' came later.

I'll explain.

Once an encounter has taken place, one has to work for days on the infinite amount of material that ensues from it. The Dreamer carefully chose sequences of images, fragments of conversation; like clips from the film of my life, He then showed me frames of film, one by one, in the light of His pitiless sincerity. Thoughts, emotions, attitudes and the smallest details from those occasions ended up under His magnifying glass. A grimace on my face, an inflection in my voice, a quickening of my heart, a soaring in my soul, a movement of my body, a mechanical reaction, a recurring expression, a hidden wretchedness in language, behaviour, emotions; the way in which I presented myself, how I sat, a detail of my dress… Nothing escaped Him. And months, even years later, if His impeccable pedagogy had deemed it necessary, He would have been able to find the most remote fragment from a meeting and project it. He then enlarged it under a microscope to let me see the danger, and at times the catastrophe hidden behind a mere trifle. With Him, I discovered the mortal trap waiting behind calm, apparently normal gestures or words; and I saw its cruel mechanisms ready to snap and imprison me.

This extraordinary work was not carefree; as a matter of fact, it was often unbearably painful, but it had the strength to force my destiny off the tracks of repetitiveness and lack of attention, and change it forever. I have to say that during the course of these operations, my resistance and most deeply-rooted prejudices came to the surface, together with the psychological rubbish accumulated over the years. Every time I seized upon some shred from my past, some ghost, I protected it, fearing it would disappear. Something in me did not want to come out into the open, it hid itself away. There was still much that I preferred not to see. And then, every time, the Dreamer would become an implacable hunter, capable of tracking down a shadow in my Being for months, until He drove it out and killed it forever.

Once I found myself at the Hotel Maurice in Rue de Rivoli. I crossed the hall to meet a businessman who was waiting for me, and for an instant, a young, attractive woman passed between us, capturing my attention. Just for a moment. That movement of my head, my glance, which for a fraction of a second caressed the woman's body, was caught by the Dreamer who made me watch it hundreds of times, close up and from afar, from above and below, until I became nauseous.

«That man – said the Dreamer, referring to me while placing those images before me for the hundredth time – *can't make it. He has failed, before he has even started… with that movement, he has already put his head on the block…»*

«The question isn't about whether it is right or wrong to admire a beautiful woman – continued the Dreamer, whose observations never mingled with ethical judgments and moral principles, nor could they ever be brought back to a time or a place – *that movement of the head, that lingering glance, are indicators of a*

lack of determination... they're symptoms of corruptibility... That gesture is the epitome of your entire life; it goes down to its origins through layer upon layer of unawareness, emotional confusion deposited over centuries.»

The Dreamer did not care at all about wounding my sensitivity, mortifying or producing states of frustration in me. He passed over my ego as gently as a caterpillar; but over time I came to bless His pitilessness. He was not only a mentor and invaluable guide, but also the inflexible accuser of every mediocrity... He represented totality.

«Learn to not take your attention away from the target... Be aware, be flawless, don't deviate... Those who fix on a point without ever deviating, either with their glance or in their mind, can do everything! They always have a target at which to aim... Do not miss the mark – enunciated the Dreamer – *To deviate is the sole, true sin.»*

On that occasion, I was surprised by an unusual excitement in Him. He was like a scientist who had finally achieved a favourable result after long research and numerous experiments. He told me that He had in His hands, a visible and observable, still wriggling, virus of the soul... one of those insidious intruders in the Being that was the true cause of each of our failures... I could see face to face one of my 'enemies,' one of the saboteurs, one of the killers I bore inside.

I heard Him say in a whisper:

«You may believe that this is an exaggeration, but in just one movement a man reveals his life and his destiny. That man is denouncing his unreliability!»

It was as if He was speaking of someone else; of a cast-off skin that I was leaving behind during the course of my transformation.

«Existence doesn't rely on men like that, men who will not only never have more but who will also lose what they believe to have.»

Here He suspended His words and I had the impression that His vision was no longer external, but inside me. Through His eyes, it was I who was looking at myself. I was the observer and the observed; both scientist and guinea pig at the same time. My thinking became confused. I do not know how, but I was sure - very sure - that that woman, who had suddenly appeared between me and the man I was about to meet, had not passed by chance but had somehow been the fruit of His production. This thought, hovering about me in virtual reality, in a kind of film directed by the Dreamer, made my legs tremble with dismay. What I called life was in actual fact a total learning environment: a School whose vision encompassed three hundred and sixty degrees.

16 Expecting from the world

For months, like a boxer training for a big match, I was sent by the Dreamer in search of those who landed the most underhanded punches; those who helped me to discover my weak points; those who were my reflection in order for me to discover what had ruled my entire life up until then. Commenting on every meeting, examining every phrase, every detail, the Dreamer helped me to focus my attention, to develop my self-observation, and to know myself. Entering further into the rules of the 'game', I ceased to see others as a reality separate from me, and I started to perceive them as bright, irreplaceable rungs, on an invisible ladder, on a vertical way to the unity of Being.

Meeting after meeting, match after match, I ascertained something incredible, something the Dreamer had revealed to me but was still too far from my ordinary vision for me to be able to accept.

«Search, search for someone who knows – He said – *and you'll discover that everyone knows nothing!»*

It disconcerted me to discover that respected men, acclaimed leaders, gentlemen with serious countenances; intelligent men, with titles and prestigious positions, had no idea where they themselves were going. They led others like the blind man immortalised by Brueghel.

On occasion, I was deceived into believing they were happy, aware or free, and I convinced myself that some of those ego-stricken men, these prisoners of their roles, had enviable lives. Forgetting reality, the world of appearances corrupted and bought me; so I became fascinated by the power of those men and women, by their wealth, by their abilities. Thus, the description of the world got the upper hand and I remained trapped with my entire Being.

Once I returned from a long journey, discouraged, without a scrap of energy and weighed down by a sense of defeat. I remember that particular meeting had made me touch my limits; it had shown my corruptibility and lack of attention, also, how little was required for me to feel humiliated, offended and disheartened.

The Dreamer explained to me that I felt like this because I still encountered the others with an expectation; I still nourished in some corner of my being the illusion that someone could help me, elect me. Very often, particularly at the beginning of that 'work', I still felt like grasping hold of someone, still encountering others in whom I sought the trust I felt lacking in me. According to the Dreamer, this was the clearest sign of my vulnerability and the reason why He was still unable to trust me.

«These aren't defeats – the Dreamer encouraged me at times – *They're only signs of what and how much there is still to do... The 'game' is directed towards making you realise that there is no one to hate, and no one to ask for help; that it's not you who depends on the world, but the world which asks you for clarity and direction. Reality is a creature of the 'dream'.»*

I noted the Dreamer's warnings about expectation and for months I worked on it, observing and studying the moments in which it came out, the forms it took, and the thousands of tricks it devised to escape my observation.

«Maintain your inner freedom – He tirelessly suggested to me – *Stop being reactive! Reacting to the world means becoming a victim of it... Those who 'expect' from the world have already lost. The biggest secret is knowing that the entire world is at your service in order to improve you; realising that everything, event or circumstance, is food, nourishment, propellant for your journey.*

It may appear that events and men are only there to obstruct you and impede you from going beyond. Those who 'see' know that the world is a gymnasium of being where they practice and practice again, where they experience and experience again, until their performance of existence becomes flawless; where they train their muscles of responsibility, until they become more integral, free. Sooner or later every man will have to affront all that is required to balance and complete him.»

«Go faster – the Dreamer urged me insistently – *Look for other encounters, create every opportunity to plug the leaks, to*

eliminate the misunderstandings and 'settle accounts' with the past.»

17 This Book is forever!

«Write! – the Dreamer ordered me roughly – *If you write, your entire life will not have been for nothing...»*

«Listen!... and write! – He ordered me again, interrupting my thoughts, sweeping away at once the emotional filth which had come to the surface – *Write a book that will be for all time... A book that can only be read by those who are ready, those who are already on their way towards a state of healing, those who have already questioned the old description of the conflict-ridden mortal world.*

Write a courageous book, in which you faithfully tell everything you have experienced with Me. A book that makes the world understand that the 'dream' is the most real thing that exists. A book that eliminates all the superficiality and falsehood, and shakes the most deeply rooted beliefs of humanity at the foundations.

Write a book that brings light to the universal rules buried in the Being of every man.»

Again, I took out my notebook and with barely enough light to see, I frantically began to write the words with which He concluded His visit to Seven Oaks.

«This book will encounter opposition from the most vehement antagonists in the establishment and the multitude. And yet, at the same time, you must believe that it will also reach that part of mankind ready to flee the hells of banality and routine.»

CHAPTER X

The School

1 The vertical Vision

«A completely transformed human species is about to appear on the scene» the Dreamer announced, the glow in His eyes reflecting life in all its fullness.

I felt an unusual excitement. I had travelled a long way to reach Him, stopping first in Buenos Aires, then in Bogota. From there, a tiny plane had taken me to a small city nestled on a plateau 2300 metres high.

The *Casa del Pensamiento*, the solitary bamboo building where our meeting was taking place, was surrounded as far as the eye could see by tall peaks covered in lush greenery. No other place could have sustained such incisive words with more absorbed participation. The arcane presence of lost civilisations was listening and the air still throbbed with their myths: the legend of Eldorado; tales of guerrillas, cocaine, emeralds, the mysteries of the Lost City.

His voice pulled me away from my ethnographical fantasies.

«The new man has shed his swaddling clothes and pierced the mental cocoon that imprisoned the old humanity for millions of years» He said with the conviction of a scientist, who at last receives proof of a theory he has pursued for decades, one in which he has been the only believer.

The distinctive element, the evolutionary characteristic of the emerging species was a new event on the planet, a true cosmic rarity: the birth in man of a psychological apparatus free from fear and conflictuality. This unprecedented characteristic, this watershed condition, was producing a true speciation in *Homo Sapiens*.

Mankind was approaching a point where its evolutionary path would diverge: two very distinct kinds of human were becoming clearly defined and growing further apart. Men would continue to call each other men for who knows how long, but from this discovery henceforth they would always belong to two co-habiting but separate species, marked by different destinies.

«The old mankind, trapped in a flat vision of reality, can see only by means of a play of opposites... it perceives and feels through polarity, antagonisms and counter-oppositions» recited the Dreamer, turning towards a point on the horizon. I had the impression that, rather than talking to me, He was performing a ritual of which only He was aware. I followed His glance. He seemed to single out one valley from all the others, one where the summit of the distant mountains loomed more abruptly. There, from civilisations more ancient than those of the Mayans and the Aztecs, was born the brilliant understanding, which still made the Dreamer's dark eyes shine.

«Vision and reality are one and the same thing» He enunciated, reiterating one of His most emblematic statements, perhaps in itself the most concise version of His entire philosophy.

«Horizontal man has a conflictual vision of the world, and this is the cause of all his disasters... The history of his civilisation is the clear reflection of a fragmented psychology... a history of wars and destruction... Even his science, the activity of which he is most proud, is only a product of friction between two antagonistic concepts... good and bad, true and false, beautiful and ugly... like a spark generated from the rubbing of two flints in the hands of a primitive man.»

The Dreamer continued to explain that ordinary mankind still uses a visual archaic apparatus. Like frogs, which are only able to perceive the world in a shadowy way, men of the old species, who as a consequence, can only understand through contrast, and the comparison of opposing elements. Their logic is conflictual, their vision of the world is always the rudimentary outcome of a game of opposites.

«The distinctive characteristic of the new man is his awareness of the illusory nature of opposites – stated the Dreamer – *Those which the old mankind consider opposites are in fact two faces of the same reality, like the two ends of a stick... Good and bad, true and false, beautiful and ugly, are not opposing forms of*

existence, but steps or levels of the real... Behind the apparent antagonisms, there lies a harmonising force capable of uniting them, and leading them to a higher order.»

The anthropogenic fact, the revolutionary characteristic that the Dreamer was revealing to me, was the appearance in some individuals of a new and subversive sense, which He called the 'vertical vision of the world'. This was a dizzying idea. I tightly gripped the bamboo balustrade, finely polished by the wind of the Muiscas, and carved His incredible account into my heart.

«To these first models, to these champions of a new mankind, reality no longer appears unambiguous, illusorily defined by polarity and oppositions, but made up of levels. Perceived with their new sense, the universe is no longer sliced into opposites, but is proven to be made up of layers of reality. Something is not true or false, but is at the same time true and false, neither true nor false, neither untrue nor unfalse...»

I accurately noted down His words, even though I needed a long time for their full meaning to reach me. To help me understand, He gave me one of the most classic antinomies as an example: the opposition of good and evil. In contrast to the ordinary, horizontal vision of the world, nothing that is objectively and permanently either good or bad exists outside us.

«The bad of today is the good of yesterday which has not been transcended» He declared. He continued to watch me as I transcribed His words, as He would do when He wanted to be sure they had been recorded correctly. He waited a little longer, before adding:

«What appears bad today in a man's life is the result of his indulging in the good of yesterday. Yesterday's perfection is only a stepping-stone towards a new perfection.»

«But one must admit – I insisted, clinging to some shreds of my life-long beliefs – that one antithesis at least is certain… that life and death are antithetical realities… two true opposites.»

«That is how horizontal man sees them» conceded the Dreamer. Then, lowering the tone of His voice and drawing closer, as if to confide a secret to me, He said:

«In reality, death doesn't exist... We're made to live forever! The clearest proof of man's omnipotence is in his power to make possible the impossible: his death... His body is indestructible. Only the absence of will... an involuntary will, an unconscious

omnipotence, can destroy it. Death is immortality seen from behind!»

I listened and trembled. Suspended on the edge of an abyss, I was a frightened creature about to take the plunge that is at the same time his simultaneous death and rebirth.

It was then that He pronounced the words that would guide and occupy every moment of my life.

«We need to educate the cells of this new humanity, one by one. The harmonisation has to take place in every man – He said gravely – *In economics as in politics, one needs to prepare a new generation of leaders, a decision-making aristocracy... men and women who have mastered 'the art of dreaming', the art of believing and creating.»*

2 A School for pragmatic dreamers

«We need forges of visionary men» announced the Dreamer decisively.

From the tightening I felt in my stomach, I knew that those words had just set a further acceleration to our meeting. His tone was like that of a command to which there could be no objection. Directed not at me, but at an invisible army ready to march on His orders.

«We need new schools – continued the Dreamer, transmitting His ardour to me, that feverish state which accompanies great events when their moment has come – *We need schools for preparing men capable of bringing solutions... schools for visionaries, solar men, 'pragmatic Dreamers'...»*

This expression pervaded me with the strength of an evangelical paradox. In the future, in the years that would see the construction of the university, I would use it in official documents and at conferences in order to proclaim the mission. But even listening to it on that first occasion, listening to it, I was sure of its mysterious power... 'pragmatic dreamers'... Here was the most concise and powerful definition of the brilliant army that the Dreamer was asking me to recruit: thousands of boys and girls, special students, in love with their own boundless dreams. 'Pragmatic Dreamers'.

For a few long moments I lingered over those two words, contrasting them mentally, savouring that sense of complicity peeping from behind their apparent contrast. Then the slight prickling of their paradoxical rationality ceased, and they became fused in a timeless unity.

«... *They will be the leaders of a new exodus* – continued the Dreamer – *a 'psychological exodus' of planetary proportions... Thousands of men and women will abandon the slavery of their conflictual logic in exchange for a vertical vision of the world founded on the ability to harmonise inner antagonisms..."*

I wrote down His words while resting my notebook on the bamboo railing. The *Casa del Pensamiento* was an ark lost in an vegetal ocean extending to infinity, breaking far away, at the foot of Andean stone giants.

«*Only visionary leaders, men free from every ideology or superstition* – He said – *can ferry mankind from the psychological shore of the ordinary, weak, irascible and bigoted man, to that of the new, integral man, inspired by the principles of a lay spirituality.*»

Here, the Dreamer ceased His discourse, and I took advantage of this pause to reorganise my notes. Bent over the page, I felt a pressure grow on every centimetre of my body, like the dangerous, green embrace of the waters of Castello Aragonese, which I had experienced during my reckless dips as a child in Ischia. Slowly, I raised my head. The Dreamer had come very close and was now standing only a few centimetres away. I was imprisoned, captured by His eyes, like an asteroid that has entered the orbit of two black moons. We fell into deep silence... The Dreamer was drawing nearer... and nearer... Every thought was suspended and I saw processions of gothic naves pass endlessly by, while centuries-old organ music resounded. An uncontrollable emotion gripped my throat as His words rang out; words that would give meaning to my life.

«*You will found a School of Being* – He announced – *a University for those who have a dream to realise... There, individuals can learn that the Dream is the most real thing there is... that what man calls reality is but the reflection of his dream.*»

I felt as if the trapdoor of a gallows had suddenly opened beneath my feet, and if I had needed a test for discovering the limits of my Being, the magnitude of that task in the Dreamer's words would be the one. It threatened to crush me before I had even begun and I felt faint at the very thought of such an undertaking.

«You will create a School of responsibility – He continued – *a school for pragmatic dreamers, philosophers of action, where to learn that happiness is economy... that wealth, harmony and beauty are every man's birthright... You'll create a School that has no end... A School for Gods... It will have My pace, My breath. Don't fear any attack. Any attack coming from the outer world is a very precious gift for those who really want to understand and change. Any harmful attack, even the most ferocious, can only happen as a healing process that you yourself have dreamed and put in act.»*

The Dreamer fell silent and waited. Like a good musician, He was giving me space to express myself. In that solitary jam session of ours, it was time for me to play a riff of my own. Time passed and I prevaricated, in the unreasonable hope that I could avoid His invitation. But the Dreamer's silence became even more pressing. I wanted to cry out my inadequacy before the magnitude of His design, and distance myself from it. So I plucked up courage, but I could only manage to stammer:

«It would seem to be a School of philosophy» implying that it was beyond my capabilities.

«So? – He sneered as usual, His tone amused and benevolently ironic – *A school of economics is a school of philosophy!... You should know that!»*

In His words, smile and tone, there was a wink, a note of innocent malice that inspired complicity. Something important was there, just out of reach, at the confines of my memory, but I was unable to seize it. In the meantime, the Dreamer drew imperceptibly closer and His gaze fixed upon me, without blinking. Suddenly, as if a membrane had been breached, the past was freed from memories. The ribbon of time rewound and distant pictures were projected on my mind's eye...

Once more, I saw my years of study and work at the University of Naples, at the side of my beloved master Giuseppe Palomba, who had helped me discover that moral values and ideas were the great motors of economics; and on the other hand, to search, in their drying up, for the true cause of every shortage and underdevelopment in vast regions across the planet. Years spent at the Università Cattolica in Milan and the London Business School also crossed my mind, not in succession, but in an explosion of images, faces, feelings and states of being. The desperate study of those years united all the schools of the past into one... The building of the Faculty of Economics in Naples, a beautiful cube of travertine stone facing the sea at Santa Lucia, was shifted to the lawn of the LBS in Regent's Park... Masters... colleagues... teachers... the Great Hall, the first-class honours degree. I saw Giuseppe and Carmela's emotion on my Graduation day, the gold Tissot ... my joy at the scholarship from the Giordani Foundation that opened the door to Columbia University... Then, as quickly as it had appeared, that kaleidoscope of images vanished and the scene changed. I saw myself in a break from lessons at the LBS: I was little more than a boy, day-dreaming under a tree, watching the clouds make furrows in the sky above the campus. A forgotten dream slowly started to take shape... That school without frontiers... the University of which the Dreamer was speaking to me... its centres and offices in the main cities of the world, and the faces of thousands of students that would study there... I had already dreamed it...

The Dreamer's voice distracted me:

«Can you remember now? It's time to make that dream come true! It's time to create a School for dreamers, where the giants of economics would love to teach.»

Those words, which I would read thousands of times in the following years, were infecting me, conquering me and making me fall in love with them. They would sustain me and give me strength during the many difficult moments I was to encounter in quest of that enterprise.

«Everything important and real in a man is invisible – He enunciated – *It's the same in economics. There's a vertical shaft that crosses the axis of economics, a plane of a superior order, a world of ideas and moral values on which economic facts depend.»*

He made me see how today, conditions of underdevelopment, which ritually appear during economic stagnation, are associated with an economy that is immersed in a system of archaic moral values. They are the other side of a problem, which, in evolved economies, manifests itself through pathological and social ills.

«It's therefore in the invisible world of ideas; ideological and moral values, philosophy and language, where we find the origin,

the motor of the facts which are visibly projected in the world of economics and business.

...Beyond the powerhouses of industry... and skyscrapers of finance... behind all that you see and touch, behind all that is useful, beautiful, and true among man's conquests... at the origin of every institution and scientific achievement, there is always one man's dream... an individual's vision.

Devote all of your efforts to the individual and his preparation! Make it the focus of your attention. The mass is a ghost... a mechanism influenced by everything and anything... It doesn't have faith; it doesn't have its own will... it can't create... And, in actual fact, the mass has never created anything. Its function and the reason for its existence, is to destroy. The individual and the crowd are two faces of the same reality, pistons of the same motor. The individual creates; the mass destroys.

It's you who must choose to which group you belong. The individual is the only reality... he is the salt of the Earth.»

According to the Dreamer, the only limitations are in one's Being. Poverty and war are the reflection of a scarcity in the being and a conflictual mind, and they will only be eliminated from the planet when they have been eradicated from the individual.

«Found a School for individuals, a School without frontiers... Bring together dreamers from around the world... regardless of nationality, colour, belief, wealth... A School where the most important subject is studying oneself and where the ability to do and act are the most concrete results of loving oneself inside.»

His words flowed quickly and I had difficulty keeping up as I transcribed them. Rather than speaking, the Dreamer was dictating, and when I noticed this, I felt wounded, humiliated... He was treating me like a copyist. A trace of resentment, the mumbling of a dull, silent complaint, rose up from the depths of my being without my being able to stifle it. I was making a huge effort to keep up with Him, but He remained unconcerned. More than anything, His seeming lack of respect, more than anything, was what exasperated me most. It seemed as though He was doing it on purpose...

«Stop that and write!» the Dreamer ordered in a terrible voice, immediately interrupting that stream of thoughts and the succession of states through which I was spinning. The Dreamer's cry came providentially to grab me at the top of the slope. I was

already slipping into the Stygian waters of recrimination, blame and complaint.

«*Write!*» He repeated. His voice had become a whisper that was even more terrifying than His roar.

«*This Book is forever! One day you'll know that your life has only had meaning because you met Me, and that writing My words was the only reason you were born.*»

The Dreamer's potent intervention set me free. In an instant I felt limpid and carefree, like a summer sky swept by the northwest wind. As always, the Dreamer's drubbings were therapeutic; possessing the power to eliminate the clutter and purge every form of pollution from my innermost parts.

In the meantime, He took up His discourse again, in a normal tone of voice.

«*Even the Schools and Universities of the first education teach one to dream*» He said, and fell silent for a moment. Then in a bitterly ironic tone, He added:

«*But the dream they project in their students is scarcity… they teach dependence, doubt, fear and limitation, and behind the mask of their presumed erudition, lurks pain and a constant song of defeat.*»

He was not talking to me anymore but addressing generations of future students, students who were beyond time. His powerful, revolutionary ideas were becoming the roots and lymph of the School, shaping its mission and its destiny.

«*All knowledge, methods and theories coming from the outside may be necessary as starting points, but must soon be abandoned for a higher source of understanding.*

It is time to disregard all teachings, ideologies, disciplines, books and ideas, any written words, and dive deeply within yourself to find your own truth and uniqueness. This alone will remove all your obstacles and leave you free from any hypnotism and in full mastery of all and everything.»

3 The dream of the Dream

His lecture continued, and I interrupted Him only to ask for occasional clarification. Invaluable thoughts, the cornerstones of an extraordinary construction, like the pieces of a mosaic, were fitting together before my eyes, forming the vision of a planetary magnitude.

He told me that schools of Being have always existed, but have been hidden, as the political climate and historic moment, have almost never allowed their manifestation. Among other stories, I was fascinated by the one of the construction of Notre-Dame in Paris, its true mission hidden behind a 'pretext' for realising that wonder. I hung on His every word as He spoke of the architects, artists and sculptors, the workers and labourers, who were all students of that extraordinary School, and I mused over that enterprise, which was carried out by men on the way towards integrity; students, researchers of their own indivisibility.

«In that construction, every detail and stone speaks of the School and reveals its laws» outlined the Dreamer. I realised that Notre-Dame, and the great masterpieces in history, were the materialisation of eternity; yet they gave only small hints of the vast 'true' work done by immortal Schools.

Progressively, like successive clicks of a zoom lens, that vision expanded and I realised that the task, which the Dreamer was entrusting to me, was only the beginning of a far grander project. The creation of a University, which would subvert the planet's traditional education at its foundations, was only a fragment of an extraordinarily larger design.

So what was the Dreamer's 'dream'? I could not even imagine it… What could it be? My imagination had reached its limit, and was halted by the flaming sword of the Cherubim… I dream, I am… If, as He had taught me, it is the dream that measures us; and no one can nourish a bigger dream than oneself, then who was the Dreamer? If inciting a revolution capable of inflaming the planet from one end to the other, overthrowing its vision, and heralding the advent of the 'vertical' man, was only one step in His journey, who then was this Being and what was His 'dream'?

«What is it?» I asked, without clarifying my question.

The Dreamer let an endless period of time go by, and I was still holding my breath when, close to my ear, He whispered:

«The 'dream of the Dream' is the conquest of death... and even before that, conquering what has always enabled it: the idea of death's invincibility…»

At those words, I felt a light trembling under my skin: ecstasy. That dream broke down millennial boundaries, and thrust ahead, beyond where man had ever dared to go, even in his imagination, and to withstand this announcement, I had to summon all of my strength, drawing upon my years of preparation at the Dreamer's School.

4 The portable paradise

Meanwhile, the Dreamer maintained His position, and was so close to me that I could hear His breathing. Suddenly I saw Him sniff the air around me. At first, He did it discreetly, then more and more blatantly, until I was unable to hide the evidence: the Dreamer was smelling my scent! An unrestrained embarrassment pervaded me when I saw a wince of disgust etch His face, as if He had discovered the source of a nauseating smell in me and I blushed, burning with shame. But when His malicious smile replaced that grimace I understood that He was pulling my leg. It was another of His pedagogical devices. That pantomime about malodours of the being was intended to brand the facility with which I still fell prey to negative thoughts and emotions.

As He spoke of paradise, His masterly lesson was in sharp contrast to my inclination to create and feed a portable hell. Who knows how long man would remain a touchy, irascible, quarrelsome being? How long would he cultivate and pass on that fragility and vulnerability to other generations? These reflections distracted me. The Dreamer had already gone further. I forced myself to abandon that dead weight, and with giant strokes I managed to traverse the liquid light that separated us.

«Life is as you dream it. We always meet what we dream...»

«It's inevitable that we meet all that we dream – He said ardently – *Life is already a terrestrial paradise for those who build and nourish a portable paradise in themselves.»*

He paused for a long time, before boldly confronting the conclusive part of our meeting.

«Mankind afflicted by poverty, criminality and endless conflicts, can only be healed cell by cell... It's an alchemical transformation which has to be performed in every man through an overturning of beliefs, and spread by the transfusion of will, light... Only individual education can do it.»

He maintained that such an undertaking cannot be realised by mass education, by what our civilisation proudly considers to be one of the most important conquests of modernity.

«A School for free men, devoted to discovering the uniqueness of every individual, a School of responsibility, can't be for the masses. Mass education is a contradiction in terms: if it's for the masses then it isn't education, if it's education then it isn't for the masses.»

«Make the School accessible to those who have a true, sincere 'dream' to realise... The true passport for admission is to believe in it fiercely, with all one's strength.»

5 The greatest economic truth

The golden sun worshipped by the Quimbaya and Muisca people, was climbing the tops of the distant Cordilleras with their round, green peaks like those in a child's drawing. The Dreamer's voice soared calm and solemn over that place sacred to ancient gods.

«Create a School founded on principles that have no end – He commanded me with the solemnity of a viaticum – *Create a true and living School, not based on books. At the core of its teachings will be the Art of Dreaming.»*

He was about to take leave of me and I experienced a feeling of loss. The enterprise still seemed enormous to me, beyond my ability. I felt a cry rise into my throat, silent and desperate, inconsolable. By entrusting me with such a task, He was revealing the thing that I loved most, the Dreamer was showing me that after a life of selfishness, I could truly achieve something special… a school for dreamers…

The Dreamer revealed that the adventure of Ulysses, the journey of Dante, the expedition of Jason and the undertakings carried out by heros and demigods through time, are the paths made by a school for transformation. Ulysses ties himself to the mast with the School's ropes, thus keeping its principles firm; and Dante abandons Hell by following Virgil and turning himself 'upside down'. This, too, is a movement of the School…

«We need to prepare men who are resolved to conquer their own integrity and free themselves from the pain, fear and anxiety that everyone bears inside. This is mankind's only hope.»

The Dreamer predicted that in the near future, all organisations, from the biggest corporations to the smallest businesses, would become schools of Being, schools of integrity. In them men will learn to transcend themselves, constantly eliminating every division, shadow and degradation of the Being. Throughout the organs of those enterprises, the diapason that engendered them will resonate again, a chord that still binds all their cells and makes them vibrate in unison.

«I see thousands of students...» the Dreamer said prophetically, showing me with a wide, slow gesture the green parvis all around the *Casa del Pensamiento*, the endless field of sunflowers and the small lake in the centre.

«They will be giants of economics and global communicators of the future. Their ability to create wealth will only be the effect of an inner state of freedom.»

«But an undertaking like that will take a long time» I protested, not knowing how else to give vent to my anxiety and the pressure of the army of doubts that was already laying siege to my good intentions. The Dreamer was inviting me to fly and, as always, He was encountering my resistance.

«Man is ready now! – He announced, causing the motors of the 'dream' to roar, instantly sweeping away my pathetic objections – *Understanding and love are already in man.»*

I would never forget those words.

Today I see them emerge in each of my students, and I know that one can only teach the young how to scratch the surface and make true knowledge emerge in the strength of their uniqueness and true nature as *winged Beings*, *real Beings*.

External teachings are only a pretext. The true work of a School is the elimination of every compromise, limit, prejudice, hypocrisy, fear and doubt that has accumulated since childhood, and which are the fruit of the old education; an education that appears intent only on suppressing the most real thing that exists: the 'dream'. A true school does not presume to give anything to its students… it knows that it cannot add anything to what they already possess within their Being… It only needs to bring it to light… It's a work of elimination of everything that hinders understanding. True education is 'remembering' one's own uniqueness, one's originality, the 'dream'.

«Economics is a way of thinking» The Dreamer announced.

«Only those who are truly alive can create wealth.»

«Material wealth is only a metaphor for true wealth, the crucial test of a state of integrity, understanding and inner prosperity.»

Only a School founded on these principles can prepare economists capable of eliminating poverty from vast regions of the planet and removing layers of ignorance from the Being, which have already thrown entire nations, and once magnificent civilisations, into scarcity and under development.

He spoke to me of the fabulous natural wealth of Columbia, of its inexhaustible silver mines, emerald deposits, immense forests and boundless plateaus, its huge coffee and tobacco plantations.

«And yet it's one of the poorest countries in the world – He stated – *The level of Being of this country has been reduced to such a low point that it can't sustain what it has... like what happens to a man who finds he possesses a wealth that is larger than his level of responsibility.»*

He made me see that the most economically developed countries are often completely without natural resources but have a store of ideas, culture, history and art.

«Economics is a state of Being» He proclaimed and paused, so He could stress the significance of that law.

«A country's economy and the level of material well-being it has achieved, are a reflection of that society's way of thinking and feeling. The system of values and quality of thought, is the cause, and never vice versa.»

«When the dream fails and the values dry up, wealth also fails» asserted the Dreamer, and then He stated the necessity of educating responsible men, capable of connecting to the dream of their country, of embodying it and feeding its roots. The life of an entire civilisation depends on the existence of these men. The breadth of their vision is reflected without limits through the economic universe, expanding its borders. Without them no progress is possible. The main obstacle against which the most ambitious projects shatter is not the lack of financing or natural resources, but a shortage of men capable of bearing that level of responsibility, containing that brave idea and believing it with all their strength.

«The School will carry in its very roots a truth that has never been expressed in the world of economics: Visibilia ex Invisibilibus. Economic wealth is only the reflection of an organisation or

nation's invisibility. Prosperity comes from within. It's a process that, like all healing, starts from the inside and moves out.»

6 Having is Being

«Having and Being are one reality, but on different planes of existence – He announced – *Having is Being.»*

According to the Dreamer, having is Being that manifests itself in time and space. This discovery opens the door to a tremendous revolution in the ordinary perception of the world, and is one of those shocks to the thinking, which is capable of changing the course of an entire civilisation. The Dreamer pointed out the extraordinary fact that each epochal passage in humanity's history has always been preceded by the overturning of ideologies, by a revolution in thought which begins in an individual and then spreads to the masses.

Relocating man from the centre of the universe to its margins, Copernicus, with his notion of heliocentricity shook the cornerstones of medieval thinking, and opened up to the modern age. Protestantism radically changed the view of work, from a biblical condemnation to an instrument of man's evolution, creating the psychological conditions for the Industrial Revolution and rational Capitalism.

«Today we find ourselves confronting a new revolution, a psychological revolution founded on the idea that being and having are two sides of the same reality – announced the Dreamer – *All that we see and touch, all that we perceive and all that we call 'reality', is none other than the projection of a world invisible to our senses, a world of ideas and values that runs vertically to the plane of our existence: the world of the Being.»*

Being is not opposed to having, but is superimposed on it: it is the cause. This explains why the countries richest in natural resources are often also the poorest, and how a man's enrichment is not a satisfactory condition to deliver him from his destiny, if it does not correspond to an elevation in his Being. It is possible, in fact, to detect a circuit regulator; a kind of mechanism for homoeostasis, that inevitably takes having back to the level of Being. An unprepared man, even if he is temporarily favoured by an event or external circumstances, is forced back again into the old poverty if having exceeds his level of Being. This is also true for nations. After more than half a century of failed international aid programmes in the Third World, even economists who specialize in development should have understood by now that it is not possible to help a country from the outside if it is not ready in their Being. It cannot be rescued from a condition of poverty if it has not already reached an adequate level of wealth in its own invisibility, richness of ideas – ethical, aesthetic, religious, philosophical, scientific – and system of values. For many of these countries, returning to their old wisdom and essence of their origins would be enough, bringing nourishment back to their oldest value system in order to improve the conditions of their lives.

The recognition that 'Having is Being' uproots one of man's oldest prejudices, and revolutionizes its conceptual schemes. However, it is not having which allows one to do and to be, but being which allows one to do and then to have. Overcoming this form of collective hypnosis means leaving behind a flat vision of the world and entering a vertical thought: there exist layers of real and infinite levels of the Being. 'Having is Being' is the key to understanding the most complex and vital arguments regarding the life of man and organisational systems, of every order and complexity, and explains the diversity of their destiny.

Man's history has always been about doing and possessing more. The advance of civilisation – in societies hypnotised by the desire to possess and guided by unappeasable predatory instincts, the echo of an animal nostalgia – coincides with the development of the ability to produce, communicate and travel and also to destroy even more. Perpendicular to this history runs the invisible dimension of ideas, the world of causes.

Every conquest in the visible and every increase in mankind's ability to do and have has always been preceded by a conquest in the being. In time, scientific knowledge and technological progress follow not only man's knowledge of himself, but also the level of awareness achieved. Science and Consciousness advance together.

«Whether it be an individual, organisation, nation or entire civilisation, the ability to know, do and have depends on the level of Being reached by that civilisation, by that nation, by that organisation, by that individual.»

The Dreamer concluded these reflections with a simple and powerful epigram.

«The more you are, the more you know; the more you do, the more you have. Doing and having depend on Being, just as a shadow depends on the dimension and form of the object that projects it.»

The Dreamer made me see that by observing a man or an organisation, everyone can perceive the dimension of what it has, but the dimension of the Being remains invisible: the depth, the magnitude of ideas, the values, the 'dream'.

What prevents one from seeing the perfect equilibrium that exists between being and having is the time factor which, like a smokescreen, illusively separates them. If, amazingly, we manage to compress time – the years of a man's life, or the centuries of a civilisation – we will see the perfect correspondence between being and having. They are the same reality on different planes of existence. The materialised Being becomes having and the having becomes being.

The discovery of the identicalness of having and being also profoundly marks economic thought. If having, and thus the production of wealth, obeys the Being, then the fundamental concepts and states of the Being, all of man's work on self-discovery and self-observation will rightfully have to be included among the legitimate subjects of scientific research, along with ethics, belief systems, moral values and, above all, intuition and the 'dream'.

«The broader a man's vision, the richer his economy. This holds true for an organisation, a country and an entire civilization.»

7 University means 'towards oness'

The Dreamer told me that 'university' means 'towards oneness'. In its etymology, I discovered some invaluable information about the nature of those institutions, which had never emerged before from any encounter, and which I had never found in any book.

«Its mission is inherent in its name: to carry forward the work of man's integration... to lead his journey towards the unity of Being.»

In the Dreamer's vision, the universities of the future will have the task of continuing, through a secular approach, the work that convents, synagogues, hermitages and mosques have undertaken for millennia and have left unfinished, thereby becoming receptacles for irresponsible individuals, men and women terrified of existence.

Many universities will disappear, and only a very few will be entrusted with the vital task of preparing new leaders to be visionaries or lay monks; they will be perfect, invulnerable warriors, capable of winning the challenges that our civilisation faces with the new senses: intuition, will and the 'dream'. The project of educating a man who is 'balanced' by apparently paradoxical qualities is thousands of years old, a man who can harmonise within himself cunning and innocence, reason and intuition, financial power and love.

«The University has to propose a system of essential ideas capable of interpreting the world, revealing man's true condition and pointing the way to his possible evolution.

The University has to prepare the cells of a new mankind, individuals inspired by the dream's principles: visionary men and women, pragmatic utopians, brilliant individuals capable of nourishing the dream of global economics and political responsibility for the planet.»

A bookish knowledge, imposed from the outside, equal for all, is a suffocation of the essence… it is false and illusory… 'True' knowledge is already in every individual. Knowing means remembering… it is a journey back in the 'vertical memory'. For the Dreamer the new education, the second education, is light years beyond traditional instruction. Its task is not to add notions but to 'remind' the students of the uniqueness, originality and innocence they already possess.

«Don't rely on any institution – the Dreamer solemnly advised, as if He were asking me to swear an oath – *Don't take money, don't ask for grants of any kind from any corporation, public or welfare institution. The traditional university system is not only obsolete, but extremely susceptible, delicate and fragile, because it is dependent.*

This is why you'll have to cut a new path, taking on the soul of a rebel, a revolutionary. True education is a subversive activity in the eyes of the Establishment. This is why you won't be able to accept the authority of tradition or adhere to any existing educational concepts.

The university you'll found will be such a revolution in the world of education that old beliefs and mentalities will disappear forever, and with them, obsolete institutions and schools. Only those who are ready for a complete change, who have prepared for accepting this revolution, will survive.

Keep hold of your integrity! Don't let anyone or anything damage it. Keep it intact. Success is a natural consequence of integrity.»

At this point, He illustrated to me that extraordinary idea for which the term 'distributed University' would be coined, the organisational model that would play such an important part in the School's success, in the achievement of its educational model in the world's academic setting.

«Future battles will not be won by employing huge ships, but with a flotilla of nimble craft» He said.

Not only did this concept allow one to pay attention to each student, welcoming each one in small athenaeums, it also realised the condition, ideal and paradoxical, of an institution that was both large and small, worldwide and local. The new University would be of planetary dimensions, organised in colleges and campuses in the world's capitals, made to welcome and prepare a small number of students who believed in themselves and their 'dreams' and knew that it was only in a 'school of Being' that they would be able to realise them.

The new School, inspired by the Dreamer's principles, pointed to the model of a future university, and heralded the advent of an Athenaeum without boundaries and no longer Aristotelian, rooted in a territory or bound to a city, language, nationality or fixed timetable, but articulated in colleges across continents, closely united by the same philosophy.

«Just as the walls of Greek cities were erected within the reach of an orator's voice, contained in the range of that communication – prompted the Dreamer – *thus the athenaeums you found will have to fit within dimensions that allow one to know of the aspirations, the 'dream' of those who want to be part of it.»*

8 The birth of the School

Little more than a year has passed since I met the Dreamer that day and received the investiture in the *Casa del Pensamiento*. Since then I have devoted myself completely to the Project. The University was born and its first athenaeum opened in the heart of London, Belgravia. The first students were enrolled and happily completed their first academic year. The School was creating itself, and every day it grew in a wonderful way. In its evolution, it seemed to escape and in fact ignore the ordinary ties and limits of time and space. Its academic formula had the ingredients of the future. In it the English academic rigor and internationalism, and solid American pragmatism, were marvellously tempered by Italian style and culture, and a millennial search for beauty and perfection of the classical civilisation. A rich programme of practical experiences, or internships, undertaken by the students since the first year, was enabling them to work, at a very young age, in the world's largest enterprises. Made powerful by the School's philosophy, they would prove themselves to be as impeccable and invulnerable as Lupelius' warrior-monks, the students that had gone through the School for Gods ten centuries before. The features of the new University, cast in the Dreamer's philosophy, have given it the glowing body of a spaceship in flight and the ancient heart of the most venerable schools of Antiquity, that same heart which used to beat in the bosom of the schools that forged the warriors and heroes of Classical Greece.

The Dreamer had put me in command of a starship that was crossing an archaic, dusty academic world; a decrepit ruin, allegorically cloaked in ermine, a world which was finding it more and more difficult to hide the emptiness of its false knowledge and anachronistic concepts. The School's appearance on the English and international academic scene, and even more so in Italy, with the opening of the first campus in Parma followed by the one in Rome and then in the 12 most important Italian towns, could be compared to the discovery of Plutarch's small book on education. The Latin translation of this work, long thought to be lost, starkly compared the Greek educational model, the projection of that civilisation's spirit, with the dogmatic obscurantism of the medieval religious schools. Then, as is happening now, two worlds came into contact, divided not just by centuries, but by light years in awareness.

'The Dream University', as the School was soon called by the media, was the only heir to the educational ideals of Classical Greece. Its firm belief and architrave of its pedagogical philosophy was that man can only evolve through a work of responsibility; a constant strain towards the unity of Being. The students came from every part of the world, attracted by the School's thoughts, and its new and ancient message. The Dreamer's words, echoed in the brochures and the explanatory material, were notes played on a magical flute. Young dreamers from around the world listened to them and began to march.

I've dreamed of a revolution.
I've dreamed of a School which 'remembers'
that the 'dream' is the most concrete thing that exists.
I've dreamed of a new generation of leaders,
capable of harmonising the age old apparent antagonisms:
Ethics and Economics,
Action and Contemplation,
Financial power and Love.

Since those pioneering times of the new University, men, events and circumstances have come prodigiously together, and the way in which the necessary resources have arrived, has never ceased to amaze me: in the fairest ways, extraordinarily punctual; with the wonder of a gestation where everything, from the most complex organs to the remotest neurons, obeys the same project of life.

9 The Mission of the School

That morning I awoke before dawn, my mind already aware of the coming day's intense commitments. Difficult situations were awaiting me, including a plenary meeting with my teaching staff, and above all the appointments with banks, which promised to be particularly trying. I felt an impulse to seek inspiration from the Dreamer's words.

I had not seen him since our encounter in South America, when, in the solemn presence of those peaks looming above transparent deeps of green, He invested me with the task of founding the School. I chose one of my notebooks at random, and immersed myself for a long time in those pages densely filled with notes I'd gathered throughout the years of my apprenticeship. As I was reading, I felt the unmistakable quiver along my skin that always felt in His presence, and before I could do anything to stop it, I felt myself being drained as suddenly realizing that I had forgotten something vital. It had been too long since I fed on His aphorisms, too long that I had strayed from the light of that intelligence that made sense of the world non-sense. And I no longer approached the immense force of His vision, able to overturn the world and bring it back to the size of an atom. There was no place on Earth where I could watch the fluttering of the banners in the wind, or hear the trumpets blowing to announce His solitary battle, His titanic challenge against what He called *the lie of death*, against the prejudice of its invincibility. The Dreamer had illuminated my life, yet perhaps I may never fully grasp the exceptional fortune of having met Him. Now I marked a few phrases and brought them with me for my first encounter: the faculty meeting at the European School of Economics.

I knew personally all the men and women whom I found waiting there for me: they were excellent professors, with the finest academic backgrounds and a wealth of experience in prestigious British and international universities. I had selected them one by one, and yet, once again, despite all my efforts, that plenary meeting would confirm how difficult it was to bring them closer to the School's core philosophy, the principles on which it was founded. All of these faculty members had studied at traditional universities, many of which were state-sponsored. The idea of leading them to change their convictions and accept the visionary pedagogy of this young university was like asking them to abjure their lifelong religion, or to cross a biological threshold to become beings of another species.

«The founding dream of the ESE, its mission to create a generation of young leaders, requires more than good programs and good teachers. Thousands of institutions already offer those things» I said, opening that difficult meeting.

Beyond the broad windows of the meeting room I could see the royal gardens at Buckingham Palace, reminding me that even a powerful entity like the British Empire can dissolve when principles are forgotten and the ruler's stop dreaming. Words I had heard the

Dreamer utter in the antique tea house in Shanghai now came clearly and strongly to my lips.

«The ESE is a School of Being. We must nourish our students with the idea of immortality, striking down the preconception that death is invincible.»

Until now all economic systems have dealt with survival,
with peoples' basic needs:
food, shelter, clothing and reproduction.
The economics of the coming decades
deals not anymore with survival,
but with immortality.

«Can you please explain to me why the idea of immortality is important to a School of Economics, especially for Business majors?» The question was asked by a young, brilliant instructor in International Strategic Management. Her scepticism that she might receive a convincing answer was obvious in her tone. Then, with courteous irony, she added:

«Maybe you're planning to announce a new Department of Philosophy within the School?»

«Vision and reality are one and the same thing» I answered. This was my favourite among the Dreamer's maxims, and it had reappeared among the notes I had been reading that morning. I didn't have the slightest concern about needing to convince her. I knew that the School was a huge ear, and that each of its cells, even the most distant one, and the very walls of Grosvenor Place, was listening. My words were aimed at its roots, at the heart of our mission:

«*The economy is a reflection of the Being*. One fragment of eternity is enough to summon vast and courageous ideas, unimaginable solutions. The conviction that death is something ineluctable is what limits us; it is at the root of our every constriction, shackling our creativity. All that we need is the idea of immortality, keeping that principle present in our own lives, and thereby freeing ourselves from the captivity of time. We can avoid being its victim, we don't have to endure its constant menace, or its corollaries such as anxiety, uncertainty, fear of being overwhelmed. Immortality is Love, Amore, *A-mors*, the absence of death. Immortality is Life in its infinite possibilities, life without limits.

This is the idea on which we should be feeding our students; it is the precious lymph that needs to circulate through every organization. A great economist, a tycoon, a prince of business – all these live totally in the moment, free from the hypnotic notions of past and future. Our civilization needs 'timeless leaders', free from the self-created prison of time, 'healthy leaders', men of integrity, capable of perseveringly raising their vision thus changing the reality, raising the financial destiny of individuals, of organizations, and of entire nations.»

While I was speaking, Chris H. shook his head slowly, indicating perplexity and a growing dissent. The movement caused the white locks of his flowing hair to undulate softly. He was one of our most influential teachers. I feigned not to notice that silent – and surely not isolated – commentary, and continued:

«What we call reality is only the reflection of our dreams, the mirror of our states of being. The mind of man is conflictual, his logic functions by means of contrasting concepts, his reason is armed. This is why we know only a survival-based economy that believes in limits and has allowed death to become the planet's leading industry, the architrave that sustains the wealth of nations. From arms manufacturing to environmental pollution, from pharmaceutical production to organized crime, men and nations are in the service of the economy of disaster, the economy of conflict. All of humanity is on the death's payroll.»

True education is freedom from every form of
hypnotism, dependence, superstition.
True education is the abandonment of one's inner conflicts.
This will liberate the world from all opposites,
will free the world from all contradictions, violence and wars.

«But are you living in this world or some other one? – burst out Chris H. as soon as I nodded to him – The wars in Iraq, in Afghanistan, terrorist attacks, hundreds of different guerrilla hot spots, racial persecution and genocide filling the papers and the media every day, what are those supposed to be? And it won't be a dream or anything we learn at ESE that ends them… this stuff isn't going to change the global economy either!»

I remembered asking the Dreamer the same question, and showing the same skepticism veined with sarcasm. Chris H. was the personification of my doubts, the mirror image of the world that denounced my incapacity to become those words, to make them enter into the flesh, to transmit the Dreamer's vision in a credible way.

"But what war are you talking about? – the Dreamer had asked me – *There is no war going on in the world except the one you're projecting right now. The conditions in the world correspond exactly to your own inner states. So don't worry about the world, worry about yourself. This is the only way you can help."*

"But at this very moment there are industries all over the world producing weapons that could devastate the planet, that could even destroy all life forms..." I replied, and in the name of all mankind I yearned to ask Him what we could do, how could we protect ourselves from such awful destructive power. I recall that the Dreamer interrupted me brusquely, not even letting me enunciate that calamitous vision.

"No power 'outside yourself' can possibly destroy you – he said, in indelible words – *'Outside yourself' nothing can take place without your consent. Be vigilant! Get rid of your ignorance, flee from obscurity. It's your own vision that needs to be corrected, not humanity. Conditions in the world correspond exactly to your own state. If you retrieve your integrity, if you become a unity, then the world is safe."*

I could feel every word burdening me with the weight of an unbearable responsibility. After listening to Him, it was impossible to keep on complaining, to accuse unknown powers and uncontrollable forces, and take refuge, trembling with fear, in the oblivion of a resigned helplessness.

"Remember! Nobody and nothing can do anything that is not commanded and directed by you. Conflicts, poverty, failure, disease, death or any other disaster are not objective realities. They do not exist outside of you. They become real only if you dream them. No war within, no war without. This is the law."

I turned my head, glancing behind me, looking for her. I knew she would be there, with the admiring glance she always had, her unquenchable faith in me, in the School, in the 'dream'. Lucia, my assistant. Were the world to collapse today, tomorrow morning she would be here to take up her tireless work again, before anyone else arrived, offering her shy attentions, often invisibly, protecting me with her gentle austerity, as if I were her most precious possession. She was the only person to whom I had spoken about the Dreamer. She constantly asked me about Him, cherishing His every word. It was she who supervised my manuscript, spending her nights transforming it into the first draft of the Book. I caught her faint smile of encouragement, and her complicity for few treasured moments shielded me from the chill of this meeting.

«It's possible to change our destiny – I said, without directly responding to Chris H., putting all the firm conviction I felt into my voice – We have to change man's psychology, the hypnotic world-story rooted in his system of convictions and beliefs. We must change the dream. Only the individual can do that. And that's why a School is needed. A School of Being, potent enough to bring about a planetary revolution in education, to overturn teaching programs and methods, exalting the vision. This is the scientific path on which we have set forth, and in which we believe.»

I said that our teachers were the first persons who would need to change.

«Old humanity cannot teach the young to free themselves from conflicted thought, prejudices and obsolete ideas, nor to teach how to upset any fence, any stockade, and cultivate in themselves an indomitable passion for greatness. It is not resources that are limited, but man who projects his own limitations onto the external world and causes his unconscious propensity to scarcity to take on concrete form.»

I concluded the long meeting with these words:

«*The wealth of a nation, the power of its economy, the level of prosperity it can achieve, is equal to the quality of its system of values and above all its capacity to produce healthy emotional individuals, visionaries, pragmatic dreamers.* The life of a nation, the future of an entire civilisation depends on the existence of these men and women. The heads of future organizations will be philosophers of action. These people will bring success and longevity to the enterprises of the world.»

I could feel my voice vibrating with the grandeur of this prophecy bestowed on me by the Dreamer.

«Our mission is to prepare them.»

I looked at them. More than perplexed, they seemed astonished. The discovery that the world functioned from inside out went well beyond the shock of the revolution announced by Copernicus more than half a millennium earlier. The Dreamer's revelations subverted not only the laws of economy, but also everything in which they had believed until that moment. They felt the menacing strength of ideas capable of derailing them from a sad and Sisyphean destiny repeating over and over until death, the task of instructing the young in fear, boredom, and their own negation of life.

As I left, taking leave of each of them individually, I could read in some of their faces the promise of a deepening commitment to this luminous adventure; in others, perhaps most of them, I saw indecision, bewilderment.

But I had other worries beyond the fractured faculty. That afternoon at Grosvenor Place, seconded by Lucia, I met with the directors of each bank that had been working with us.

The creation of an academic space without frontiers having branches in the great business capitals of the world, had been a triumphant idea. The School the Dreamer had dreamed of had the well-founded ambition of competing with the finest and most respected business schools, surpassing them within a few years, and attracting students from all nationalities. The banks had liked the project, had witnessed its growth, had continued to grant credit for as long as possible, but they were not ready to support the growing investments required by its expansion internationally, not only in Europe but also overseas. This was an enterprise on a scale that not even the greatest English universities had ever confronted. Recently the pressure to reduce our credit had become stronger, and the M Bank, the most deeply committed one of the group, had already informed that they were not going to extend the credit they had already granted us.

10 Believing without believing

Lucia helped me slip into my raincoat and handed me a few documents as I was going out the door. From the top of the steps at the School's main entrance, I scanned the street for one of the taxis rushing through the intense traffic of Grosvenor Place. I had an appointment with my lawyers and time was getting short. I spotted the first available cab and hurried down the steps to capture it, just as a city bus pulled up right in front of me and prevented me from reaching it. I waited for a few passengers to get out and for others to board it, but the bus continued to linger there for an infuriatingly long time. Impatiently, I began walking in the direction of Knightsbridge when suddenly my glace fell on a huge poster that took up the whole side of the bus, it had been too large and too close to have noticed it earlier.

In huge letters it proclaimed, ‘There is probably no God’. Had the adverb been inserted by a punctilious supervisory authority? “Well, what if God happens to exist after all?” he may have asked himself. Without ‘probably’ the poster might be considered simply as hype, like an ad for some hair tonic that offers a 100% guarantee against baldness. With the additional aggravating circumstance that, bald or not, this text was also offering damnation and a journey to hell for an as yet undetermined number of souls. Were that the case, the devil himself could have done no better. That flash of humour, of intimacy with myself, unleashed a moment of lightness, a flicker of relief from my thorny preoccupations.

The ‘thing’ happened in an instant. A bottomless tunnel sucked me into its darkness, devouring space and time, drawing me onward, only to cast me up within the sacred walls of the School for Gods. I had arrived in time to witness the formidable exchange between Lupelius and his disciple Amanzio.

Lupelius: *“No! He is much more than that!*
He has God in his service…”

Amanzio: “What does that mean?”

Lupelius: *“It means that you can ask Him*
for all that you desire,
and God will obey, granting your every request…
without limits….
God is a good servant but not a good master…
God loves to serve…He loves to love…”

With these few remarks, Lupelius had overcome the insoluble question of God’s existence, formulating a luminous heresy that scandalized his contemporaries and gave matter for reflection to generations of scholars and ascetics over the subsequent thousand years and beyond. He had dared to conceive that something exists beyond God, his master: *You!* It was a dizzying vision , a whirlpool in which thought itself came to death, kicking and dangling, like a hanged man when the trapdoor has been sprung.

With great effort I extricated myself from those fantastic recollections, from the fragrant silence of the cloisters and the deep musings of the School, I brought myself back, feet planted firmly on the ground. I had great many other things to think about: the raising of resources for the ESE Foundation I had established in New York; the need to seek new funding for the School's international development, to upgrade our technology, supervise the hiring and training of new faculty members, confront pressure from our banks. And, last but not least of my difficulties, resolve my personal situation.

That very afternoon, in fact, my lawyers were waiting for me to celebrate the funeral rites for my marriage. For some time things had not been going well between Heleonore and myself. We had been living far from each other for more and more longer periods and one day, while she was speaking to me on the phone from her mother's house, we arrived at the only possible conclusion: a definitive parting. The worst thing, however, was that what by all means was expected to be a consensual separation, and a quite simple and straightforward divorce, became more and more complicated by Heleonore's attitude who had become ever more aggressive and rapacious, exhibiting a greediness that I had never recognized in her. It was as though, once she had renounced playing her wifely role, and once the thin coat of color had brushed across our relationship had been stripped away, a monstrosity had emerged, one I had lived with, unsuspiciously.

"You lied to yourself, pretending to be in love with her, and you used her as a pretext for leaving Kuwait and returning to your own Hells" the Dreamer once told me, back when I still believed I loved her. That opinion wounded me, and I thought that, at least about my feelings, the Dreamer was wrong. At that time Heleonore and I were working together, tirelessly, for the School project, and I would have wagered anything on the solidity of our marriage.

"Your union was born out of disobedience and falsehood. It was stillborn. Under these circumstances, there is nothing that can be given to you, and you will also lose whatever you think you possess."

The bus pulled away and finally I could see the street again. I didn't have to signal for a taxi, one suddenly stopped in front of me and unlatched the door. I leaped inside and gave him my lawyers' address.

Once inside I again sank into my cloud of troubles, but now the *infernal regions* of my personal life, with their attendant cortège of afflictions, difficulties, and bitterness, had no temporal consistency, enclosed in a droplet of time without a *before* or an *after.* These came into my mind not like separate situations and events, but *en bloc*, clustered together, like a single constant defeat, without any remedy.

A feeling of impotence came over me. That taxi was the compression of my existence, the physical trap where it was imprisoned, the only difference being that my life had no door through which I could make my escape… Doubt, fear of defeat, irresistible need to give up, I knew well; they were like old friends in whose company misfortune is leavened. They had been the inseparable companions of all my years, and only in the presence of the Dreamer was I able to recognize, transform, and conquer them.

At one of the traffic lights along our route, while the red light stayed on for an infinity, seeming that it would never change to green, I glanced out the window. There, on the side of a bus, just at eye level, I saw another slogan of the atheism campaign: "The bad news is that God is dead. The good news is that you don't need him." I resumed my thinking about this, and something the Dreamer once told me came to mind:

"The attempt to eliminate God by those who call themselves atheists is their attempt, secret even to themselves, to exorcize their fear of death. A fear that grips and torments them more than any others."

Thus the Dreamer overturned the common prejudice viewing the atheist as a person of strength, one who refuses to lean on the illusory crutch of a God, unlike the rest of humanity. He was affirming that in reality weakness was the common denominator and the explanation of that doctrine.

For an ordinary man,
for those who have not attained an interior unity,
believing and not believing are the same lie…

The atheist has first transferred divinity outside himself,
and then denied it.
The mortal sin of atheism therefore is not disbelief in God,
denial of His existence, but disbelief in oneself.

These words recalled something else the Dreamer had said on that subject, something of such vastness that I could hardly believe to have forgotten it for such a long time. I couldn't visualize where, or in which of our encounters I had heard those words from Him, but they were deeply incised within me and now they were resurfacing in my memory.

"To believe is not difficult...everyone believes in something... But obliging oneself to believe is for the few..." the Dreamer had said, expressing a concept capable of thrusting thought to heights beyond reason. The paradox he had coined, 'believing without believing', concealed a cathedral's powerful structure beneath butterfly's wings.

At that time I had been unable to absorb the greatness of this message, but now its pitiless light was showing me how much encomiastic rhetoric was bound up with belief, and how perilously close it came to the root of all fanaticism.

"*Outside of you, every creed, any faith, enlists you in the army of liers. Belief makes you a follower of the doctrine of lying.*"

In the Dreamer's vision, believing induces membership in the masses of those who profess faith, the multitude of persons who spend their lives in a state of identification, of belonging, that sticks them to the flypaper of time. Even "disbelief" in God, as the atheists assert, is a belief that equally sinks them in the *mare magnum* of fundamentalists, dogmatists, the intolerant, and ideologues of every persuasion.

The Dreamer had never wanted to meet or otherwise have any contact with those who characterized themselves as spiritual persons or "seekers after truth." He told me once, "How much better off they'd be, and what greater benefit they'd derive if they'd stop looking for the truth outside and find the lie inside themselves." Not in opposition, but in a dimension vertical to the supine flatness of belief, there is "*believing without believing,*" the Dreamer's liberating vision of enfranchising the individual, setting him free from the captivity of superstition and credulity.

There is no fault, no sin, no karma or punishment.
There is no life beyond and no universal judgment,
no heaven and no hell.
There is only this instant, sacred, infinite, and omnipotent.
Use it well! For this is your only chance.

'Believing without believing' means to choose one's own intention and following it to the end, unshakably. It is a high state of being that demands the elimination of falsehood, and it can only be attained only by men of integrity who know and practice the *Art of Acting.*

Now I asked myself if I had ever touched that state of liberty, if I had ever been capable of believing in an idea, doctrine, or principle; or filling a role, without needing to identify myself with it, without yielding myself slavishly to it. In reality, the atheists' slogans were precisely denouncing belief in the hypnotic tale told by the world, more than to oneself . I was the atheist, the man who had asked to escape from the ordinary, from every kind of dependency, to be near the Dreamer, and instead I had continued to believe in limits: the man who had promised to be faithful to the 'dream' he had forgotten about for years. It was a lump of bitterness I had to swallow.

In different occasions, I gathered on this topic copious notes, of such an interest that I thought of compiling them into a pamphlet. In the end, I'd decided to keep them to myself rather than make revelations that might exceed the reader's capacity for acceptance.

And also, in regard to the content of this Book, I have sometimes hesitated over recounting certain episodes, facts, and circumstances; revelations by the Dreamer that might seem to go too far, possibly awakening the antagonism of political, academic, or religious institutions, or fundamentalism of all kinds. I have therefore tried to select those that, however revolutionary, can nonetheless enter the understanding of present day humanity.

One day you will write immortal pages
that no one has ever written before.
My words, the most unacceptable ones, will flow out of your pen,
and like a river in flood, sweep away every obstacle
until at last they reach those who seek,
those who already know.

11 The Secret of doing

Deep in these musings, I had not even glanced at the taxi driver until he spoke to me.

«You're Italian, right?» he asked with his Cockney accent and the satisfied smile of one who has just won a bet with himself.

«My dad was Italian – he went on without waiting for my answer – He's the one who named me Fiorello.»

And as the cab proceeded slowly through the City traffic, he told me the story of his family: the illiterate grandfather who emigrated first to Australia and then to England founded a shoe factory and became very rich. His father let three squash-playing buddies to invest everything he had in the stock market and within few weeks was left without a penny. Fiorello confided in me about the resentment he felt towards his father; his never-forgotten disappointment at having had to give up singing so that he could start earning a living at a very early age. He told me about his taxi license, his father's only bequest to him; of his hope that his own son might achieve the dream he had been forced to abandon; about his twin grandsons, as alike as two drops of water, who showed exceptional intelligence in their studies and at home, and who were surely destined for great things. They will undoubtly rebuild the empire founded by their industrialist ancestor.

The cab-driver's voice began to fade into the background of my concerns, and as his story continued, I saw myself as a child in the talcum-scented shop of Saverio the barber, with its powdery mirror set in a gilded frame. Within that looking-glass only a few traces of former splendor remained: bright islands afloat on the darkening surface. Therein my imagination could perceive a map of unknown continents, the scratched borders of new archipelagoes. As a little boy, I would observe Saverio at work amid infinitely repeated images of my neck being mercilessly shaved according to my mother's unyielding instructions. That procession of *me* in the slightly tilted mirror behind me, *me, over and over,* like the repeated generations in the cabdriver's tale, seemed to burst forth from a wound in time.

That succession of senseless lives, passed down from father to son, the wretchedness of that immortality on instalments, actually nauseated me. I felt the rejection to exist on those conditions. At that moment I realized, with startling vividness, the incessant recurrence of images and happenings, always the same, in the lives of ordinary men, crushed by anxiety, flailing between schedules and sums, the prey of negative emotions. Men doomed to grow old, fall ill, and die, one after the other, from father to son, inexorably.

I recognized the labyrinth of my existence, that insidious prison I had created myself, of which paradoxically I was both jailer and inmate, and from which, by definition, there was no exit. The difficulties and the problems that I thought I had solved, left behind me forever, were instead still present, still recurring ever more painfully, with no apparent solution. I saw in myself the shameful repetition of my impulse to flee every time I sensed the painful sensation of going uphill, whenever I had to confront challenges and problems that appeared larger than I was, and ready to crush me. Something the Dreamer had said brought a flash of light into my dread.

Only those who are forced to face their own horror
and can bear to contemplate their impotence and incompleteness,
can succeed.

I couldn't bring myself to pursue this, I had to interrupt the analysis. I could see that in performing this interior scrutiny, I was actually observing a lab animal, a guinea pig, some grotesque animal life form, related to me by blood I would never have wanted to see or know.

Triggered by Fiorello's story, born out of some unknown part of me, I felt the impulse to reread one of the notes I had chosen that morning:

"Memory creates fate... Fate creates memory... So long as you believe in your remembrances and continue inwardly to tell yourself the imaginary story of your life, you will keep on projecting it ahead of you and convince yourself that you have a future, which is indeed only the past repeating itself. Memory and fate, past and future, are illusions. Recognize them as nothing other than simultaneous projections of this moment, of the Now, and you will be free. In the Now there is no defeat, only victory."

At this point Fiorello began to sing, in a beautiful tenor voice. The aria was from the last act of Puccini's *Turandot,* when the unknown prince, in love with the beautiful but cruel Turandot, affirms his victory:

"Tramontate, stelle! All'alba vincerò...vinceroooooò..." Fiorello sang on, every so often glancing back at me, enjoying my surprise and waiting for my approval. But the singular coincidence of that song of victory's arrival concurrently with the Dreamer's words, in vivid counterpoint to my defeatist thoughts, flung me into a state of agitation. I perceived that this corpulent man with the pretty name had been fitted between the seat and the steering wheel of his taxi, filling the space so completely with the gelatinous mass of his body that it seemed as he were such an integral part of the taxi that he would never be able to leave it. When I looked more carefully at him in the rear-view mirror, I saw that he was looking at me, and I felt the blood chill in my veins. Those eyes had nothing in common with that fat face. It was as if an alien had taken over this nice fellow's body, and now it was studying me. My brow damp with sweat, I tried to swallow, but my saliva had become something sticky, rubbery; it was choking me. I could see an obscure menace in those eyes... expressing shrewdness and a calm ferocity... Those eyes I couldn't escape from, those eyes that were penetrating me... those were the eyes of the Dreamer. I felt as though I'd suddenly been awakened, interrupted from an ancestral sleep. I came to a quick decision.

«Forget about that address» I told Fiorello, who had stopped singing and had also, to my relief, stopped watching me. I wasn't going to meet with anyone, at least not with the lawyer to discuss my divorce. In a whirlpool of thoughts, as the taxi went on without any destination, I was feverishly assembling the tesserae of that day. I saw that from the first light of dawn, when I had felt that premonitory shiver under my skin as I read the dreamer's words, up until this very moment, there had been a succession of steps, an itinerary whose every event, encounter, and thought, each tiny detail, had been a step on an invisible stair that would bring me to Him. I had never so intensely felt the desire to see him. I would have reached Him anywhere in the world, if I knew where to find Him. In an instant of dazzling, unexpected light, from the heart of the kaleidoscope of the hundred places where I'd met the Dreamer, an image exploded inside me. Now I knew where I'd heard him say the words that had marked that day.

«Take me to Spaniards Road» I told the driver, unable to control the emotion in my voice. I was following the sudden idea of looking for Him where we had seen each other the last time in

London. And as the taxi was bearing me to that destination, following that single fragile clue, the absurd certainty grew in me that I was going to find Him that evening, right there, in the old inn at Hampstead.

I had learned from the Dreamer that dreaming is the birthright of every man. And now I was feeling in my flesh, my joints, my breath, that sense of certainty which transformed that remote possibility into the most precise of appointments; and turned the frail thread that attached me to Him, into a steel cable. This was the integrity in action that the Dreamer had sought to transmit to me; the living seed of the Art of Dreaming that for years had found me such infertile ground. If this was completeness, vitality, then I'd been dead for months and years. A state in which I would never have been able to find him. I was beginning to realize that the day had served as a kind of hyperbaric chamber; its various moments had been stages in decompression that allowed me to rise up from the abysses of quotidian death until I came to Him, to integrity, to life. I held my breath, trying to hold on to that huge discovery. To keep oneself there, vigilant, alive, without letting a single atom of death to penetrate the Being, was the *Secret of doing*.

When the taxi dropped me at the entrance to Spaniards Inn, I was sure that the Dreamer would be arriving, or that He was already inside, punctually meeting my intentions and my fervent request that He be near me now, as great waves threatened to crash against my life.

12 The past is a lie

I paused on the threshold to calm the beating of my heart before going inside. This is where the 'game of encounters', with the unforgettable teachings I had received from the Dreamer, had started, inside those beer-stained walls, amid the reek of rancid bacon and the noisy, idle talk of the pub customers.

The area where they served food welcomed me into a warm semidarkness. It seemed smaller than I remembered. I saw only a few clients in the dining room, some of them sitting at tables; most of them standing at the bar, silently intent on drinking from outlandishly huge mugs. I looked quickly around the room, into its every corner, hoping that He was already there, then I started firmly up the stairs. I could hear the conversations and general noise growing louder. This time, remembering our former meeting and the Dreamer's preference, I chose a table in the middle of the most crowded room on that floor, where the alcohol-fueled public was at its noisiest. It occurred to me that I should ask the host or one of the waiters to let me know when He arrived, and only then did I realize that I had no idea how to describe the Dreamer, nor could I guess what aspect he might have, nor even his age. I quickly abandoned that idea.

Lupelius used to disguise himself as a slave, a vagabond, a political man, a banker, a rich merchant, and he used these roles strategically. Be it a kingly crown or a priest's habit, Lupelius wore them and made his disciples wear them, teaching them how to 'become' a given personage, in order to explore and come to know that subject's every hidden corner, every secret, while never forgetting the game, never remaining imprisoned by it.

I sat where I could see the street from the window, and the green of Hampstead Heath. I had no idea how long I would have to wait. I closed my eyes for an instant, to calm the emotions of that day and I found myself in the Great Hall of the School. The Dreamer was entering, flanked by two wings of warrior-monks. He was wearing a robe, something between a monk's habit and a knightly tunic, his long hair hidden by a broad cap. I saw the figure of Lupelius come forward and melt into him. Across the distance of a thousand year, the School for Gods had passed the baton of its immortal principles, the witness of its timeless pursuit.

It seemed as though only a few minutes had passed, but now I saw that it was dark outside. A lanky red-haired waiter came across the room, shuffling heavily across the uneven floorboards: a gentleman had arrived and was waiting for me downstairs.

I saw him sitting in the most distant corner of the room; still wearing His coat, a short one, made of some light and soft material, of impeccable cut. I walked towards him with short steps, hesitant with emotion. I saw that the table he had chosen was the one farthest from the bar; above it was a trophy, a display of crossed harquebuses, an eighteenth-century vestige of the Kenwood's revolt. I had so yearned to see him, but now, as had often happened in the past, I felt torn between the joy of seeing him and my anxiety at having to face that pitiless mirror that was going to denounce my forgetfulness, my every limitation. Our meeting began with no need of words or preamble, and as the silence continued, I felt all distance recede, all time shrink away until it disappeared. Now, seated beside him, it seemed to me that our South American meeting, in the *Casa del Pensamiento,* had taken place only an eye blink ago.

I had so many things to tell him, but the Dreamer signaled me to keep quiet before I could even open my mouth.

«*What happened in Kuwait, when you abandoned your post, bartering a kingdom for the illusory protection of a job, is repeating itself. And today, once more, you're ready to abandon everything that's been entrusted to you for the sake of saving yourself*» said the Dreamer. His tone was severe, without hardness, but I felt the weight of his words, like blocks of stone.

«*Circumstances and events of your life are reproducing themselves, identical down to the smallest detail, in a perverse perfection, following the pattern of an imaginary recurrence, a circular destiny that doesn't exist, but in which you believe and from which you cannot free yourself.*»

I didn't need to tell him about the hundred problems that were causing such tribulation in my existence. The Dreamer knew. My life was still the same because nothing in me had really changed. I thought that I'd come here to hear him tell me this, instead the Deamer's words were coming to set me free, sweeping away the oppression that came from the thought of recurrence, so close to the superstition of Karma, and with it, the regret and self-pity that were already darkening my Being.

«*Only apparently does the past repeat itself. In reality here is no past, neither in a man's life nor in the history of a civilization. The past is a lie. There isn't any karma and there isn't any former life, any guilt, any sin, or any punishment. There's no afterlife or universal judgment, no hell, no paradise. There is only this instant, sacred, infinite, omnipotent. Use it well! There will never be another chance. Outside of the Now, we're helpless, dependent on time, limited, vulnerable, mortal.*

The past is a lie. And all that belongs to memory is a fiction. What ever you believe has happened in the past, has never really happened. All that you believe happened in the past is happening right now, in this very instant. There is no moment before and none after. Everything happens Now because nothing is outside of Now. Now is the timeless beginning and endless end of every cycle, from electron to God.»

13 State is place

During that meeting at Spaniards Inn, I scribbled timeless words on the back of the menu and on napkins that I still cherish as precious relics.

During a pause, and in an atmosphere that felt lighter now, I thought I could tell the Dreamer how surprised I was at His having chosen this out of the way inn as our meeting-place. The Dreamer lived strategically. I knew that every choice He made, even the apparently least important ones, was in the service of His intent. A quiet laugh preceded His answer. Teasing me, He suggested that the principal reason was the quality of the beer; this was one of the few remaining London establishments that could boast of having offered the best dark beer, still produced by the artisans on the premises, for the last four centuries. For a few seconds, before He went on, He lifted the pewter tankard to His lips. But, as he did with food, he hardly tasted it, He took not even one actual swallow. Then He told me that the Spaniards Inn had been a famous hideout that generations of brigands, thieves and highwaymen had supped at this very table. And a number of them, summarily tried and sentenced, had been hanged from a tree a few steps outside.

I didn't quite see the connection between my question and his story until when He uttered the word 'thieves'. The Dreamer deliberately paused, looking at me in silence. His smile had vanished, and from the fierceness of his stare, I knew that I was going to endure a difficult moment. Pierced by his eyes, I could feel myself beginning to take short quick breaths. When he began to speak again, he said:

«You are the thief of your own self. You're robbing yourself from within. In business or in love, your associates and partners will always be the perfect reflection of your condition, your states of Being. A man can possess only what he is, and he can choose and be chosen only by what he deserves.»

That reference to the course of my life could not have been more explicit. The painfulness of what I was hearing was already unbearable when the Dreamer lunged again, striking even harder.

«The worst partner in the world would never be able to cheat you or rob you more thoroughly than you are cheating and robbing yourself.»

Even though every one of these hammer blows hit home, I wrote down each of His words as I heard it. A pause gave me time to complete my notes and take in this tough lesson. Then, in only three words, he distilled the intelligence of that moment:

«State is Place – he announced – A man occupies a physical space that corresponds to his Being. The place where he is, the environment surrounding him, the people he meets, all demonstrate a remarkable correspondence with his states of Being, the quality of his emotions, of his thoughts.»

The silence that had surrounded us until that moment, sealing our meeting inside a bubble of discretion, split open, and the life of the pub began to rush past us like images from an old film clattering freely through a jammed projector. I glanced around us, looked searchingly at people and objects as if they had only just appeared in my personal universe, and the Dreamer had invented them for me at that moment. The room was filled with an improbable mingling of humanity, a universe by Toulouse-Lautrec, misshapen as its creator. Creatures that were frighteningly thin or exaggeratedly fat cawed and chattered together, or else stared helplessly, lost in silence and the void. Threadbare shirts hung limply from thin shoulders that might just well have been hangers; while others were stretched to bursting point across bodies that were hugely obese. Bright red lips, open like wounds, kept imitating smiles. Young lives, already withered simulacra of men and women, breathless. They were there to look for a moment of reprieve from their hell, hovered between two dolours, past and future.

One stocky man was hoisting a heavy tankard to his mouth, gulping down the foamy liquid, eyes half-closed and with a look of stupefaction, as if he'd been drugged. His swollen stomach kept him at some distance from the bar. These characters from whom until that moment I had felt separated, as if by a glass through which I could watch them fluctuate, scattered through the liquidity of life; those presences that I might have glimpsed from far off, flectingly, whom I had believed I could forget and leave behind at any moment, I now recognized as belonging to me. I saw dull fibers, starting from my body, connecting to each of those beings, to every detail of that setting, weaving themselves together to form an intricate and dense arterial system that nourished all of us as if we made up a single organism, uniting us in a horrible, indissoluble symbiosis.

I had the sensation that the Dreamer was no longer at my side. I was unable to move a single muscle, but I could tell that he was no longer in my field of vision... A pressure on the back of my neck scrambled my five senses; now they no longer perceived that world but *were emanating it,* as if persons and things, and all the atoms of the universe were coming together and dissolving in every blink of my eyes. Here the Dreamer's absence became breath, sound, voice.

«What you see here is the multitude, the legion that you carry inside of yourself – he said – *They are your Being made visible, the physical representation of your condition...»*

In that faceless crowd, in that grimace of pain beyond time, I saw social distinctions dissolve, along with racial and religious differences all the divisions among men that throughout the millennia have been pretexts for wars and killing, and I saw the various roles melting before my eyes, like waxen masks. What remained were simply men and women whose only purpose was to portray my own oblivion. That motley and noisy circus, that spectacle, had been arranged so that I could observe something that in all this time I had never wanted to see or touch in myself. *'State is Place',* I repeated, penetrating into the deep reaches of the motto that was striking down the illusion of an external, extraneous world that was separate from me. I felt lost.

Through a new lucidity, I was able to link the theatrical staging of the pub, that warehouse of despair, with what I had been able to observe in school and university classrooms. The worn-out humanity that came here to drown their own degradation in alcohol, was precisely similar to the category of pedants, masters of doom and gloom, obsolete mechanical repeaters geared out to perpetuate the archaic education they had received. They pretend to teach young people what they themselves do not know, and to explain what they don't understand and have never applied to themselves. A theatre of the absurd where bald pitchmen sell lotions guaranteed to grow hair; and worshippers of scarcity, economists, with clumsy patches stitched on their Being instruct in the art of creating wealth.

«The School I entrusted to you isn't becoming anything other than this place of idleness and boredom – said the Dreamer – *Change, otherwise people will keep replicating it everywhere you go, because it's not outside of you. Get rid of this inner rot, and you'll see the world float away like dust when you blow on it. The world that you see and touch is a product of your dream. Your*

thoughts and emotions, beliefs and actions, history and fate, the events and the people who surround you, are all produced and shaped by your inner Being. If you indulge in negative states, you will be defeated by the very same world that you dream and project.»

«Make a clean sweep. You can cancel this degradation right now, in this very instant. You can only do it now – the Dreamer urged – *The Now is the only time that exists and the only world wherein you can act. If there were any other 'Now', a second before, it would be a world completely different from this one, and totally forgotten one second later.»*

I renewed my promise to the Dreamer. The new university would never fall into a chasm, nor would it be suffocated by the living blob we had witnessed. It would be a School of Being, a planetary organ capable of generating new cells for a humanity cured of conflict, fear, and doubt; it would engender philosophers of action, pragmatic dreamers, the visionary leaders of whom the Dreamer dreams, and whom our civilization needs.

«All existing ideologies of left and right are outdated and obsolete. Powerful forces coming from the individual and not from the masses are steadily rewriting he fundamentals of life. You as an individual are called to create through your integrity a new humanity, and to redesign a new economics within yourself, project a brand new era and remember a new destiny.»

14 Be a King, the Kingdom will come

It was the Dreamer who brought up the subject of the School. I seized the occasion to speak to Him at length about various aspects of its governance, its development, its needs. I tried to stick to the facts and maintain a healthy detachment from the account, but inevitably the words and my tone began to slide into complaint. Speaking to Him in particular about the financial aspects of the project, and the urgent necessity of finding new capital, I mentioned the difficulties in our relations with the banks.

At this point the Dreamer intervened, interrupting that *cahier de doleances,* my self-indulgent complaining about problems and obstacles.

«The School is already done. There is nothing you can do, nothing you can add, other than obeying the design dictated by the 'dream!'» he cried in such a loud angry voice that I was afraid all the other customers would turn and look at us. No one seemed to have heard, however.

«The University is only one fragment of the 'dream'. For you, as for all those who are part of it, its realization is not the ultimate goal, but an instrument for change, a guide, a path towards a higher vision of existence.»

Then, with a weary glance at me, like a scientist observing a ailed experiment, He said:

«I placed you at the tiller of the School, in command of a starship capable of traveling at the speed of dreams, and you turned it into a prison where you yet again enforce the tyranny of roles and re-create all the usual doubts and fears.»

Realizing that I had grasped nothing of what He'd been saying, and that even now I was still waiting stubbornly for an answer from Him, a concrete solution to the problems I had mentioned, he said:

«Our Being is the true Creator of all that happens to us. Heighten your level of responsibility, renew your promise, and you will see that the economy and business obey the laws of Being. This is the solution! Don't blame the world, circumstances, other people, looking for guilt outside yourself. You have to regain lost ground now, and reassemble the fragments of your lost integrity. This is the solution. Integrity is a state of Being, a sense of certainty, of completeness, vitality, the absence of fear. You feel it in your flesh, your heart, the way you breathe. Governments and nations, organizations and enterprises guided by integrity are prosperous, and they pursue long and happy lives.»

«Be a King, the Kingdom will come» he said, uttering the words that would become emblematic in my life and the lives of my students.

«Royalty of the Being always precedes the birth of a reign. 'Being' comes before 'Having', never vice versa. Don't ever wish for the kingdom to appear before kingliness: it would crush you into dust.»

Those words sounded as clearly as the tones of a great bell there in the semidarkness of the pub, and it seemed to me that the words themselves were raising shields to protect me from an imminent peril.

«When you find yourself facing something that appears insurmountable, impossible to withstand... remember Me!... my words, the principles of 'the Dream'. All limitations can be pinpointed in your interior states. If you are aware of this, they'll disappear! Don't worry about the lack of money. The money is lacking because you're worrying about it! Observe yourself, and don't change from that moment. Everything is already done. There is only one obstacle: and that is you.»

15 The Bank

«Your commitment, your inner promise, will obtain for you all the resources you need – was the Dreamer's reply to the most urgent of my questions – *Commitment is investment... Commitment is luck... Wager everything... don't leave one single atom out of the orbit of your responsibilities... Bet everything you have, everything you don't have yet, on yourself, on your ideas, and the whole world will bet on you too.»*

I remembered what he had said to me in the *Casa del Pensamiento*: the principal obstacle against which the most ambitious projects shattered was not the absence of financial backing, but the lack of men who were capable of containing a luminous idea, of bearing the responsibility of a great dream, of believing the impossible, committing all their energies to bringing it about, all the while knowing that it might exact a huge and early price from them, and that price has to be paid in advance.

«When you find yourself facing a financial problem, don't be discouraged... Be still ... Breathe deeply... Focus all your attention on your being, and be aware of your inner deaths, which are the veritable cause of all your misfortune... and win! You'll see help and prodigious resources come abundantly and promptly each time you ask.»

The cool air of a late August evening surrounded us as I followed him out into the garden for a brief pause before we took leave of one another. It was late at night. I saw moonlight shining on the branches of a cherry tree, picked bare by now, and on the pale shirtfront that showed under the Dreamer's dark coat. I wanted this moment, this suspended time, this state of liberty, that I was feeling in His presence and so rare for me, not to end. His voice floated easily over the dense hubbub from inside.

«*Let's go* – He said, drawing his soft coat around him – *This garden smells of vomit!*» That comment made me blush to the very roots of my hair. I knew that brusque remark had less to do with the garden than with a bitter verdict about my existence.

As I walked beside him for the few metres that separated us from the end of this meeting, the Dreamer completed that evening's discourse, going straight to its essence.

«*Money is not real. It makes visible in time whatever a man has conquered in his Being, through his commitment, his responsibility, the victories he has won over himself. In the same way, the smallest crack in the dream can shake a financial empire off its foundation.*»

Then he added:

«*Go to the bank and ask for whatever you need* – were his final words to me – *On the other side of the desk, you'll find Me!*»

I could see those words scurrying across my mind, like electronic letters on a screen, as I climbed the steps to M Bank. At a certain point I noticed that I was actually reciting them like a mantra to fend off the swarm of doubts that were poised to penetrate the 'dream' and jam the powerful but delicate engine of *the marvellous.* The Dreamer had suggested the sum I should ask for: it seemed enormous to me, disproportionate. I could not imagine that the same bank which had hardly been willing to support our original credit was going to decide *d'emblée* to give us ten times as much so that we could make the new investments required by the School's expansion.

Once more my reason was struggling against the miracles that unfailingly, day after day, had accompanied the project's growth and transformed my life all over these years. At His side I had seen giants brought down, with only the dust a dwarf might leave floating in the air; I had seen mountains shift or reshape themselves into gentle mounds a child could climb. How many intricate, hopelessly lost situations had I seen the Dreamer resolve, undoing knots with the skilled fingers of a helmsman! And how many impossible duels I had won with him at my side.

And yet, I was still doubtful.

The obstacles you find outside are the limits within you.
Be complete, a totality! Invest what you have,
bet everything on the 'dream'.
You will see there are no limits to the bank's commitment.

Inspired by these words, and the difficult meeting with M Bank ever more imminent, I could feel a powerful acceptance growing in me. The Dreamer called this the 'yes attitude'.

When you forget the principles of the Dream,
you can only give up and disappear from My vision.
Put yourself into a state of integrity!

The thought that I might actually fail, betraying the Dreamer's faith in me, was unbearable. I gathered my courage and strengthened my resolve, remembering His words:

I am the banker you are about to meet.
I'm sending you, I will greet you, and I will listen to you.
If I like you, the bank will like you, too.
If you remember My presence, and My words,
they will tell you 'Yes'.

The thin crust of daily existence split open, and all at once I spied the source; the magic lantern that projects the shadows of our lives, the facts and circumstances that men call reality.

I was poised on the threshold, not of a bank, but the narrow gate to the invisible that can be crossed only by a humankind freed from the description of the world and its hypnotisms, the Biblical eye of the needle through which a camel can pass more easily than a man 'rich' in ignorance, superstition, doubt, and fears.

16 Money is not real

This time the Dreamer was extremely quick, almost brusque, in telling me what he expected from me.

«*It's time to bring the School to Italy* – He said in a lapidary tone – *There you will face the most brooding and merciless Antagonist you could wish for. With his irreplaceable help, you will have the greatest chance of confronting your limitations and conquering yourself.»*

From the start, the Dreamer had informed me that the School should be an academic space without frontiers, with branches in the great world capitals of business, but I could never have imagined that in addition to the two Georgian manors in the heart of London, the School's next setting would be a castle in the middle of nowhere.

The property the Dreamer had suggested was splendid but isolated. More than an aristocratic country residence, Villa del Ferlaro was a royal palace. Napoleon I had given it to his wife, Marie-Louise of Austria, the heiress to empires. The property, last remnant of an industrial fortune shattered in a financial crash, had been the subject of vacant judiciary auctions for years. Despite the beauty of the Villa and its dropping price no one had dared to acquire it – in part because of a local superstition, to avoid the legacy of the unfortunate destiny of its successive owners, but even more to avoid to go against the powerful elite that actually ran the city. As I learned later, they had been maneuvering for a long time to ensure that the auctions remained deserted while they worked out an agreement about how to divide this rich booty.

While I was getting ready to leave for Italy to attend the auction, I assembled and studied every possible image of the Villa, so that I came to know every detail of the interior with its lovely frescoes, the great terraces, the English garden designed by Barvitius two centuries before, and the immense park surrounding it.

The property fascinated me, but it was also burdening my thoughts. If the academic formula of the new university, beyond the academic English rigor and internationality, was to include an Italian culture and sense of beauty, no one could imagine a more appropriate setting, nor at the same time one more difficult to conquer. The vision of its beauty, the great rooms, the paintings, the stuccoed decorations, were all obscured by a fog of fear and anxiety at the thought of becoming the successor to so many men's and women's lives; all those ephemeral histories; their fragile existences and the desperate castaways which intertwined for two hundred years with the Villa del Ferlaro.

When I learned that after the fall of Napoleon Marie-Louise had lived and reared her children from her second marriage to Colonel Neipperg, I realized even more profoundly that winning the auction would not only mean acquiring the building and its lands, but participating in the history of nobility and style that could crush someone who might incautiously take on ownership without a required level of responsibility. More than a royal residence, it was a symbol, the very abbreviation of a city's entire history. To come there from London and subdue it was among the most arduous tasks the Dreamer could have given me; a task that immediately struck me as impossible, not only because of the financial scope of the operation, arduous in itself; but because of the great and local veneration that still persisted for every vestige of that imperial princess who had loved her subjects and been loved by them in return. It was she who had laid the base of the region's economic and cultural activity, attracting the greatest scientific and artistic influences of her century.

«The impossible is the possible viewed from underneath» the Dreamer said at that time, exhorting me.

«Aim higher, elevate the Being. You will understand that the art of dreaming, the art of believing and creating, is precisely that: the capacity to transform the impossible into the possible, and at last into the inevitable. This is the first condition for your integration.»

He spoke the next words slowly and carefully, to force them through the hard barrier of my understanding, making them penetrate deeply.

«You do not need money to purchase that property. You need commitment, an inner vow! Your commitment must be total. Your inner responsibility and integrity determine the extent of your financial means, and produce all the necessary resources. Money is not real. What is real is a man's commitment, the strength of his convictions. Resources and money are merely the natural consequence of these qualities...they align themselves and take on the proportions of his dream.»

These words of the Dreamer were revealing something extraordinary to me, not found in any textbook and not taught in any school of economics. For the first time I was realizing that there had never been any social, scientific, or economic conquest, any human undertaking among those recognized as the very emblems of success, which had been accomplished with money. The money arrived naturally, as a consequence.

Behind every apparently impossible victory there has always been the dream of one man, one individual, and the strength of his flawless certainty, of his capacity for believing totally. My mind wandered, then stayed suspended, like a caught breath, at the thought of all the great enterprises and adventures that had apparently been carried out with no resources except for the visionary strength of one man, and his unshakable faith. These musings were making room in the attic, where obsolete things are stored, for the principles of rational capitalism and the decisional theories founded on economic calculation and return on investment.

«*All things are possible to one who is whole. If you bet on yourself and your ideas, the entire world will bet on you* – said the Dreamer, reaching me in the whirlwind of my thoughts – *Commitment to your ideas has to be total. The quality and success of your life depend on your level of commitment.*»

«*The art of dreaming, the art of believing and creating, is a state of liberty, a state of certainty, the total absence of doubt* – the Dreamer continued – *Inner commitment is investment, is the only real money. It is your commitment that makes things happen! It's your commitment that attracts all opportunities and necessary resources. The success of your actions in the external world is only the reflection of your commitment.*»

17 Believe, then see

At the thought of this task I felt an unbearable stomach cramp. The lucidity, the cool certainty emanating from His words, alleviated it. After a few seconds, though, the pain returned, even more sharply.

I couldn't sleep the night before the auction. Following the precepts of the School for Gods, I also refrained from eating anything. I knew Lupelius's words by heart: *"You must fast on the eve of battle!"*

The food of the Being is will.
The food of the mind is silence.
The food of the body is fasting.

Even with my whole-hearted commitment, not even these rituals proved efficacious, and I could feel anxiety growing inside me, along with concern about what the outcome of the auction was going to mean. The sum I had had to put up as a guarantee that would allow me to bid on the property had wiped out a large part of the credit I'd obtained from M Bank. But the most tormenting thought was that even if I won the auction and the property were to come to me, I would need to pay the entire residual amount in cash within a few months.

'Believe, then See' is the ineluctable law of Kings,
and it is the law of those who govern themselves...
Have faith, belief, partake of the Art of Dreaming
these are intimate qualities of the Dreamer.
A man who takes a step into the abyss must believe,
without even a single second of doubt,
that the ground is going to take shape beneath his foot
to prove that his daring move, his luminous madness, was right.

These were the amazing words I had heard from the Dreamer as I prepared for my departure. And yet I still felt the sensation of proceeding along a narrow ridge between two dizzinesses. If I won, I would have to find the money very quickly indeed; but if I didn't try, I would be missing an opportunity that would never come again, one of the most important ones the Dreamer had ever created for me. I was emboldened by the thought that, in all the years I had spent near Him, every problem that I had believed unsolvable had always resolved itself quickly and in the simplest way.

I envied the strength of Lupelius and his warrior-monks, the absence of fear that assured them invulnerability in the most perilous and mortal activities. I had been studying The School for Gods for years now, the manuscript by Lupelius, seeking the secret for transforming the fragile and insecure man within us into a hero, a demigod who sees the world as his creature looking for his orders. This is how I lived, walking a tightrope between soaring peaks and bottomless depths. A part of me was drawn to the world of audacity and freedom, where the Dreamer's voice resounded with the force of a warrior's shout; and another part of me was being sucked into a state of impotence, imprisoned by fear and doubt, languished in a condition of painful uncertainty.

«You will find the certainty you're looking for only within yourself – the Dreamer told me – *The sense of safety is an inner victory which cannot come from anything or anybody out there, but only from you.»*

Then, just for a little while, I felt I could fly freely, and in a flash of light I saw the way out of the labyrinth.

But all my determination, the courage I'd gathered into my two hands, sank away in a second when, having entered the courtroom, I found it crowded with people; and furthermore I saw that there was a large group of people who intended to bid on the Villa, whereas I had expected to be the only one. I felt a desperate choking sensation in my throat as the judge called for bidders. One name after another was announced. I had to fight against that feeling of defeat I knew so well. I could feel it invading my Being like a poison, chilling every fiber and sickening every cell, draining me of all my energy.

Despite its being officially a secret, it hadn't taken the city any time at all to learn that an intruder, an outsider, someone from London, had put up the amount of money required to participate in the bidding. And for the first time in years, instead of being deserted, the auction room had drawn a crowd of eleven interested bidders, all of whom had deposited the necessary guarantee. Naturally, the really interested parties were hidden behind these straw men. The Union of Industrialists, the state university, the two leading banks, and all the other strong players were present. Each of them was one of the Hydra's heads, with the eyes and fangs of a single animal that was monitoring the *status quo* and controlling the city's every breath. A monstrous creature with nine heads I would soon be facing.

I mentally tried to calculate my chances of beating all these contenders. I weakened imagining they had limitless financial capabilities, and that the price would go higher with each counter-offer, forcing me out. The very thought of it made me feel helpless… Insecurity, the fear that I might not be able to accomplish this feat, were shrinking me to dwarf size, just as the outside world was becoming infinitely huge and menacing.

18 The Auction

I made my final bid. The sum echoed through the crowded room, and the audacity of that offer provoked fresh mutterings, more fervent comments. Then the murmuring died down, stopped. Time was suspended.

In that atom of universe beyond time, the judge's ritual gestures went on slowly, solemnly. I watched him extinguish the first candle, then the second. Before his gavel struck, signaling the transfer of the historic property and the end of the auction, that instant fell, like a drop of infinity. All of my life appeared to me. I saw the intoxication of my self-destructivity, the unconscious sabotage behind every abasement, each fall, and all the impossible victories that constellated the tempestuous voyage to the discovery of an opening through which I could escape, showing all men that it's possible to change our fate. We need not accept being condemned to grow old, sicken, and die. I felt infinite gratitude to the Dreamer, for having led me by the hand into the world of courage and impeccability, where time and death do not exist, where wealth knows neither 'thief nor decay'.

In the silence that followed my bid, when it began to seem that every other contender had yielded, I felt a rush of exultation at the prospect of victory. At that moment, it seemed certain; but I didn't even have time to confect a few atoms of happiness before the thought of the responsibilities I was assuming burst upon me, projecting a vortex of fear. An eclipse of being dimmed all my certainties, cancelling the sense of omnipotence that had sustained me until that moment. In the darkness of that instant, while the world dimmed and its colours became livid, what I had done, acting with determination and courage, now seemed merely reckless and irresponsible. In my imagination, now rushing out of control, the price I had offered grew to enormous size, something colossal, unthinkable. And now that I was a breath away from winning and owning this property that had been so bitterly contested, I could feel my knees giving way. I had to fight down a wave of nausea. I even cursed my meeting with the Dreamer and the decision to get involved in this rash enterprise.

Something sticky coated my mouth, and I felt the unmistakable pain that had always governed my life. The fear of losing was transformed into the fear of winning, still smeared with that same cloying sweetness, the same affliction. I felt my world threatened by panic, terror, desolation; my limbs blood sucked by a fatal illness. I would have liked to abandon my body, leave it there like a shed skin, and go away.

«You may think that fear is a natural reaction to something that frightens or threatens you from the outside – the Dreamer had

told me in other circumstances – *In reality, it is your fear that is the source and the true cause of what you will be afraid of.*»

I blamed the Dreamer for having given me yet another insurmountable task, another ocean to cross, another peak to scale. Why had I come here? Why had I ostentated a confidence that I didn't possess?

The 'dream' that had led me to this place was dissolving. I saw that infinite instant expire, its eternity slip from my fingertips, to dissolve, a droplet in time's River Styx. I sank back into the next act in the courtroom's proceedings, a shade among the shadows crowding the room, an unknowing actor in my own drama.

I turned my head to glance furtively at the door. I felt a flicker of relief, it was still ajar.

I saw my face, pilloried and distorted with fear, projected against an immense crystal pyramid for just an instant, before it exploded with the roar of a stormy sea. The air was still raining shards of crystal when I heard the Dreamer's voice over the blast, closer to me than my own breath.

«*'Here' there is no time, no death* – He said – *In my world there is no space to fall back, to accuse or regret. 'Here', close to the Dreamer, there is no space to indulge in any weakness, doubt, or fear.*»

These words of His were still vibrating when I heard the voice of one of the last remaining bidders, loud and confident, making an offer much higher than my own. I felt a growing desperation: victory was vanishing from, right before my eyes. Inner and outer worlds were revealing their identity, knocking down the barrier that had given the illusion of separating them. The sense of defeat that I always carried within me was materializing again. Another fraction of a second, and I would have lost the bidding definitively.

It took an infinity for the judge to raise his gavel. I saw it lifted, ready to come down. It wasn't the auction that was ending, but an implacable judgment that would condemn me to perpetual slavery.

A sudden inexplicable pain clutched the left side of my neck with talons of steel. I had never felt such atrocious and total pain. I was about to faint. I barely heard the hiss of His words:

«*I am the lethal threat to everything in you that's decided to die, and all in you that lives on death. The supreme goal of the School for Gods is Victory over Death.*»

The air grew darker. On the faces of the other bidders I could see sneers of ferocity and derision; they were the first wave of an enemy falange ready to crush me. The walls of the chamber fell away, and I was in an open field, surrounded by the crash of arms and the trumpet calls to battle, while the earth trembled under the potent tread of armies and the hooves of a thousand maddened steeds.

Amid the horror of that butchery, among arms and legs hacked off and flung aside, I found myself with Lupelius' warrior-monks. They were armed with swords, but wore no armor and no shields, as the School demanded. They were passing through ranks of invisible militias, protected by their incorruptible belief in their own invulnerability. The opposing falanges were waves of a tempestuous sea, clad in screaming colors. The air was heavy with the stench of blood and the screams of the wounded; it was impossible to breathe. An immense cloud of arrows, horribly sibilant, flew upwards, darkening the sky.

In that supreme moment, the Dreamer appeared beside me.

«No retreat!» He shouted in a voice louder than the din of battle. In His voice I could hear the enthusiasm, the intoxicating joy of one who recognizes the root of his own life, which he has forever sought and for which he has long prepared.

«Move it! Get out of that deathly state, or you'll be eliminated. Return to the totality of your Being, take back your oneness, only that way will you be invulnerable. Don't waver for even a second, because the outcome of this battle, defeat or victory, depends completely on you.»

I remembered reading about the discipline of invulnerability in the 'School for Gods' manuscript: "*Lupelians did not do battle for supremacy, control, or power over others. Lupelius summoned his monk-warriors to fight not for the poor, the needy, or the oppressed, but as a litmus test to express on the battlefield their inner achievement as real conquerors of death. Lupelius' discipline was not aimed at preparing people to lay down their lives and become martyrs or heroes in the name of some ideology or faith, but for the sole purpose of opening a gateway to immortality, first in their hearts and, consequently, in their physical bodies.*"

«For a warrior there is nothing greater than a battle that comes without his provoking it and that opens the portals of the infinite to him» the Dreamer concluded.

Swarms of arrows were falling all around us, in murderous waves, and I observed the miracle of our safety while soldiers and mounted knights fell around us by the hundreds. The battle had reached its paroxysm. At the core of the army, with a thousand victorious banners fluttering, I was crossing the rushing waters of the Granico, at the gates of Asia, in pursuit of the routed enemy. In every fiber I could feel the courage, the certitude, the sense of victory that had pulsed in the veins of heroes since the world began, and for a fraction of a second I knew the ineffable joy of an immortal.

That was when an arrow, swifter than the wind and razor-sharp, struck me, slicing off my earlobe and leaving a burning pain behind. I felt it as a memento of my vulnerability, an announcement of death. Suddenly the wind changed. Among all the other sounds, I could hear the thunderous gallop of a warhorse, preceding the apparition of a huge rider emerging from the mists. His armour flashed in the firelight. He approached me, making the horse rear up, so close that one of the hooves brushed past my face. I moved slightly backwards, just in time to avoid him. I felt the inevitability of defeat and my own resignation even before a mute howl of terror rose within me. With a rapid movement, he pulled off his helmet and flung it away, making it fly like a mechanical bird, and then he drew his sword. The long ashen hair was loose and waving in the wind, and now I recognized him. That mortal foe, It was He: the Dreamer. There was no expression on his face, just a slight glint in his eyes, when he raised his sword to strike me. I felt the blade penetrate deeply into my flesh. The myriad fragments that had composed my life until that moment fused together, and those scraps of me cried out in unison before their certain extinction. With a cry of horror I put my hands tightly around my neck, in the desperate attempt to hold the sides of that mortal wound together and stop the gush of blood. From that world pulsing with epos and death, with heroism and tragedy, I fell back into the unreality of the courtroom.

Everyone was watching me, waiting for my next move.

I felt the slumbering coverlet of the world lifted off me, like a curtain rising on the play externally symbolized by the auction, although in reality this drama was entirely internal. Now I knew what the real wager was. I was barely in time to make a final offer, an unbeatable one, which left my last rival behind me, along with fear and doubt. The Villa dei Ferlaro and its huge surrounding park had a new owner now: The European School of Economics.

This was the end of the long years of neglect for that royal residence, and the beginning of its new destiny. A long, intense rustle of applause accompanied the adjudication of that property that had been so bitterly contested.

Generations of philosophers and ascetics, esoteric schools of thought, monasteries and ashrams had labored for centuries to bring their Dream here, to bring the School back to Italy. That was the only thing that counted now. Journalists were the first to make their way through the crowd and dart out to spread the news to the city and the nation. It would be the lead story in all media and in the newspapers which had been following the varying fortunes of the property and the misadventures of its many owners.

And as the pendulum swung upwards to its highest point, the opposing forces were already loading their weapons. The Antagonist was already setting forth on his apparently opposing path. His actions would be merciless and essential, just as the Dreamer had foreseen.

"Everything happens for your final victory" He told me when in the months succeeding the auction I told Him about the powerful opponents I was confronting, the fight against the nine-headed Hydra, and the obstacles proliferating along my path, planted there as shields and barricades against the success of the School in Italy.

«Even those who appear to be against you play a purposeful role in bringing the Dream to reality. They offer a meaningful opportunity for your growth and understanding. There is no antagonist, enemy, or demon outside of yourself. Dig out the enemy in the most hidden recesses of your Being, and conquer him. There are no thousands of enemies, there is only one, and there is also only one victory to be won: the conquest of death. When you stop doing damage to yourself, when you stop polluting your Being with conflictual thought, negative emotions and destructive attitudes, those antagonists will disappear.»

Some time later, the Dreamer, referring to the other bidders at the auction, remarked:

"Those men came, or they were sent, to buy only what's visible. They were hypnotized by money, by the value of the property, the cupidity of possessing it. Desire is time, and all that belongs to time is false. Nothing can be possessed in time, nor is

there any solution or remedy. You can only understand this when the Now, the true time, will rule in you."

"You, when you replaced the 'dream' with vanity and desire" he said, forcing me to relive that moment of eclipse of the Being that had diminished me and stripped me of all strength at the most crucial moment of competing for the Villa.

"*You became one of them, and you were going to suffer the same fate as all those who tried to possess it without responsibility. Un crack economico è sempre preceduto da un crack nell'Essere. A man can only possess what he is responsible for."* This aphorism on which He suspended His discourse made me think of R. Salvi – the last owner of Villa del Ferlaro – and it seemed the perfect epitaph to mark the ending of every industrial empire.

«Connect yourself to the 'dream' – he went on – *The 'dream' is the absence of time, it's the absence of death...You aren't here to satisfy some desire of yours, or your possessiveness, or to acquire a new seat for the School. You are here to overcome the most dreadful of all man's superstitions, his most deeply rooted lie.»*

Here the Dreamer stopped and gazed hard at me, as if watching for a signal to go on before passing on to me such a potent message. The Dreamer was about to reveal the final stage of my apprenticeship, a sense of the infinite efforts demanded if one were to live near Him and the essence of His vision. A wave of pain swelled in the region of my heart. I carefully transcribed His message so that I could transmit to all those who seek and are ready to listen to the breath of the infinity, of immortality.

When He spoke again His tone was grave, his voice vibrant.

«You are here to derail your inflexible fate, to change the impossible: the unchangeable you! Here is the occasion for you to conquer time and affirm your victory over the interior deaths that are prelude to and the sole cause of physical death. You are here for the sole purpose of opening a gateway to deathless life, to infinity.

When you stop dying within, there will no longer be a 'time' outside of yourself... a time that imposes a cadence on your life, makes you grow old, get sick, and die. When you stop dying within, real life will overwhelm you and occupy all the atoms of your Being.

There aren't any hundred problems to solve, but only yourself! The true victory, the solution, is one: return to youself! Return to being integral, complete, unique... A warrior can't permit himself to lose even a single atom of his integrity... he can only be complete!

Love yourself within with all your strength, and everything in the world will be perfect. Everything, I say: everything, including the past, will take on your aspect and will be created in your image, in perfection.

Be very careful! You asked to be closer to the Dreamer, and this no longer allows you to do what you used to do, not even think or feel in the way you used to feel and think. Living close to the Dreamer is only for the few.It is risky. Living near the Dreamer is the most difficult task you could ever undertake.

Here, if you forget yourself, you will instantly be catapulted into your infernal past, and be lost.

Here, closer to the Dreamer, there is no space for you to indulge in weakness, regret, doubt or fear.

Here, you have to be strong. Here, closer to the Dreamer, you can only be pure and whole.

The 'dream' is the most real thing there is. Dreaming is the most real thing there is. Its timeless action will create everything you've desired for years and failed to achieve.»

I promised myself that I would never again forget.

Dream, dream, dream... never stop dreaming.
Reality will follow.

The School for Gods

First published in Great Britain in 2009

The University of Buckingham Press
Buckingham MK18 1EG
www.ubpl.co.uk

The European School of Economics
8/9 Grosvenor Place
London SW1X7SH - UK
www.eselondon.ac.uk

© The European School of Economics 2009
© The University of Buckingham Press 2009

visibilia ex invisibilibus
European School of Economics

All rights reserved. No part of this publication may be reproduced or transmitted, stored or introduced into a retrieval system or transmitted in any form or by any means without the prior written permission of the publishers nor may be circulated in any form of binding or cover other than the one in which it is published and without a similar condition including this condition being imposed on the subsequent purchaser.

A CIP catalogue record for this book is available at the British Library

For more information:
www.theschoolforgods.com

Printed in Italy by
International Punto Grafico
www.i-puntografico.com